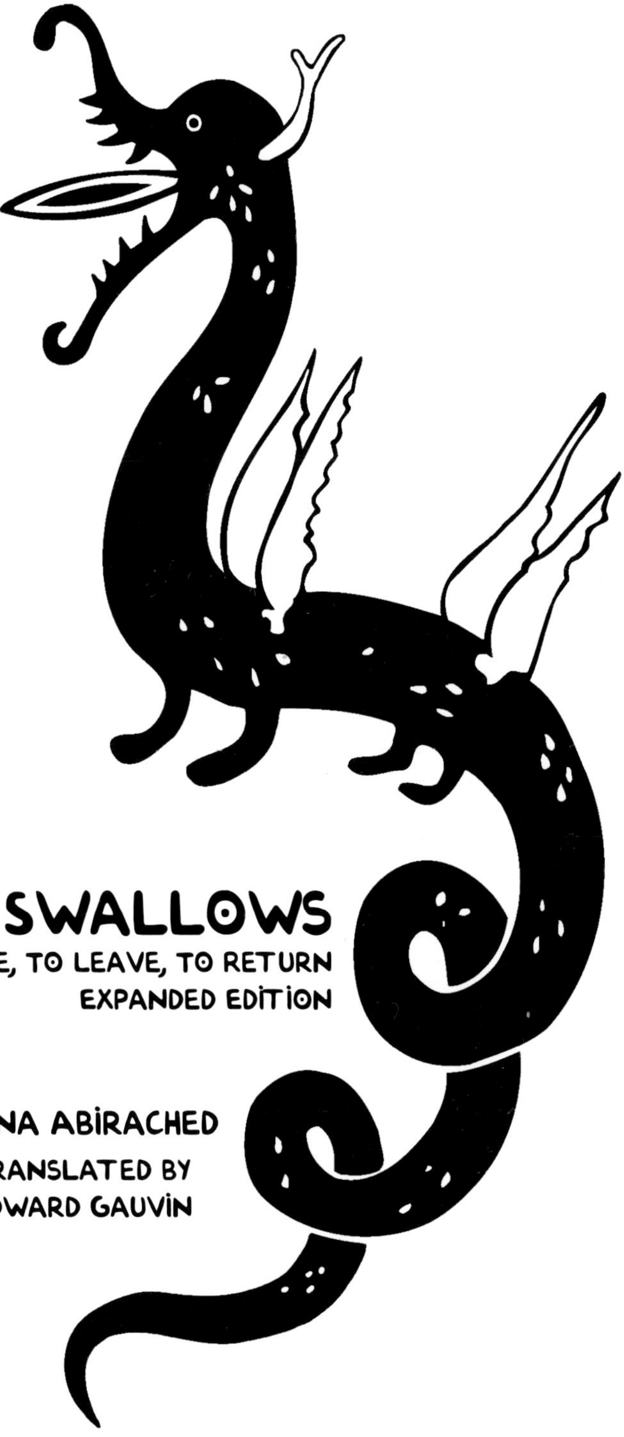

A GAME FOR SWALLOWS

TO DIE, TO LEAVE, TO RETURN

EXPANDED EDITION

ZEINA ABIRACHED

TRANSLATED BY
EDWARD GAUVIN

GRAPHIC UNIVERSE™ • MINNEAPOLIS

FRENCH VOICES

FRENCH VOICES

THE FIRST AMERICAN EDITION OF THIS WORK, PUBLISHED AS PART OF A PROGRAM PROVIDING PUBLICATION ASSISTANCE, RECEIVED FINANCIAL SUPPORT FROM THE FRENCH MINISTRY OF FOREIGN AFFAIRS, THE CULTURAL SERVICES OF THE FRENCH EMBASSY IN THE UNITED STATES, AND FACE (FRENCH AMERICAN CULTURAL EXCHANGE).

FRENCH VOICES LOGO DESIGNED BY SERGE BLOCH

THIS TITLE RECEIVED A 2013 BATCHELDER HONOR AWARD FOR THE FIRST EDITION PUBLISHED IN THE PREVIOUS YEAR IN 2012

STORY AND ART BY ZEINA ABIRACHED
TRANSLATION BY EDWARD GAUVIN

FIRST AMERICAN EDITION PUBLISHED IN 2012 BY GRAPHIC UNIVERSE™.
EXPANDED AMERICAN EDITION PUBLISHED IN 2022 BY GRAPHIC UNIVERSE™.
PUBLISHED BY ARRANGEMENT WITH ÉDITIONS CAMBOURAKIS. RIGHTS ARRANGED THROUGH NICOLAS GRIVEL AGENCY.

A GAME FOR SWALLOWS
© 2007 BY ÉDITIONS CAMBOURAKIS
ENGLISH TRANSLATION COPYRIGHT © 2012 BY LERNER PUBLISHING GROUP, INC.
AFTERWORD ENGLISH TRANSLATION COPYRIGHT © 2022 BY LERNER PUBLISHING GROUP, INC.

QUOTATIONS FROM EDMOND ROSTAND'S *CYRANO DE BERGERAC* ADAPTED FROM THE 1899 TRANSLATION BY GLADYS THOMAS AND MARY F. GUILLEMARD.

MAP P. 8 © LAURA WESTLUND/INDEPENDENT PICTURE SERVICE

GRAPHIC UNIVERSE™ IS A TRADEMARK OF LERNER PUBLISHING GROUP, INC.

GRAPHIC UNIVERSE™
AN IMPRINT OF LERNER PUBLISHING GROUP, INC.
241 FIRST AVENUE NORTH
MINNEAPOLIS, MN 55401 USA

FOR READING LEVELS AND MORE INFORMATION, LOOK UP THIS TITLE AT WWW.LERNERBOOKS.COM.

LIBRARY OF CONGRESS CATALOGING-IN-PUBLICATION DATA

NAMES: ABIRACHED, ZEINA, 1981– AUTHOR, ARTIST. | GAUVIN, EDWARD, TRANSLATOR.
TITLE: A GAME FOR SWALLOWS : TO DIE, TO LEAVE, TO RETURN | ZEINA ABIRACHED ; TRANSLATED BY EDWARD GAUVIN.
OTHER TITLES: JEU DES HIRONDELLES. ENGLISH
DESCRIPTION: EXPANDED EDITION. | MINNEAPOLIS : GRAPHIC UNIVERSE, 2022. | AUDIENCE: AGES 12–18 | AUDIENCE: GRADES 10–12 | SUMMARY: "WHEN ZEINA'S PARENTS DON'T RETURN ONE AFTERNOON AND BOMBING IN BEIRUT GROWS CLOSER, HER NEIGHBORS CREATE A COMFORTABLE WORLD INDOORS FOR ZEINA AND HER BROTHER. THIS EXPANDED EDITION FEATURES A NEW, ILLUSTRATED AFTERWORD"— PROVIDED BY PUBLISHER.
IDENTIFIERS: LCCN 2022000021 (PRINT) | LCCN 2022000022 (EBOOK) | ISBN 9781728446134 (PAPERBACK) | ISBN 9781728460987 (EBOOK)
SUBJECTS: LCSH: ABIRACHED, ZEINA, 1981-—JUVENILE FICTION. | LEBANON—HISTORY—CIVIL WAR, 1975–1990—JUVENILE FICTION. | BEIRUT (LEBANON)—JUVENILE FICTION. | CYAC: GRAPHIC NOVELS. | ABIRACHED, ZEINA, 1981-—FICTION. | LEBANON—HISTORY—CIVIL WAR, 1975–1990—FICTION. | BEIRUT (LEBANON)—FICTION. | LCGFT: AUTOBIOGRAPHICAL COMICS. | HISTORICAL COMICS. | GRAPHIC NOVELS.
CLASSIFICATION: LCC PZ7.7.A256 GAM 2022 (PRINT) | LCC PZ7.7.A256 (EBOOK) | DDC 741.5/95692—DC23/ENG/20220121

LC RECORD AVAILABLE AT HTTPS://LCCN.LOC.GOV/2022000021
LC EBOOK RECORD AVAILABLE AT HTTPS://LCCN.LOC.GOV/2022000022

MANUFACTURED IN THE UNITED STATES OF AMERICA
1-50339-49887-1/6/2022

iNTRODUCTiON

A song I used to love back in 1969 asks what war is good for. The answer: absolutely nothing. My politics are pretty simple: people have the right to love one another, regardless of gender; basic health care is a human right; women have the right to control over their own bodies; it is unfair for 1 percent of the population to have all the wealth while 99 percent have nothing; and war is bad.

But I don't understand wars. OK, I get the reasons for World War II and the American Civil War, but I will never understand World War I. What was Bosnia all about? Why did Iran and Iraq fight with each other? And what was the reason for the Lebanese Civil War? Are there *justifiable* reasons for wars?

From my untutored viewpoint, a bunch of old guys send a bunch of young guys out to kill and die while ordinary people like you and me, caught in the middle, simply try to survive. And sometimes, in the course of surviving, we do beautiful things.

In a crisp, accessible black-and-white style, reminiscent of Marjane Satrapi's *Persepolis*, Zeina Abirached shows us both the horror and the beauty that can emerge from war. It's 1984 in East Beirut. Very young Zeina has never known anything but war. She lives in the middle of the war zone with her parents and her even younger brother. The family has closed off most of their apartment and moved into the foyer, the only safe room in the house. They've dragged in their mattresses, their chairs and rugs. Hanging on the wall is the family heirloom, a tapestry depicting Moses and the Hebrews fleeing Egypt. The tapestry is separated into panels, like the comic page that contains it: a comic within a comic.

Zeina's parents have gone out to visit her grandmother, who lives a few blocks away—and they have not returned, although they left for home an hour ago. And here's where the beauty comes in.

The neighbors all filter down in ones and twos, to stay with the kids. Soon, nine people fill the tiny foyer. Some of them have lost loved ones to the war. Some of them are preparing to flee to Canada, like Moses and the Hebrews in the tapestry.

They drink strong Turkish coffee and listen to the bombardment outside. Anhala, an old woman, makes a Lebanese cake called *sfouf* that sounds delicious. Should the worst happen, these kids will be loved and cared for!

As I write this, the newspapers and the Internet are full of tributes to Marie Colvin, the journalist who was killed by shelling in Syria on February 22, 2012, along with a French photojournalist named Rémi Ochlik. With her black eye patch, which she wore after losing her eye to shrapnel while covering conflicts in Sri Lanka in 2001, she cut a dashing figure. She always seemed to me like the heroine of a comic book. The *Washington Post* describes her as risking her life "to cover wars from the perspective of ordinary people, particularly women and children." In other words, people like Zeina and her neighbors.

Here is an excerpt from Colvin's last dispatch, to the *Sunday Times* of London three days before she was killed:

> *They call it the widows' basement. Crammed among makeshift beds and scattered belongings are frightened women and children trapped in the horror of Homs, the Syrian city shaken by two weeks of relentless bombardment. . . .*
>
> *Snipers on the rooftops . . . shoot any civilian who comes into their sights. Residents were felled in droves in the first day of the siege . . . but have now learnt where the snipers are and run across junctions where they know they can be seen. . . .*
>
> *No shops are open, so families are sharing what they have with relatives and neighbours.*

The story sounds so much the same as Zeina's.

I found a recipe for *sfouf* on the Internet. It looks pretty easy to make, but you need semolina flour and turmeric. I shall walk two blocks to the supermarket for the flour and spice, and nobody will shoot at me. Doesn't everybody deserve to live like that?

—Trina Robbins
March 2012

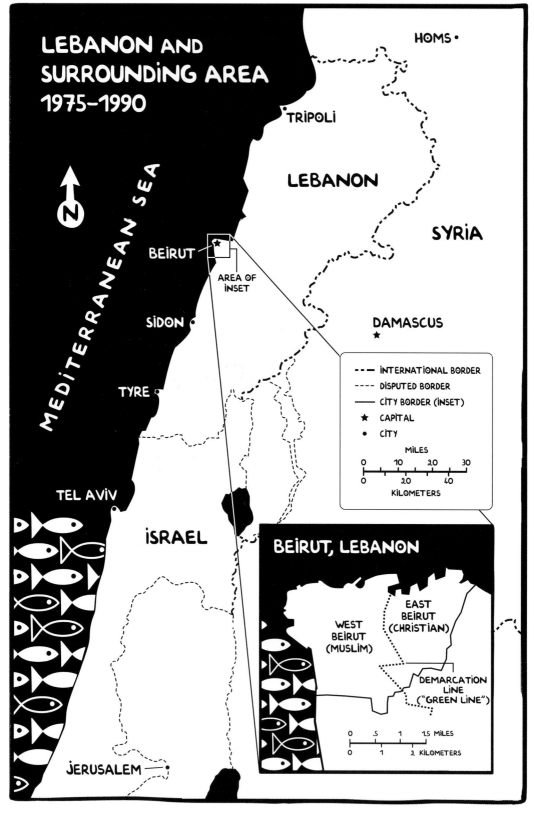

LEBANON AND SURROUNDING AREA 1975–1990

N

HOMS •

TRIPOLI •

LEBANON

SYRIA

MEDITERRANEAN SEA

BEIRUT
★
AREA OF INSET

SIDON •

DAMASCUS
★

- - ·- - INTERNATIONAL BORDER
- - - - DISPUTED BORDER
──── CITY BORDER (INSET)
★ CAPITAL
• CITY

MILES
0   10   20   30
0   20   40
KILOMETERS

TYRE •

TEL AVIV •

ISRAEL

BEIRUT, LEBANON

WEST BEIRUT (MUSLIM)

EAST BEIRUT (CHRISTIAN)

DEMARCATION LINE ("GREEN LINE")

0   .5   1   1.5 MILES
0   1   2 KILOMETERS

JERUSALEM •

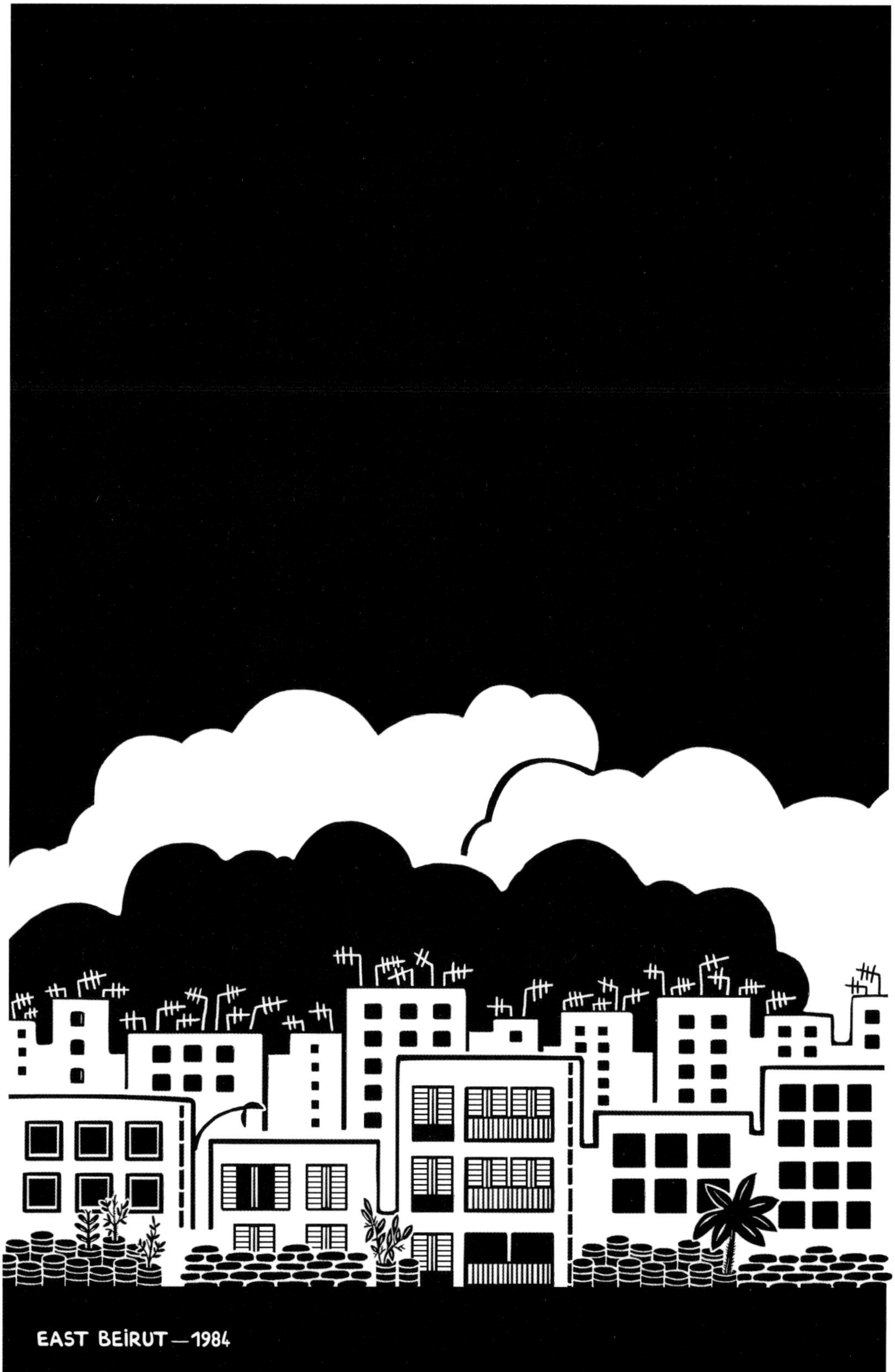
EAST BEIRUT—1984

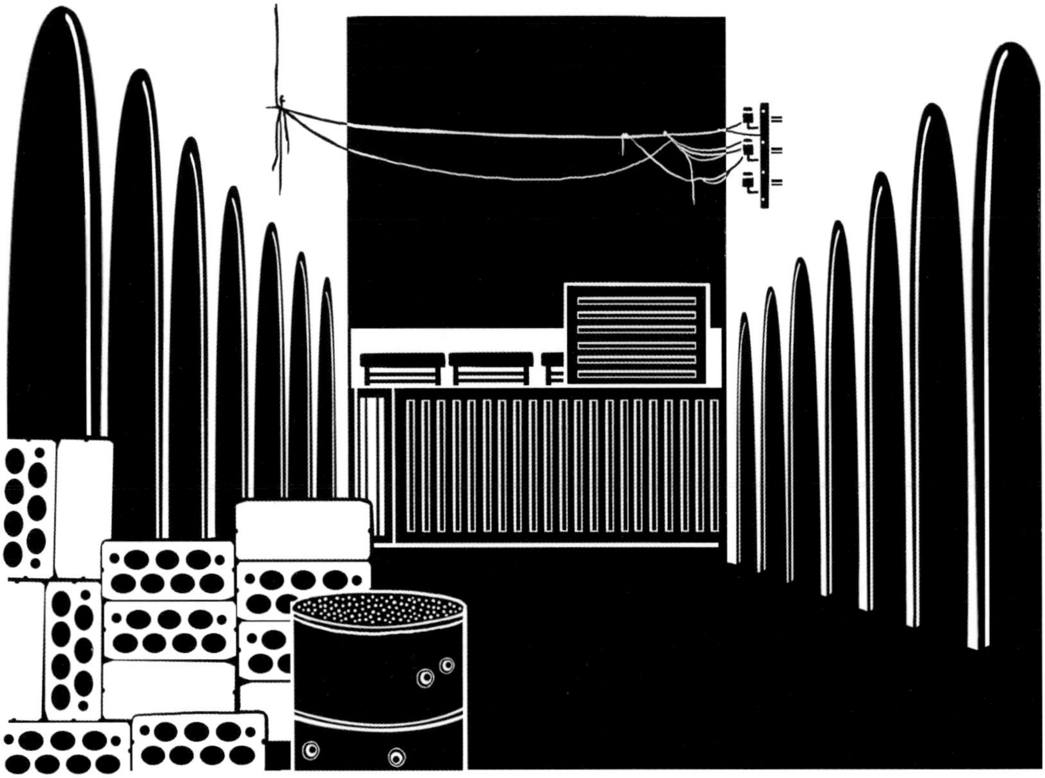

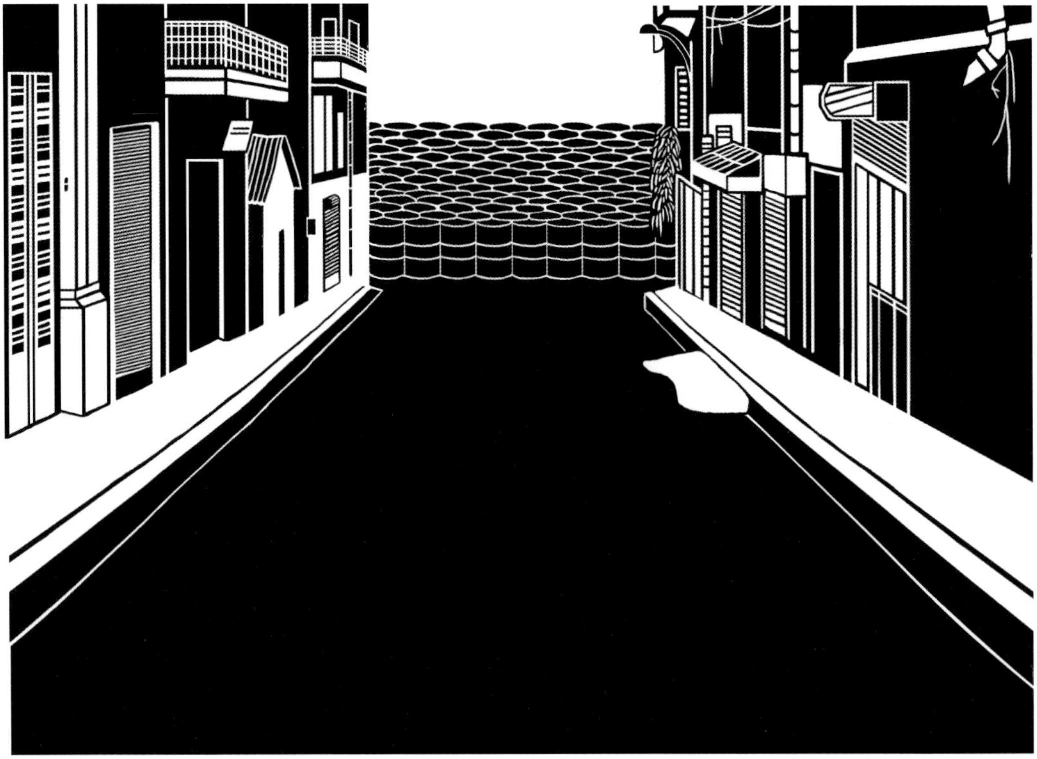

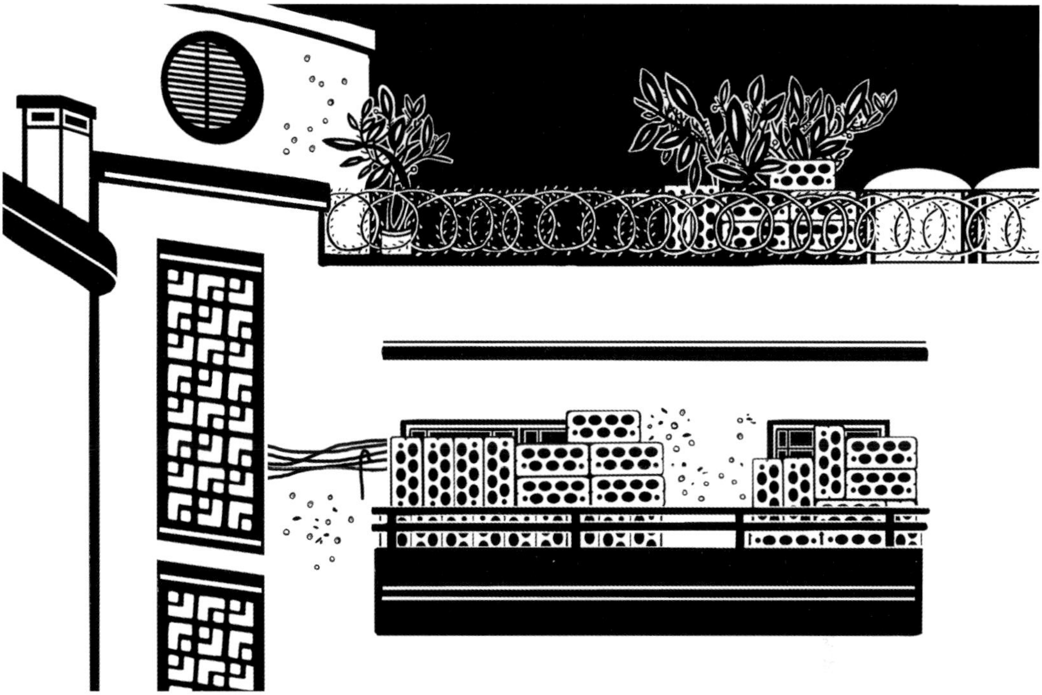

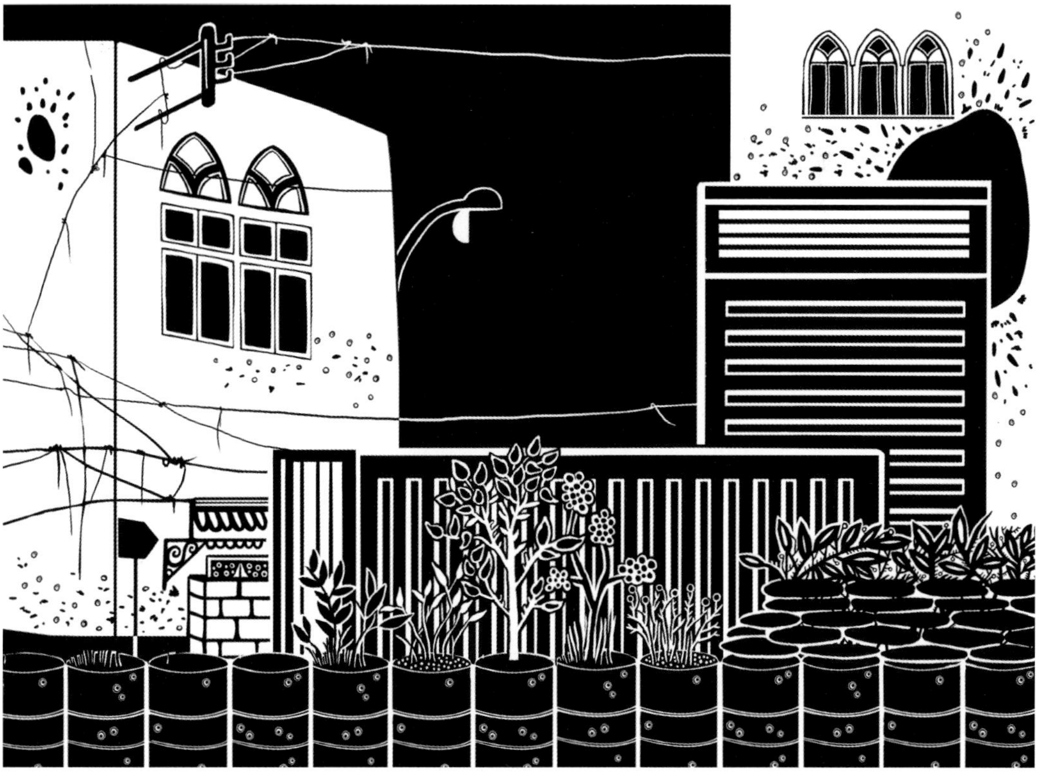

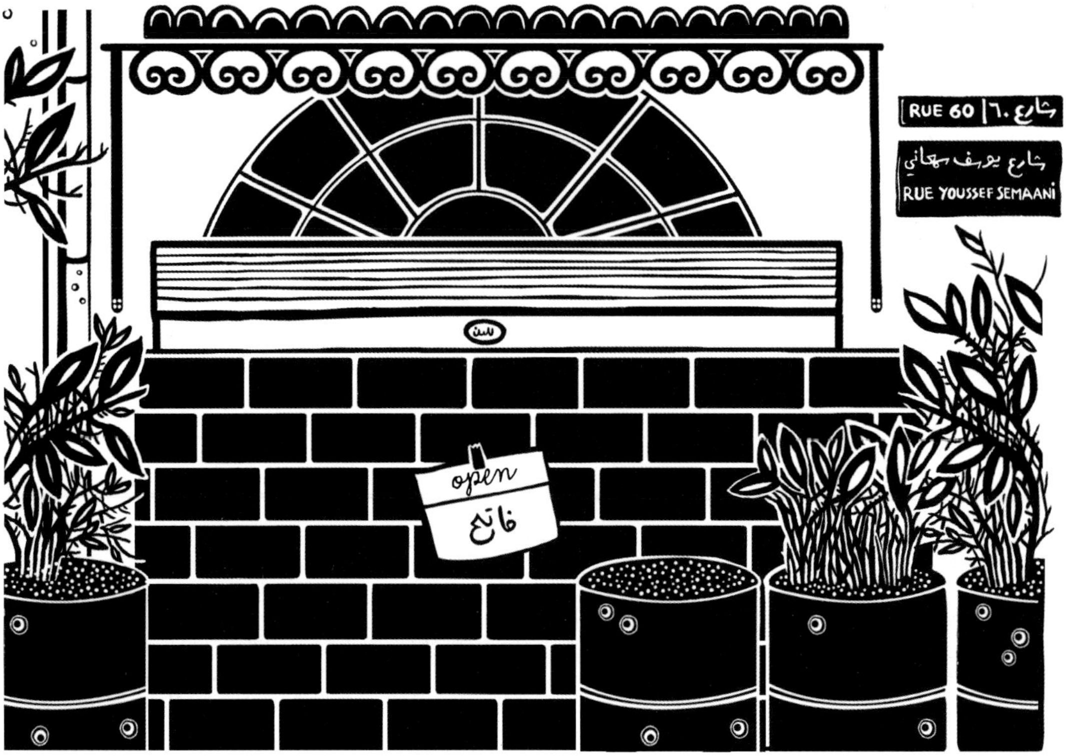
RUE 60 | شارع ٦٠
شارع يوسف سمعاني
RUE YOUSSEF SEMAANI
open
فاتح

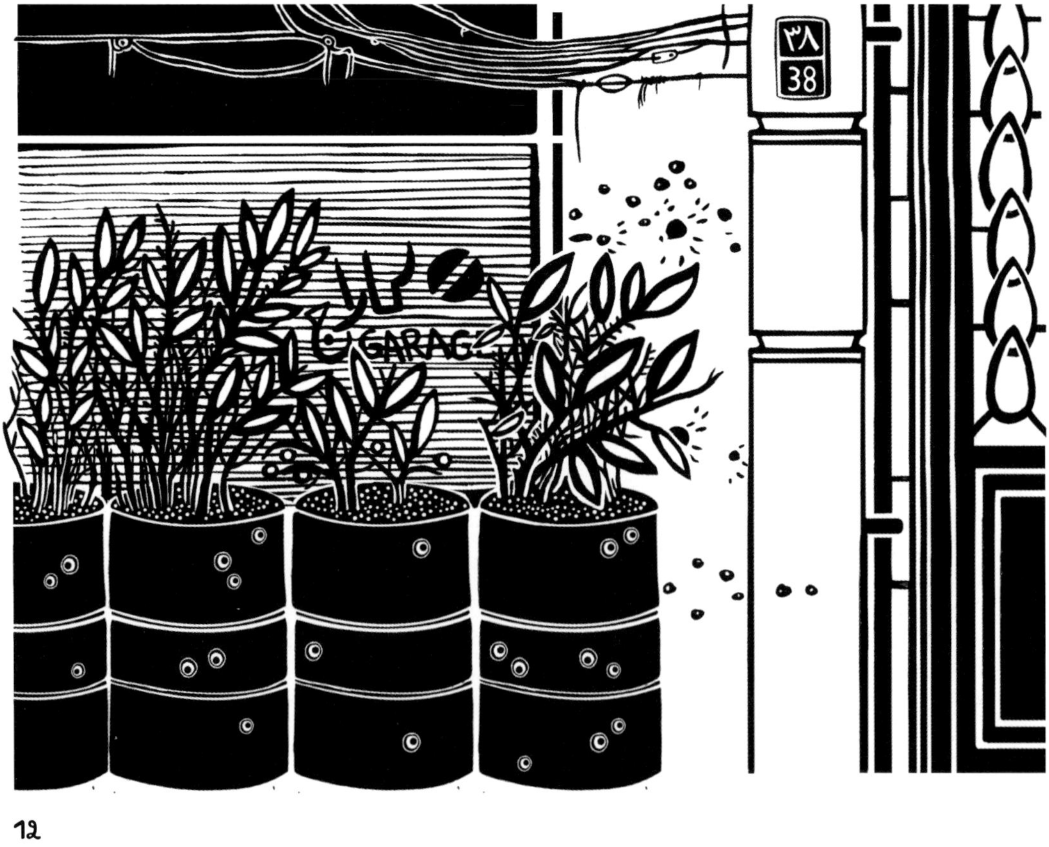
٣٨
38
GARAG

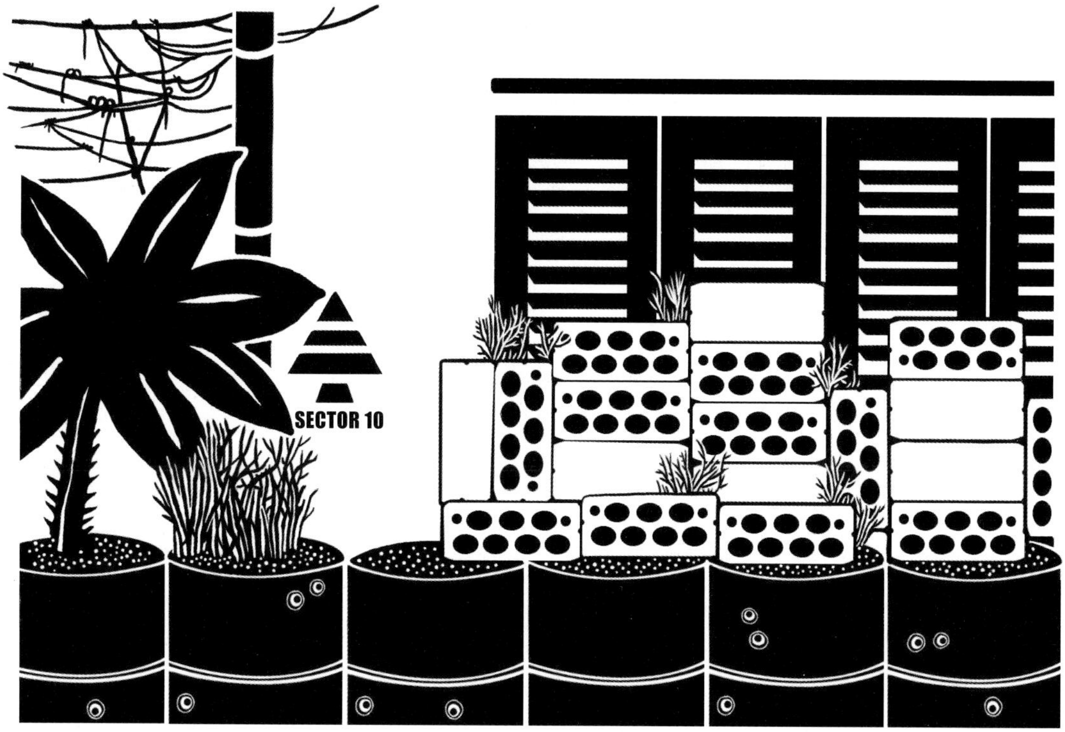
SECTOR 10

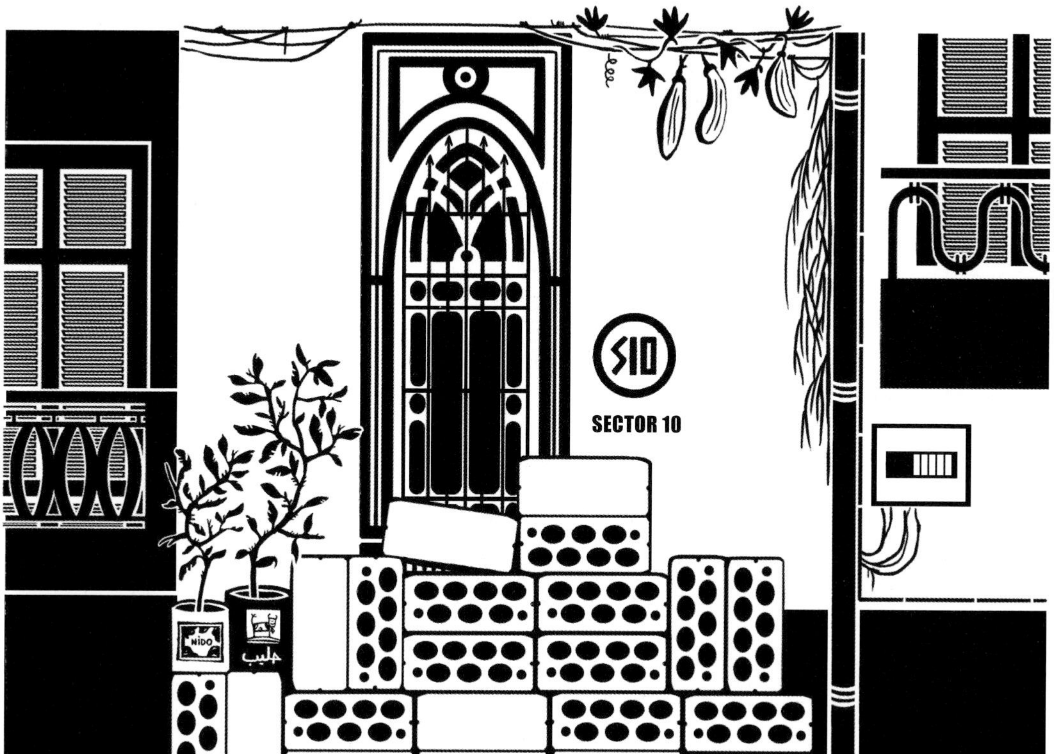
S10
SECTOR 10
NIDO
حليب

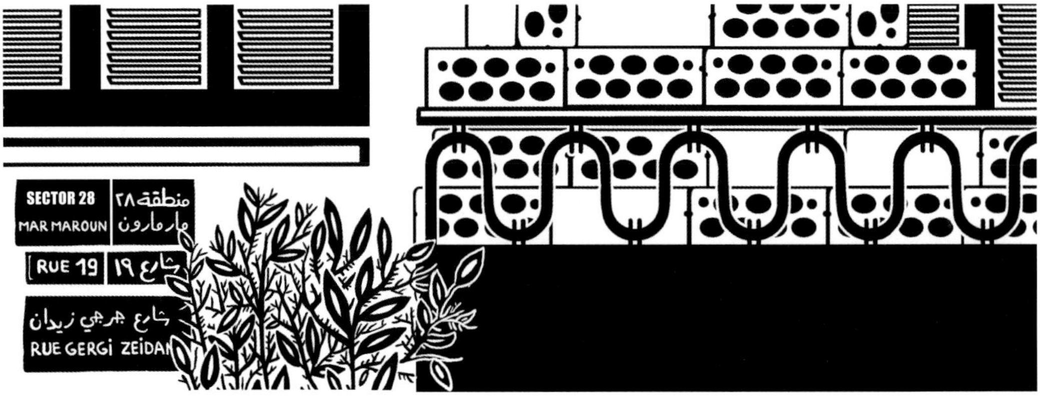
SECTOR 28
منطقة ٢٨
MAR MAROUN
مار مارون
RUE 19
شارع ١٩
شارع جرجي زيدان
RUE GERGI ZEIDA

IN THE NEIGHBORHOODS ALONG THE DEMARCATION LINE, WALLS OF SANDBAGS SEVER THE STREETS.
CONTAINERS TAKEN FROM THE DOCKS OF THE DESERTED PORT STAND IN THE MIDDLE OF ALLEYS TO PROTECT RESIDENTS FROM SNIPERS' BULLETS.
BUILDINGS SHUT THEMSELVES AWAY BEHIND WALLS OF CINDER BLOCKS AND METAL DRUMS.
INSIDE THESE DIVIDED SECTORS, LIFE IS ORGANIZED AROUND THE CEASE-FIRES.

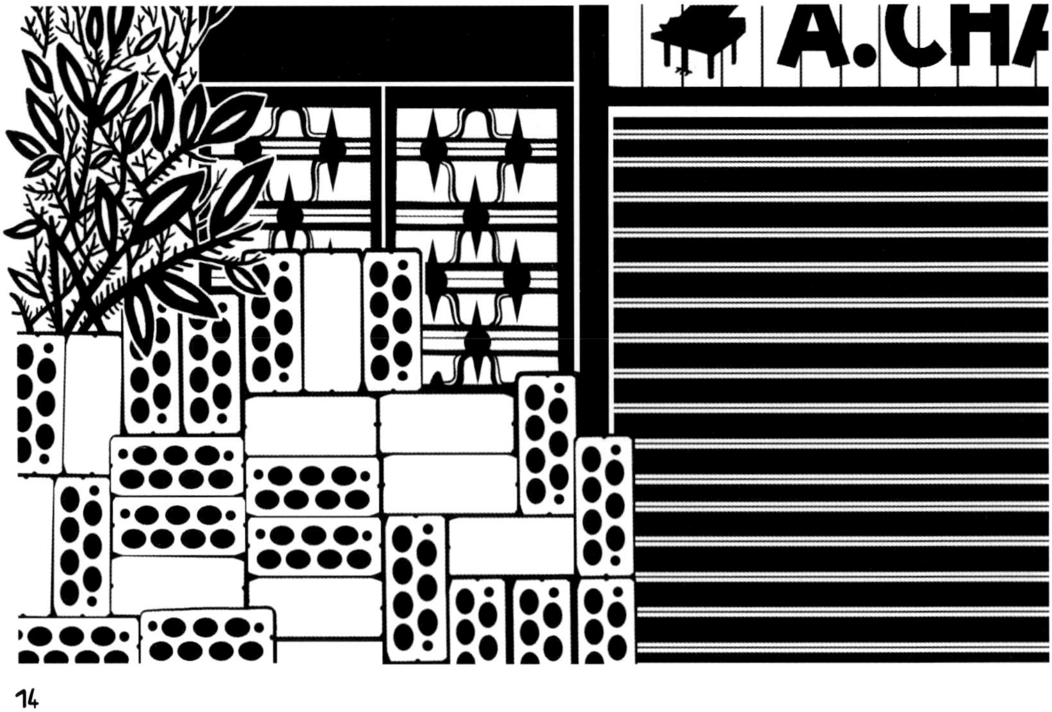
A.CHA

THAT DAY, MY PARENTS HAD GONE TO VISIT GRANDMOTHER ANNIE. VIOLENT BOMBARDMENT HAD KEPT THEM FROM COMING HOME.

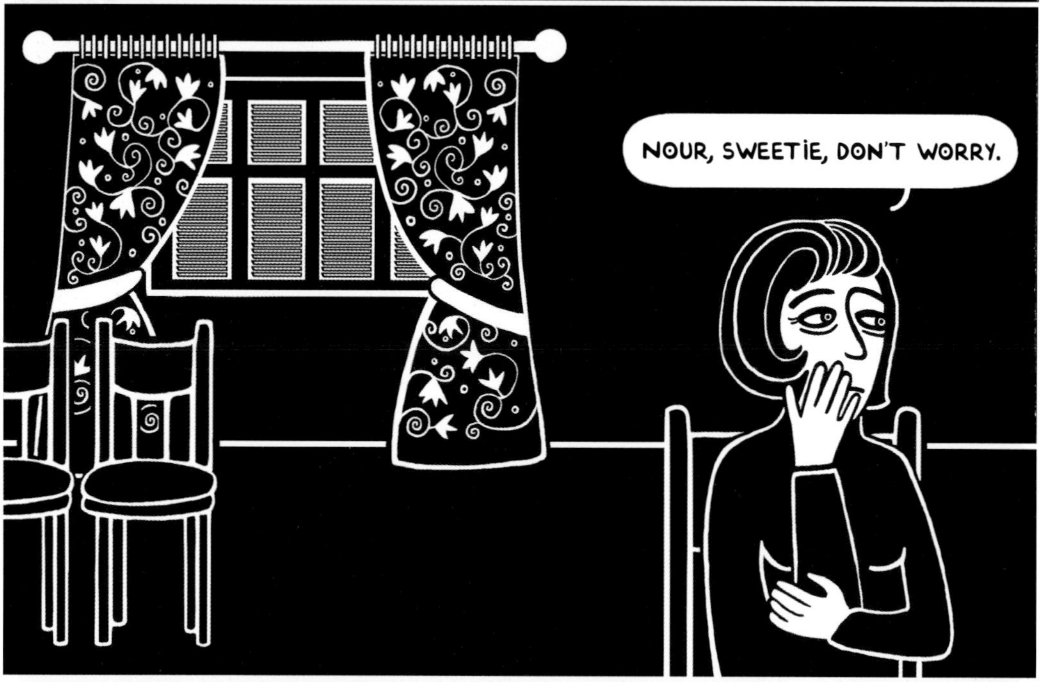
NOUR, SWEETIE, DON'T WORRY.

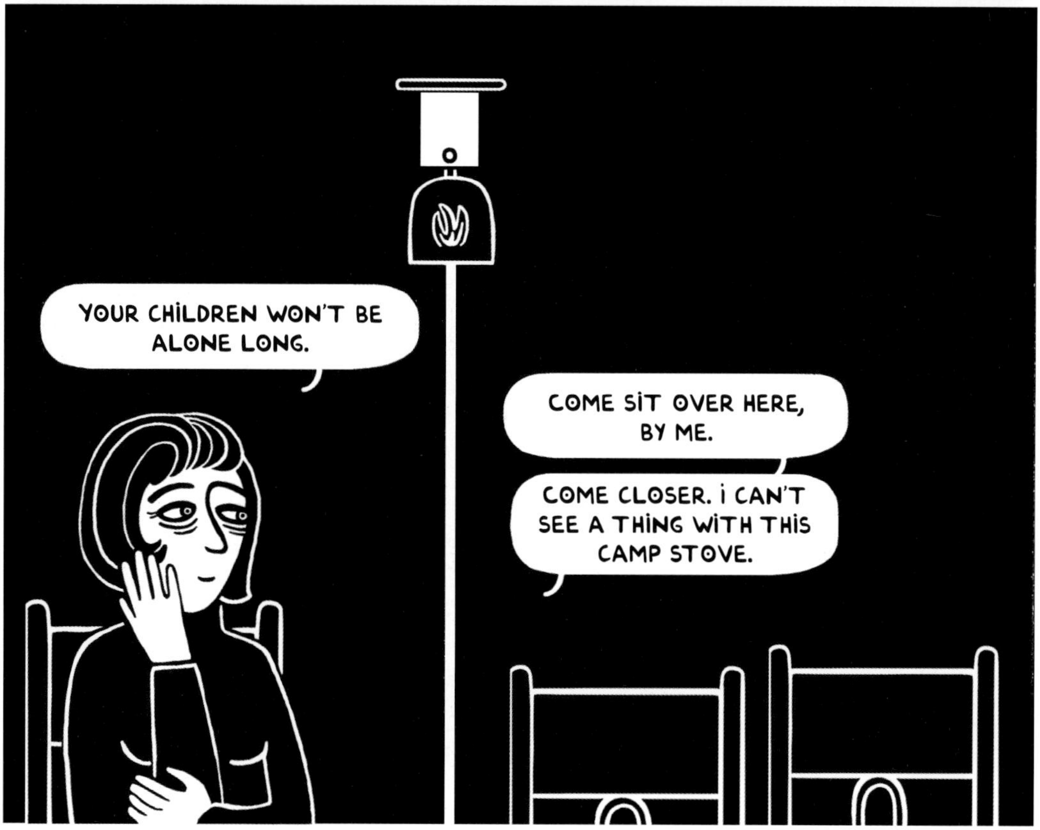
YOUR CHILDREN WON'T BE ALONE LONG.
COME SIT OVER HERE, BY ME.
COME CLOSER. I CAN'T SEE A THING WITH THIS CAMP STOVE.

MY GRANDPARENTS ON MY MOTHER'S SIDE LIVED A FEW STREETS AWAY FROM US.

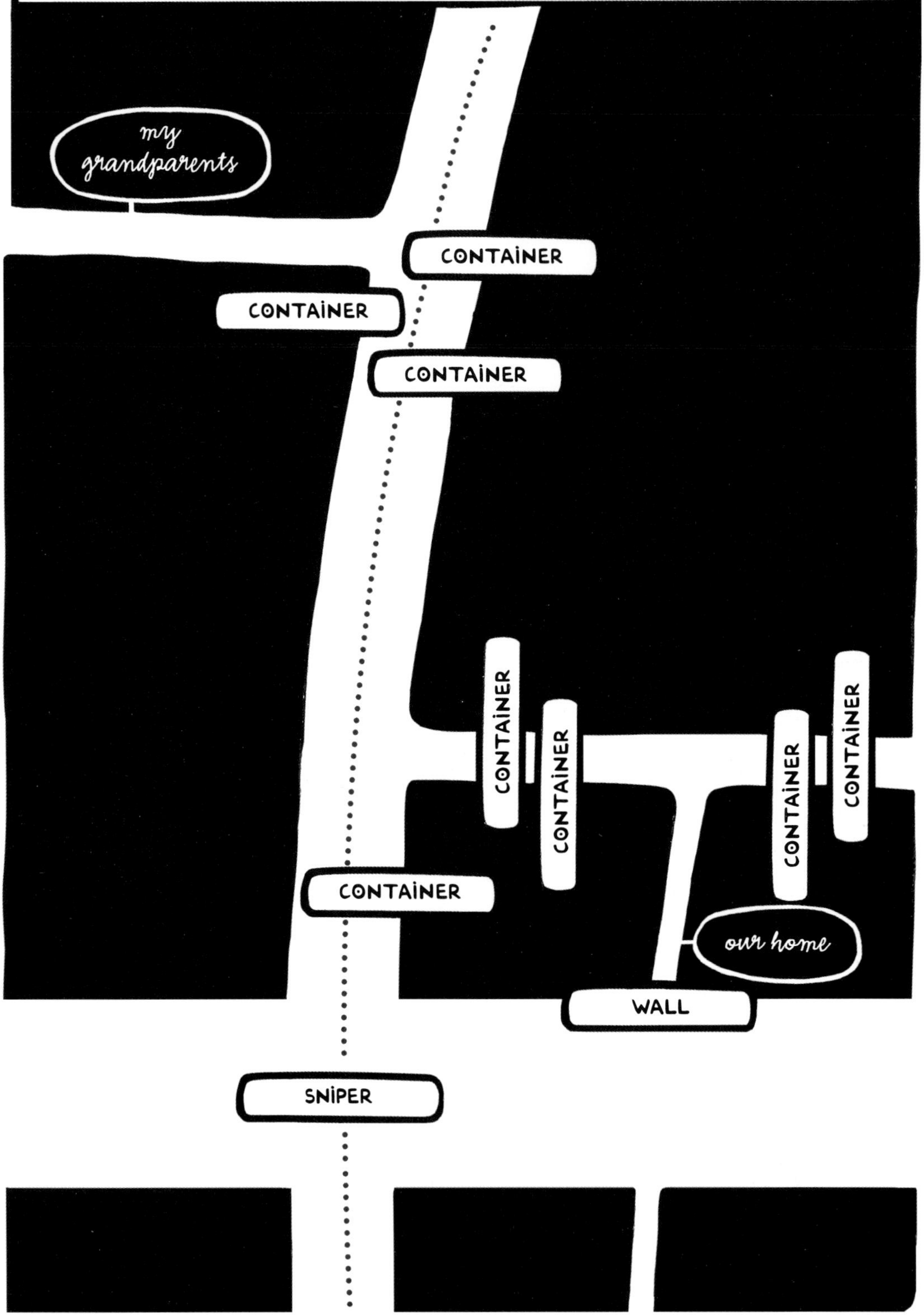
my grandparents
CONTAINER
CONTAINER
CONTAINER
CONTAINER
CONTAINER
CONTAINER
CONTAINER
CONTAINER
our home
WALL
SNIPER

TO AVOID THE SNIPER, PEOPLE HAD PERFECTED A WAY OF MOVING BETWEEN BUILDINGS.

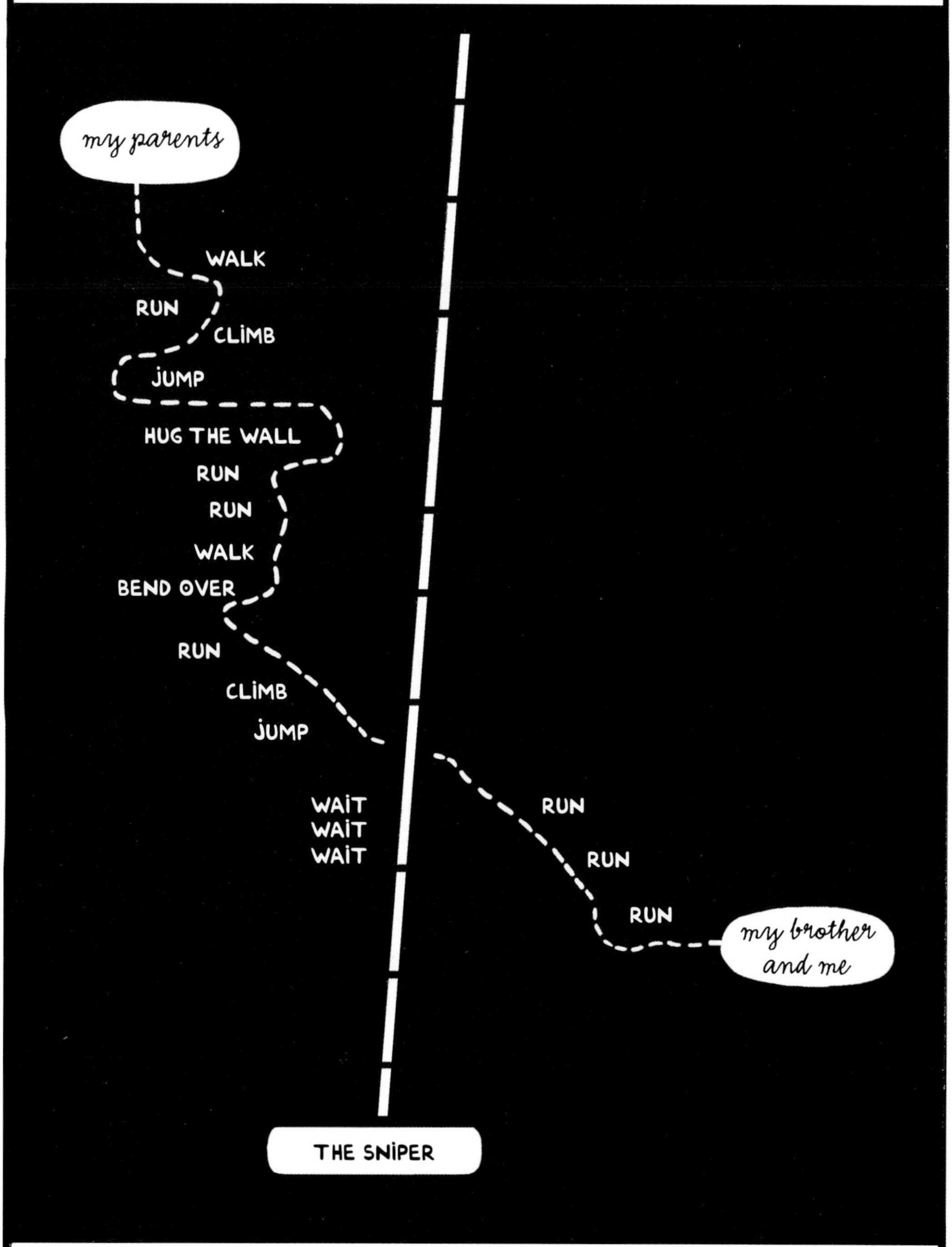
my parents
WALK
RUN
CLIMB
JUMP
HUG THE WALL
RUN
RUN
WALK
BEND OVER
RUN
CLIMB
JUMP
WAIT
WAIT
WAIT
RUN
RUN
RUN
my brother and me
THE SNIPER

CROSSING THE HANDFUL OF STREETS BETWEEN US MEANT FOLLOWING COMPLICATED AND PERILOUS CHOREOGRAPHY.

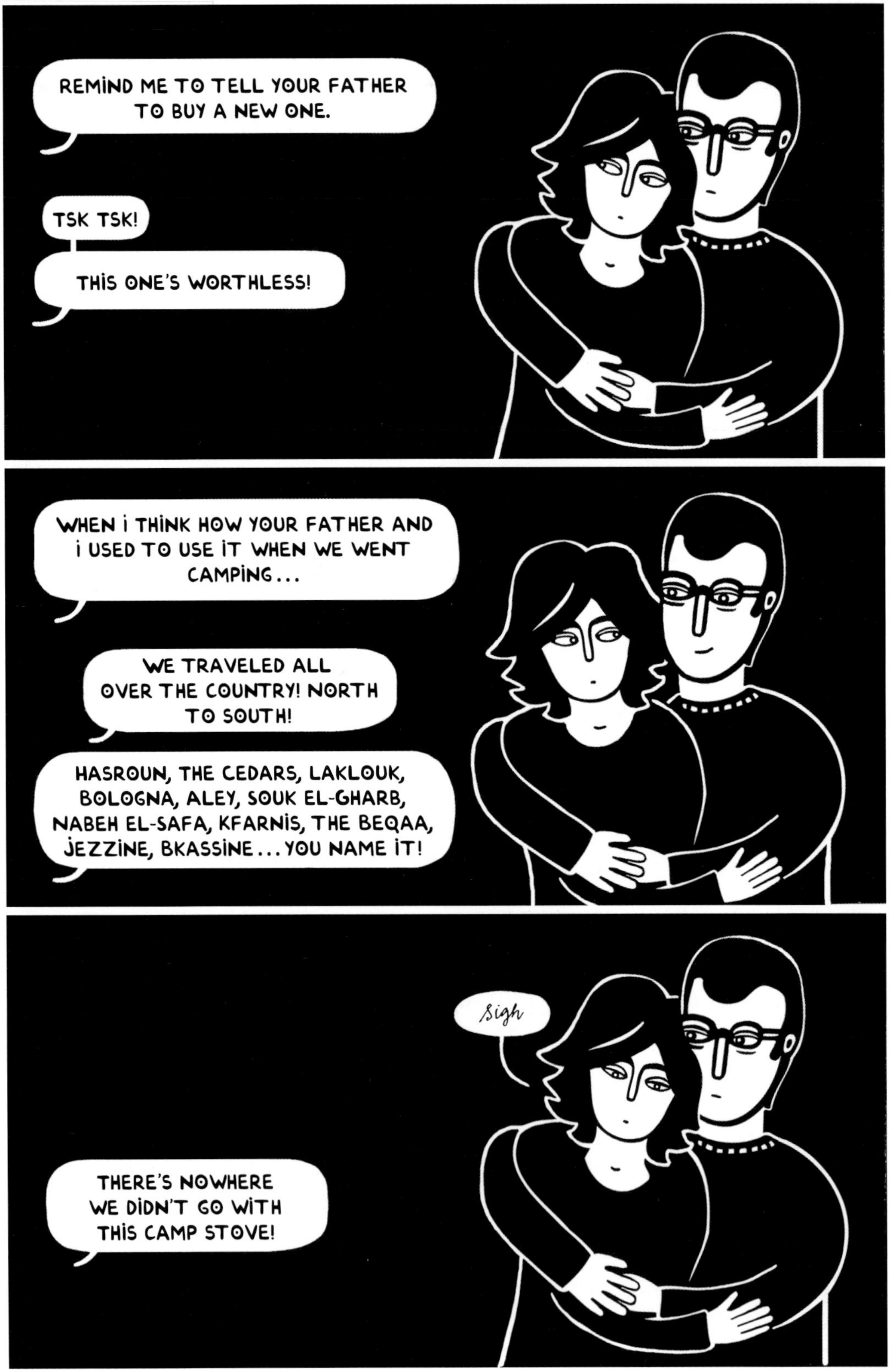
REMIND ME TO TELL YOUR FATHER TO BUY A NEW ONE.
TSK TSK!
THIS ONE'S WORTHLESS!
WHEN I THINK HOW YOUR FATHER AND I USED TO USE IT WHEN WE WENT CAMPING...
WE TRAVELED ALL OVER THE COUNTRY! NORTH TO SOUTH!
HASROUN, THE CEDARS, LAKLOUK, BOLOGNA, ALEY, SOUK EL-GHARB, NABEH EL-SAFA, KFARNIS, THE BEQAA, JEZZINE, BKASSINE... YOU NAME IT!
Sigh
THERE'S NOWHERE WE DIDN'T GO WITH THIS CAMP STOVE!

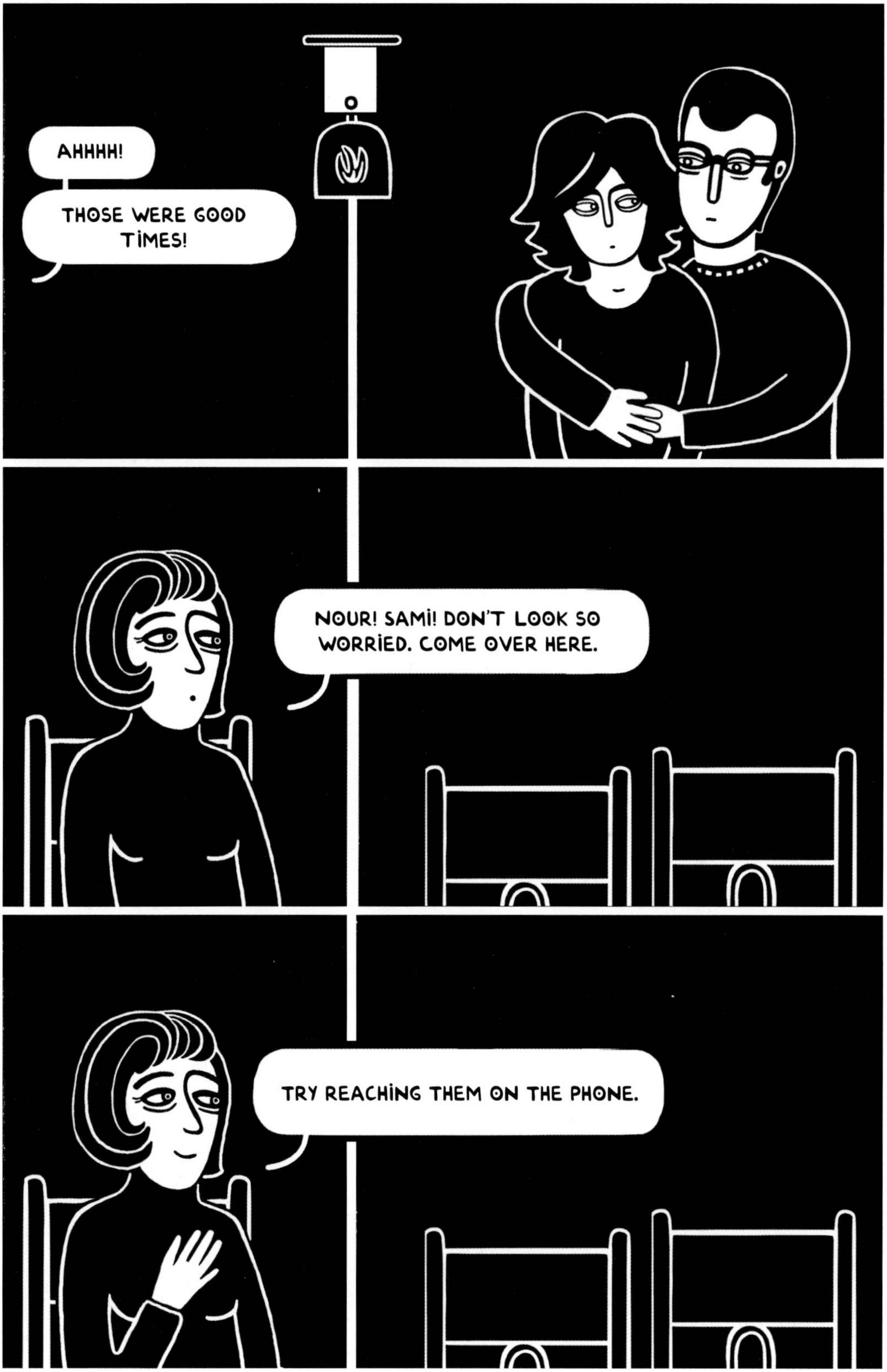
AHHHH!
THOSE WERE GOOD TIMES!
NOUR! SAMI! DON'T LOOK SO WORRIED. COME OVER HERE.
TRY REACHING THEM ON THE PHONE.

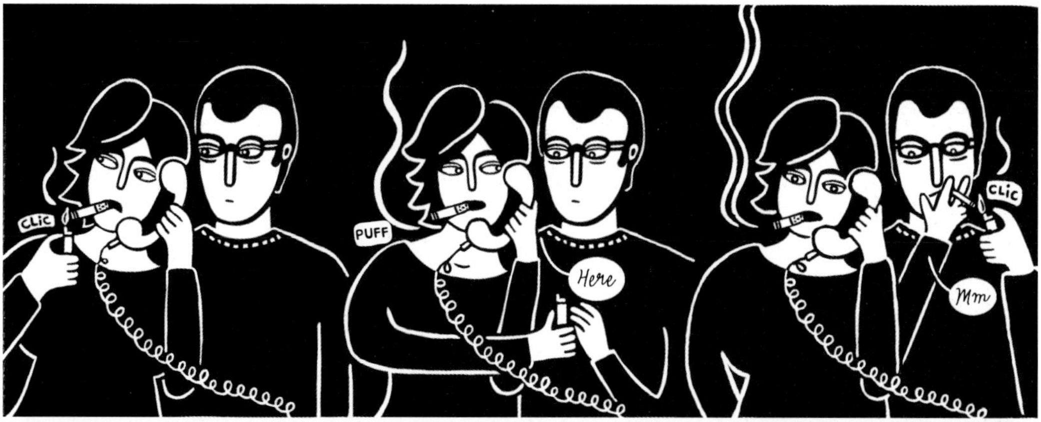
CLiC
PUFF
Here
CLiC
Mm

BACK THEN, IT WAS VERY HARD TO REACH SOMEONE BY PHONE.

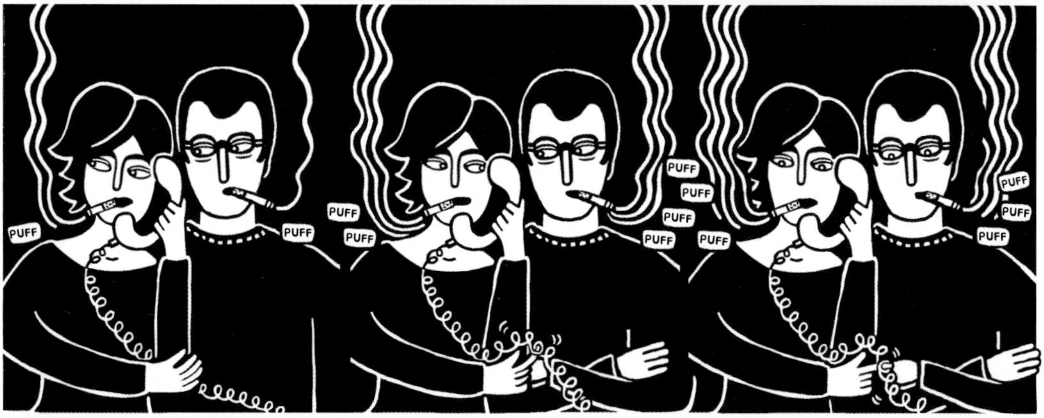
PUFF
PUFF
PUFF
PUFF
PUFF
PUFF
PUFF
PUFF
PUFF
PUFF
PUFF
PUFF

YOU COULD WAIT HOURS ON END JUST FOR A DIAL TONE.

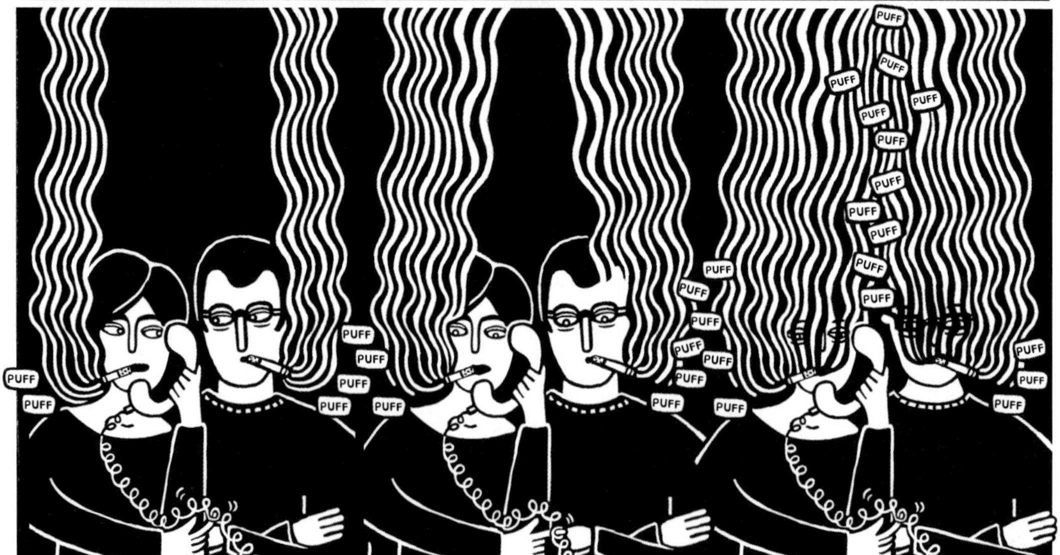
PUFF
PUFF
PUFF
PUFF
PUFF
PUFF
PUFF
PUFF
PUFF
PUFF
PUFF
PUFF
PUFF
PUFF
PUFF
PUFF
PUFF
PUFF
PUFF
PUFF
PUFF
PUFF
PUFF
PUFF
PUFF
PUFF
PUFF
PUFF
PUFF

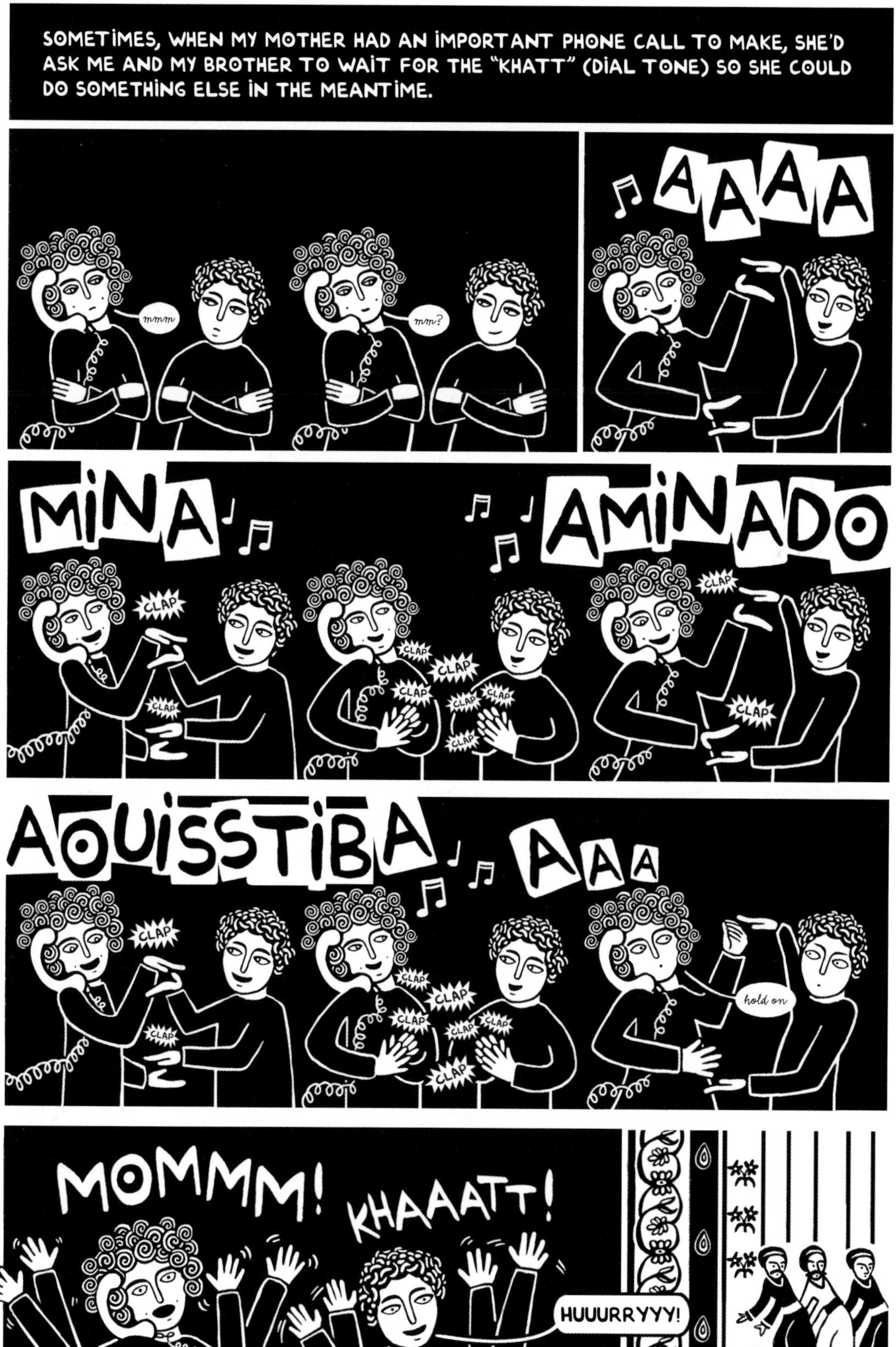

SOMETIMES, WHEN MY MOTHER HAD AN IMPORTANT PHONE CALL TO MAKE, SHE'D ASK ME AND MY BROTHER TO WAIT FOR THE "KHATT" (DIAL TONE) SO SHE COULD DO SOMETHING ELSE IN THE MEANTIME.
mmm
mm?
AAAA
MINA
CLAP
CLAP
AMINADO
CLAP
CLAP
CLAP
AOUISSTIBA
CLAP
CLAP
AAA
CLAP
CLAP
hold on
MOMMM!
KHAAATT!
HUUURRYYY!

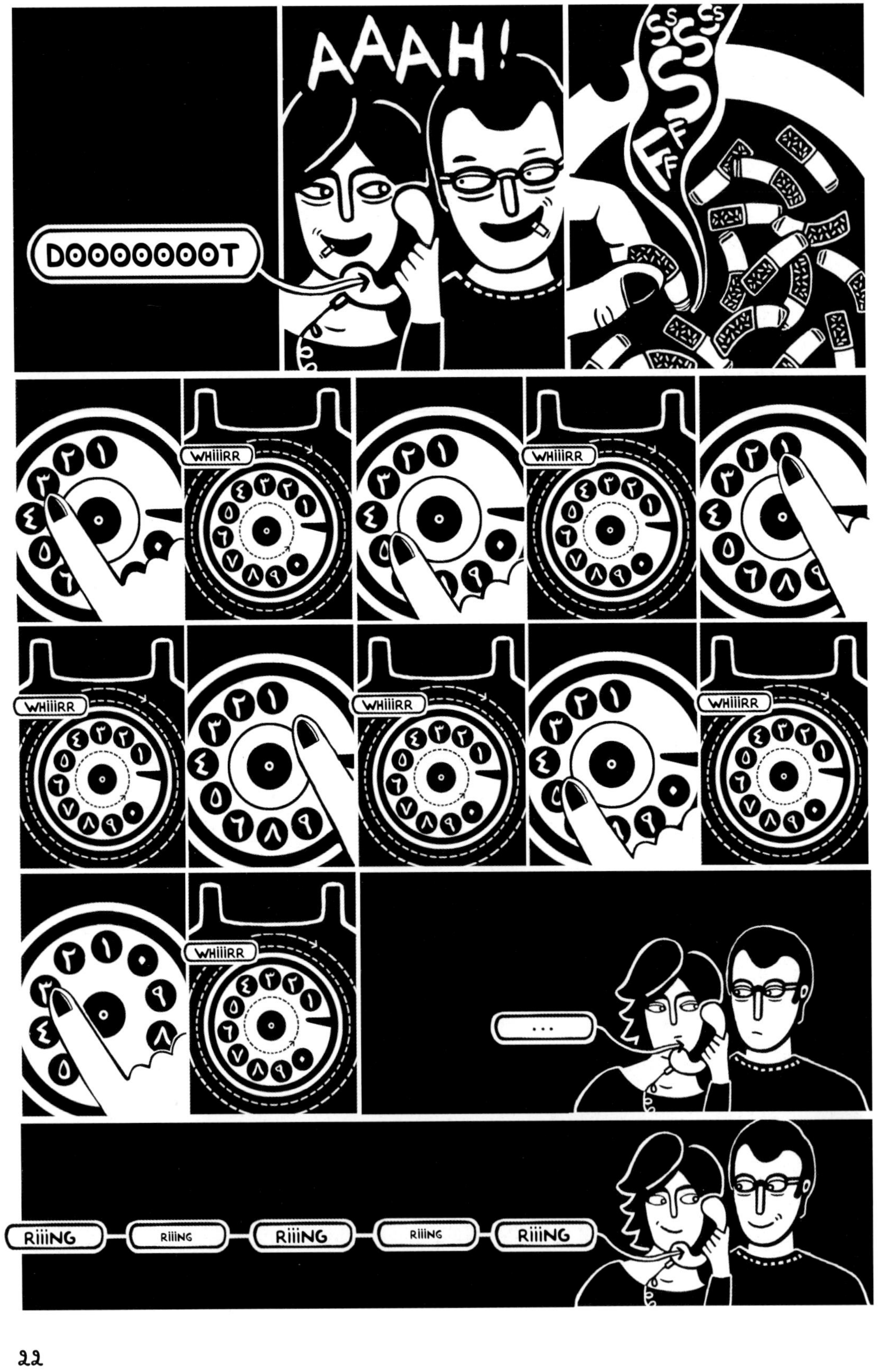
DOOOOOOOT
AAAH!
SSSSS
FFF
WHiiiRR
WHiiiRR
WHiiiRR
WHiiiRR
WHiiiRR
WHiiiRR
...
RiiiNG
RiiiNG
RiiiNG
RiiiNG
RiiiNG

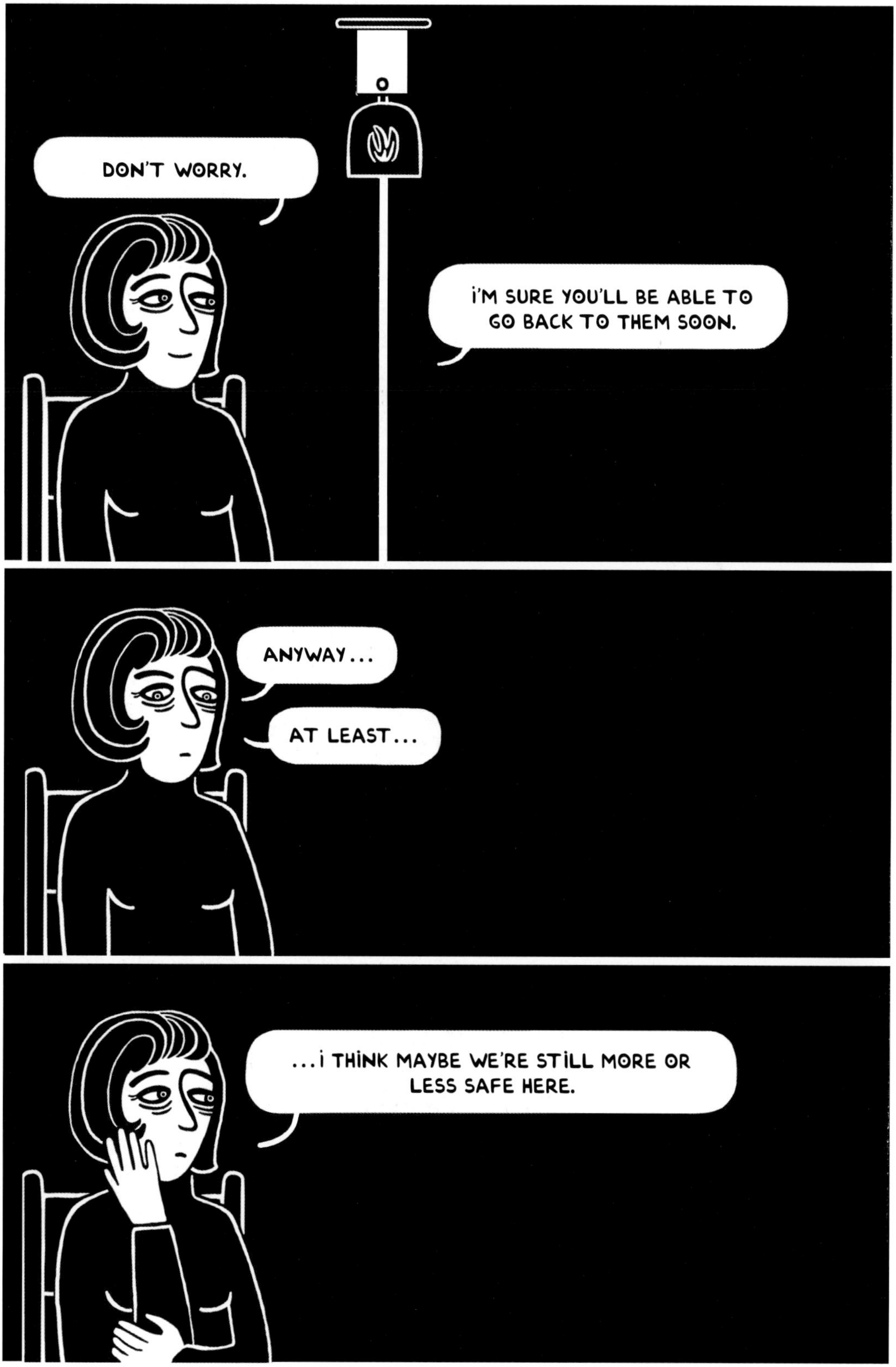
DON'T WORRY.
I'M SURE YOU'LL BE ABLE TO GO BACK TO THEM SOON.
ANYWAY...
AT LEAST...
...I THINK MAYBE WE'RE STILL MORE OR LESS SAFE HERE.

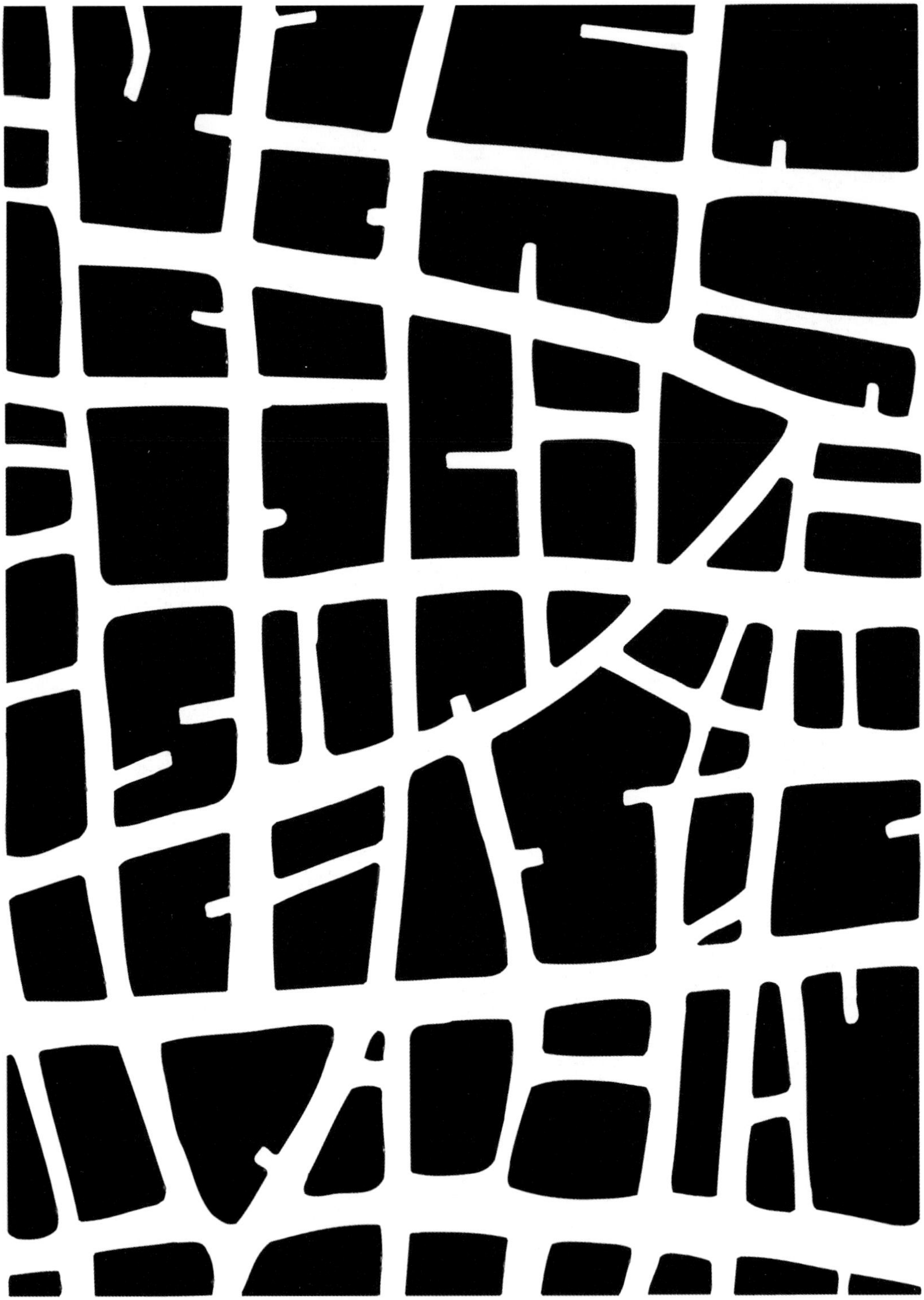

HERE IS ALL THE SPACE WE HAVE LEFT ...

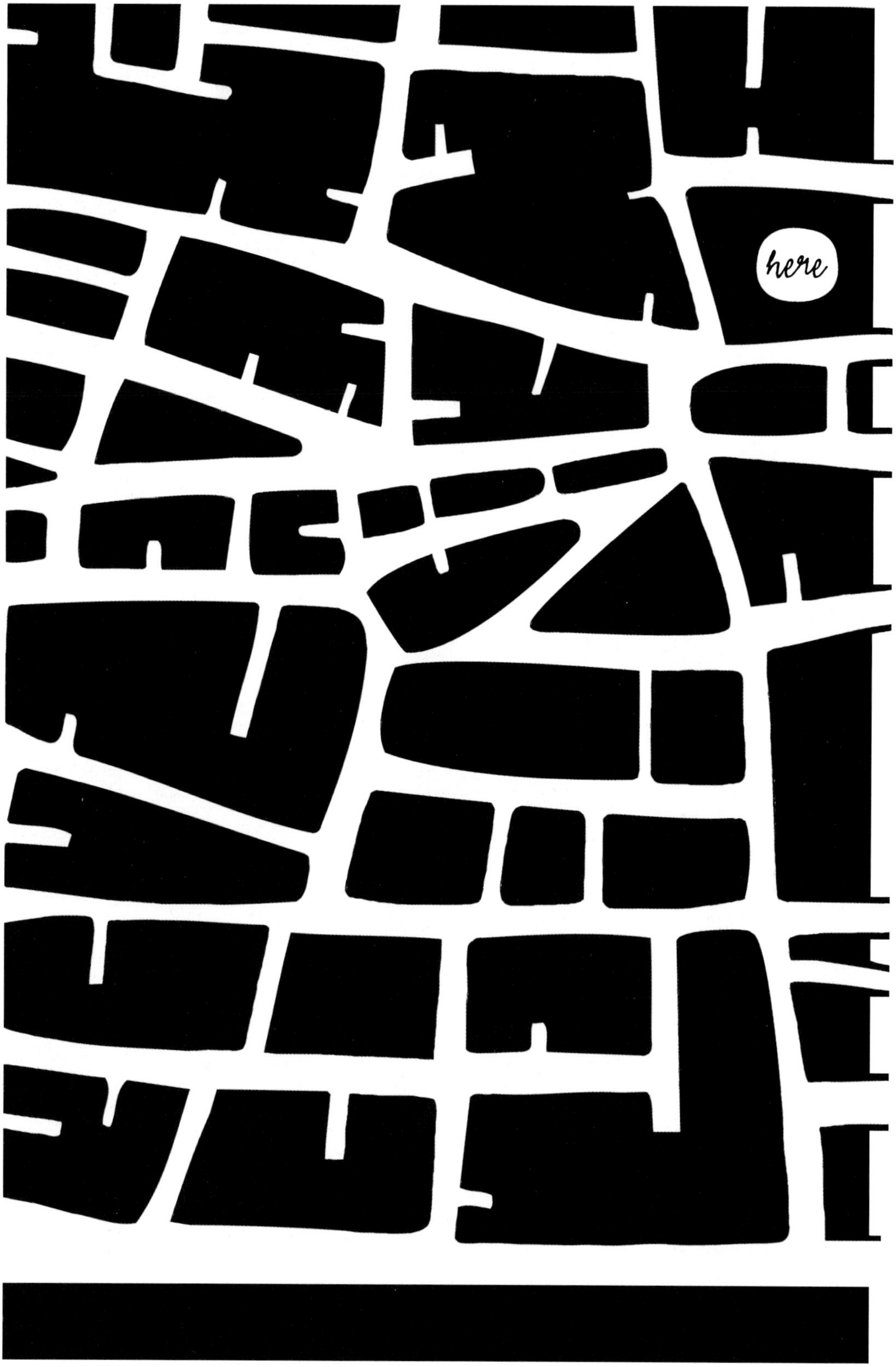
here

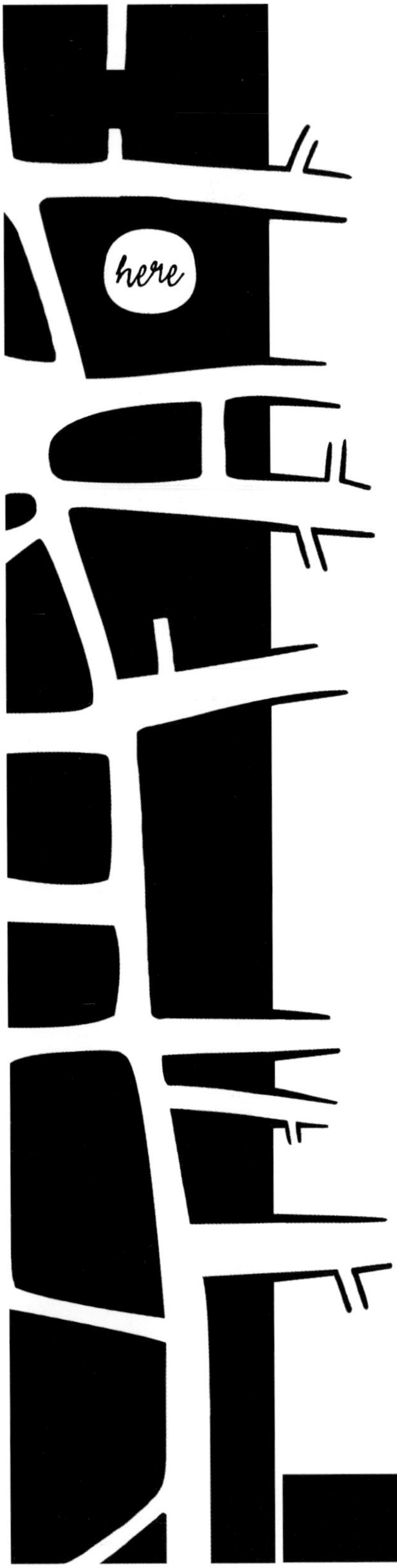
here

...IN THIS STRANGE HALF CITY.

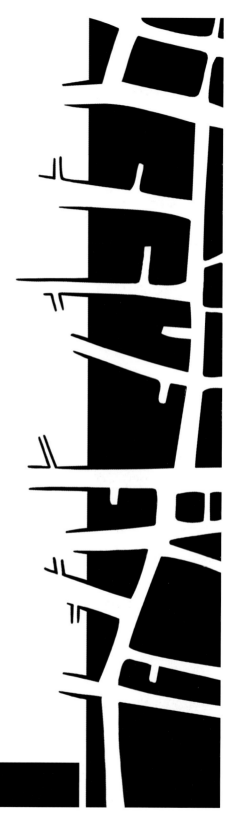

SNIPERS,

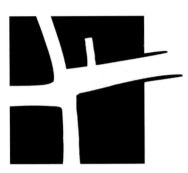

OIL DRUMS,

CONTAINERS,

BARBED WIRE,

SANDBAGS

CARVE OUT A NEW GEOGRAPHY.

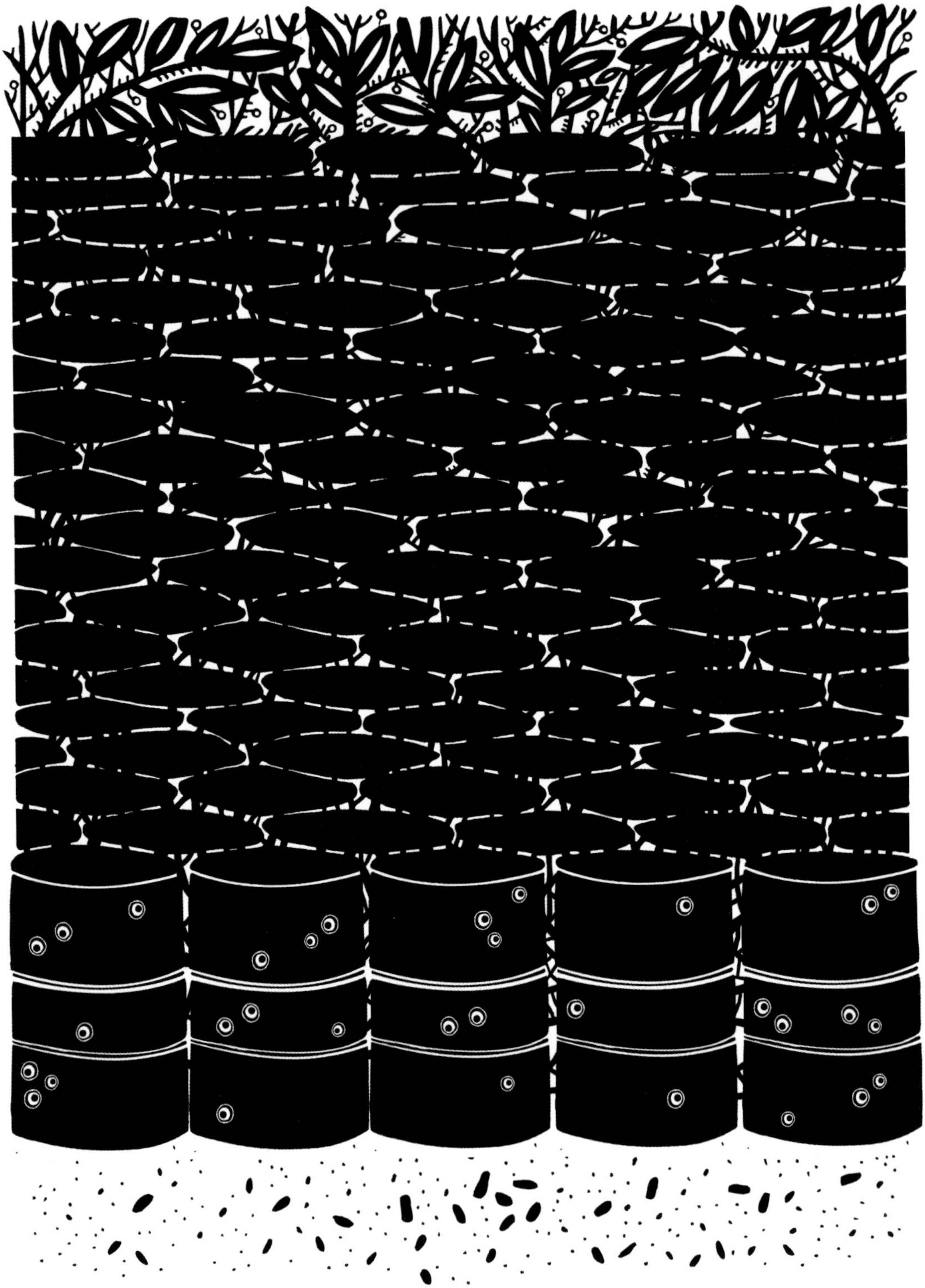

OUR APARTMENT BUILDING LOOKED OUT ON THE DEMARCATION LINE.

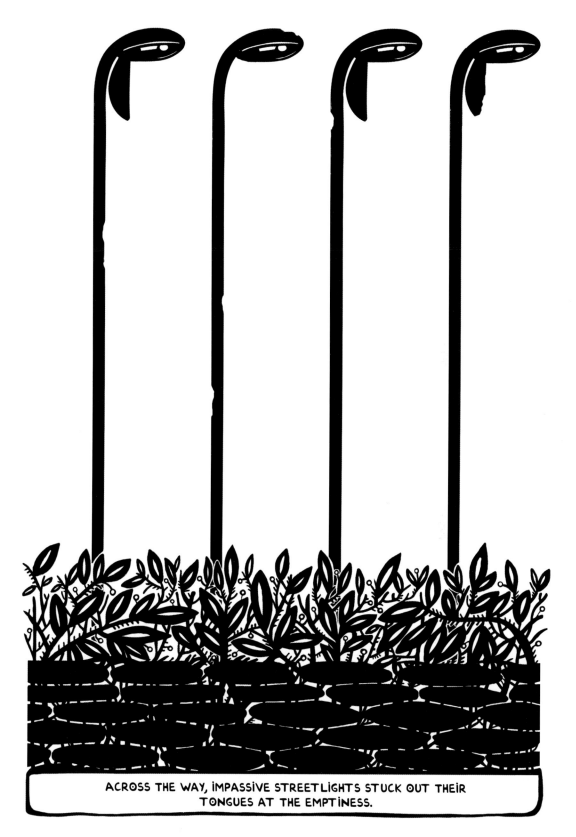

ACROSS THE WAY, IMPASSIVE STREETLIGHTS STUCK OUT THEIR
TONGUES AT THE EMPTINESS.

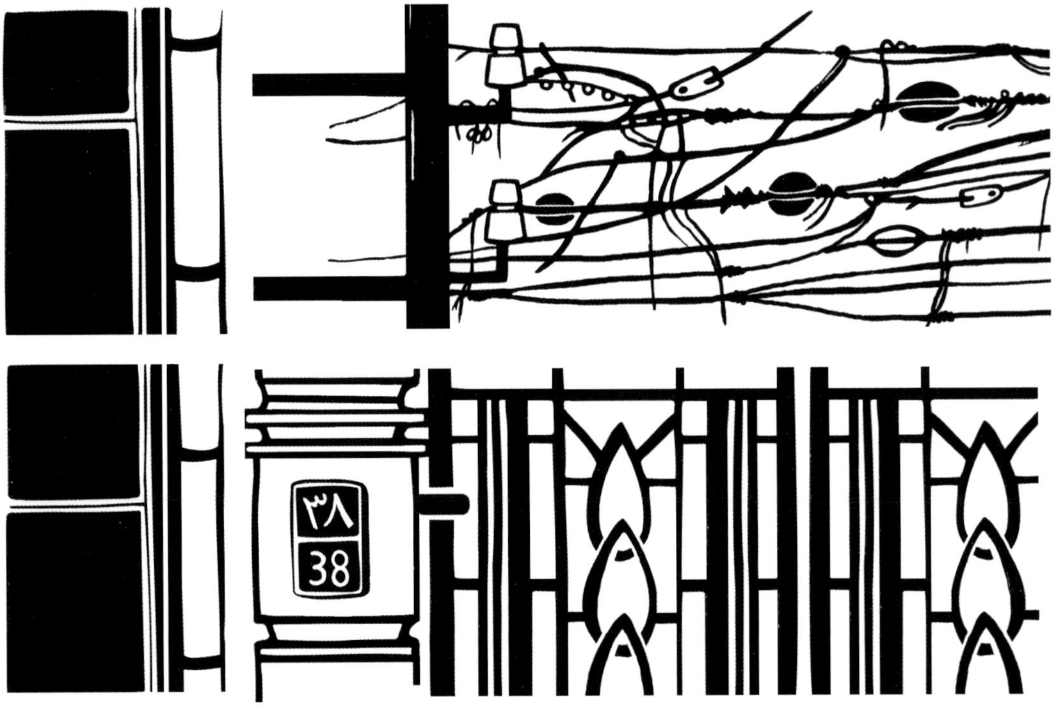
٣٨
38

IT WAS A BUILDING FROM THE 1940S. MY FATHER'S PARENTS HAD LIVED THERE ALL THEIR LIVES.

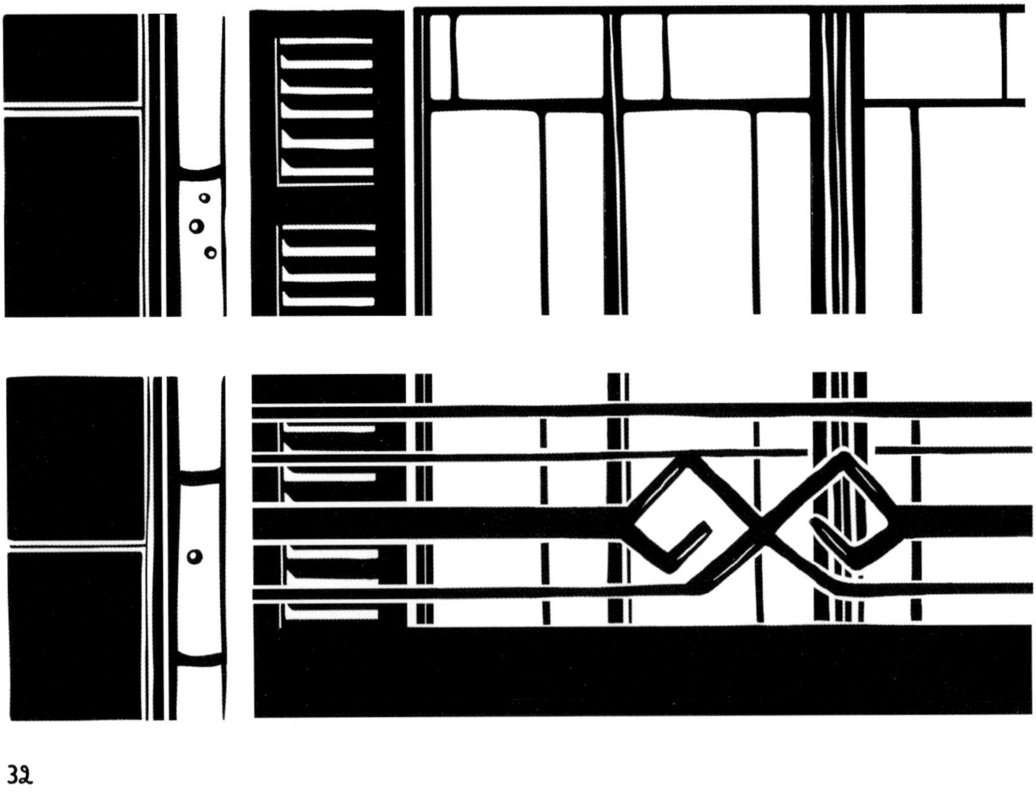

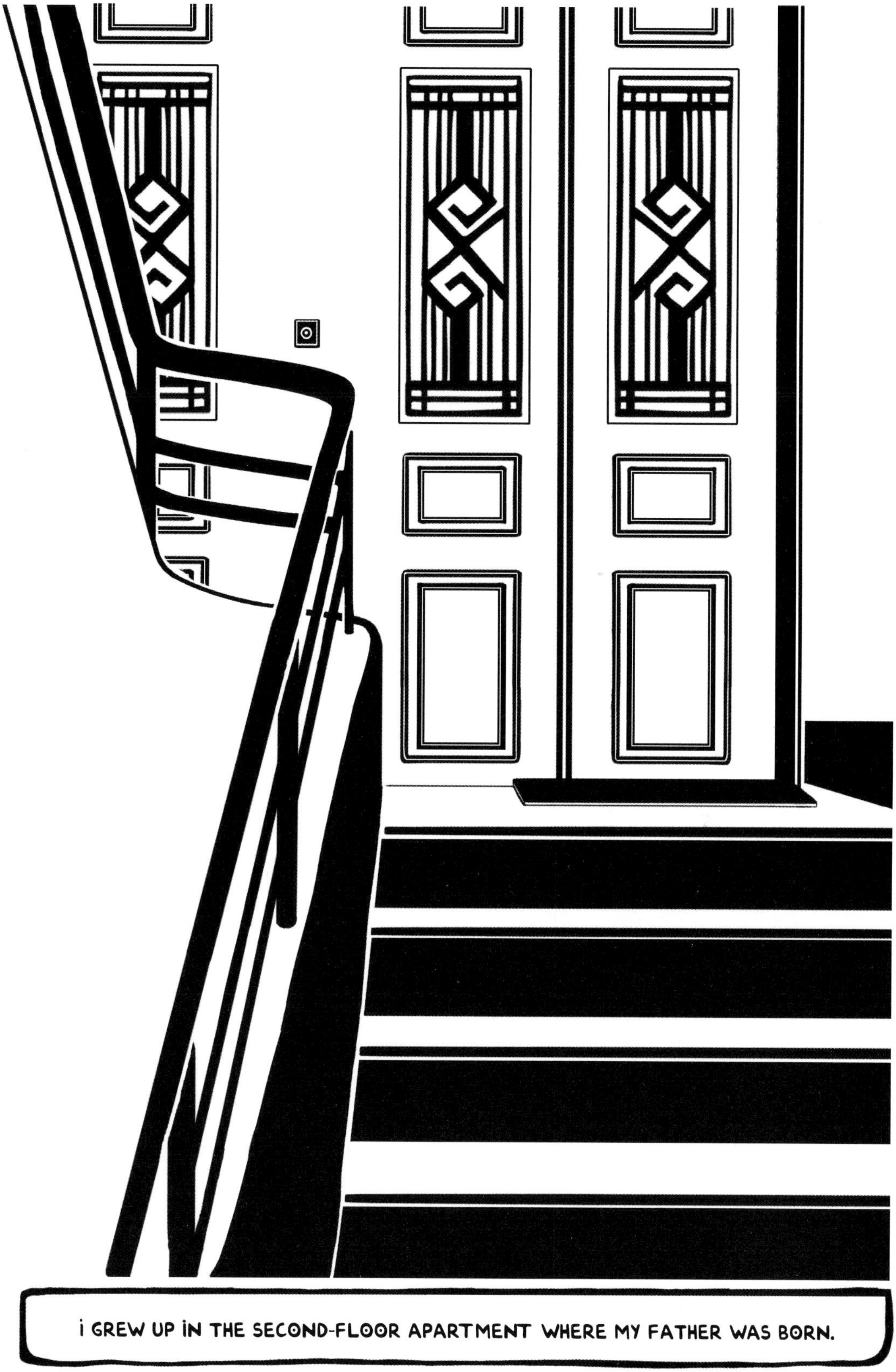
I GREW UP IN THE SECOND-FLOOR APARTMENT WHERE MY FATHER WAS BORN.

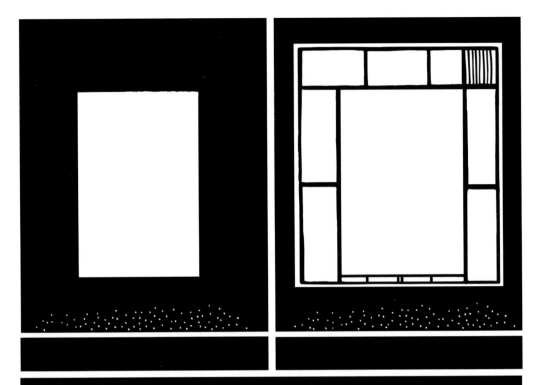

LAID OUT IN THE STYLE OF THE TIME, THE APARTMENT WAS ORGANIZED AROUND THE LIVING ROOM, A LARGE RECTANGLE THAT LINKED THE TWO MAIN PARTS OF OUR HOME.

kitchen
foyer
dining room
bedroom
bedroom
bedroom

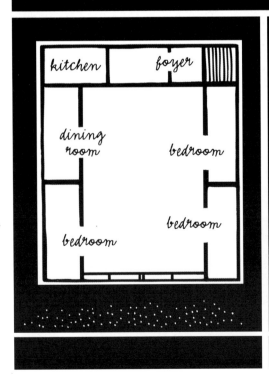

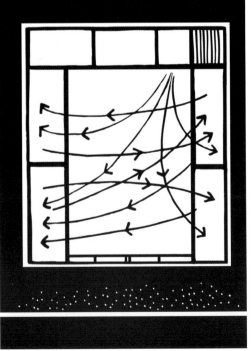

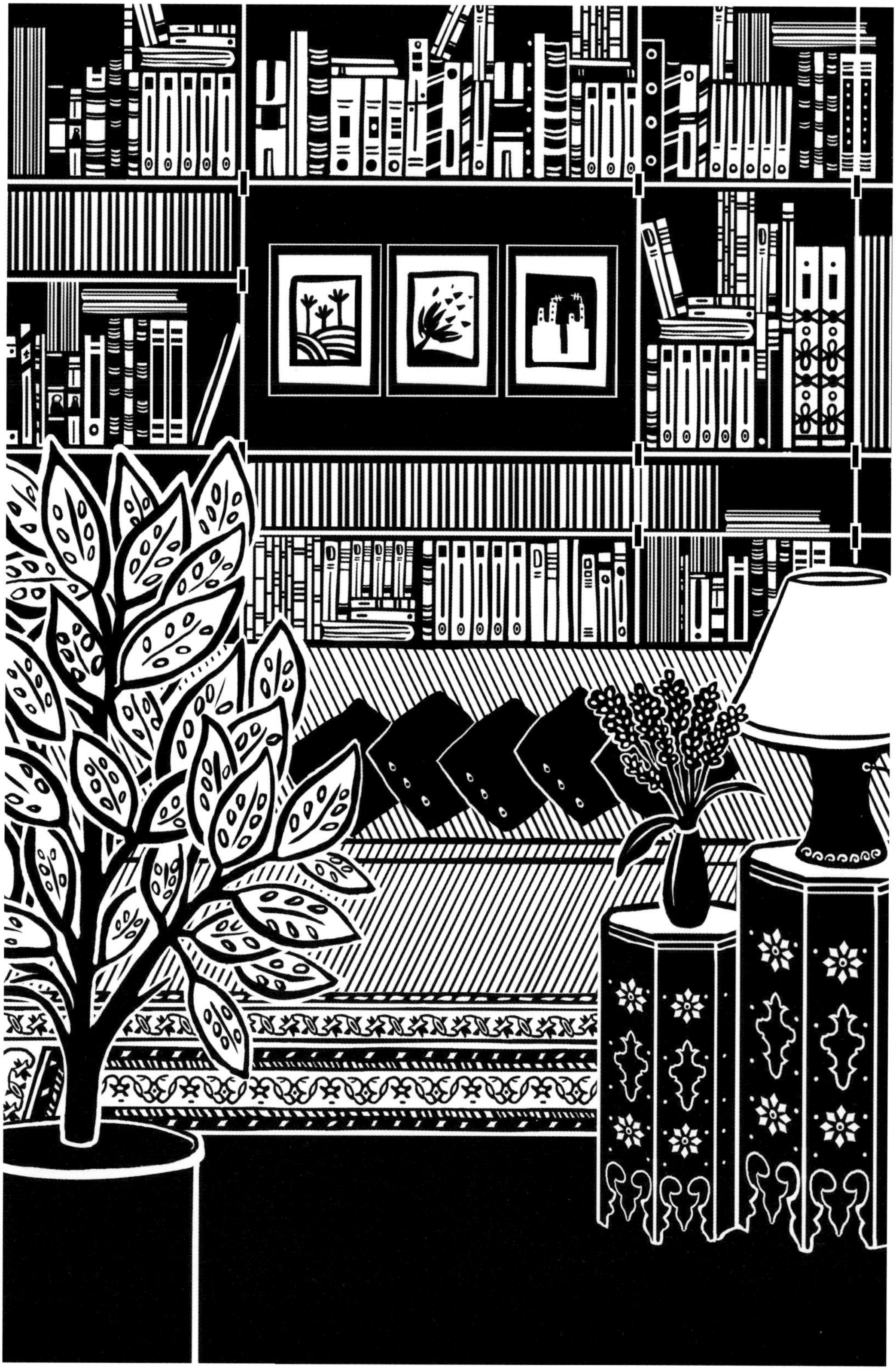

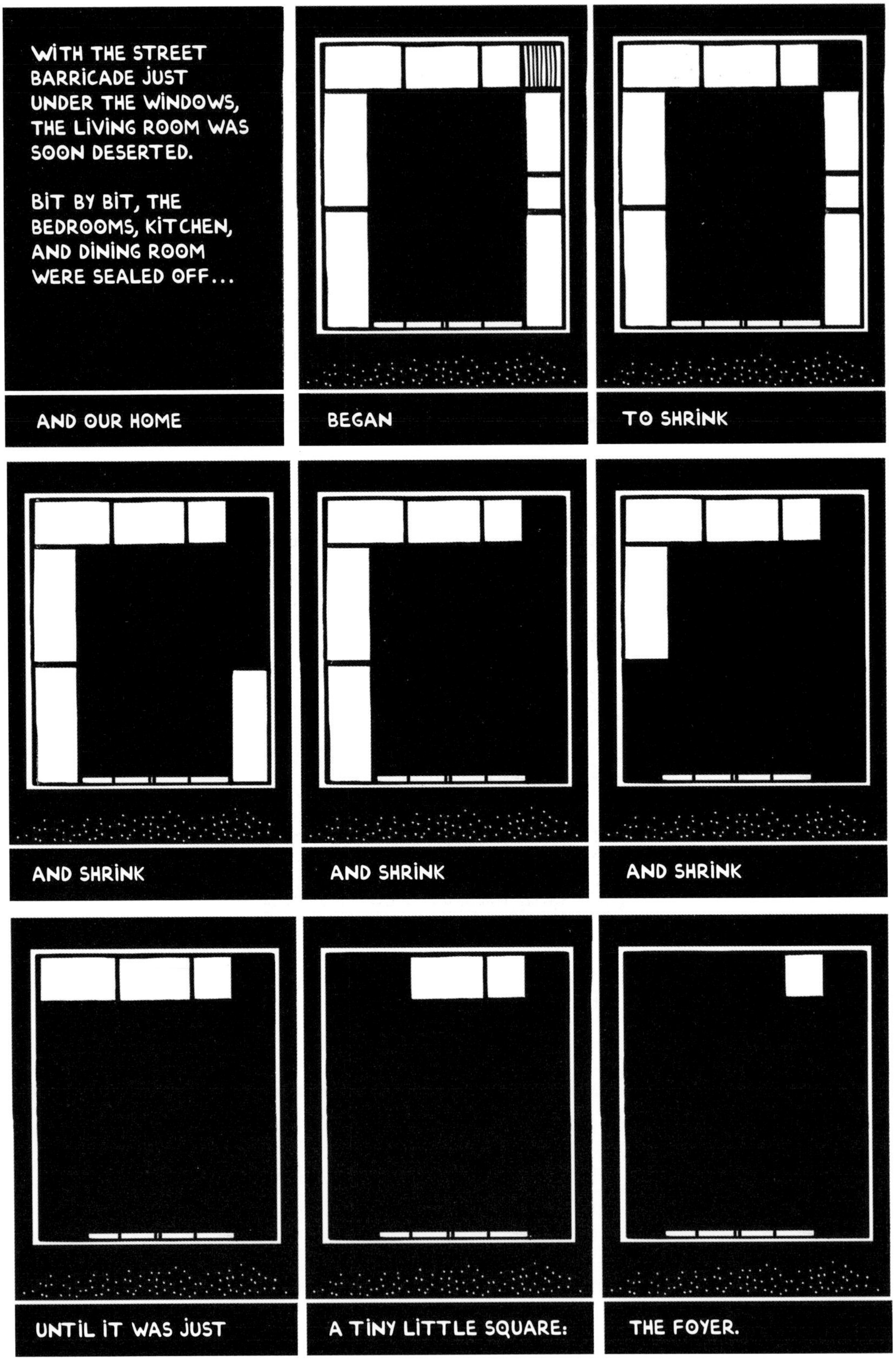
WITH THE STREET BARRICADE JUST UNDER THE WINDOWS, THE LIVING ROOM WAS SOON DESERTED.
BIT BY BIT, THE BEDROOMS, KITCHEN, AND DINING ROOM WERE SEALED OFF...
AND OUR HOME
BEGAN
TO SHRINK
AND SHRINK
AND SHRINK
AND SHRINK
UNTIL IT WAS JUST
A TINY LITTLE SQUARE:
THE FOYER.

SOON THE FOYER NO LONGER LOOKED LIKE A FOYER.

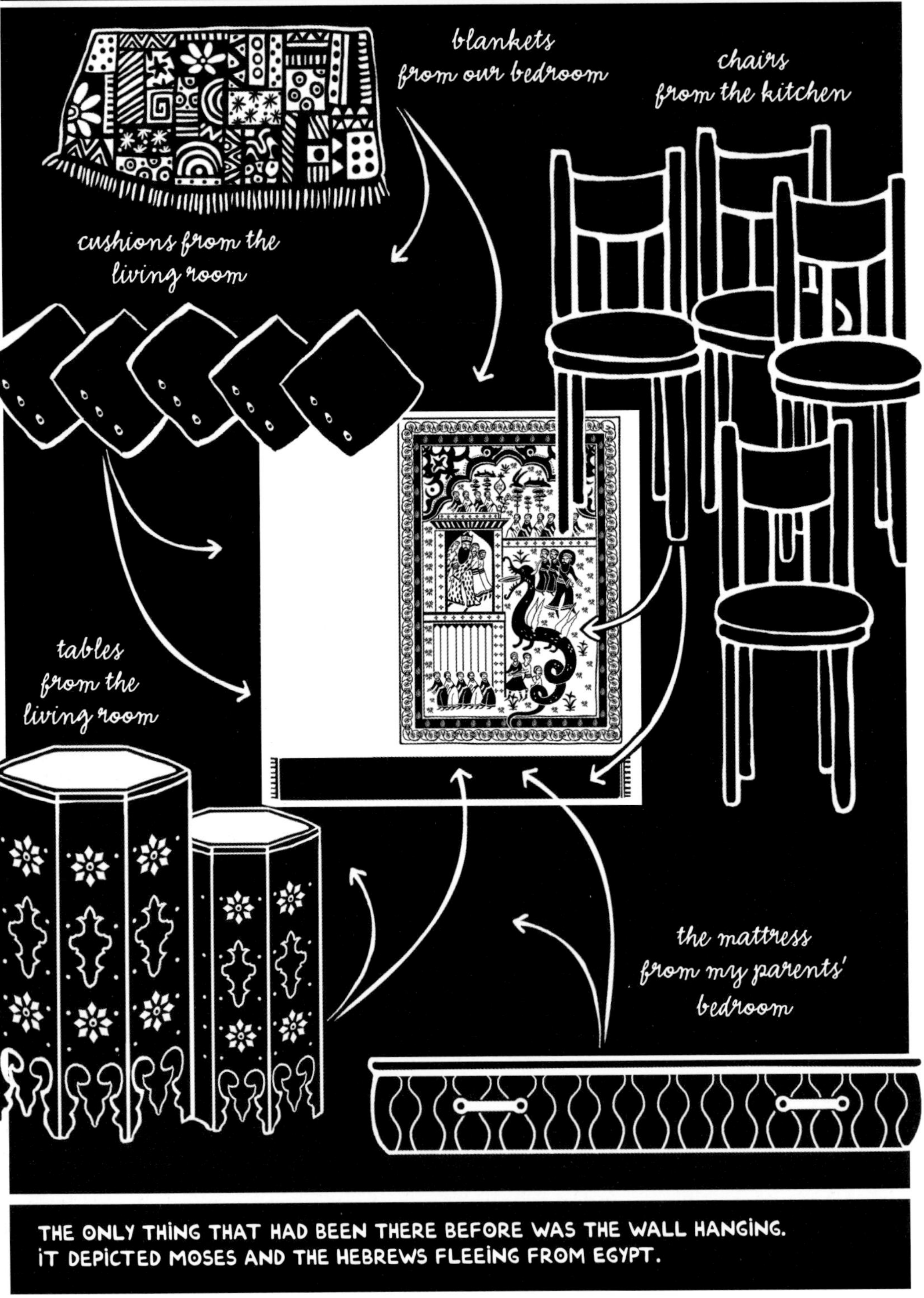
blankets from our bedroom
chairs from the kitchen
cushions from the living room
tables from the living room
the mattress from my parents' bedroom

THE ONLY THING THAT HAD BEEN THERE BEFORE WAS THE WALL HANGING.
IT DEPICTED MOSES AND THE HEBREWS FLEEING FROM EGYPT.

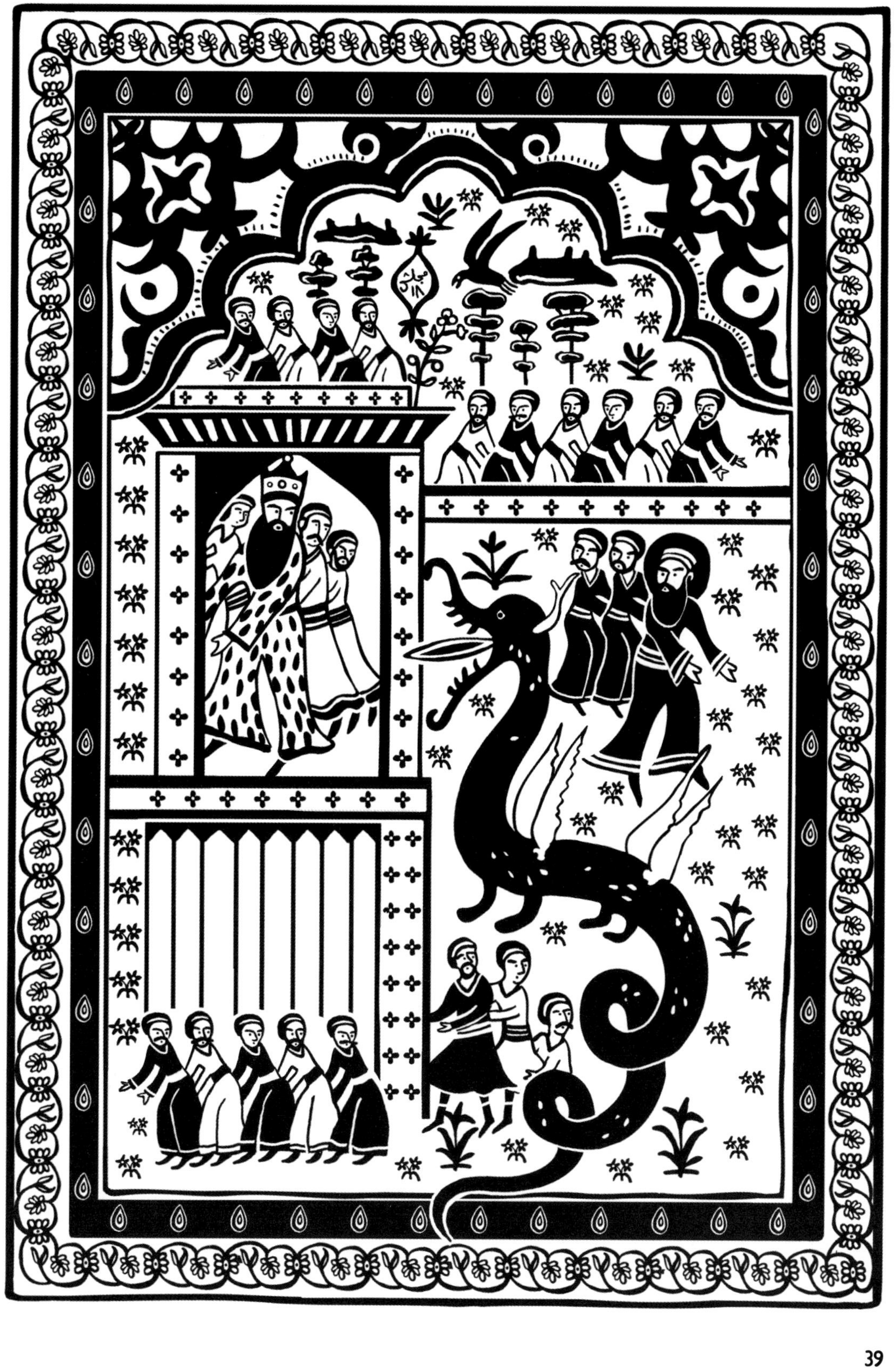

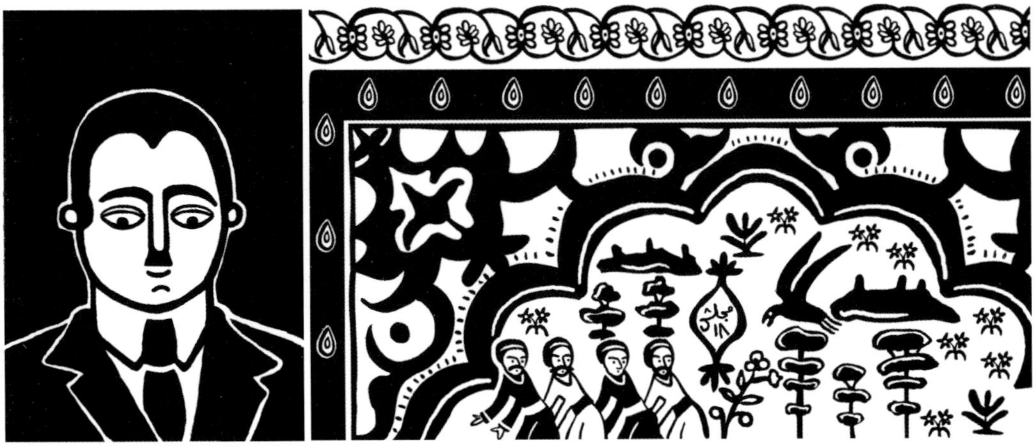

THAT WALL HANGING WAS THE ONLY THING OF MY FATHER'S FATHER LEFT TO US.

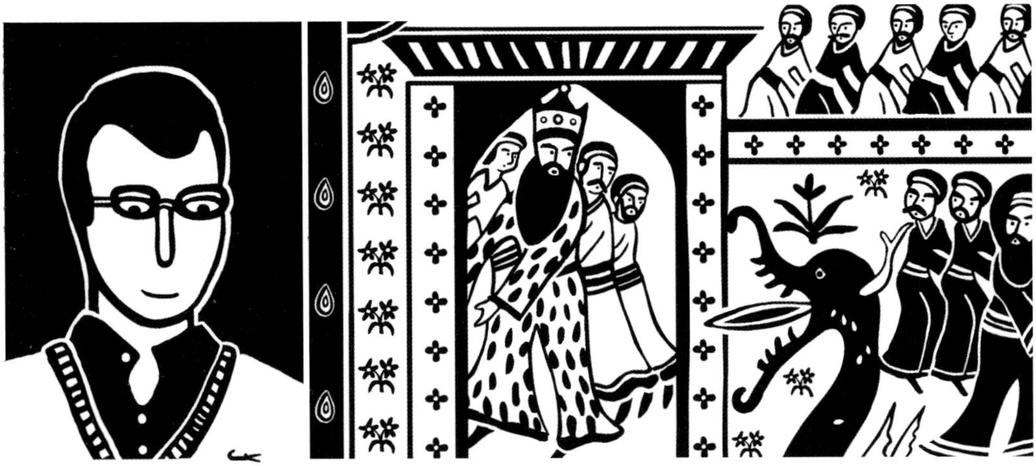

AFTER HIS PARENTS DIED, MY FATHER FOUND IT FOLDED UP IN A BOX IN THE ATTIC.

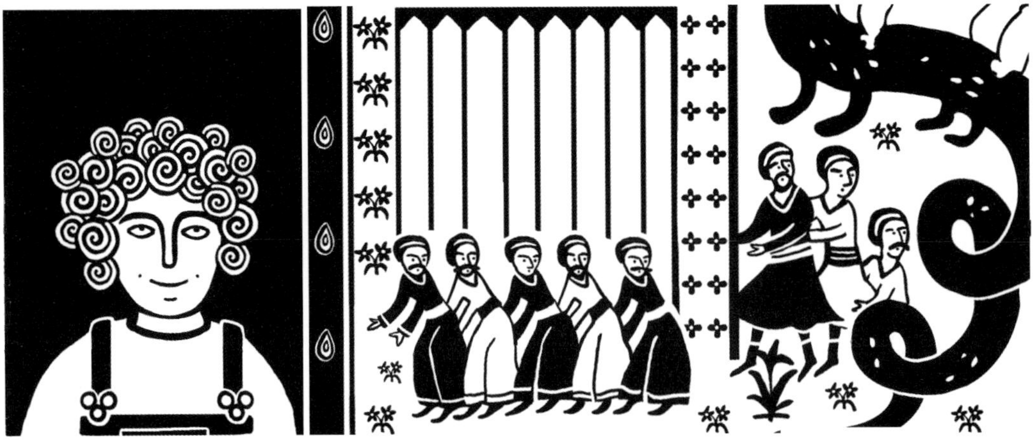

IT WAS ALREADY HANGING IN THE FOYER WHEN I WAS BORN.

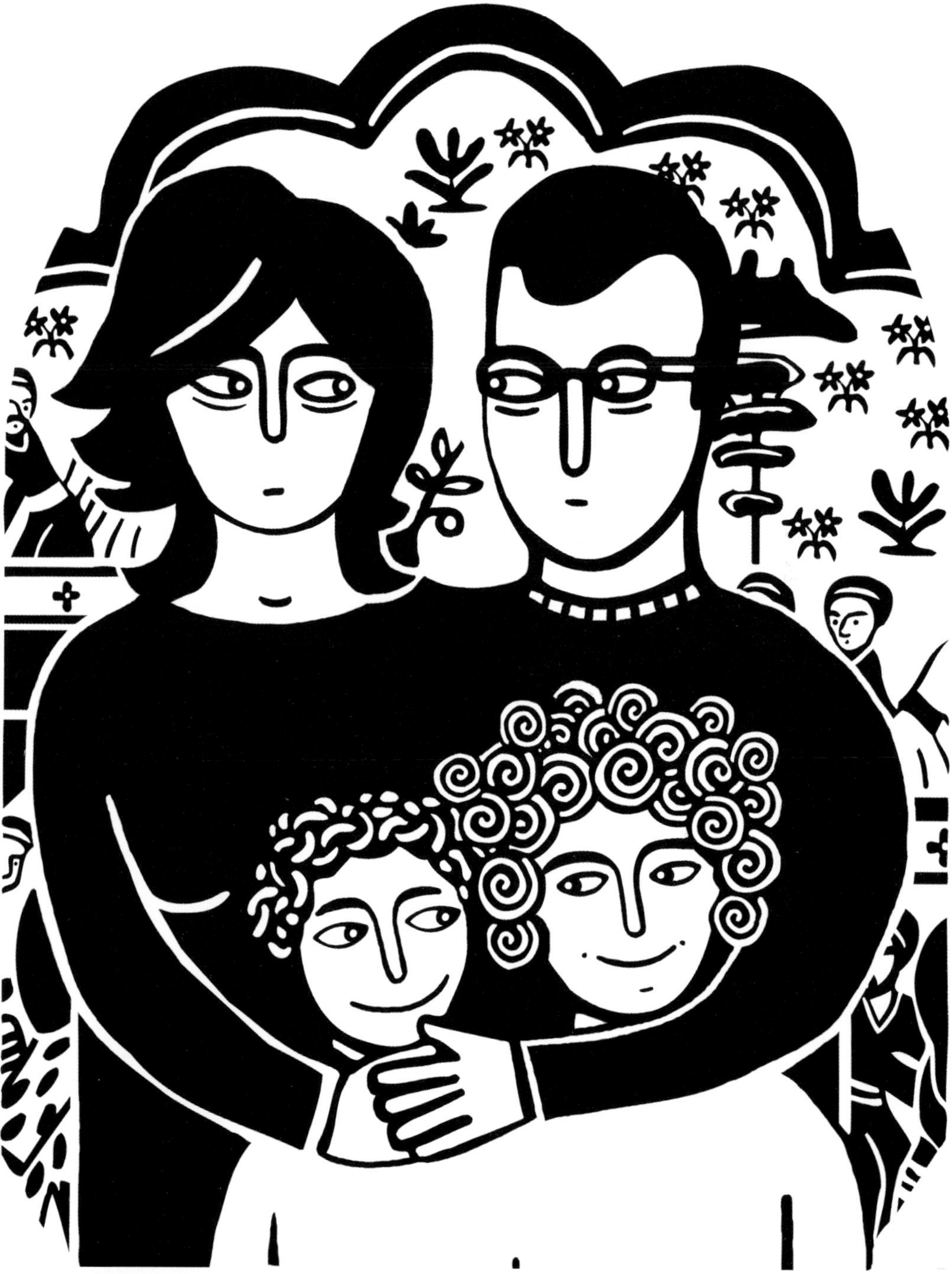

I NEVER KNEW MY FATHER'S PARENTS, AND I ALWAYS ASSOCIATED THEM WITH THAT WALL HANGING.
GATHERED TOGETHER IN THE FOYER, WE WERE SAFE.

- HELLO?
- ...
- MOMMMM!
- ...
- YES, EVERYTHING'S FINE. WE'RE TOGETHER, AND ANHALA'S WITH US.
- ...
- NO. NO, I'M NOT AFRAID.
- ...
- ...OF COURSE I'LL WATCH OUT FOR HIM.
- ...
- DO YOU WANT TO TALK TO ANHALA?
- ...
- MOM?
- ...
- WHEN ARE YOU AND POP COMING BACK?

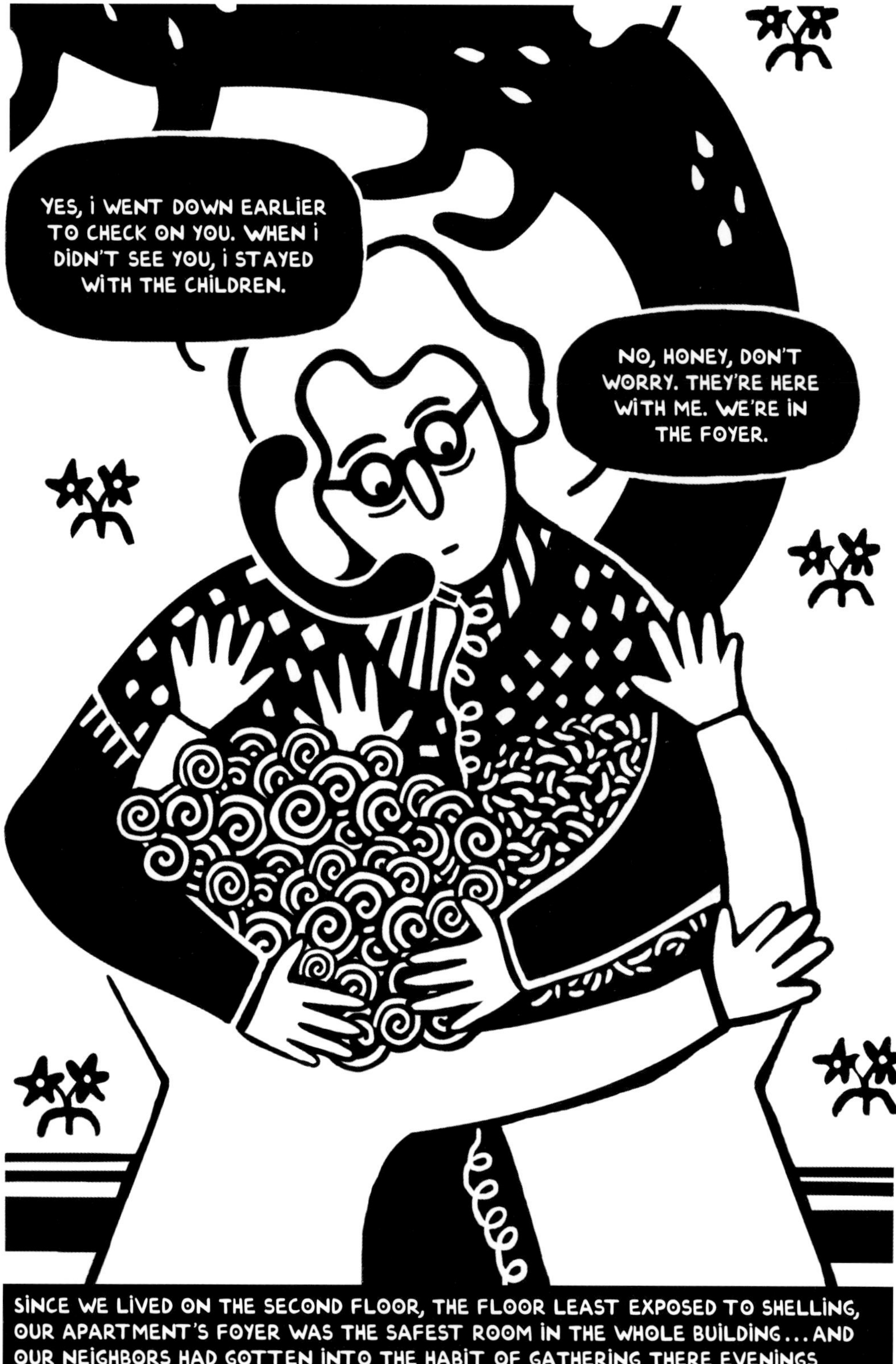
YES, I WENT DOWN EARLIER TO CHECK ON YOU. WHEN I DIDN'T SEE YOU, I STAYED WITH THE CHILDREN.
NO, HONEY, DON'T WORRY. THEY'RE HERE WITH ME. WE'RE IN THE FOYER.
SINCE WE LIVED ON THE SECOND FLOOR, THE FLOOR LEAST EXPOSED TO SHELLING, OUR APARTMENT'S FOYER WAS THE SAFEST ROOM IN THE WHOLE BUILDING... AND OUR NEIGHBORS HAD GOTTEN INTO THE HABIT OF GATHERING THERE EVENINGS WHEN THERE WAS BOMBING.

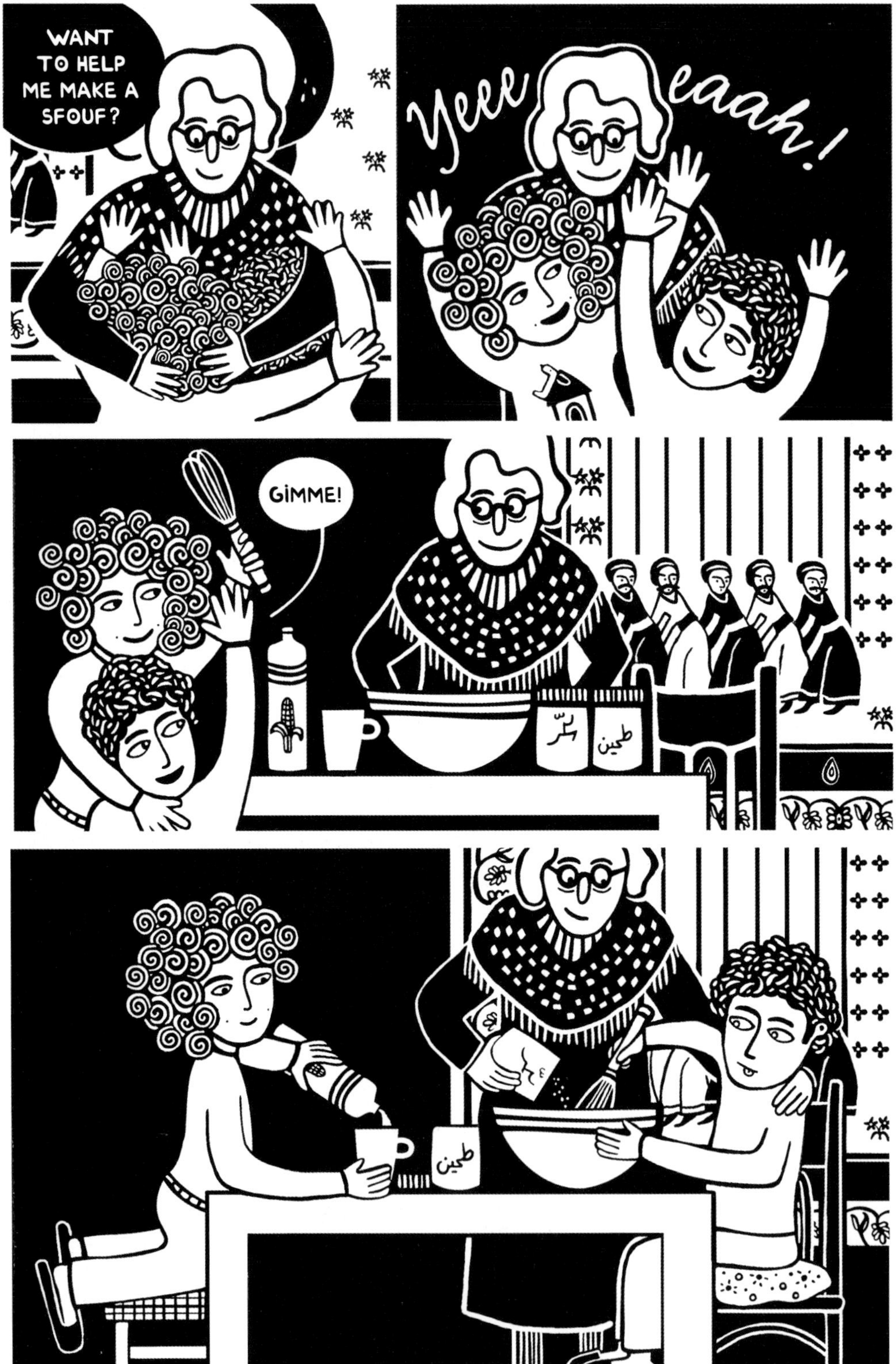
WANT TO HELP ME MAKE A SFOUF?
Yeeeaaah!
GIMME!
طحين
طحين

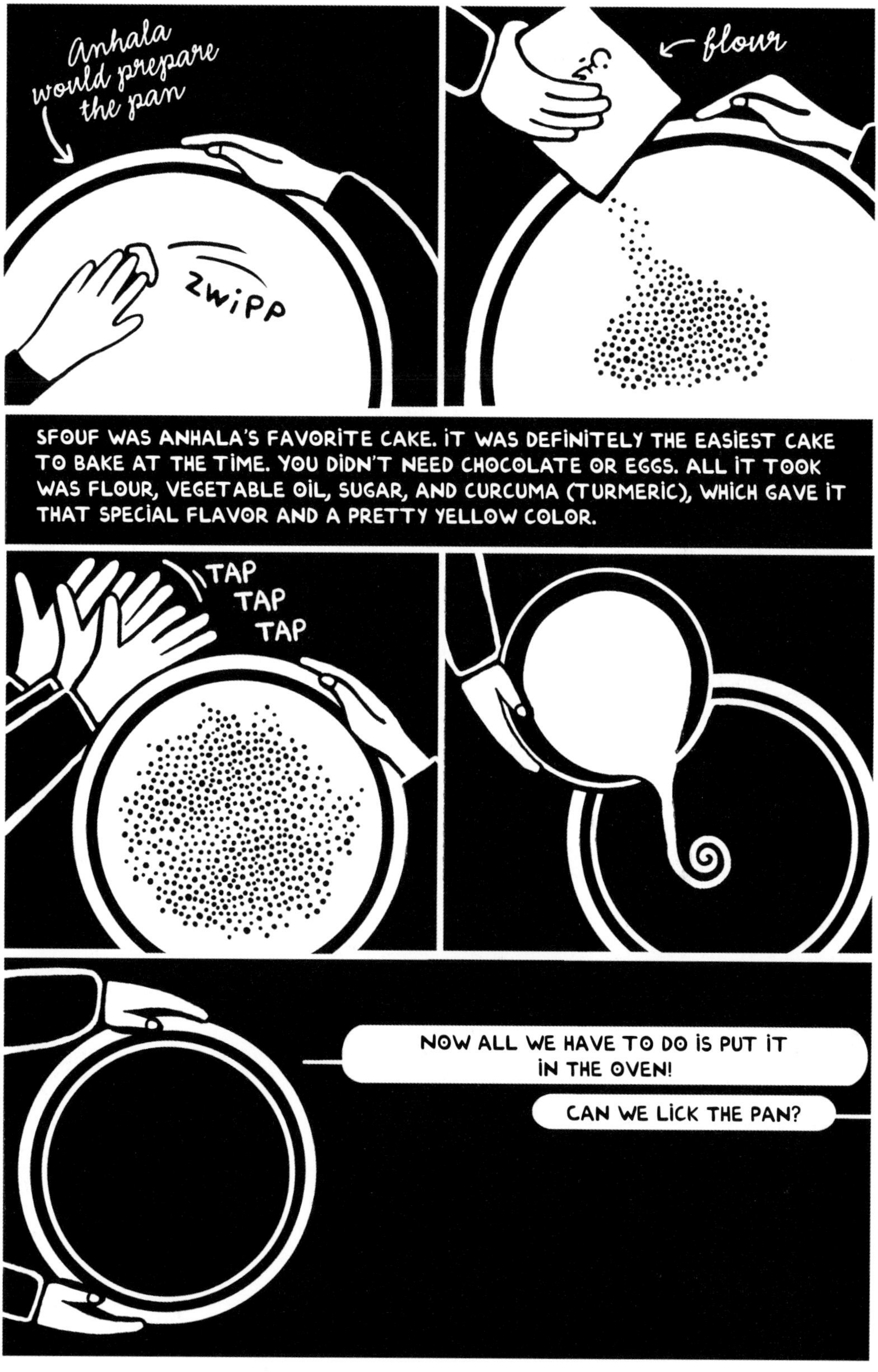
Anhala would prepare the pan
ZWIPP
flour
SFOUF WAS ANHALA'S FAVORITE CAKE. IT WAS DEFINITELY THE EASIEST CAKE TO BAKE AT THE TIME. YOU DIDN'T NEED CHOCOLATE OR EGGS. ALL IT TOOK WAS FLOUR, VEGETABLE OIL, SUGAR, AND CURCUMA (TURMERIC), WHICH GAVE IT THAT SPECIAL FLAVOR AND A PRETTY YELLOW COLOR.
TAP TAP TAP
NOW ALL WE HAVE TO DO IS PUT IT IN THE OVEN!
CAN WE LICK THE PAN?

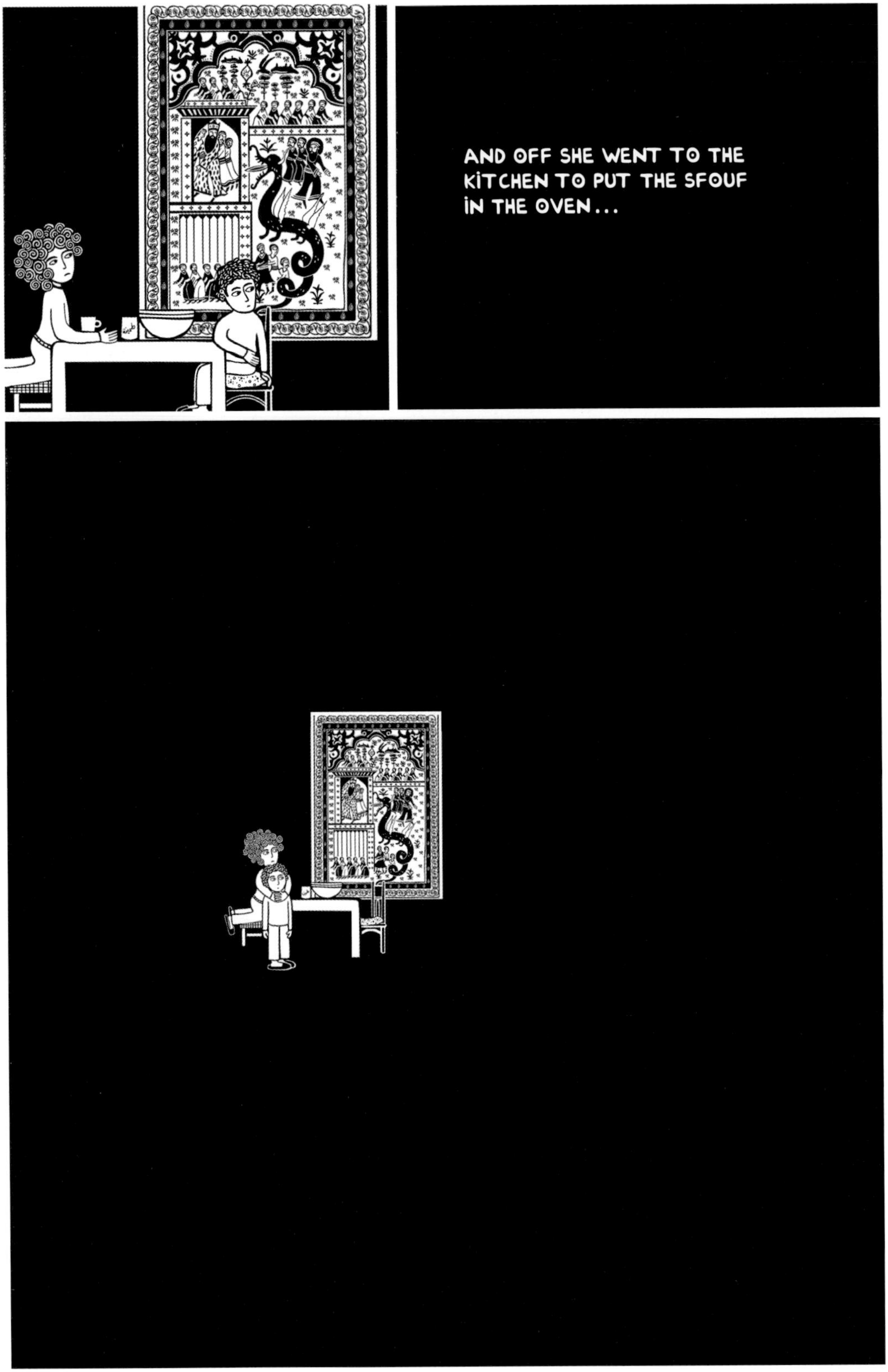
AND OFF SHE WENT TO THE KITCHEN TO PUT THE SFOUF IN THE OVEN...

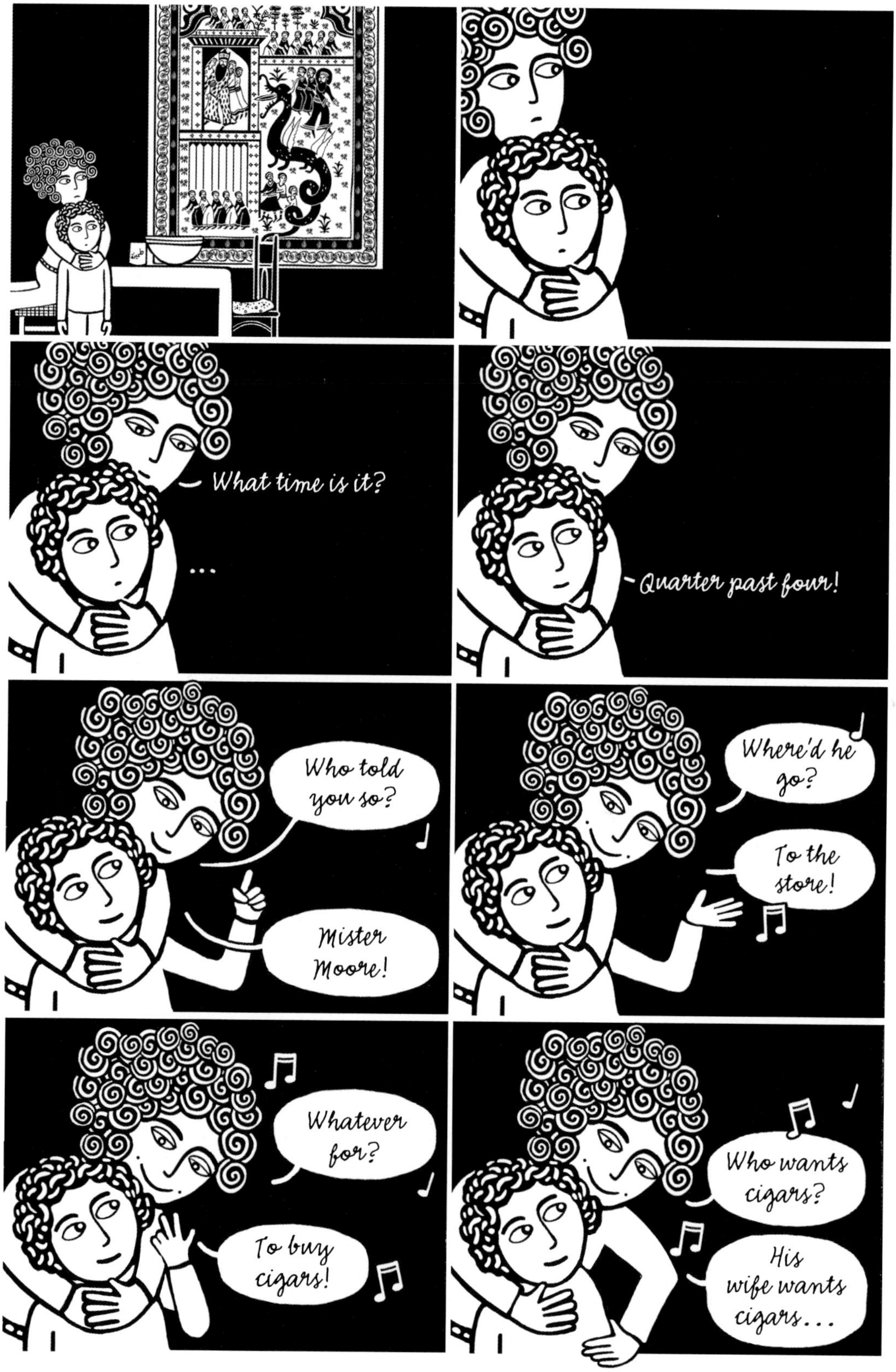
What time is it?
...
Quarter past four!
Who told you so?
Mister Moore!
Where'd he go?
To the store!
Whatever for?
To buy cigars!
Who wants cigars?
His wife wants cigars...

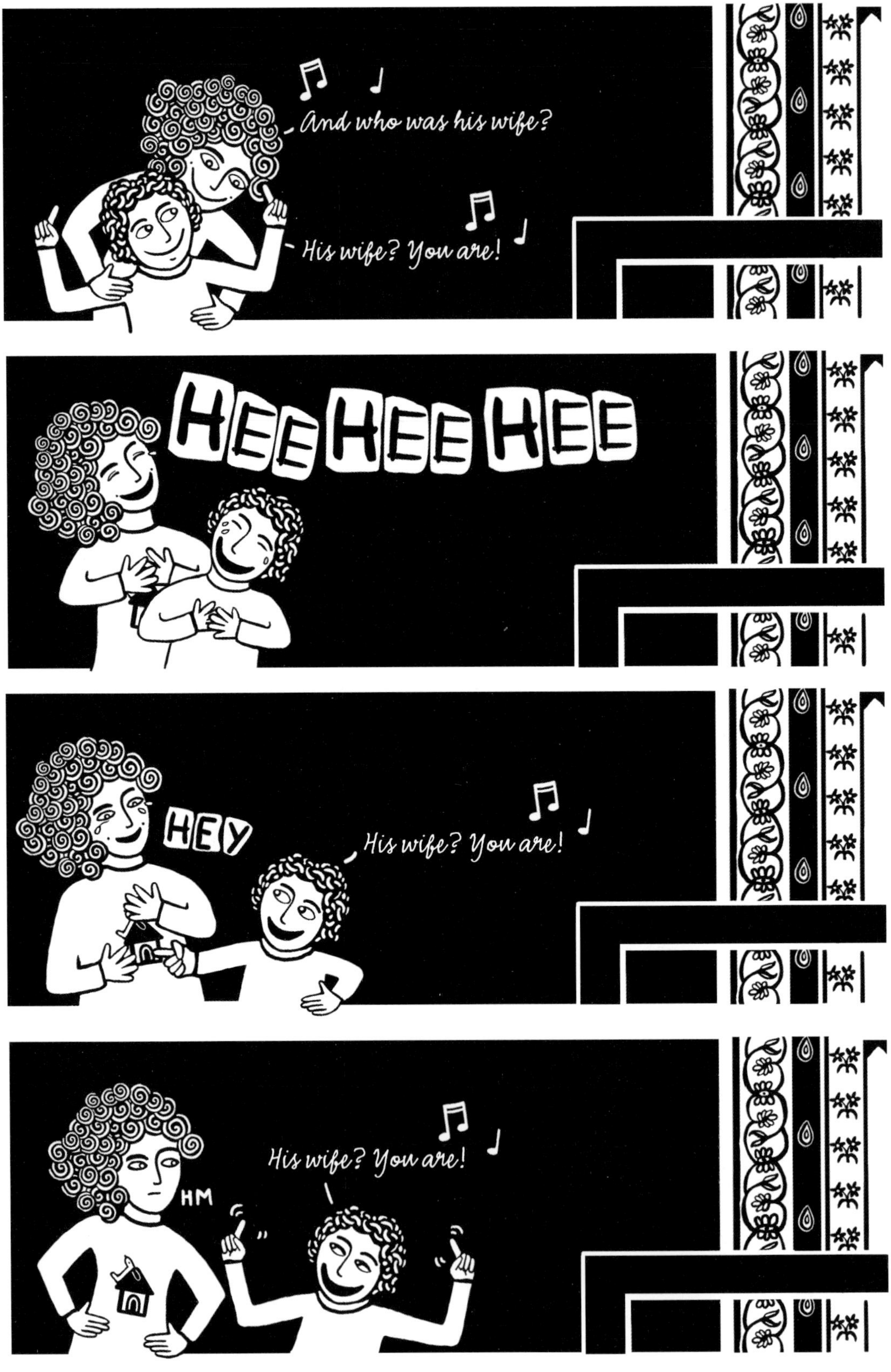

And who was his wife?
His wife? You are!
HEE HEE HEE
HEY
His wife? You are!
HM
His wife? You are!

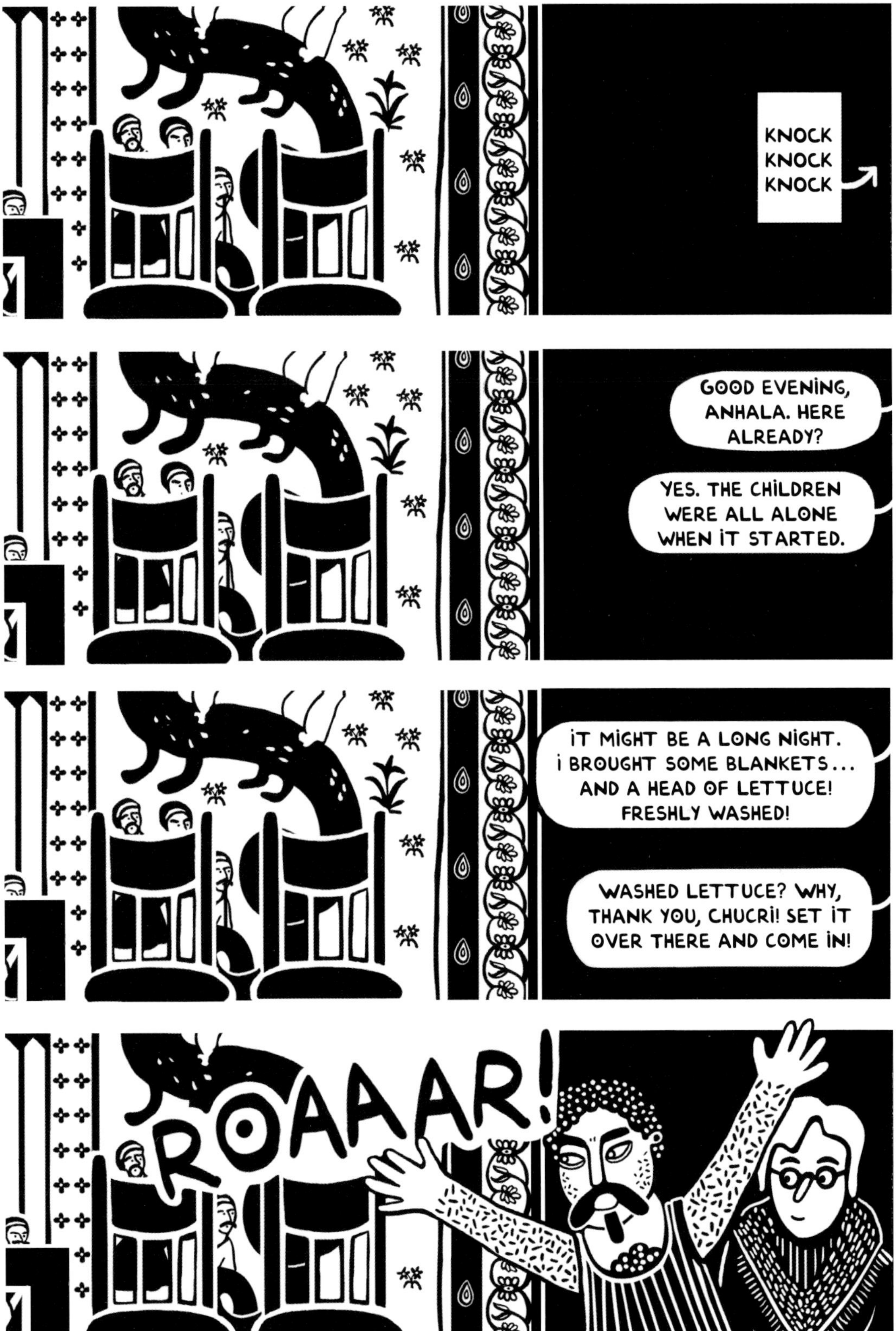
KNOCK KNOCK KNOCK
GOOD EVENING, ANHALA. HERE ALREADY?
YES. THE CHILDREN WERE ALL ALONE WHEN IT STARTED.
IT MIGHT BE A LONG NIGHT. I BROUGHT SOME BLANKETS... AND A HEAD OF LETTUCE! FRESHLY WASHED!
WASHED LETTUCE? WHY, THANK YOU, CHUCRI! SET IT OVER THERE AND COME IN!
ROAAAR!

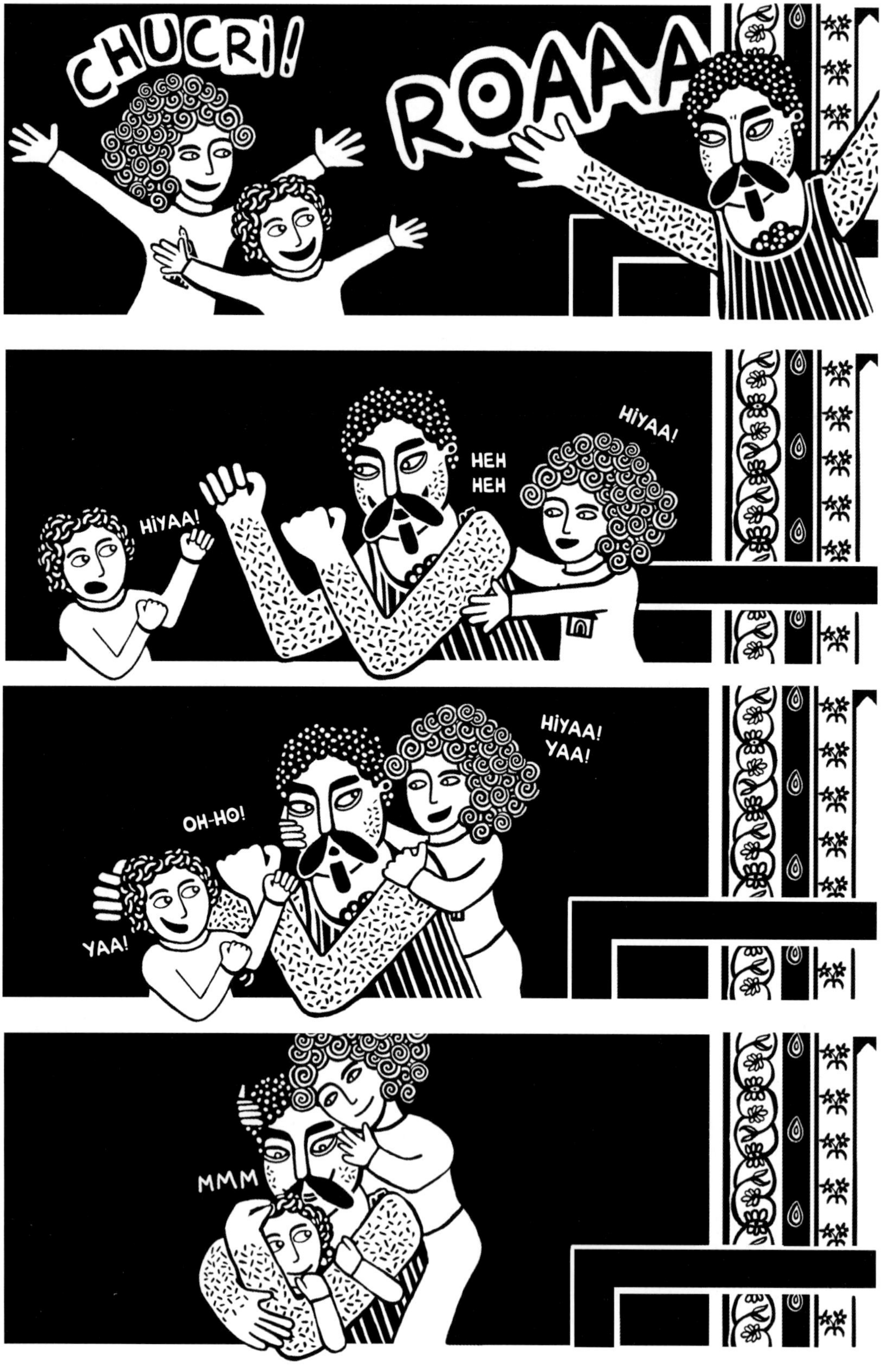
CHUCRI!
ROAAA
HIYAA!
HEH
HEH
HIYAA!
OH-HO!
HIYAA!
YAA!
YAA!
MMM

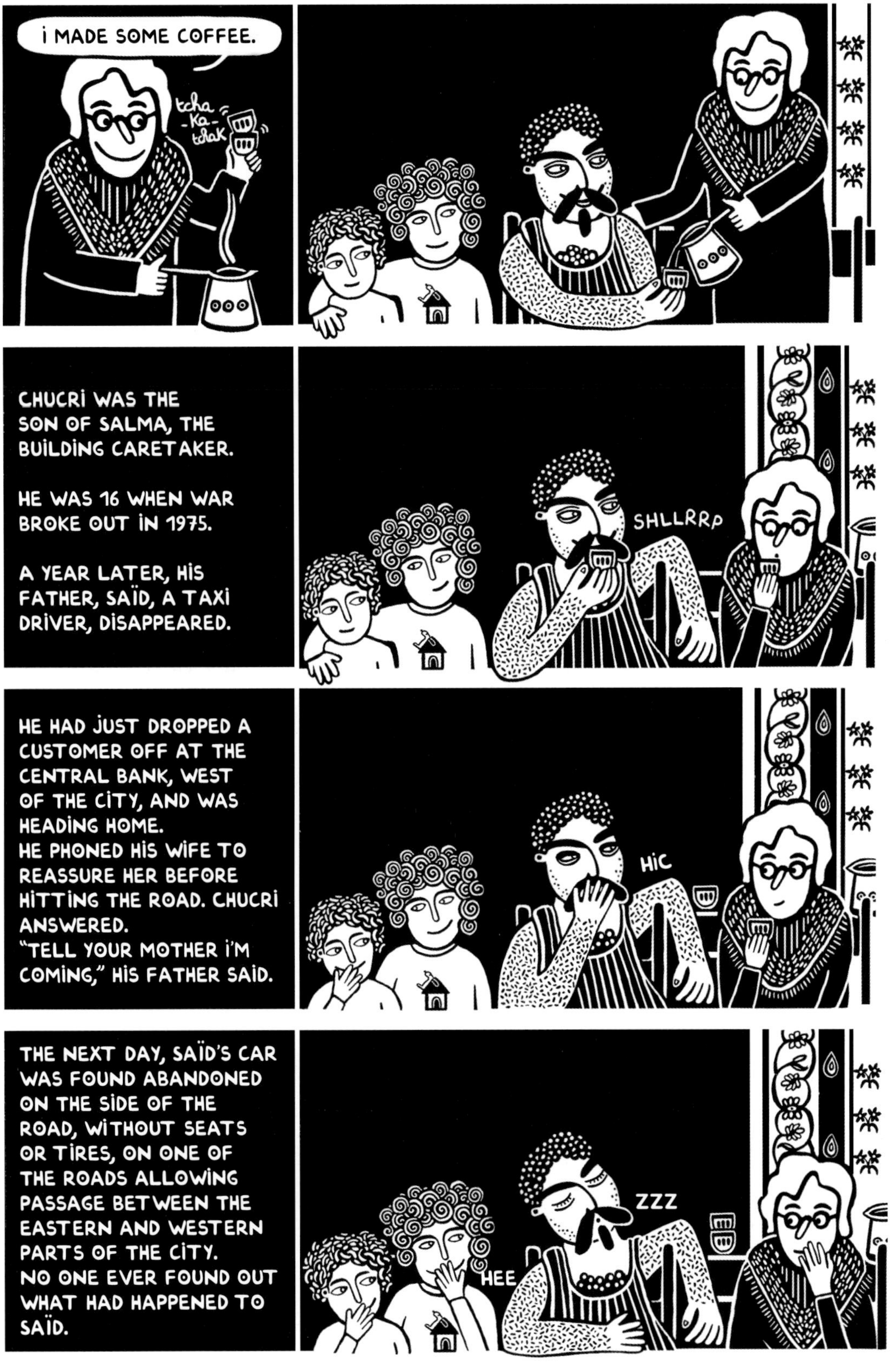
I MADE SOME COFFEE.
tcha -ka- tchak
CHUCRI WAS THE SON OF SALMA, THE BUILDING CARETAKER.
HE WAS 16 WHEN WAR BROKE OUT IN 1975.
A YEAR LATER, HIS FATHER, SAÏD, A TAXI DRIVER, DISAPPEARED.
SHLLRRP
HE HAD JUST DROPPED A CUSTOMER OFF AT THE CENTRAL BANK, WEST OF THE CITY, AND WAS HEADING HOME.
HE PHONED HIS WIFE TO REASSURE HER BEFORE HITTING THE ROAD. CHUCRI ANSWERED.
"TELL YOUR MOTHER I'M COMING," HIS FATHER SAID.
HIC
THE NEXT DAY, SAÏD'S CAR WAS FOUND ABANDONED ON THE SIDE OF THE ROAD, WITHOUT SEATS OR TIRES, ON ONE OF THE ROADS ALLOWING PASSAGE BETWEEN THE EASTERN AND WESTERN PARTS OF THE CITY.
NO ONE EVER FOUND OUT WHAT HAD HAPPENED TO SAÏD.
HEE
ZZZ

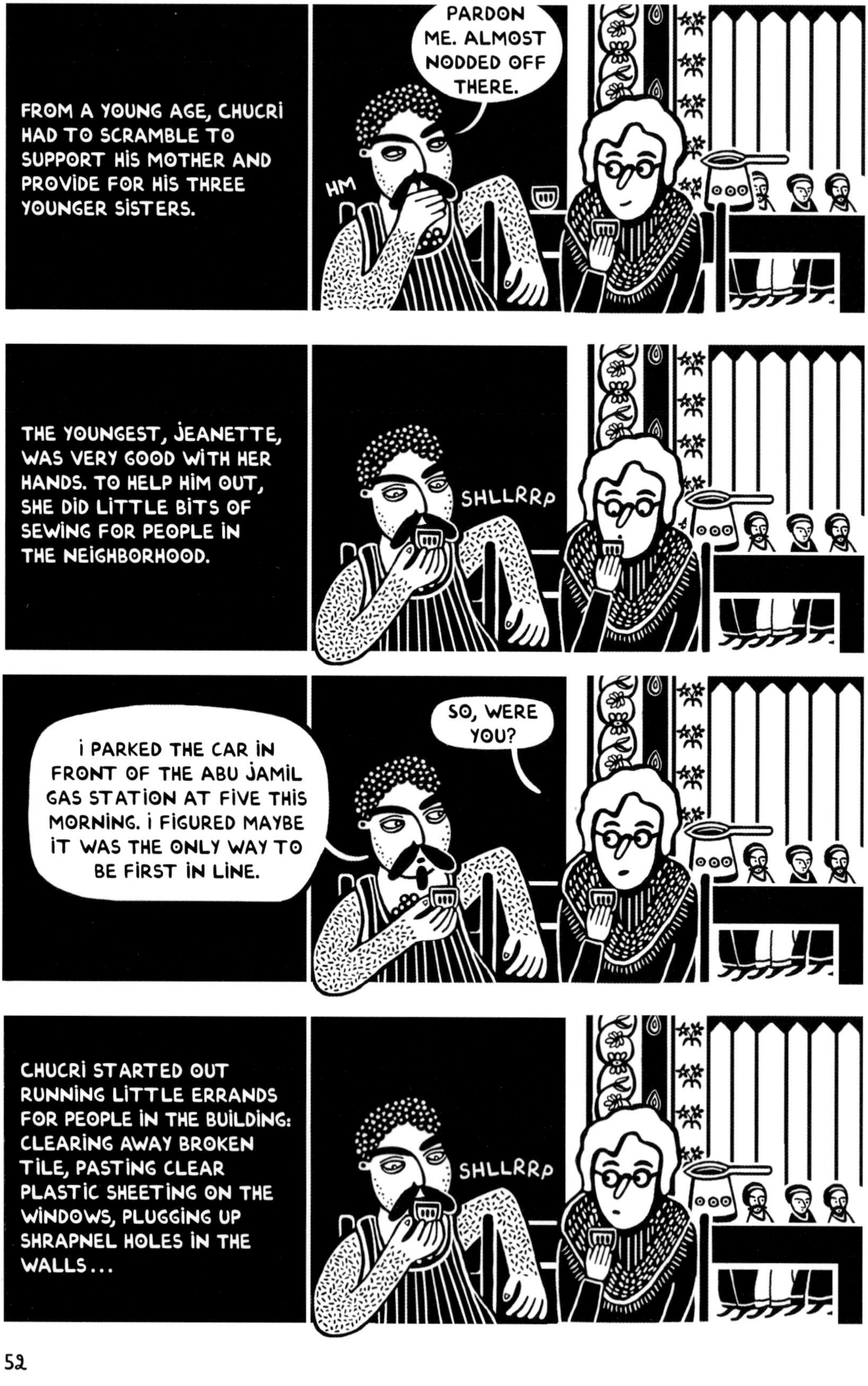
FROM A YOUNG AGE, CHUCRI HAD TO SCRAMBLE TO SUPPORT HIS MOTHER AND PROVIDE FOR HIS THREE YOUNGER SISTERS.
PARDON ME. ALMOST NODDED OFF THERE.
HM
THE YOUNGEST, JEANETTE, WAS VERY GOOD WITH HER HANDS. TO HELP HIM OUT, SHE DID LITTLE BITS OF SEWING FOR PEOPLE IN THE NEIGHBORHOOD.
SHLLRRP
SO, WERE YOU?
I PARKED THE CAR IN FRONT OF THE ABU JAMIL GAS STATION AT FIVE THIS MORNING. I FIGURED MAYBE IT WAS THE ONLY WAY TO BE FIRST IN LINE.
CHUCRI STARTED OUT RUNNING LITTLE ERRANDS FOR PEOPLE IN THE BUILDING: CLEARING AWAY BROKEN TILE, PASTING CLEAR PLASTIC SHEETING ON THE WINDOWS, PLUGGING UP SHRAPNEL HOLES IN THE WALLS...
SHLLRRP

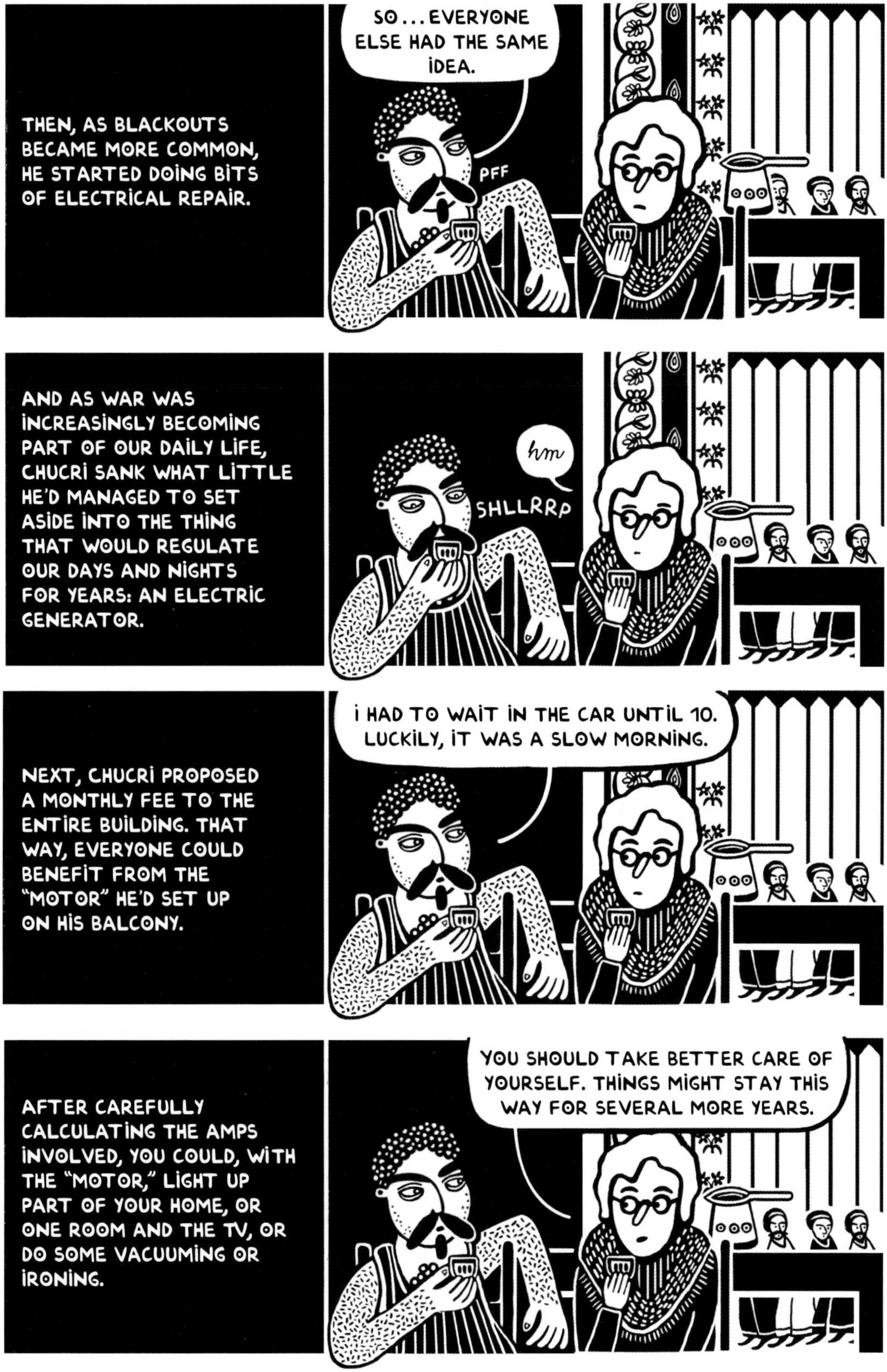
THEN, AS BLACKOUTS BECAME MORE COMMON, HE STARTED DOING BITS OF ELECTRICAL REPAIR.
SO... EVERYONE ELSE HAD THE SAME IDEA.
PFF
AND AS WAR WAS INCREASINGLY BECOMING PART OF OUR DAILY LIFE, CHUCRI SANK WHAT LITTLE HE'D MANAGED TO SET ASIDE INTO THE THING THAT WOULD REGULATE OUR DAYS AND NIGHTS FOR YEARS: AN ELECTRIC GENERATOR.
hm
SHLLRRP
NEXT, CHUCRI PROPOSED A MONTHLY FEE TO THE ENTIRE BUILDING. THAT WAY, EVERYONE COULD BENEFIT FROM THE "MOTOR" HE'D SET UP ON HIS BALCONY.
I HAD TO WAIT IN THE CAR UNTIL 10. LUCKILY, IT WAS A SLOW MORNING.
AFTER CAREFULLY CALCULATING THE AMPS INVOLVED, YOU COULD, WITH THE "MOTOR," LIGHT UP PART OF YOUR HOME, OR ONE ROOM AND THE TV, OR DO SOME VACUUMING OR IRONING.
YOU SHOULD TAKE BETTER CARE OF YOURSELF. THINGS MIGHT STAY THIS WAY FOR SEVERAL MORE YEARS.

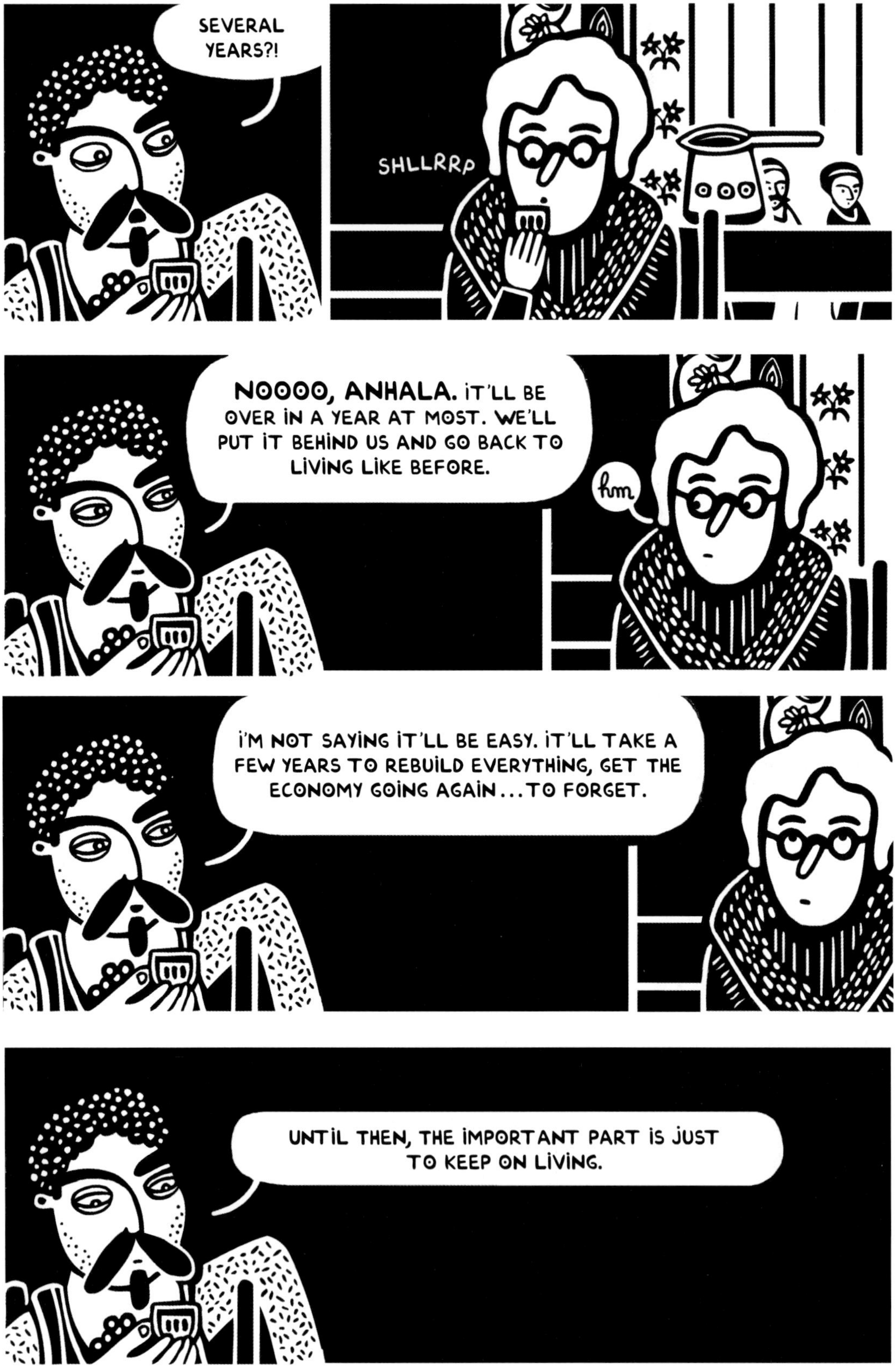
SEVERAL YEARS?!
SHLLRRP
NOOOO, ANHALA. IT'LL BE OVER IN A YEAR AT MOST. WE'LL PUT IT BEHIND US AND GO BACK TO LIVING LIKE BEFORE.
hm
I'M NOT SAYING IT'LL BE EASY. IT'LL TAKE A FEW YEARS TO REBUILD EVERYTHING, GET THE ECONOMY GOING AGAIN . . . TO FORGET.
UNTIL THEN, THE IMPORTANT PART IS JUST TO KEEP ON LIVING.

SHLLRRP

BUT IT WON'T BE LONG NOW, THAT'S FOR SURE!

OTHERWISE, DO YOU THINK I'D HAVE GONE TO ALL THIS TROUBLE? **NOT AT ALL!** I'D HAVE LEFT THE COUNTRY TOO!

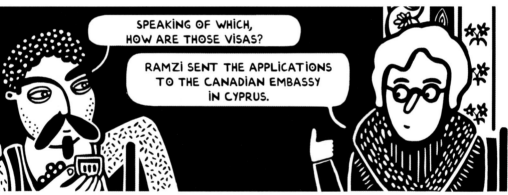

SPEAKING OF WHICH, HOW ARE THOSE VISAS?

RAMZI SENT THE APPLICATIONS TO THE CANADIAN EMBASSY IN CYPRUS.

SHLLRRP

MADAME LINDA GAVE THE ENVELOPE TO ZIAD, A RED CROSS AMBULANCE DRIVER SHE KNOWS. HE'S MADAME HYAM'S SON. YOU KNOW, THE WOMAN WHO RAN THE STATIONERY SHOP BY SAINT JOSEPH UNIVERSITY.

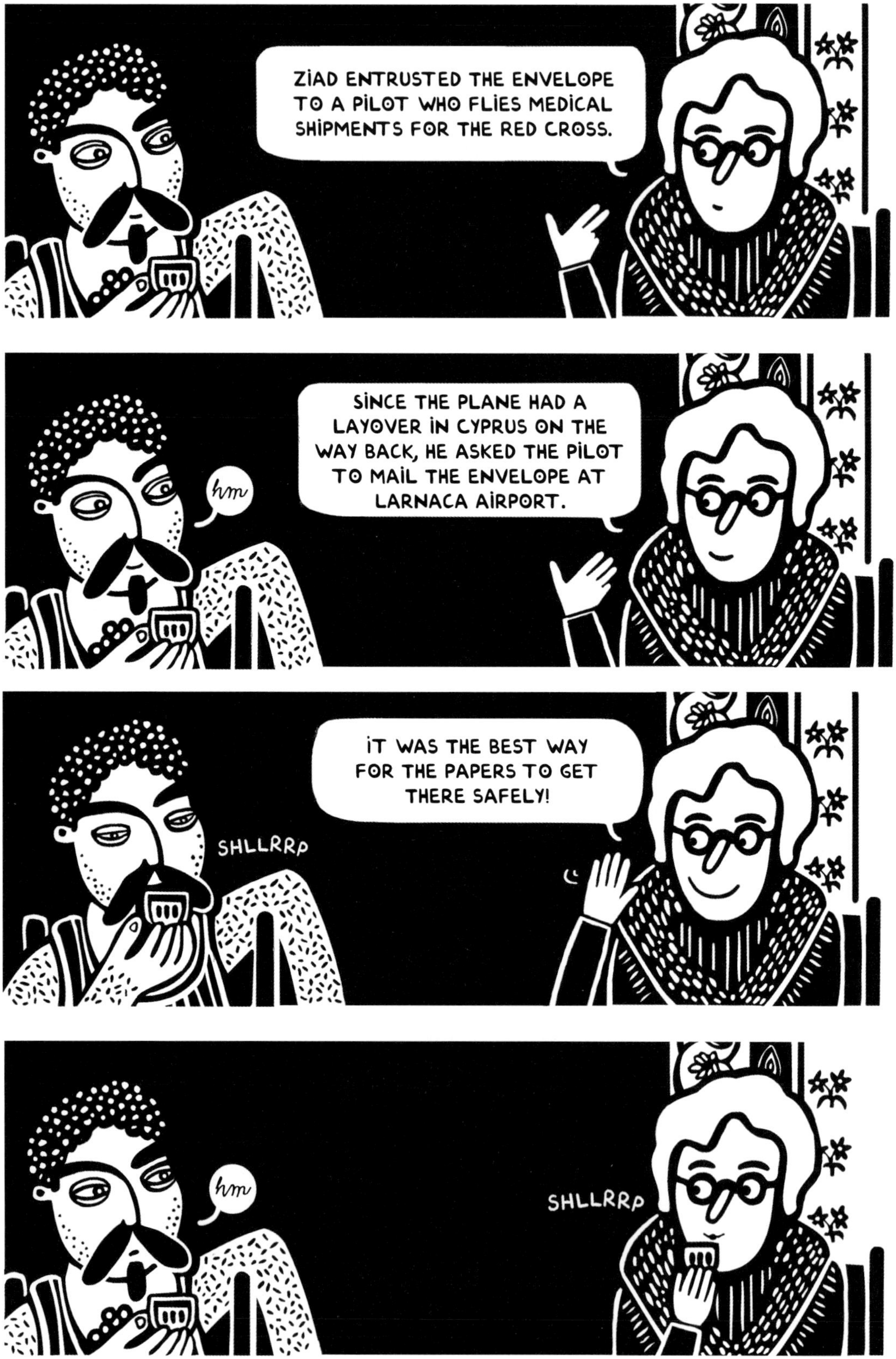
ZIAD ENTRUSTED THE ENVELOPE TO A PILOT WHO FLIES MEDICAL SHIPMENTS FOR THE RED CROSS.
SINCE THE PLANE HAD A LAYOVER IN CYPRUS ON THE WAY BACK, HE ASKED THE PILOT TO MAIL THE ENVELOPE AT LARNACA AIRPORT.
hm
IT WAS THE BEST WAY FOR THE PAPERS TO GET THERE SAFELY!
SHLLRRP
hm
SHLLRRP

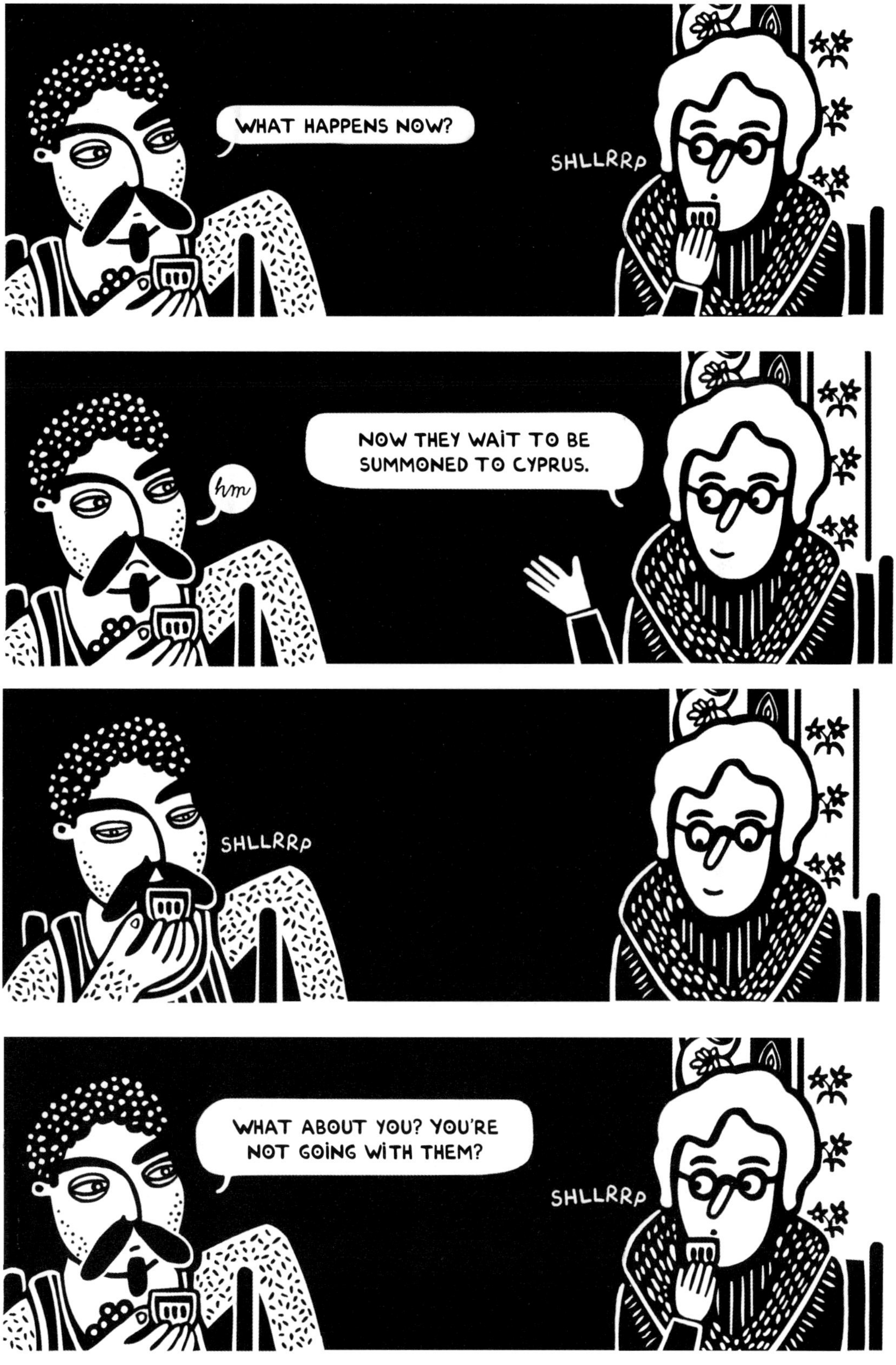
WHAT HAPPENS NOW?
SHLLRRP
hm
NOW THEY WAIT TO BE SUMMONED TO CYPRUS.
SHLLRRP
WHAT ABOUT YOU? YOU'RE NOT GOING WITH THEM?
SHLLRRP

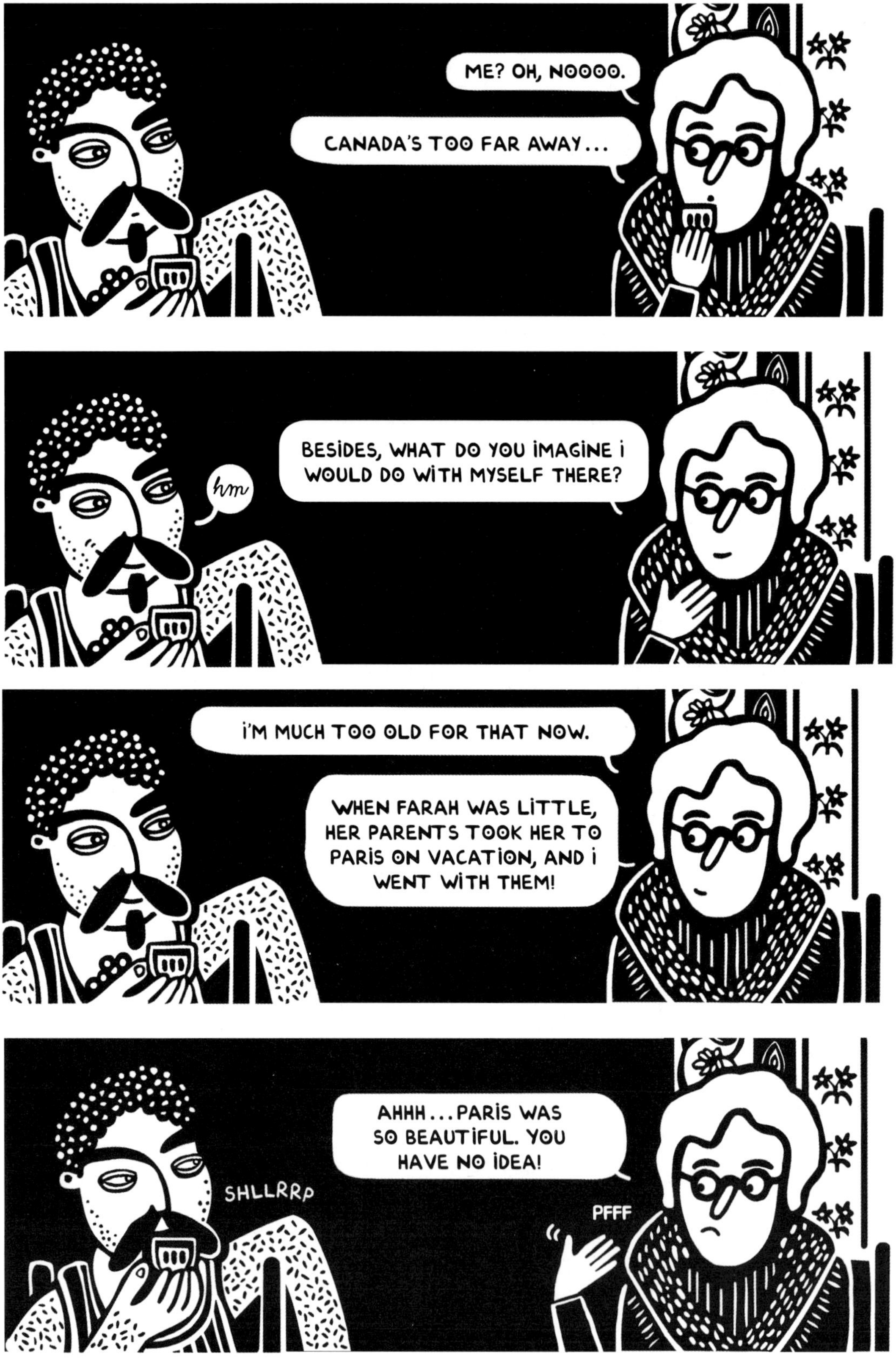
ME? OH, NOOOO.
CANADA'S TOO FAR AWAY...
hm
BESIDES, WHAT DO YOU IMAGINE I WOULD DO WITH MYSELF THERE?
I'M MUCH TOO OLD FOR THAT NOW.
WHEN FARAH WAS LITTLE, HER PARENTS TOOK HER TO PARIS ON VACATION, AND I WENT WITH THEM!
AHHH...PARIS WAS SO BEAUTIFUL. YOU HAVE NO IDEA!
SHLLRRP
PFFF

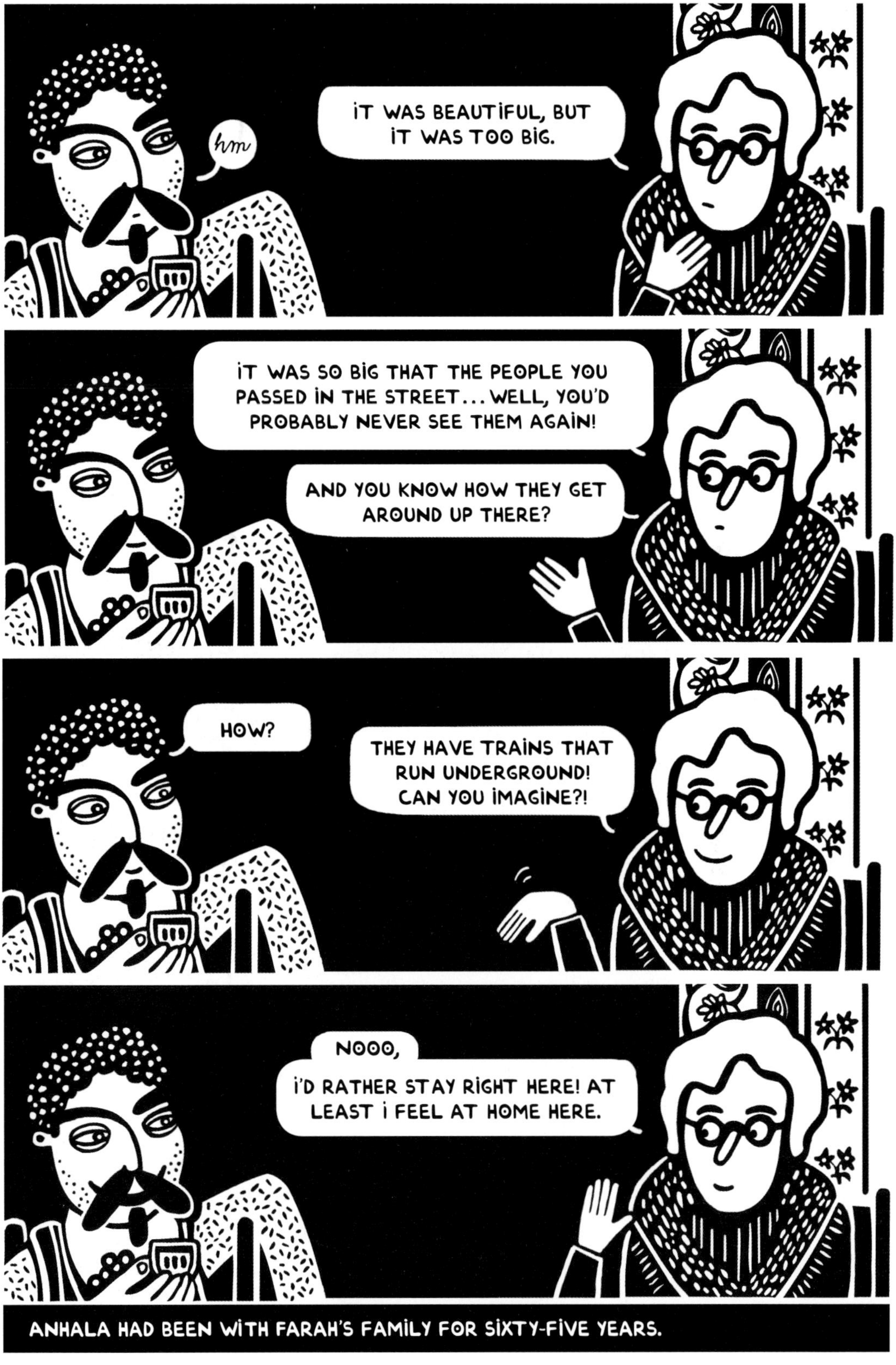
hm
IT WAS BEAUTIFUL, BUT IT WAS TOO BIG.
IT WAS SO BIG THAT THE PEOPLE YOU PASSED IN THE STREET... WELL, YOU'D PROBABLY NEVER SEE THEM AGAIN!
AND YOU KNOW HOW THEY GET AROUND UP THERE?
HOW?
THEY HAVE TRAINS THAT RUN UNDERGROUND! CAN YOU IMAGINE?!
NOOO,
I'D RATHER STAY RIGHT HERE! AT LEAST I FEEL AT HOME HERE.
ANHALA HAD BEEN WITH FARAH'S FAMILY FOR SIXTY-FIVE YEARS.

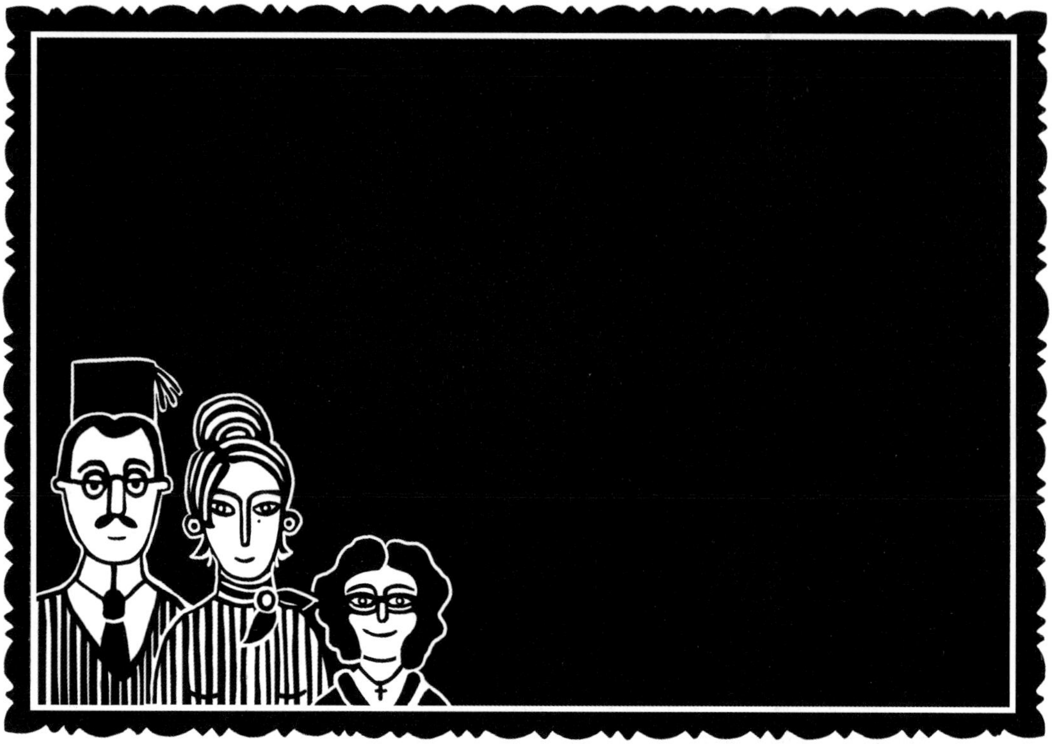

SHE STARTED WORKING AT THE AGE OF 10 FOR FARAH'S GREAT-GRANDPARENTS.

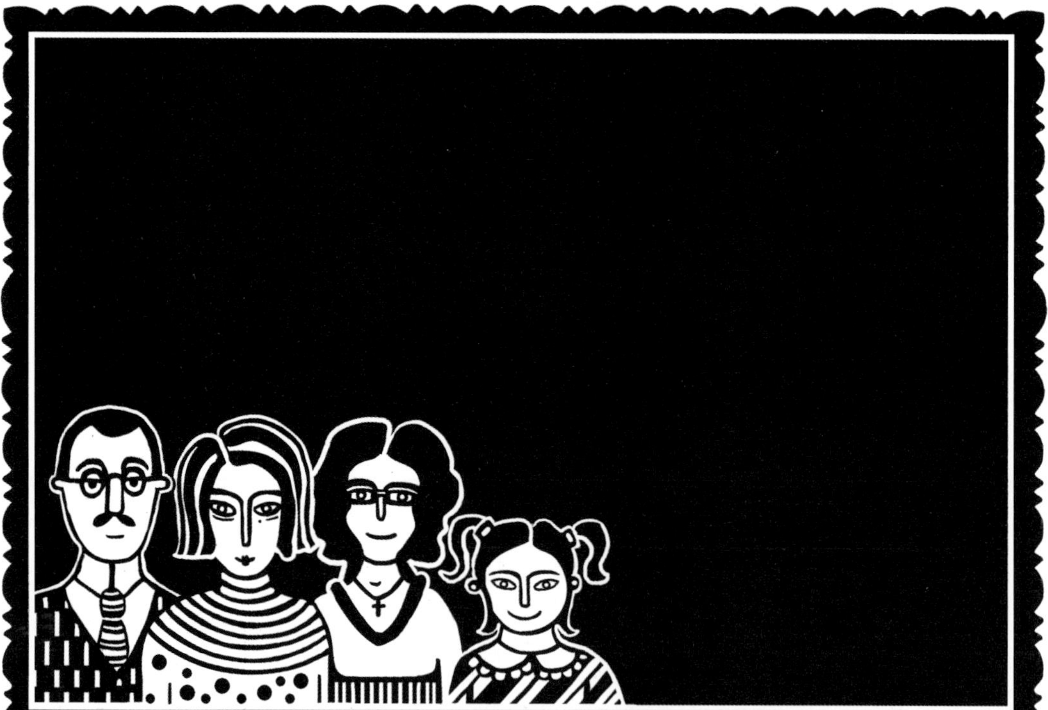

SHE WAS THERE WHEN SONIA, FARAH'S GRANDMOTHER, WAS BORN.

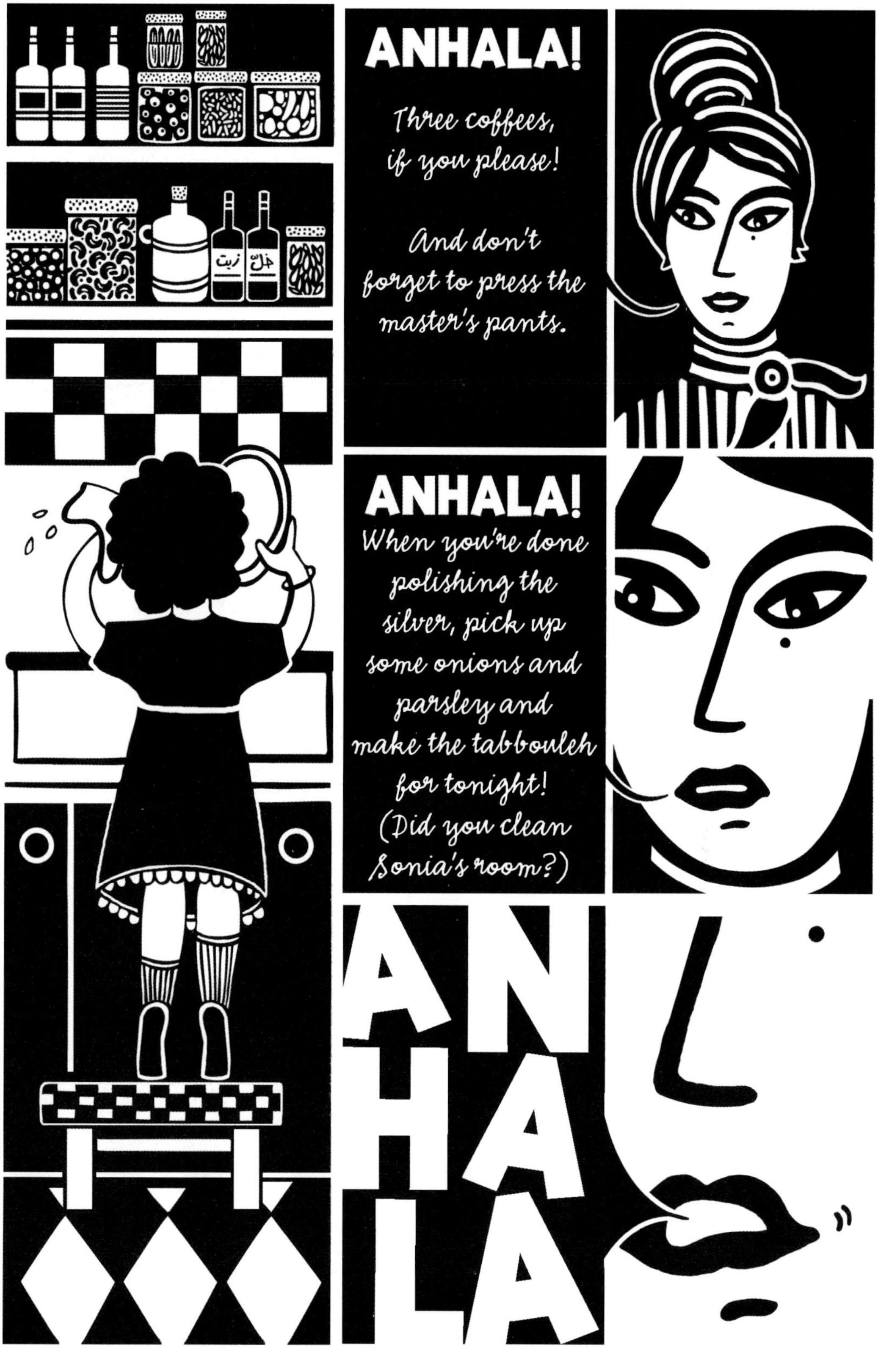
ANHALA!
Three coffees, if you please!
And don't forget to press the master's pants.
ANHALA!
When you're done polishing the silver, pick up some onions and parsley and make the tabbouleh for tonight!
(Did you clean Sonia's room?)
ANHALA

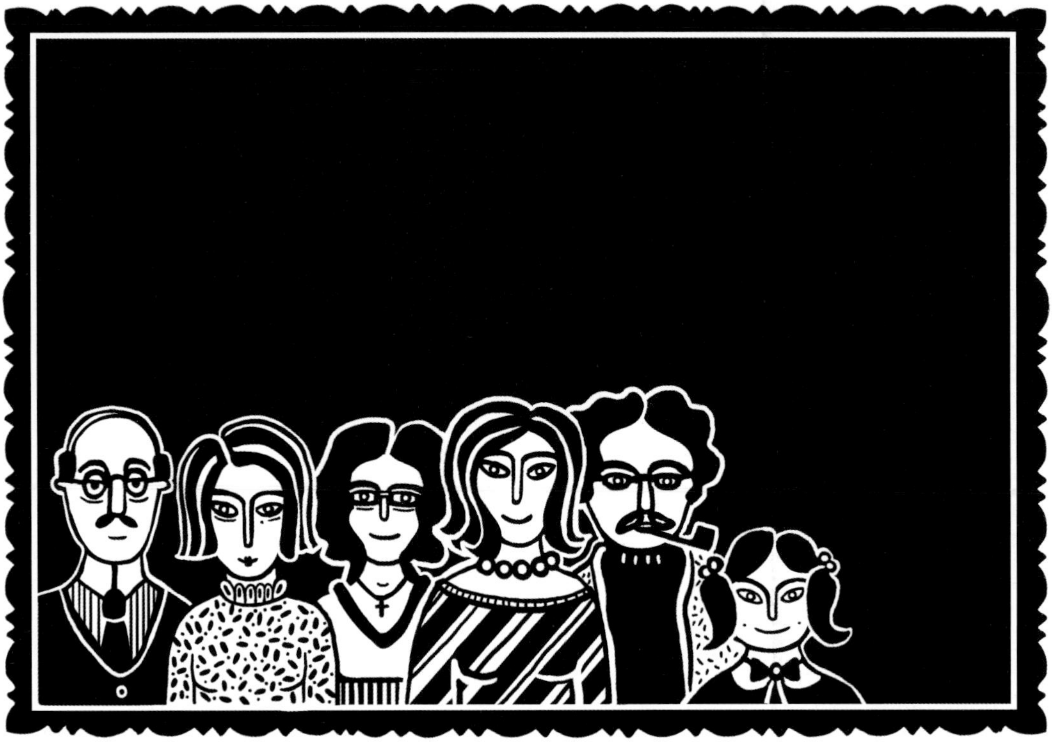

SHE WAS THERE WHEN LENA, FARAH'S MOTHER, WAS BORN.

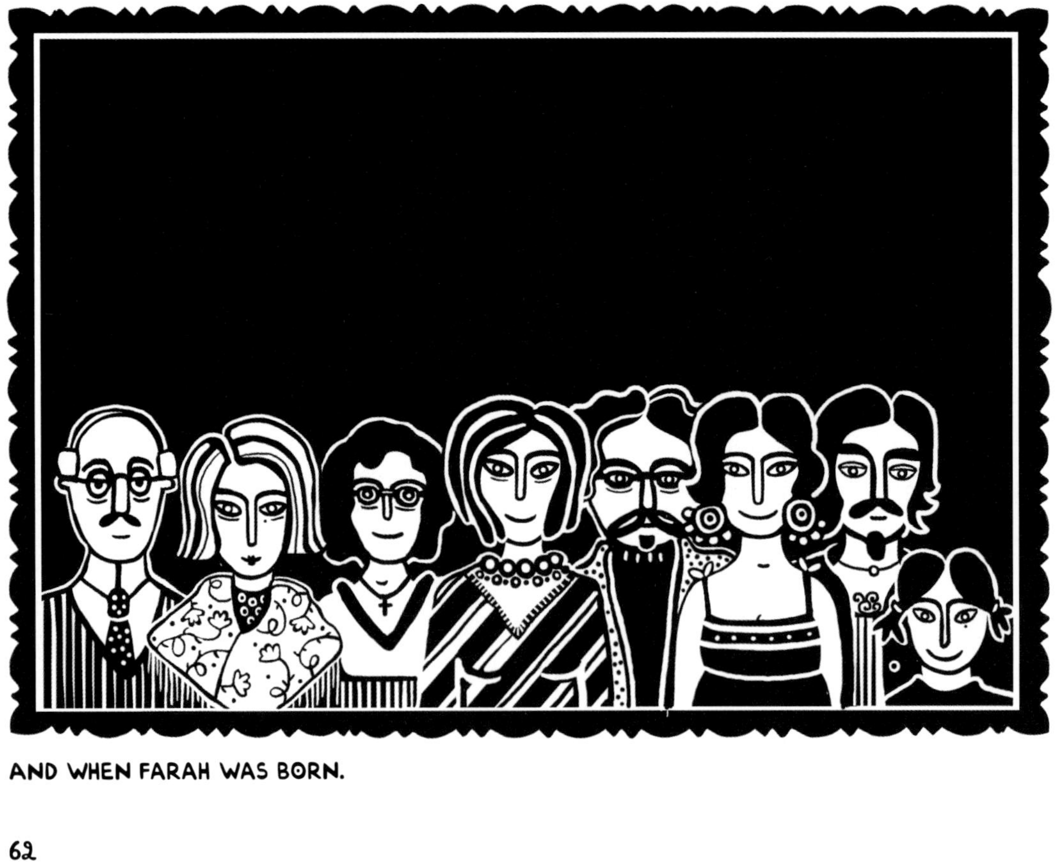

AND WHEN FARAH WAS BORN.

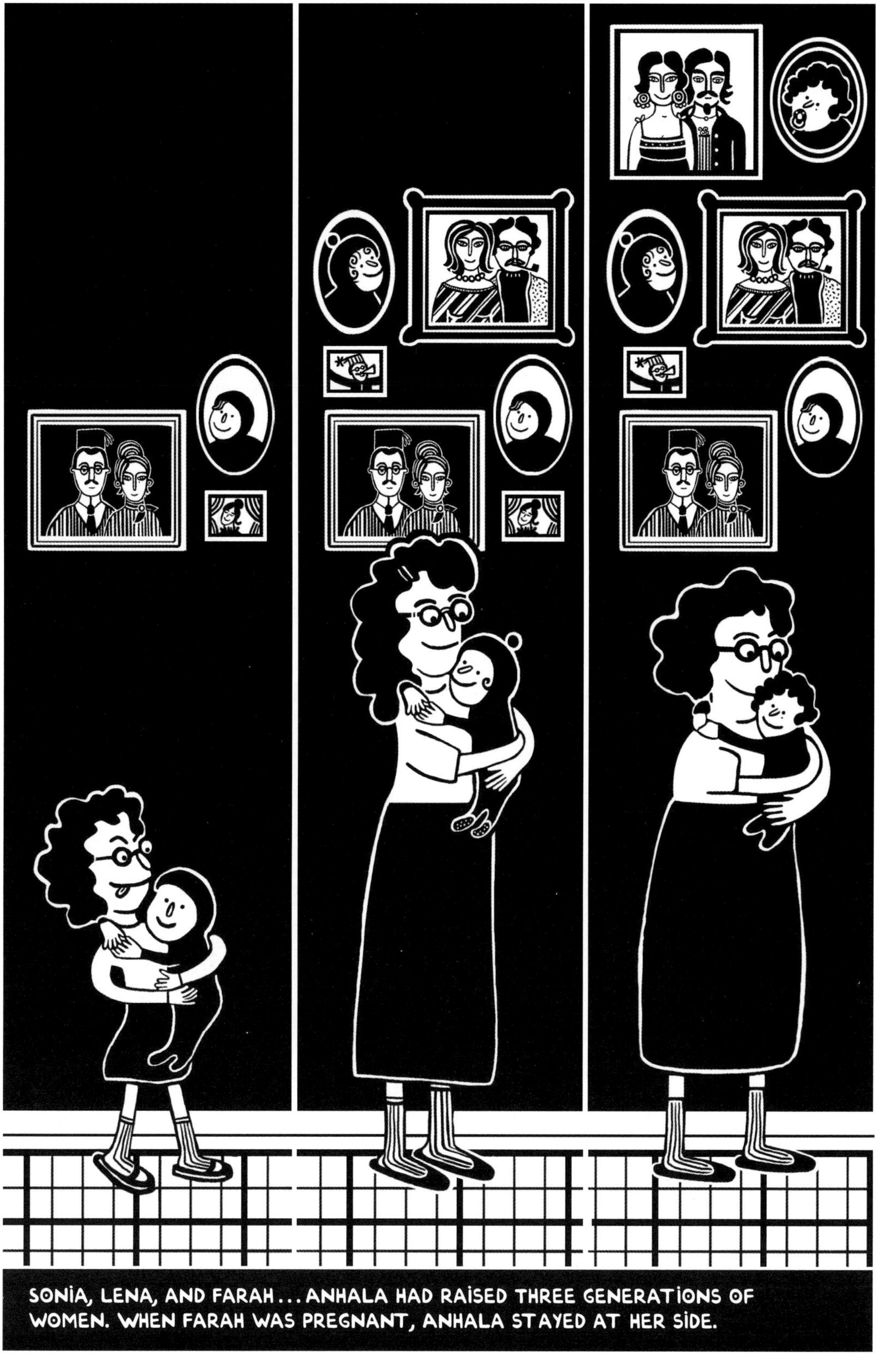
SONiA, LENA, AND FARAH... ANHALA HAD RAiSED THREE GENERATiONS OF WOMEN. WHEN FARAH WAS PREGNANT, ANHALA STAYED AT HER SiDE.

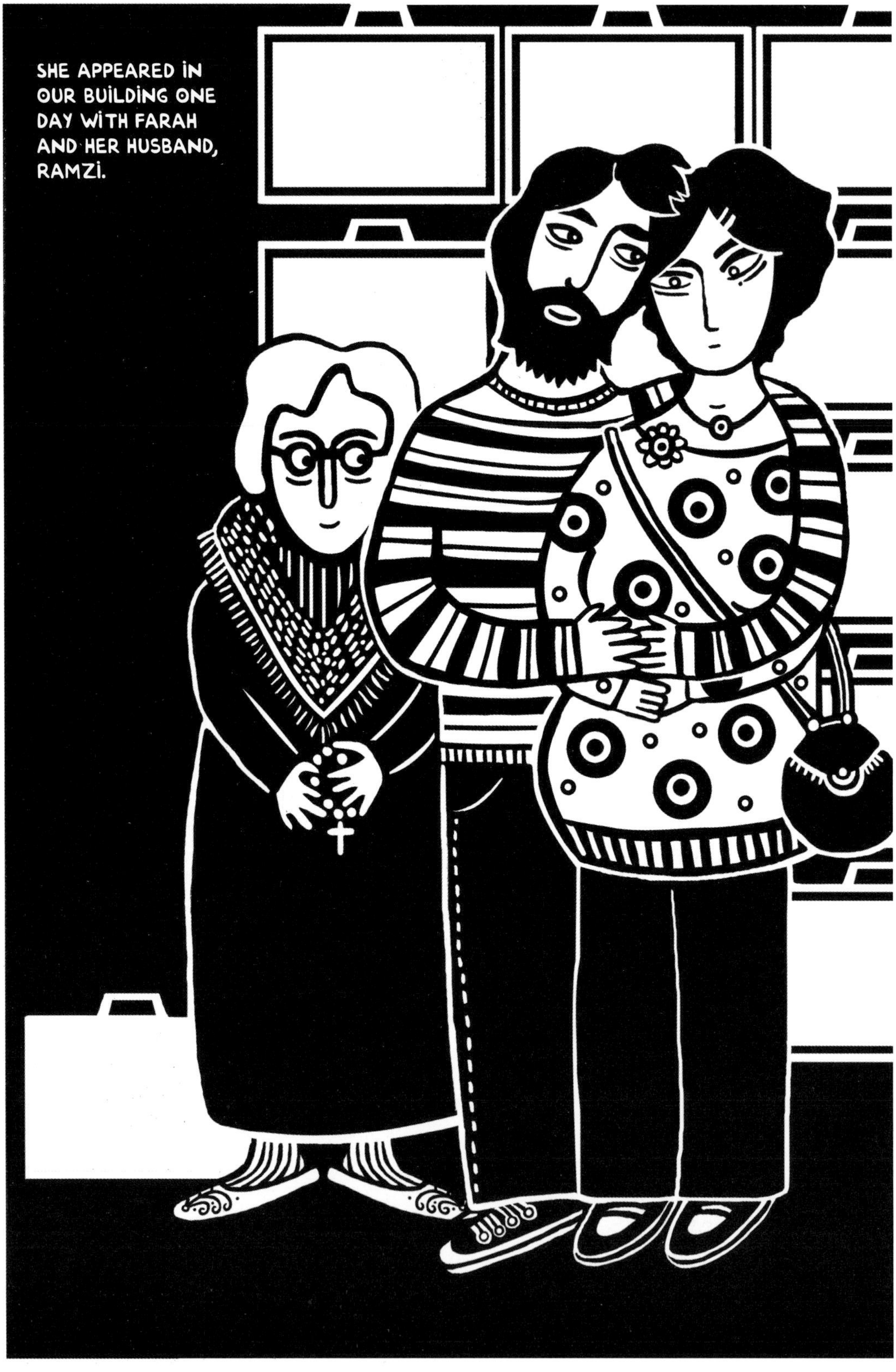
SHE APPEARED IN OUR BUILDING ONE DAY WITH FARAH AND HER HUSBAND, RAMZI.

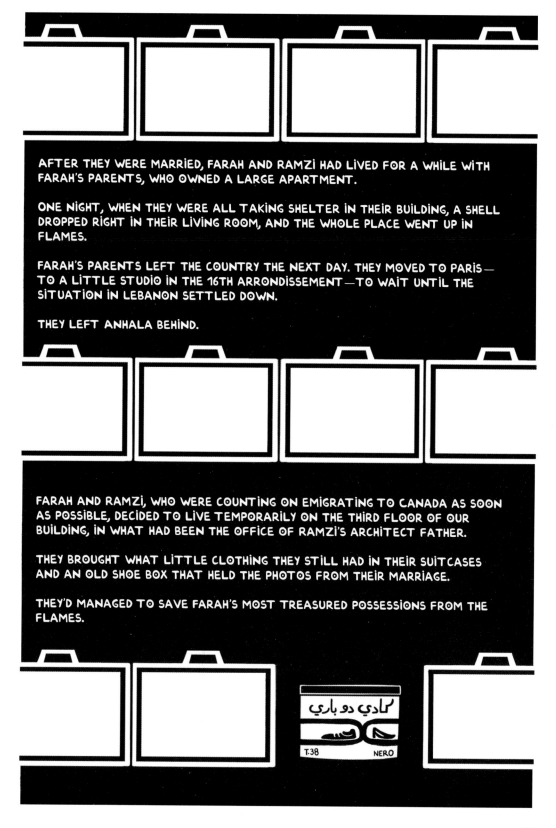

AFTER THEY WERE MARRIED, FARAH AND RAMZI HAD LIVED FOR A WHILE WITH FARAH'S PARENTS, WHO OWNED A LARGE APARTMENT.

ONE NIGHT, WHEN THEY WERE ALL TAKING SHELTER IN THEIR BUILDING, A SHELL DROPPED RIGHT IN THEIR LIVING ROOM, AND THE WHOLE PLACE WENT UP IN FLAMES.

FARAH'S PARENTS LEFT THE COUNTRY THE NEXT DAY. THEY MOVED TO PARIS— TO A LITTLE STUDIO IN THE 16TH ARRONDISSEMENT—TO WAIT UNTIL THE SITUATION IN LEBANON SETTLED DOWN.

THEY LEFT ANHALA BEHIND.

FARAH AND RAMZI, WHO WERE COUNTING ON EMIGRATING TO CANADA AS SOON AS POSSIBLE, DECIDED TO LIVE TEMPORARILY ON THE THIRD FLOOR OF OUR BUILDING, IN WHAT HAD BEEN THE OFFICE OF RAMZI'S ARCHITECT FATHER.

THEY BROUGHT WHAT LITTLE CLOTHING THEY STILL HAD IN THEIR SUITCASES AND AN OLD SHOE BOX THAT HELD THE PHOTOS FROM THEIR MARRIAGE.

THEY'D MANAGED TO SAVE FARAH'S MOST TREASURED POSSESSIONS FROM THE FLAMES.

كادي دو باري

T.38   NERO

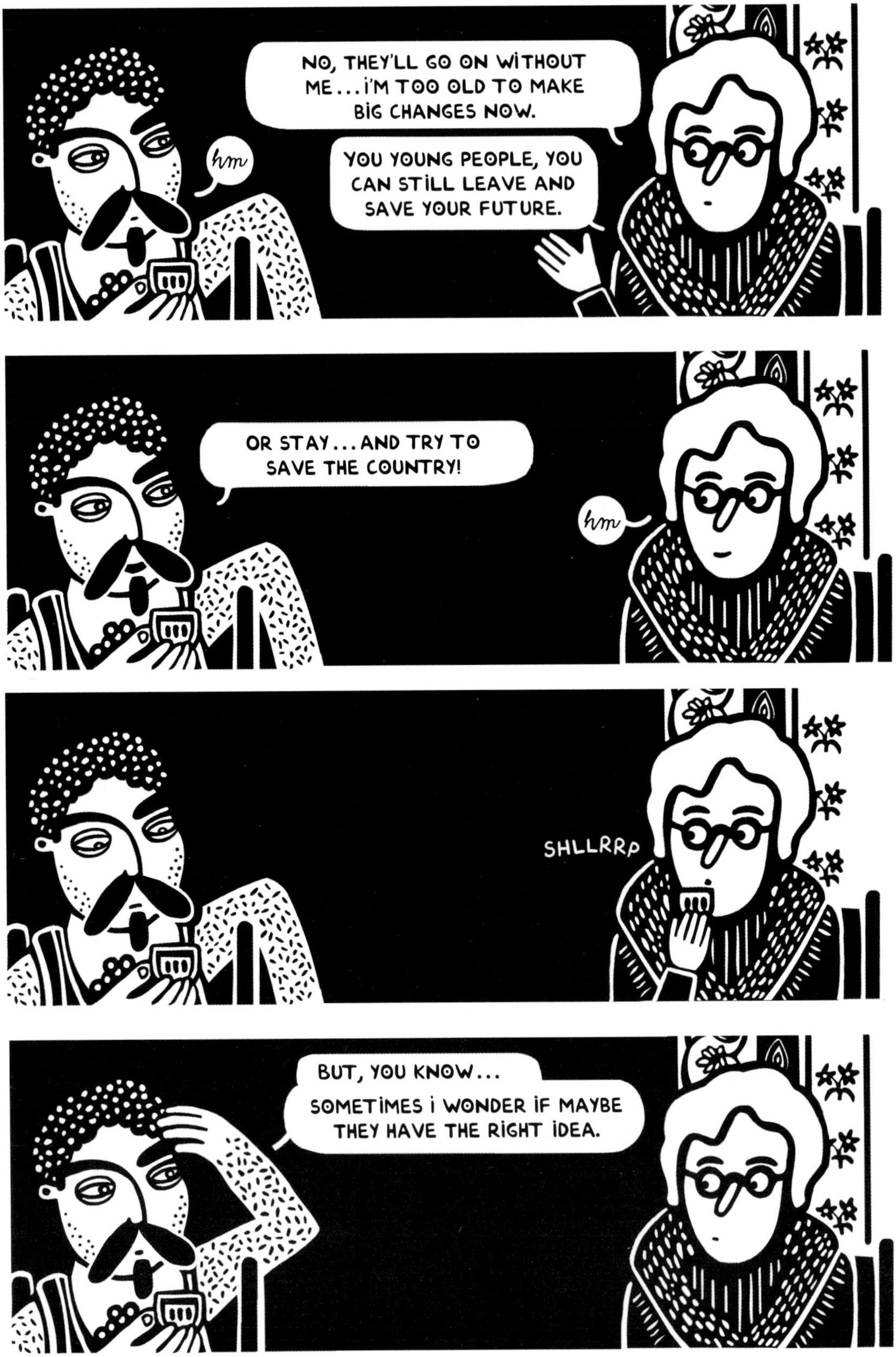
NO, THEY'LL GO ON WITHOUT ME... I'M TOO OLD TO MAKE BIG CHANGES NOW.
hm
YOU YOUNG PEOPLE, YOU CAN STILL LEAVE AND SAVE YOUR FUTURE.
OR STAY... AND TRY TO SAVE THE COUNTRY!
hm
SHLLRRP
BUT, YOU KNOW...
SOMETIMES I WONDER IF MAYBE THEY HAVE THE RIGHT IDEA.

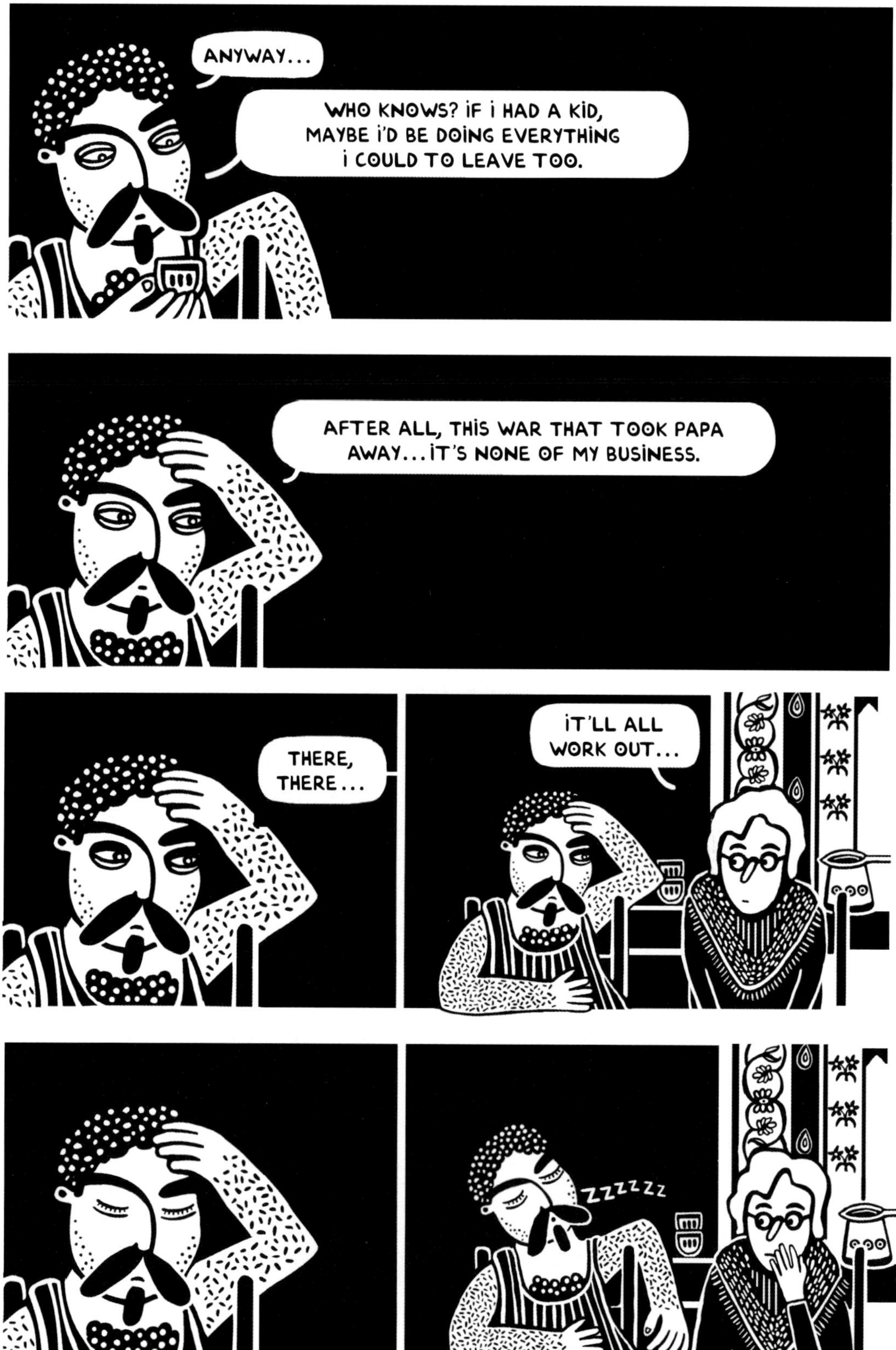
ANYWAY...
WHO KNOWS? IF I HAD A KID, MAYBE I'D BE DOING EVERYTHING I COULD TO LEAVE TOO.
AFTER ALL, THIS WAR THAT TOOK PAPA AWAY... IT'S NONE OF MY BUSINESS.
THERE, THERE...
IT'LL ALL WORK OUT...
ZZZZZZ

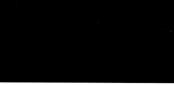

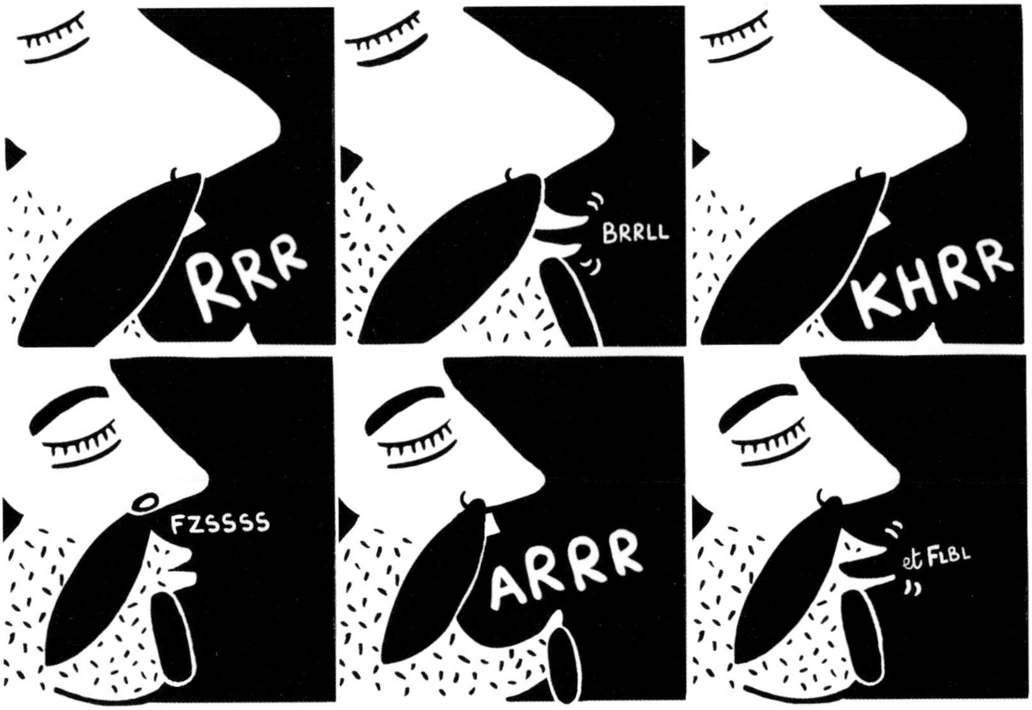
RRR
BRRLL
KHRR
FZSSSS
ARRR
et FLBL

WHEN HIS MOTHER DECIDED TO LEAVE BEIRUT AND TAKE HIS SISTERS TO LIVE WHERE IT WAS CALMER—BACK TO THE VILLAGE WHERE SHE'D GROWN UP ON THE NORTHERN COAST OF LEBANON—CHUCRI GOT HIS FATHER'S CAR OUTOF THE BUILDING'S GARAGE. HE PATCHED IT UP, CLEANED IT OUT, AND PUT A DRIVER'S SEAT BACK IN.

THE LITTLE APARTMENT ON THE GROUND FLOOR WAS MUCH MORE COMFORTABLE NOW WITH ONLY ONE PERSON IN IT, BUT CHUCRI SPENT MORE TIME IN HIS CAR THAN AT HOME.

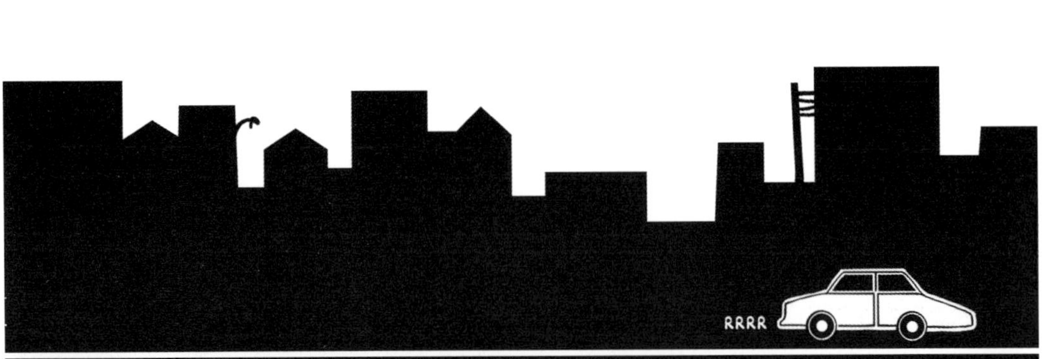
RRRR

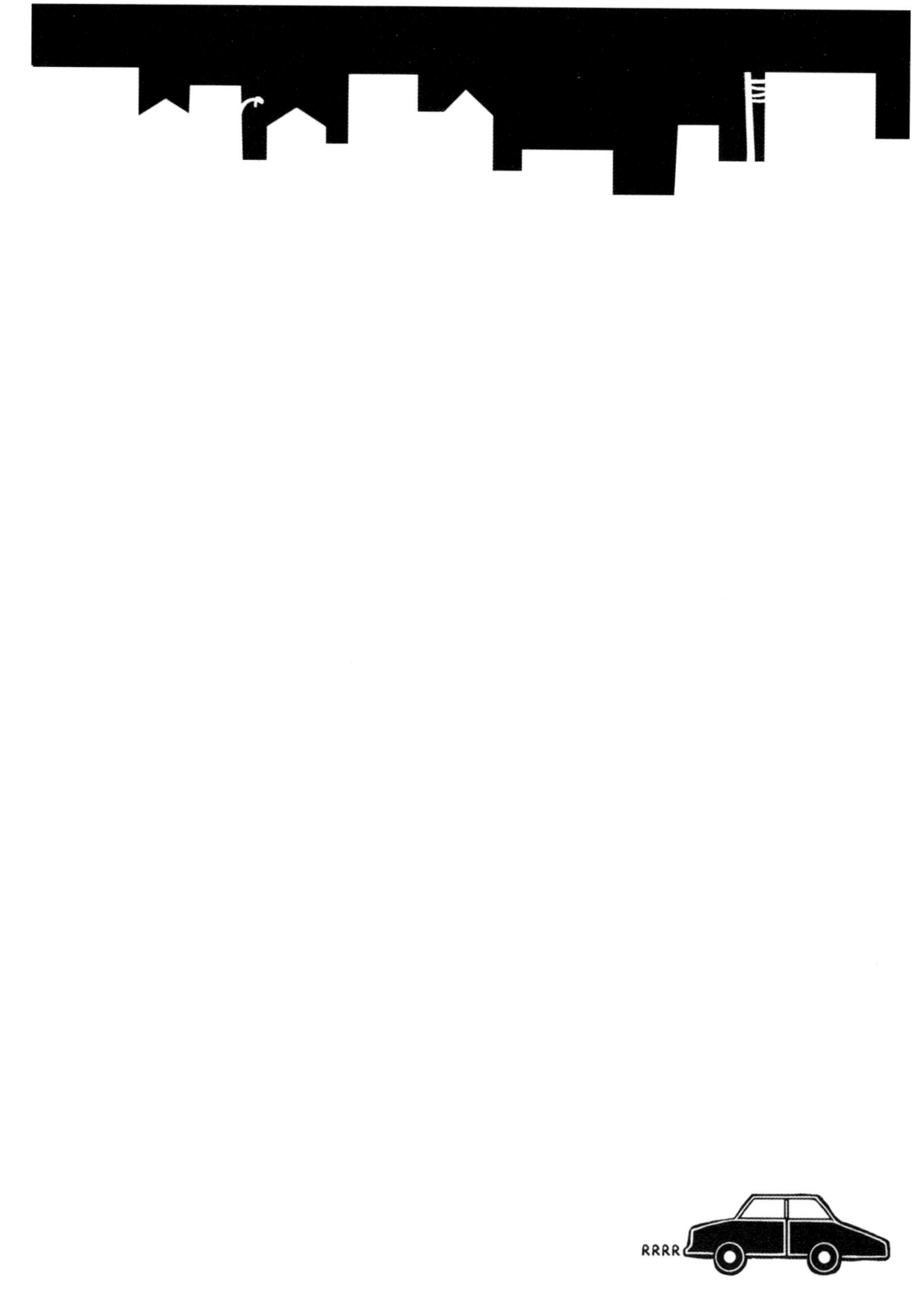
RRRR
DURING CEASE-FIRES, HE WOULD ROAM THE DESERTED CITY...

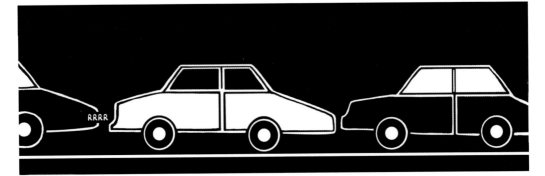

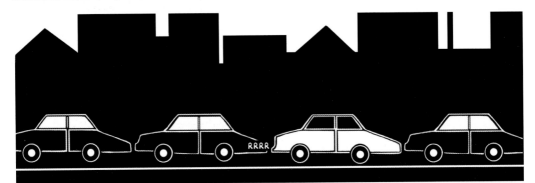

...OR WAIT IN LINE IN FRONT OF STORES FOR BREAD, RICE, SUGAR, CANNED FOOD, CIGARETTES, COFFEE, MATCHES, CANDLES, GAS CANISTERS FOR CAMP STOVES, BATTERIES FOR FLASHLIGHTS, AND RADIOS...

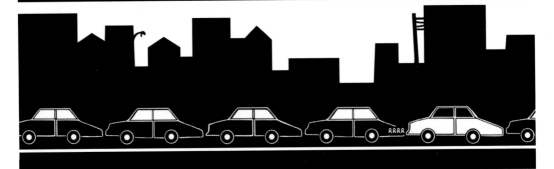

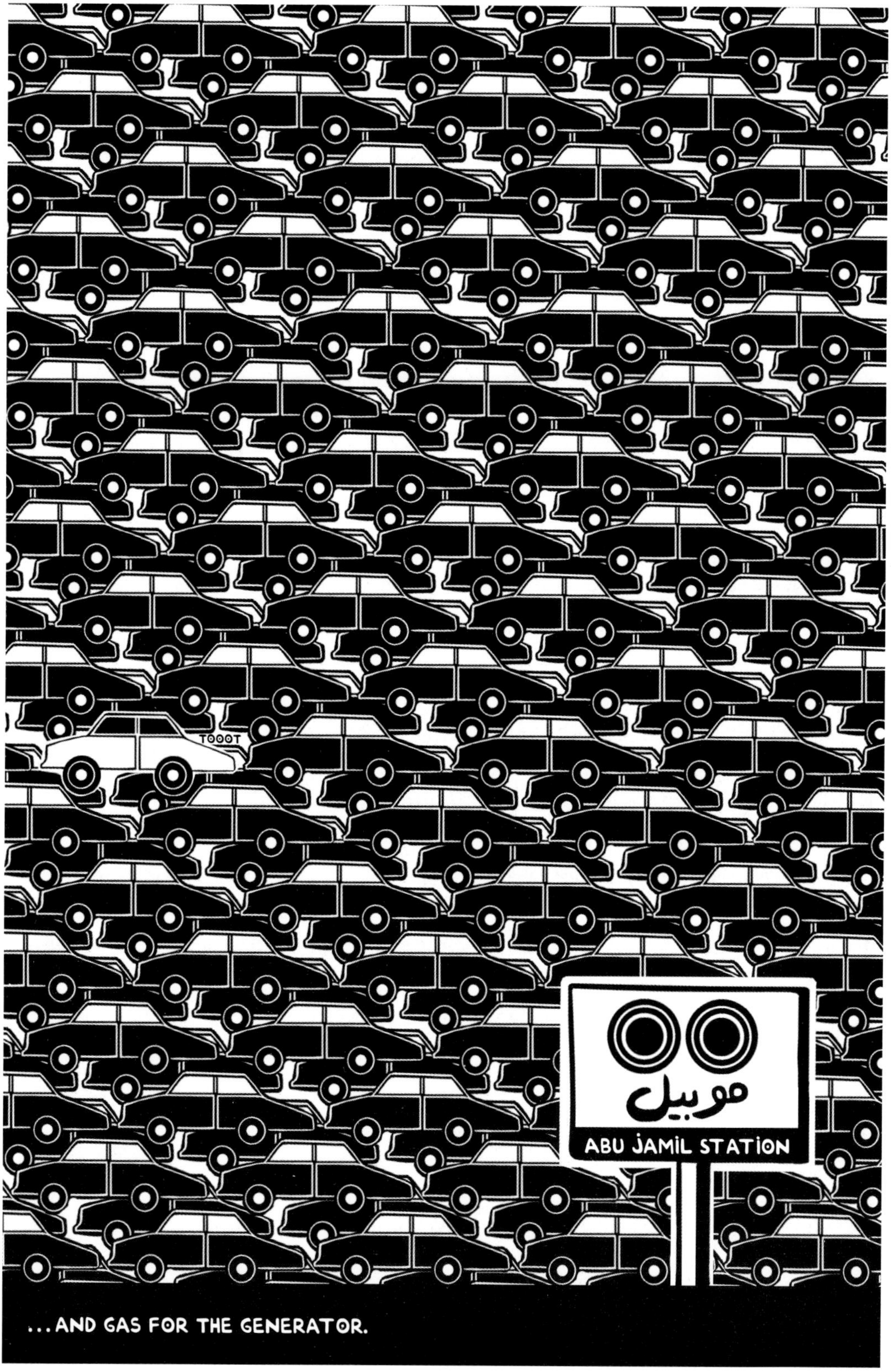
TOOOT
موبيل
ABU JAMIL STATION
...AND GAS FOR THE GENERATOR.

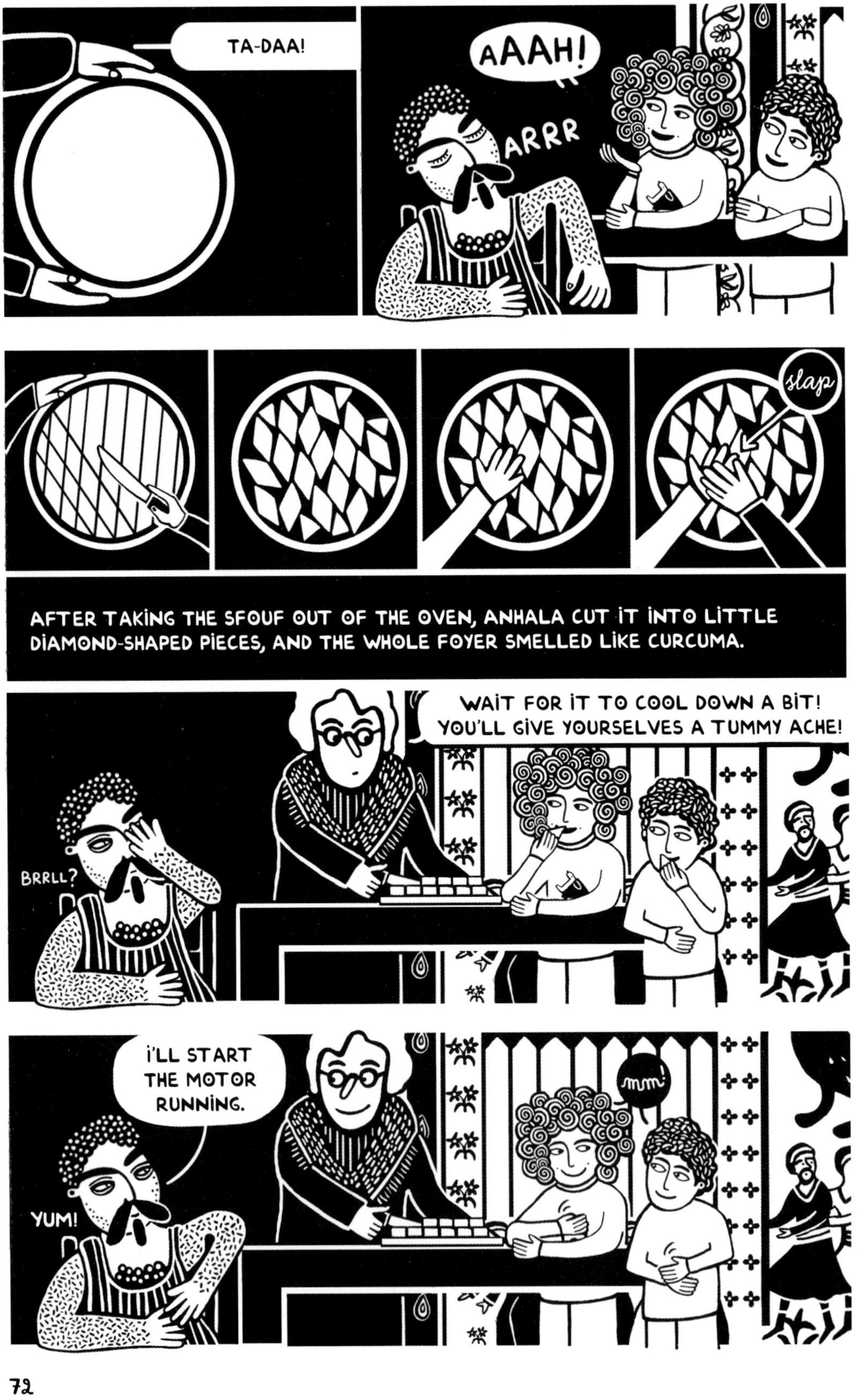
TA-DAA!
AAAH!
ARRR
slap
AFTER TAKING THE SFOUF OUT OF THE OVEN, ANHALA CUT IT INTO LITTLE DIAMOND-SHAPED PIECES, AND THE WHOLE FOYER SMELLED LIKE CURCUMA.
WAIT FOR IT TO COOL DOWN A BIT! YOU'LL GIVE YOURSELVES A TUMMY ACHE!
BRRLL?
I'LL START THE MOTOR RUNNING.
mm!
YUM!

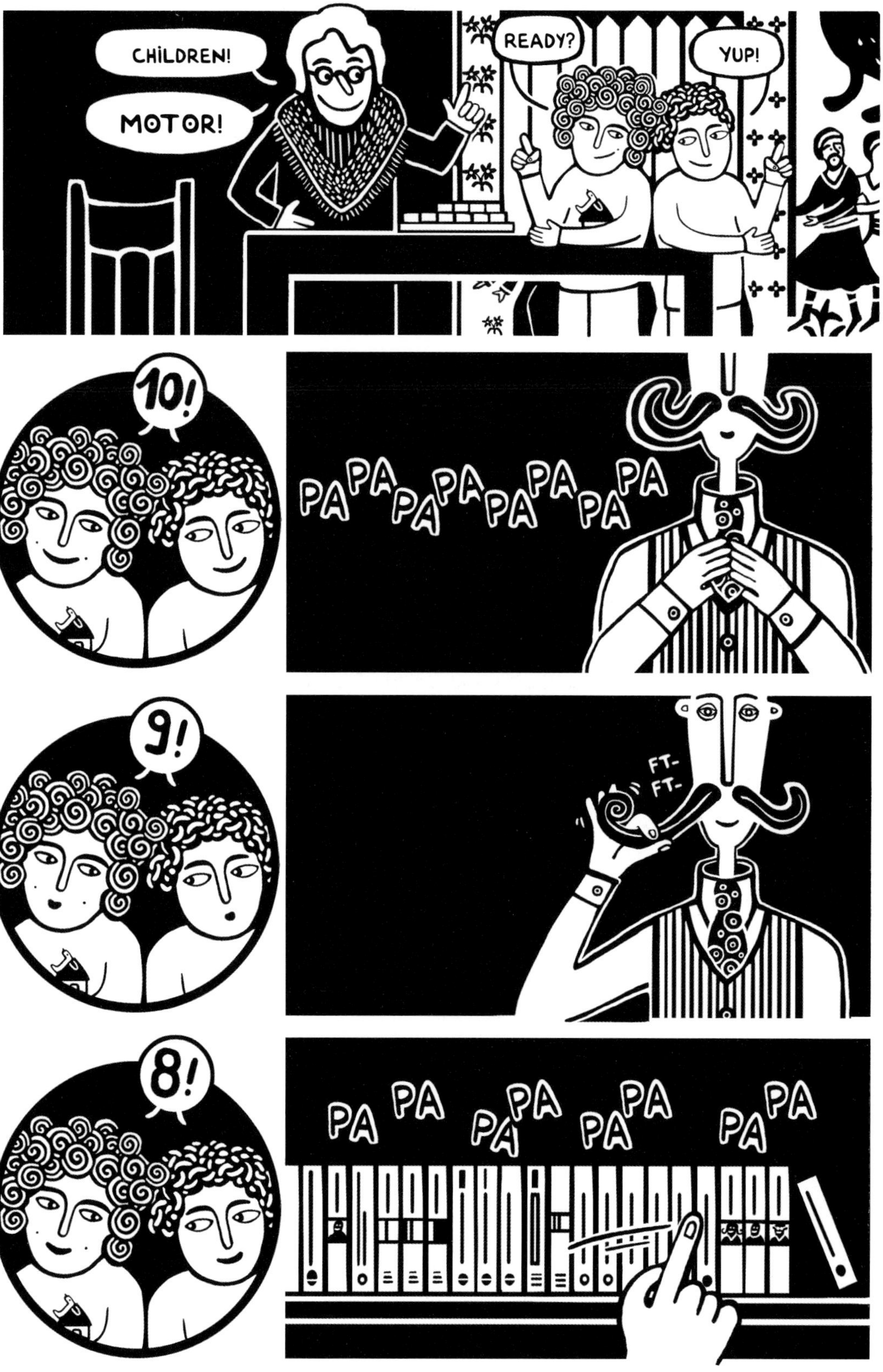
CHILDREN!
MOTOR!
READY?
YUP!
10!
PA PA PA PA PA PA PA PA PA
9!
FT-
FT-
8!
PA PA PA PA PA PA PA PA

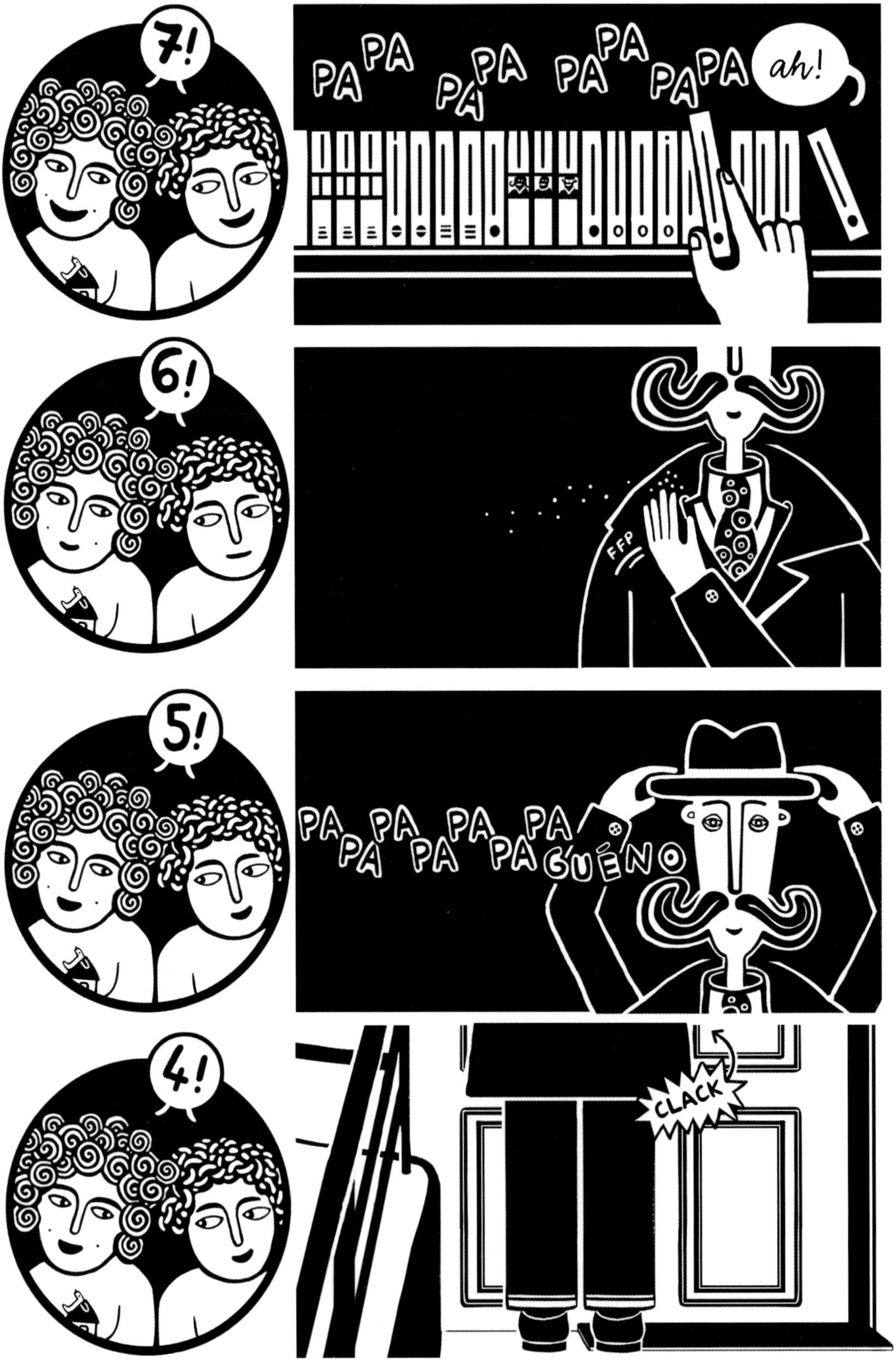
7!
PA PA PA PA PA PA PA PA
ah!
6!
FFP
5!
PA PA PA PA PA PA PA PAGUÉNO
4!
CLACK

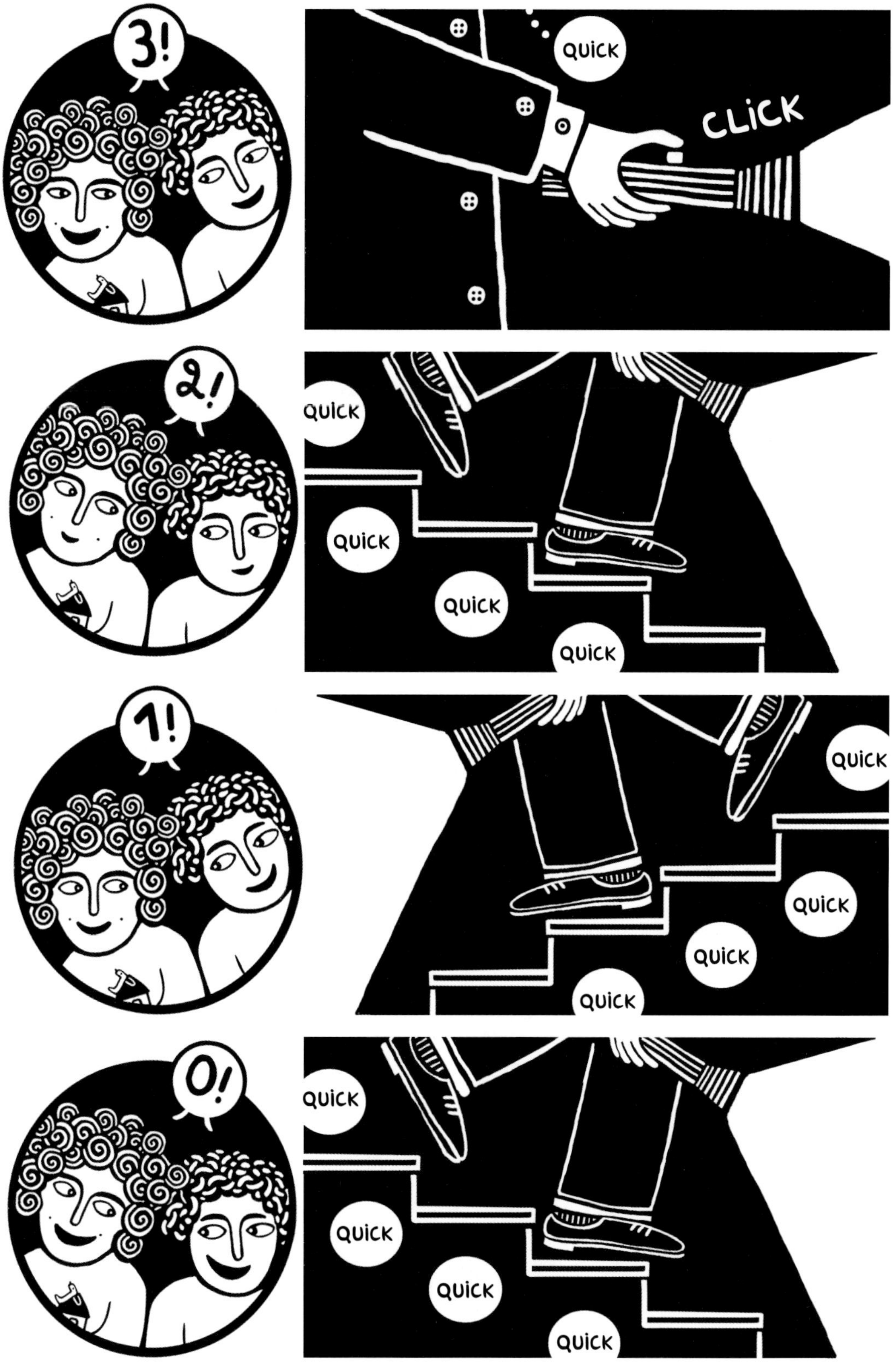
3!
QUICK
CLICK
2!
QUICK
QUICK
QUICK
QUICK
1!
QUICK
QUICK
QUICK
QUICK
0!
QUICK
QUICK
QUICK
QUICK

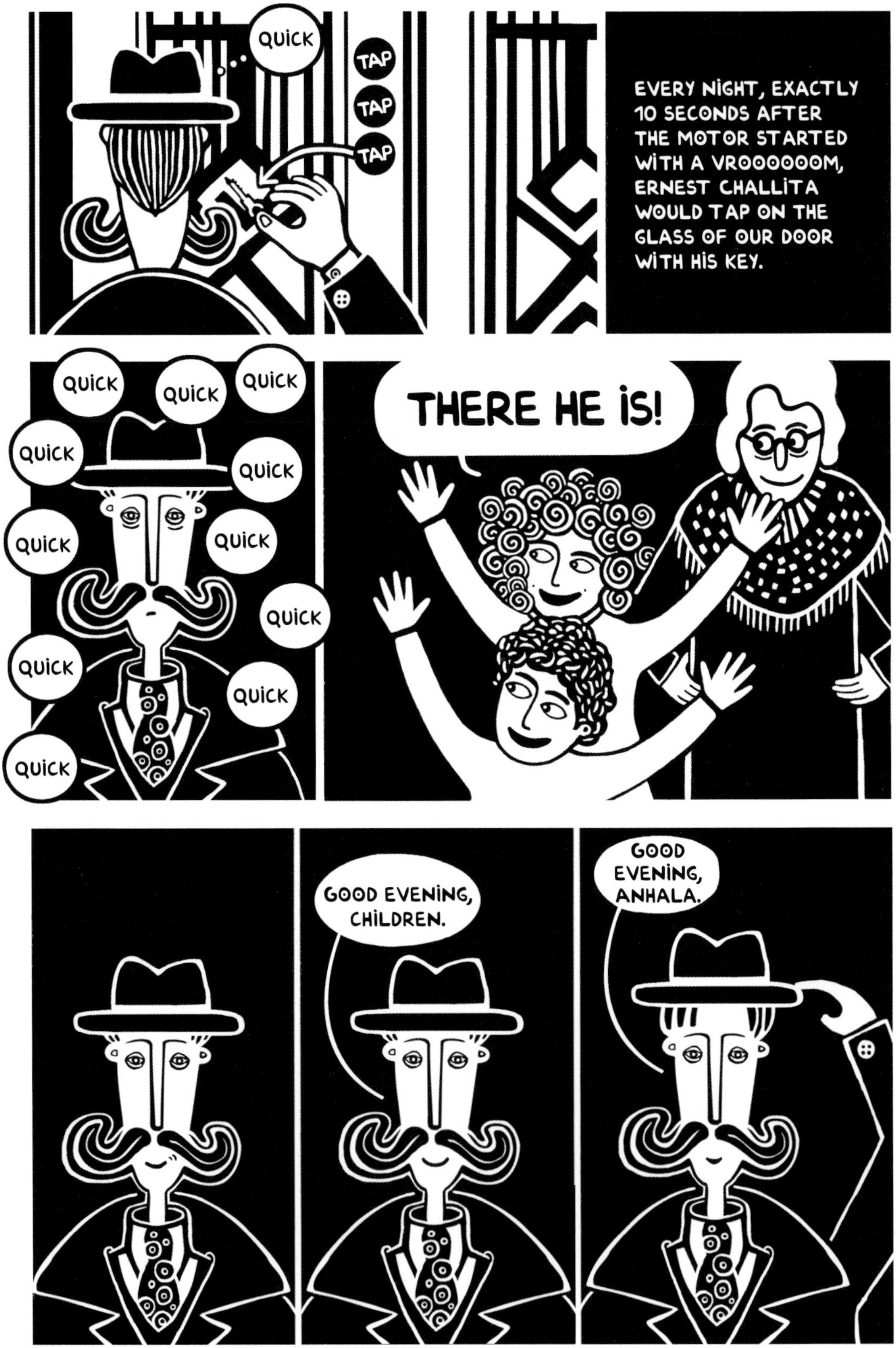
QUICK
TAP
TAP
TAP
EVERY NIGHT, EXACTLY 10 SECONDS AFTER THE MOTOR STARTED WITH A VROOOOOOM, ERNEST CHALLITA WOULD TAP ON THE GLASS OF OUR DOOR WITH HIS KEY.
QUICK
QUICK
QUICK
QUICK
QUICK
QUICK
QUICK
QUICK
QUICK
QUICK
QUICK
THERE HE IS!
GOOD EVENING, CHILDREN.
GOOD EVENING, ANHALA.

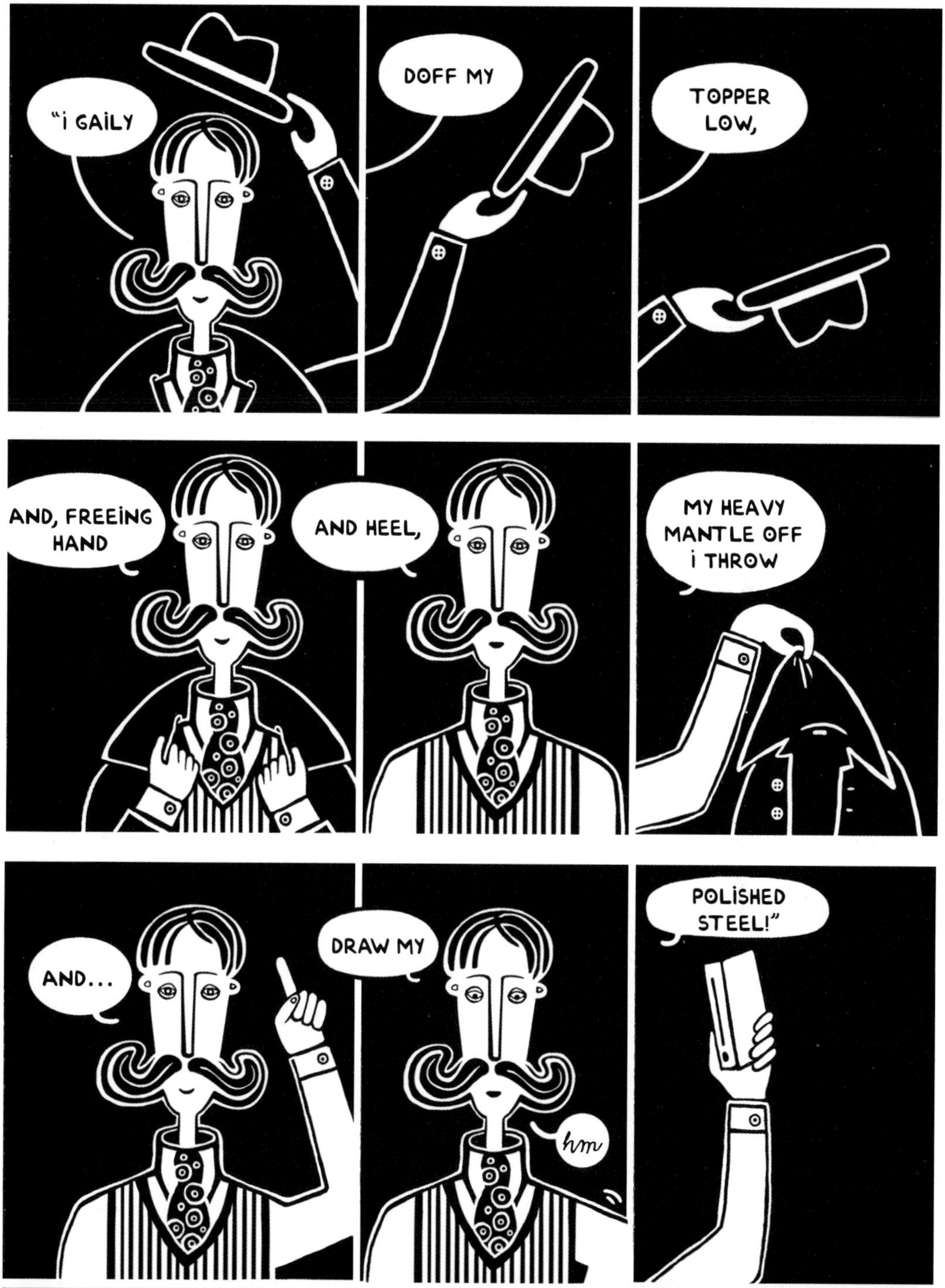
"i GAILY
DOFF MY
TOPPER LOW,
AND, FREEiNG HAND
AND HEEL,
MY HEAVY MANTLE OFF i THROW
AND...
DRAW MY
hm
POLiSHED STEEL!"

ERNEST CHALLiTA WAS OUR FOURTH-FLOOR NEiGHBOR. BEFORE THE WAR, HE TAUGHT FRENCH AT THE HiGH SCHOOL ON BAYDOUN STREET.

"COME, YOUNG HEROES!

ERNEST KNEW WHOLE SECTIONS OF *CYRANO DE BERGERAC* BY HEART.

EVERY NIGHT, IN THE FOYER, HE'D PERFORM A SCENE FOR US. (HE WAS AFRAID OF MEMORY LAPSES, SO HE ALWAYS BROUGHT THE BOOK WITH HIM, BUT HE NEVER NEEDED IT.)

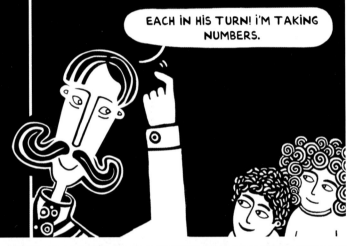

EACH IN HIS TURN! I'M TAKING NUMBERS.

NOW, WHICH OF YOU WILL COME TO OPEN THE LISTS?"

TAP TAP

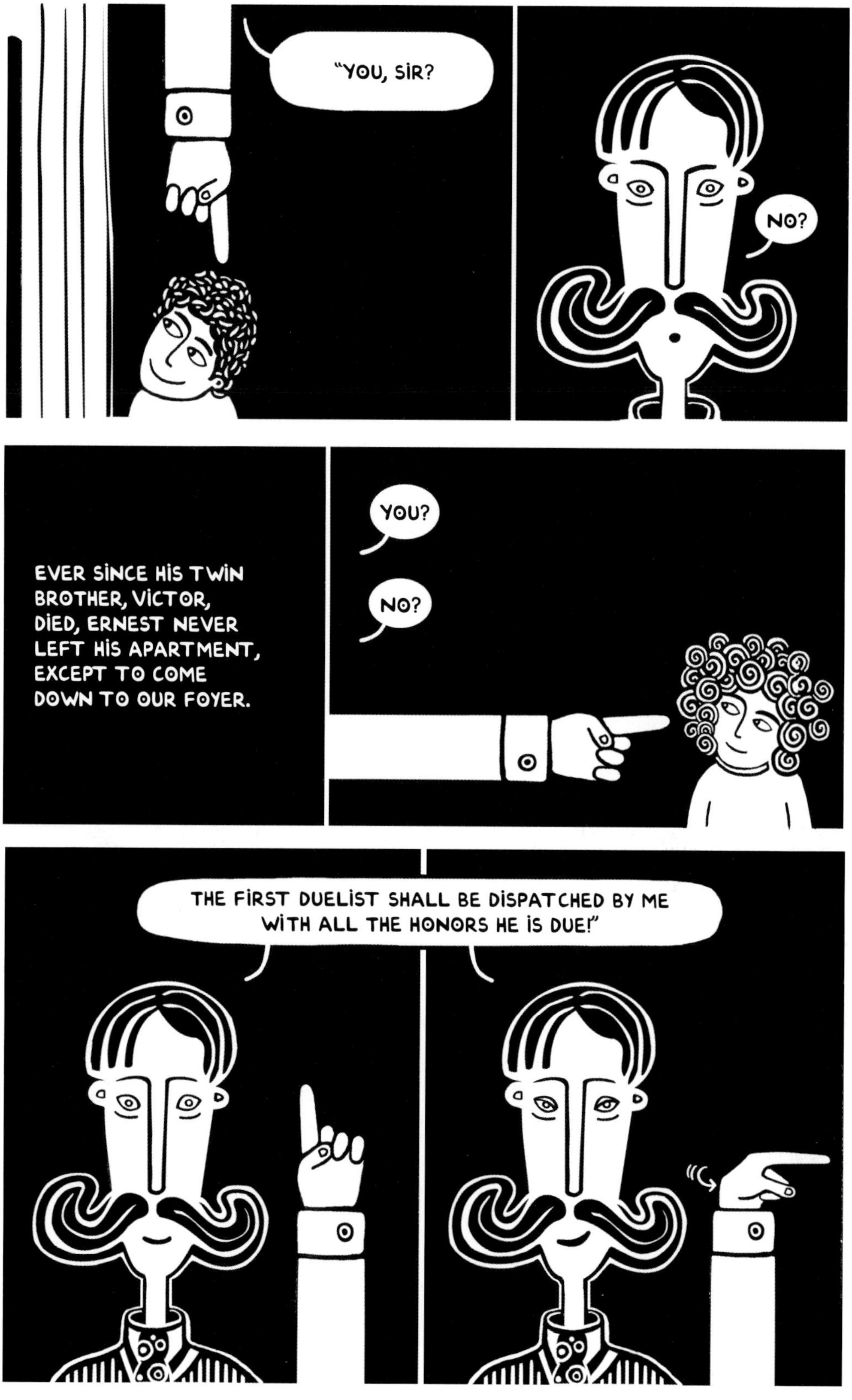

"YOU, SIR?
NO?
EVER SINCE HIS TWIN BROTHER, VICTOR, DIED, ERNEST NEVER LEFT HIS APARTMENT, EXCEPT TO COME DOWN TO OUR FOYER.
YOU?
NO?
THE FIRST DUELIST SHALL BE DISPATCHED BY ME WITH ALL THE HONORS HE IS DUE!"

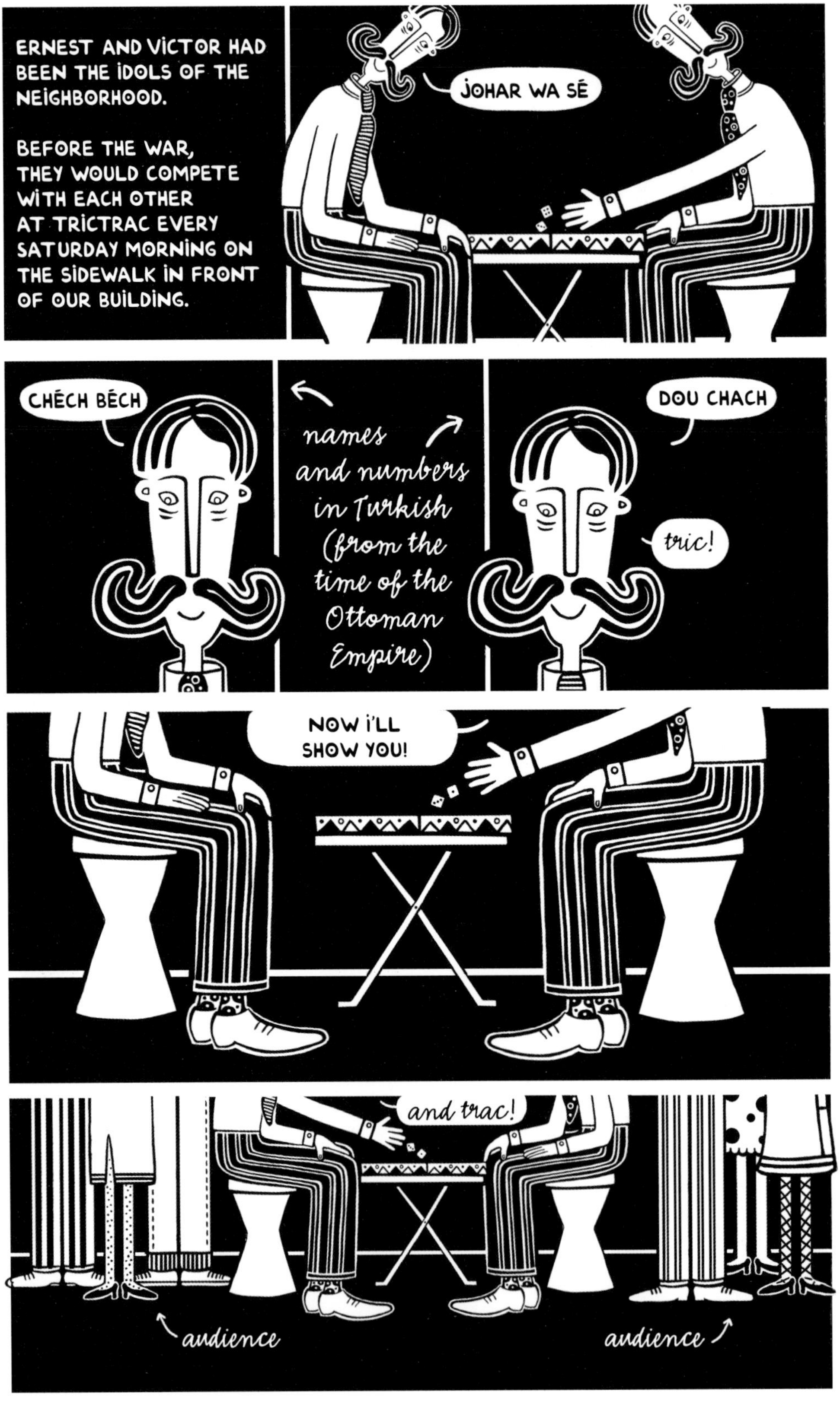
ERNEST AND VICTOR HAD BEEN THE IDOLS OF THE NEIGHBORHOOD.
BEFORE THE WAR, THEY WOULD COMPETE WITH EACH OTHER AT TRICTRAC EVERY SATURDAY MORNING ON THE SIDEWALK IN FRONT OF OUR BUILDING.
JOHAR WA SÉ
CHÉCH BÉCH
names and numbers in Turkish (from the time of the Ottoman Empire)
DOU CHACH
tric!
NOW I'LL SHOW YOU!
and trac!
audience
audience

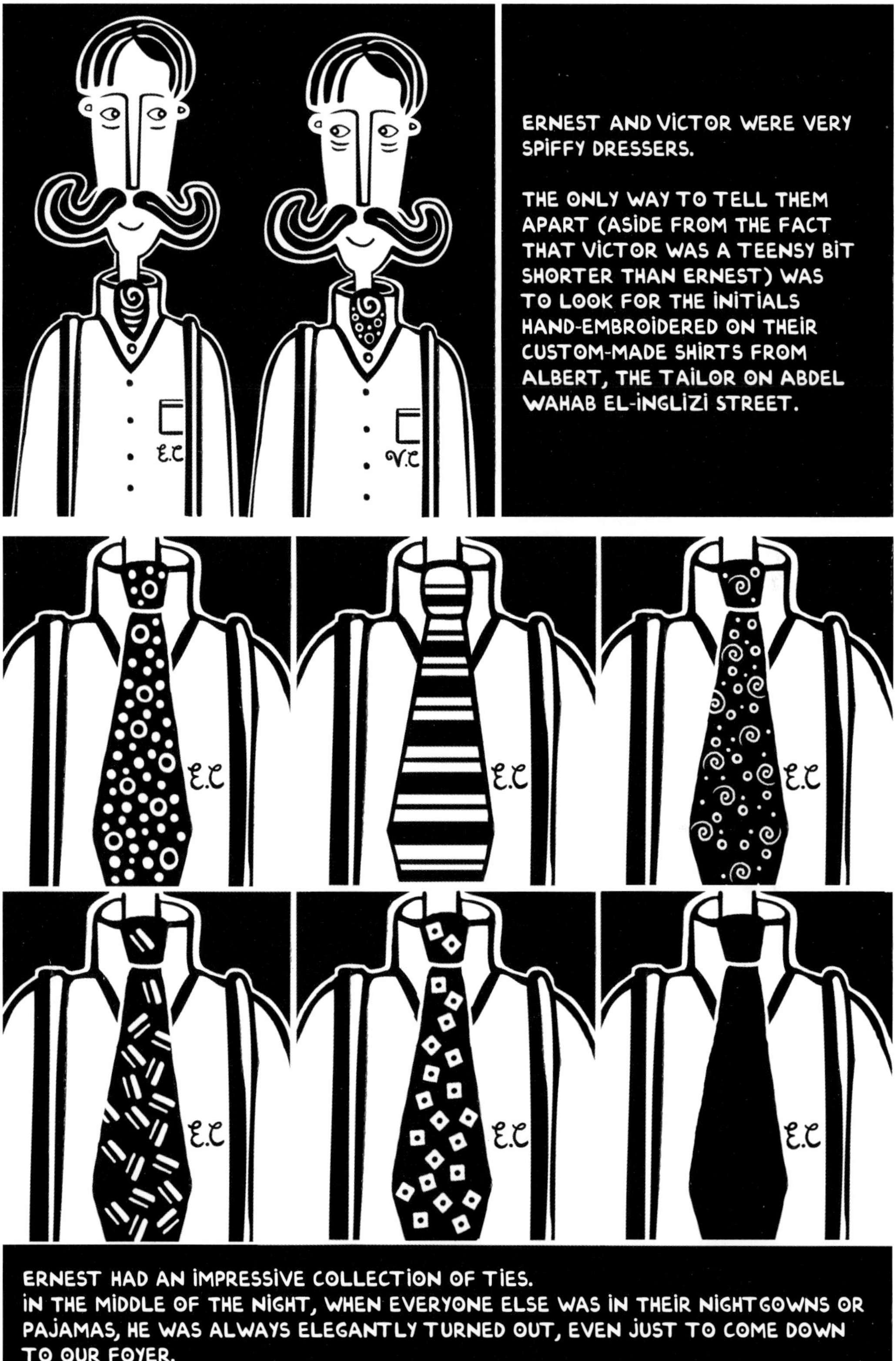
E.C
V.C
ERNEST AND VICTOR WERE VERY SPIFFY DRESSERS.
THE ONLY WAY TO TELL THEM APART (ASIDE FROM THE FACT THAT VICTOR WAS A TEENSY BIT SHORTER THAN ERNEST) WAS TO LOOK FOR THE INITIALS HAND-EMBROIDERED ON THEIR CUSTOM-MADE SHIRTS FROM ALBERT, THE TAILOR ON ABDEL WAHAB EL-INGLIZI STREET.
E.C
E.C
E.C
E.C
E.C
E.C
ERNEST HAD AN IMPRESSIVE COLLECTION OF TIES.
IN THE MIDDLE OF THE NIGHT, WHEN EVERYONE ELSE WAS IN THEIR NIGHTGOWNS OR PAJAMAS, HE WAS ALWAYS ELEGANTLY TURNED OUT, EVEN JUST TO COME DOWN TO OUR FOYER.

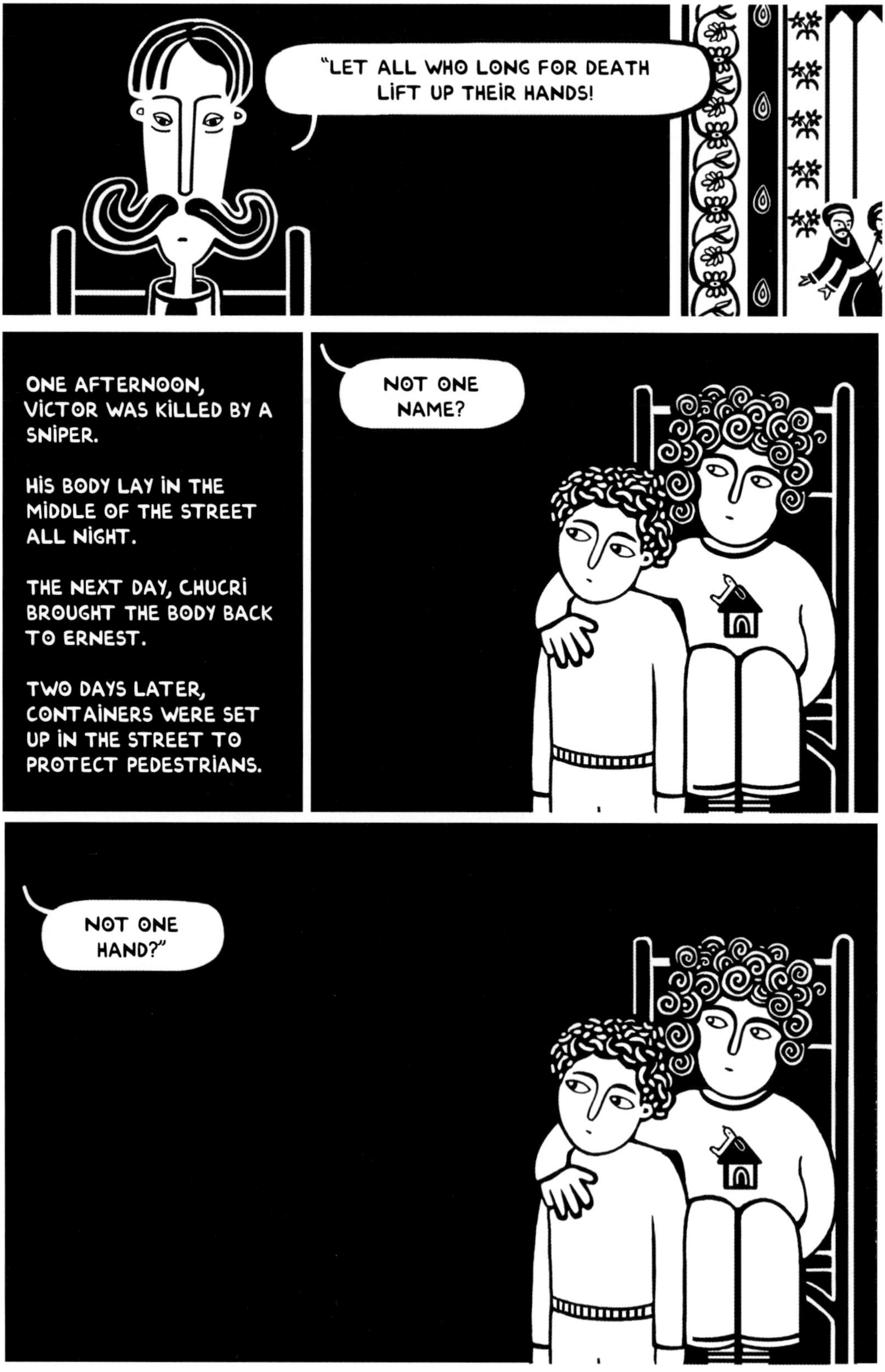
"LET ALL WHO LONG FOR DEATH LIFT UP THEIR HANDS!
ONE AFTERNOON, VICTOR WAS KILLED BY A SNIPER.
HIS BODY LAY IN THE MIDDLE OF THE STREET ALL NIGHT.
THE NEXT DAY, CHUCRI BROUGHT THE BODY BACK TO ERNEST.
TWO DAYS LATER, CONTAINERS WERE SET UP IN THE STREET TO PROTECT PEDESTRIANS.
NOT ONE NAME?
NOT ONE HAND?"

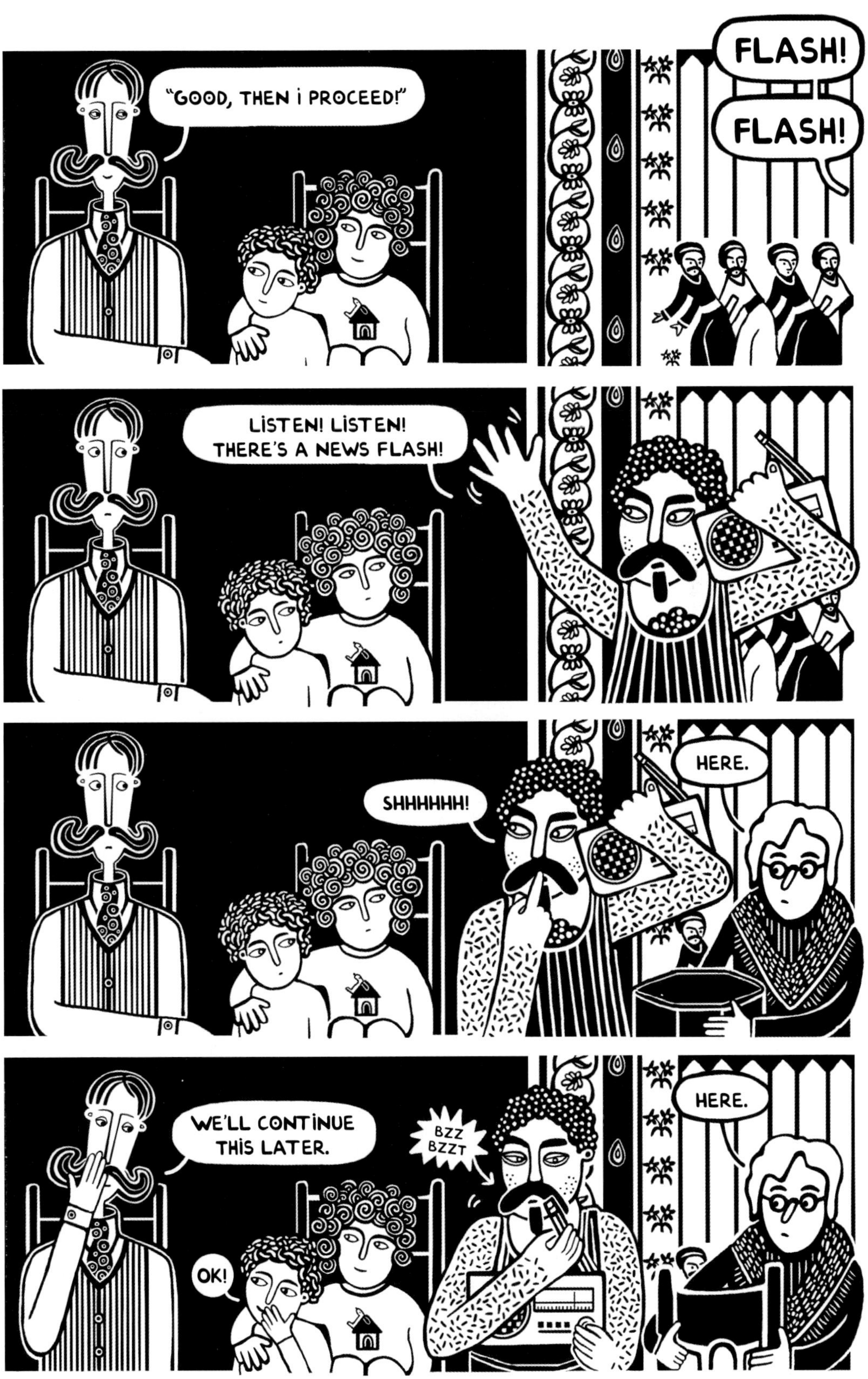
"GOOD, THEN I PROCEED!"
FLASH!
FLASH!
LISTEN! LISTEN! THERE'S A NEWS FLASH!
SHHHHHH!
HERE.
WE'LL CONTINUE THIS LATER.
BZZ BZZT
HERE.
OK!

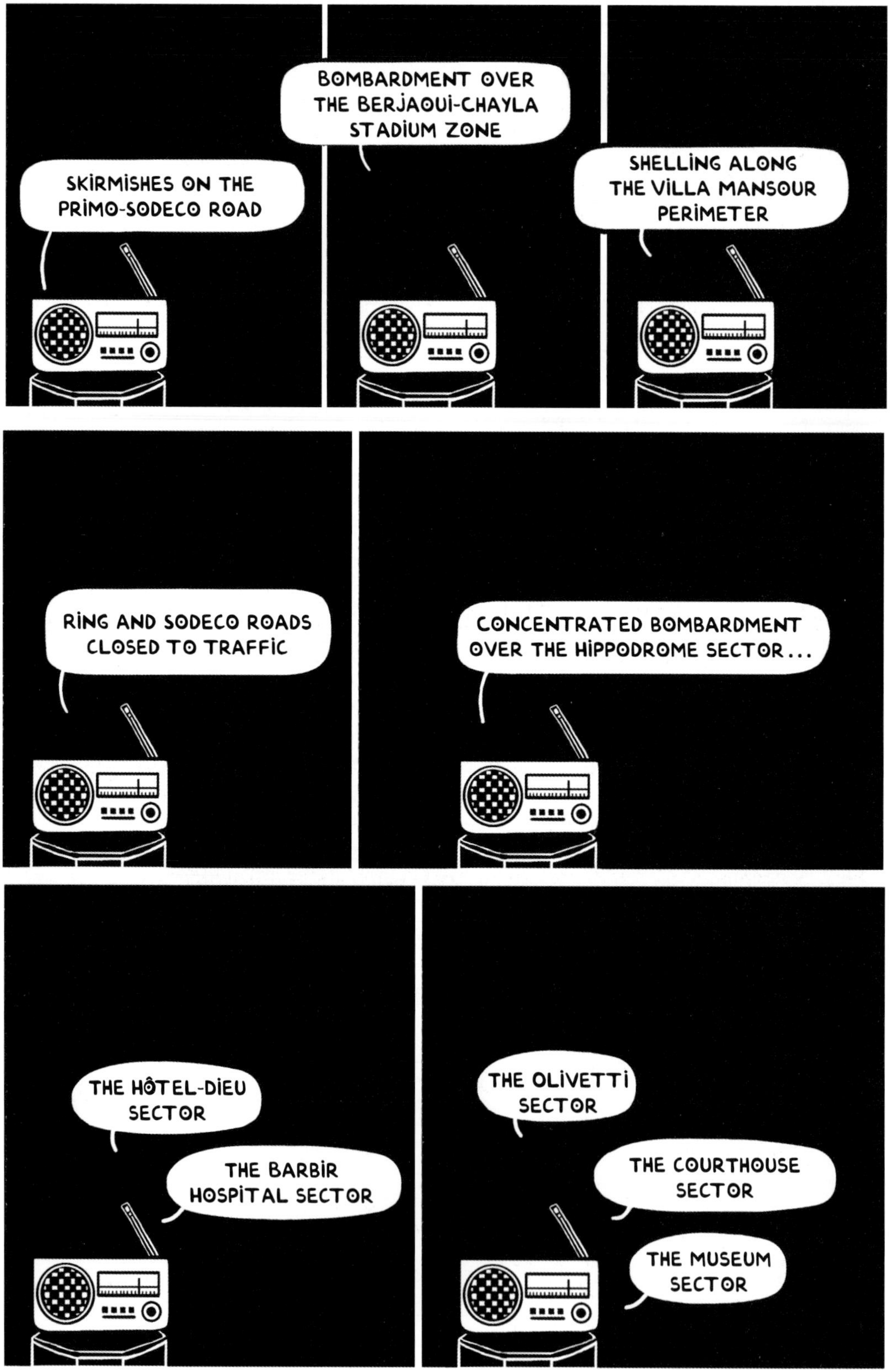
SKIRMISHES ON THE PRIMO-SODECO ROAD
BOMBARDMENT OVER THE BERJAOUI-CHAYLA STADIUM ZONE
SHELLING ALONG THE VILLA MANSOUR PERIMETER
RING AND SODECO ROADS CLOSED TO TRAFFIC
CONCENTRATED BOMBARDMENT OVER THE HIPPODROME SECTOR...
THE HÔTEL-DIEU SECTOR
THE BARBIR HOSPITAL SECTOR
THE OLIVETTI SECTOR
THE COURTHOUSE SECTOR
THE MUSEUM SECTOR

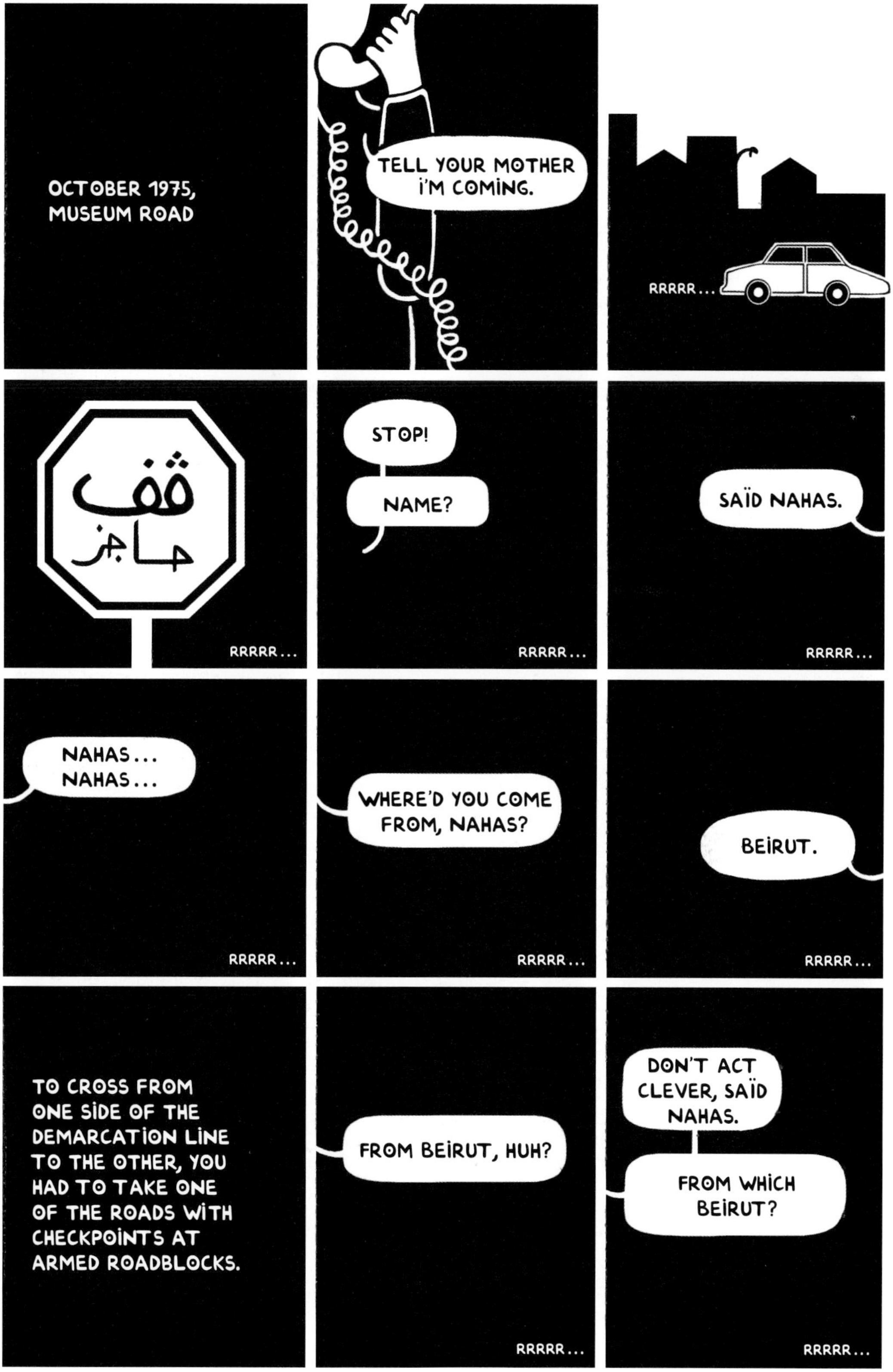

OCTOBER 1975, MUSEUM ROAD
TELL YOUR MOTHER I'M COMING.
RRRRR...
قف
حاجز
RRRRR...
STOP!
NAME?
RRRRR...
SAÏD NAHAS.
RRRRR...
NAHAS... NAHAS...
RRRRR...
WHERE'D YOU COME FROM, NAHAS?
RRRRR...
BEIRUT.
RRRRR...
TO CROSS FROM ONE SIDE OF THE DEMARCATION LINE TO THE OTHER, YOU HAD TO TAKE ONE OF THE ROADS WITH CHECKPOINTS AT ARMED ROADBLOCKS.
FROM BEIRUT, HUH?
RRRRR...
DON'T ACT CLEVER, SAÏD NAHAS.
FROM WHICH BEIRUT?
RRRRR...

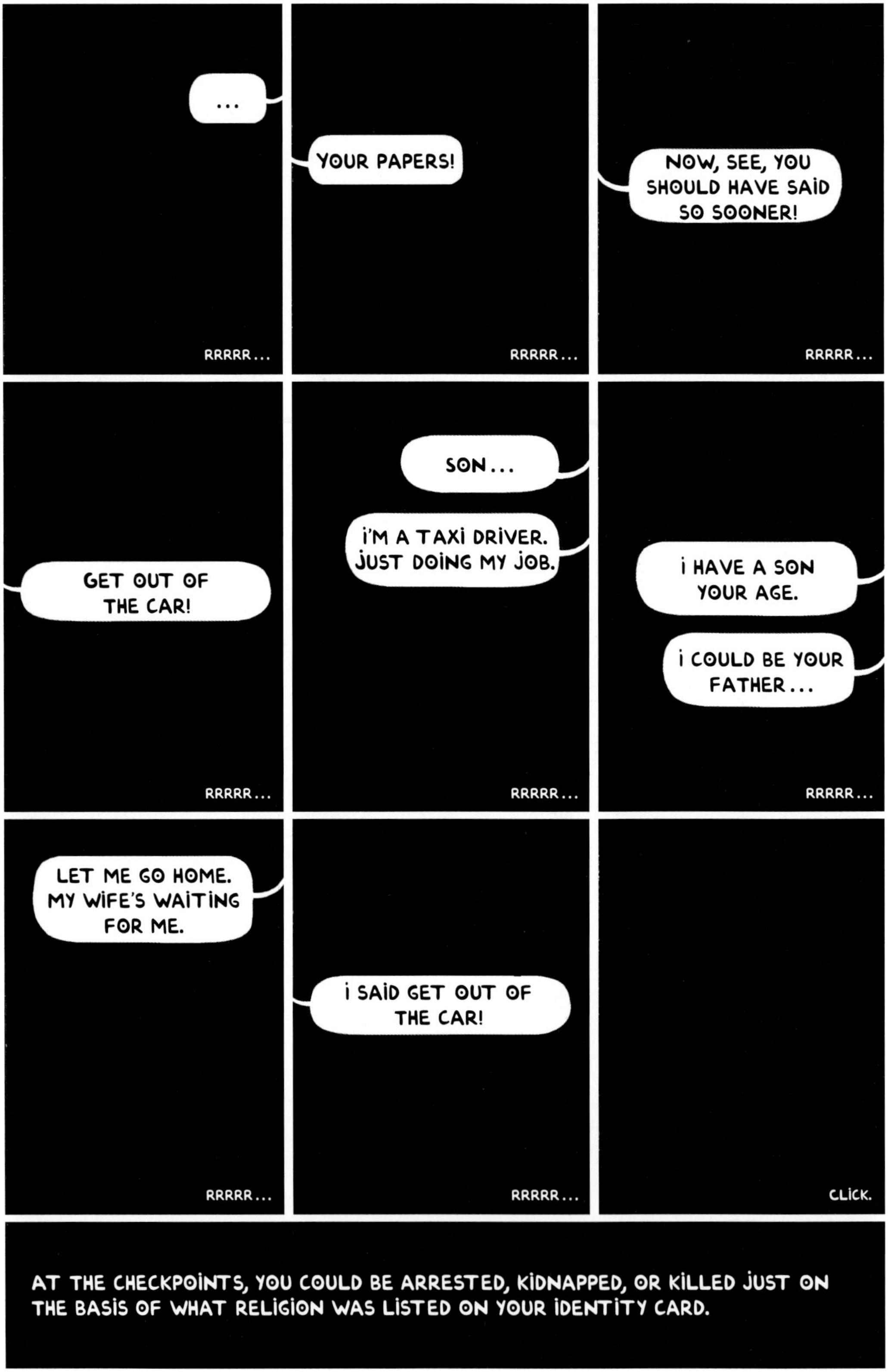
...
RRRRR...
YOUR PAPERS!
RRRRR...
NOW, SEE, YOU SHOULD HAVE SAID SO SOONER!
RRRRR...
GET OUT OF THE CAR!
RRRRR...
SON...
I'M A TAXI DRIVER. JUST DOING MY JOB.
RRRRR...
I HAVE A SON YOUR AGE.
I COULD BE YOUR FATHER...
RRRRR...
LET ME GO HOME. MY WIFE'S WAITING FOR ME.
RRRRR...
I SAID GET OUT OF THE CAR!
RRRRR...
CLICK.
AT THE CHECKPOINTS, YOU COULD BE ARRESTED, KIDNAPPED, OR KILLED JUST ON THE BASIS OF WHAT RELIGION WAS LISTED ON YOUR IDENTITY CARD.

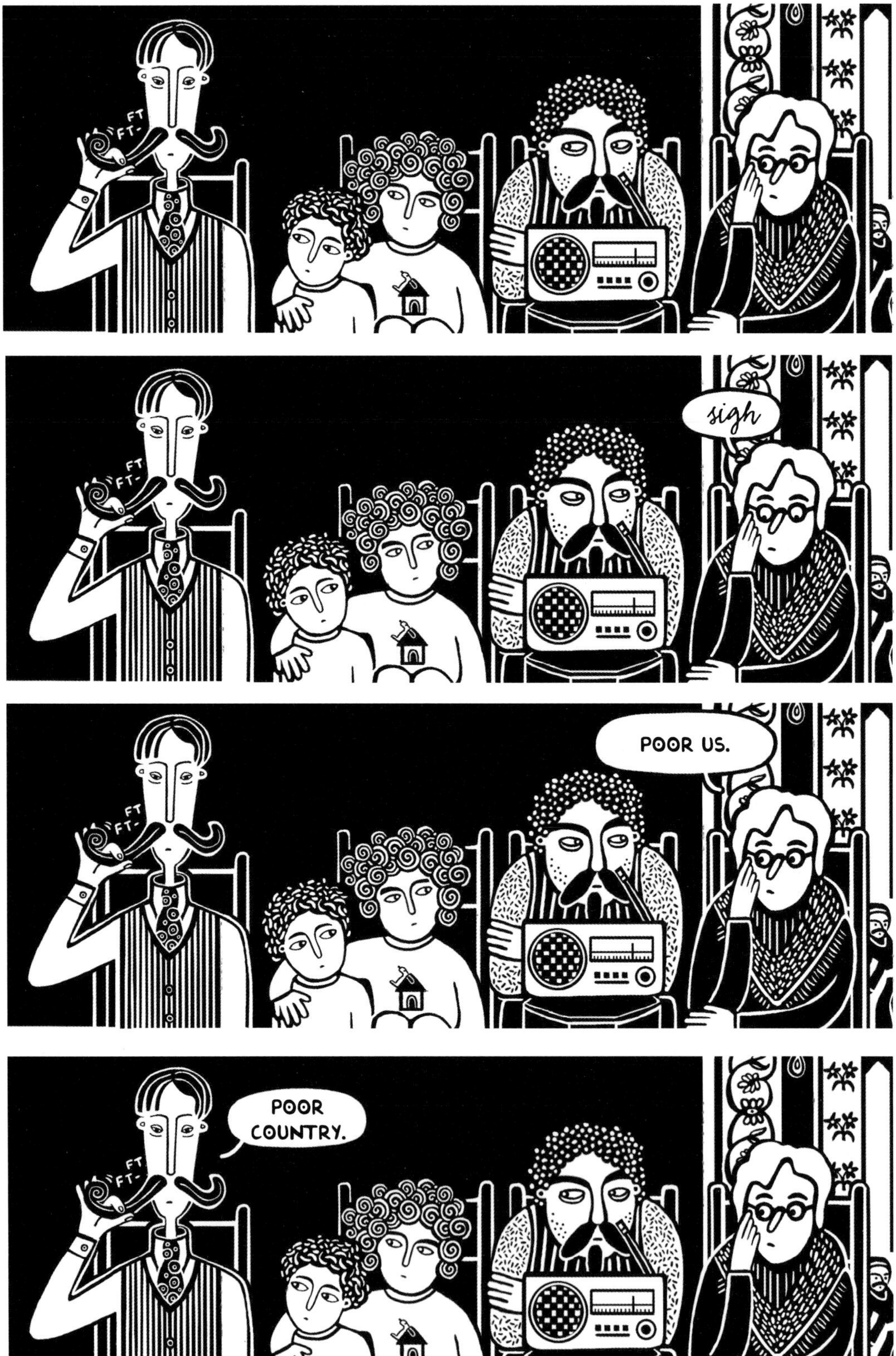
FT
FT-
FT
FT-
sigh
FT
FT-
POOR US.
FT
FT-
POOR
COUNTRY.

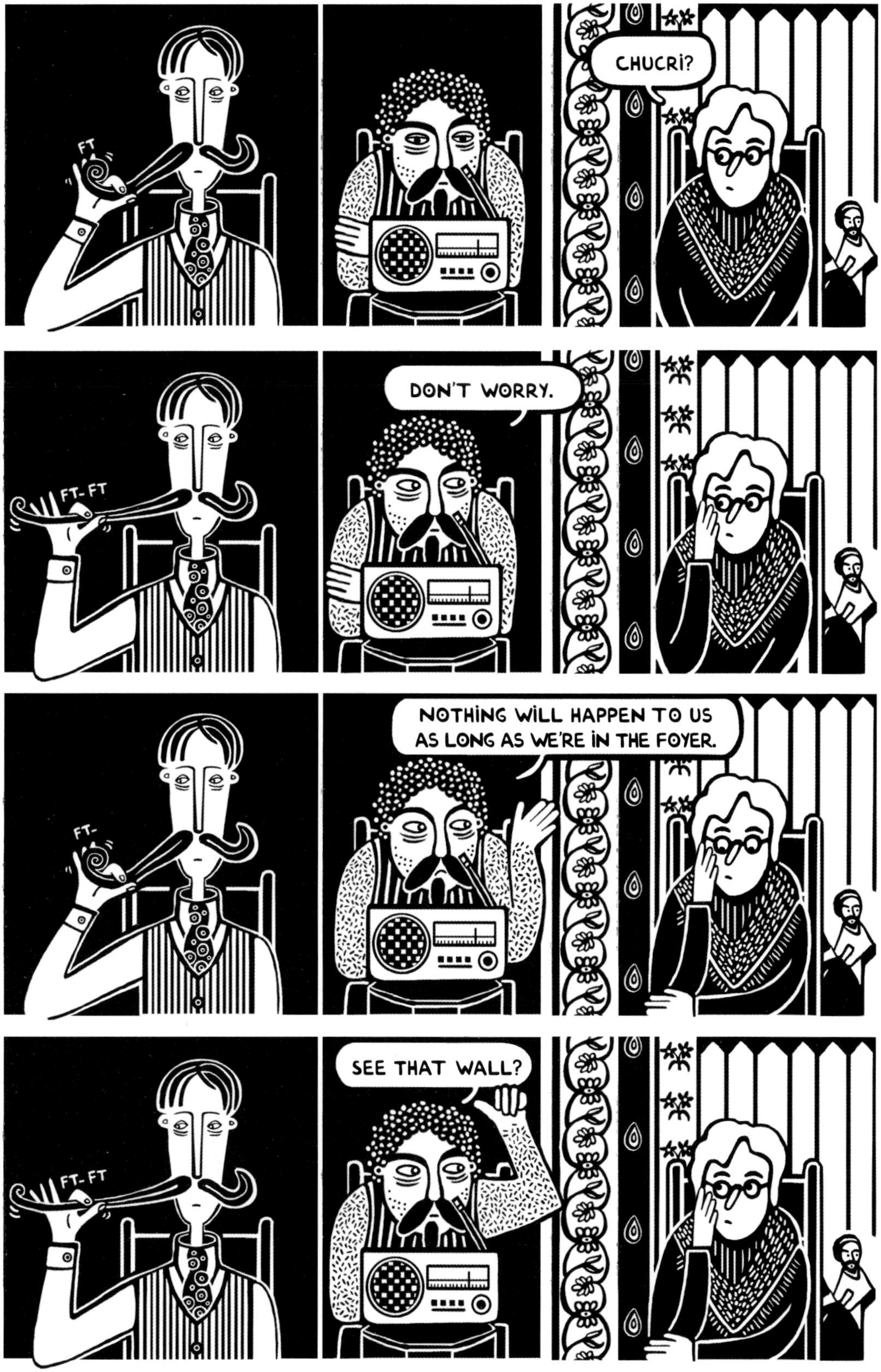
FT
CHUCRI?
FT- FT
DON'T WORRY.
FT-
NOTHING WILL HAPPEN TO US AS LONG AS WE'RE IN THE FOYER.
FT- FT
SEE THAT WALL?

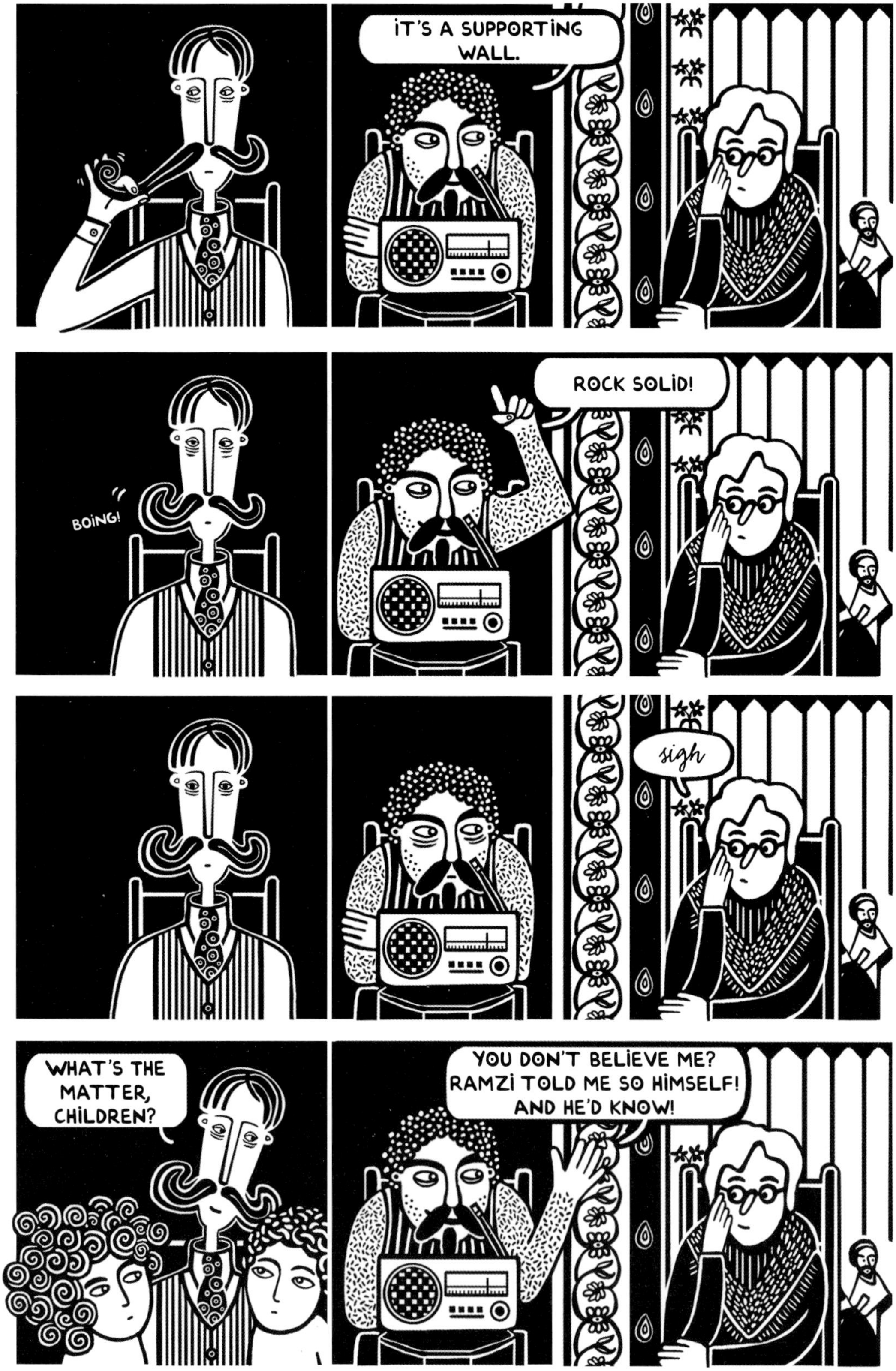
IT'S A SUPPORTING WALL.
ROCK SOLID!
BOING!
sigh
WHAT'S THE MATTER, CHILDREN?
YOU DON'T BELIEVE ME? RAMZI TOLD ME SO HIMSELF! AND HE'D KNOW!

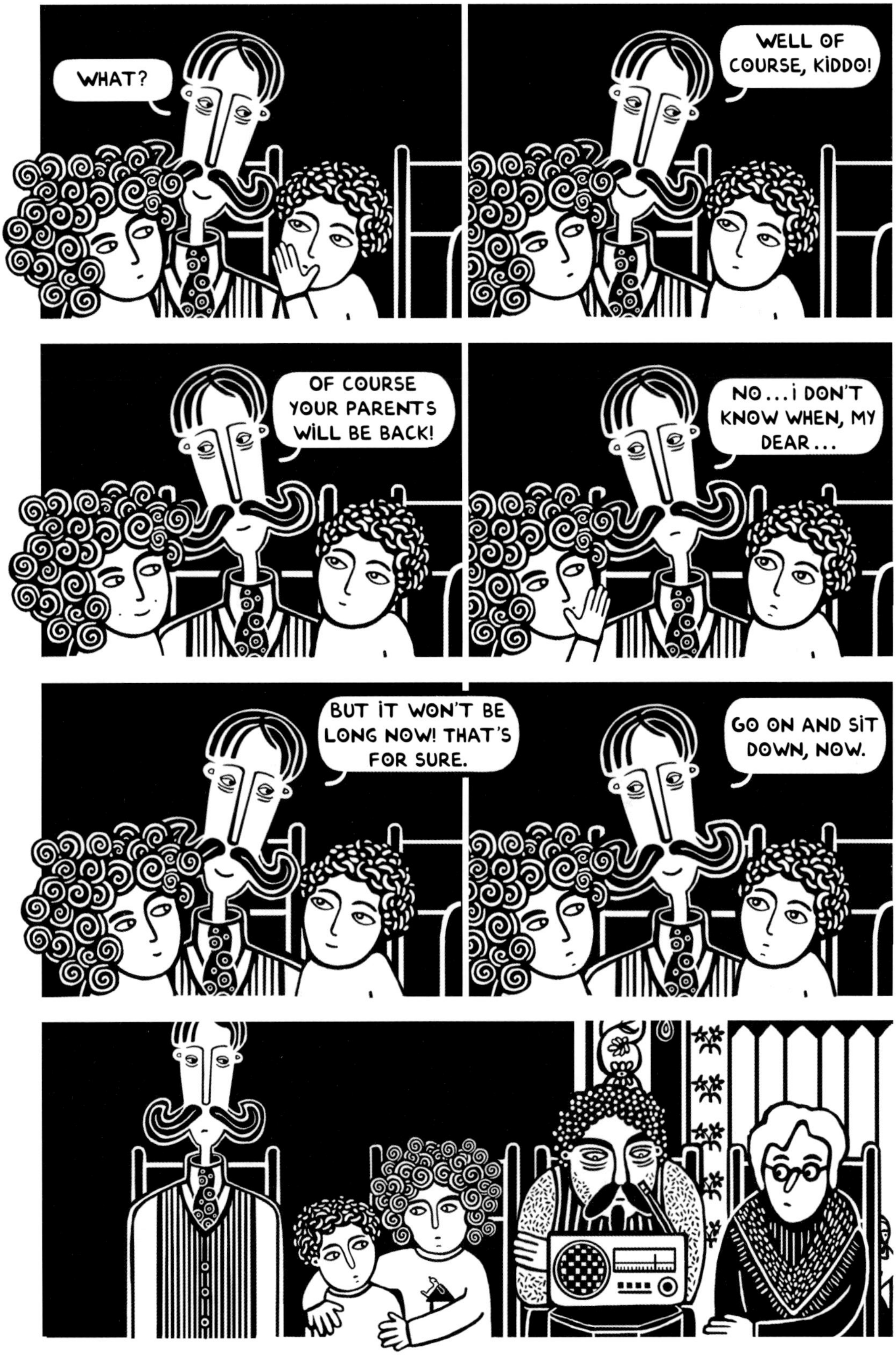
WHAT?
WELL OF COURSE, KIDDO!
OF COURSE YOUR PARENTS WILL BE BACK!
NO... I DON'T KNOW WHEN, MY DEAR...
BUT IT WON'T BE LONG NOW! THAT'S FOR SURE.
GO ON AND SIT DOWN, NOW.

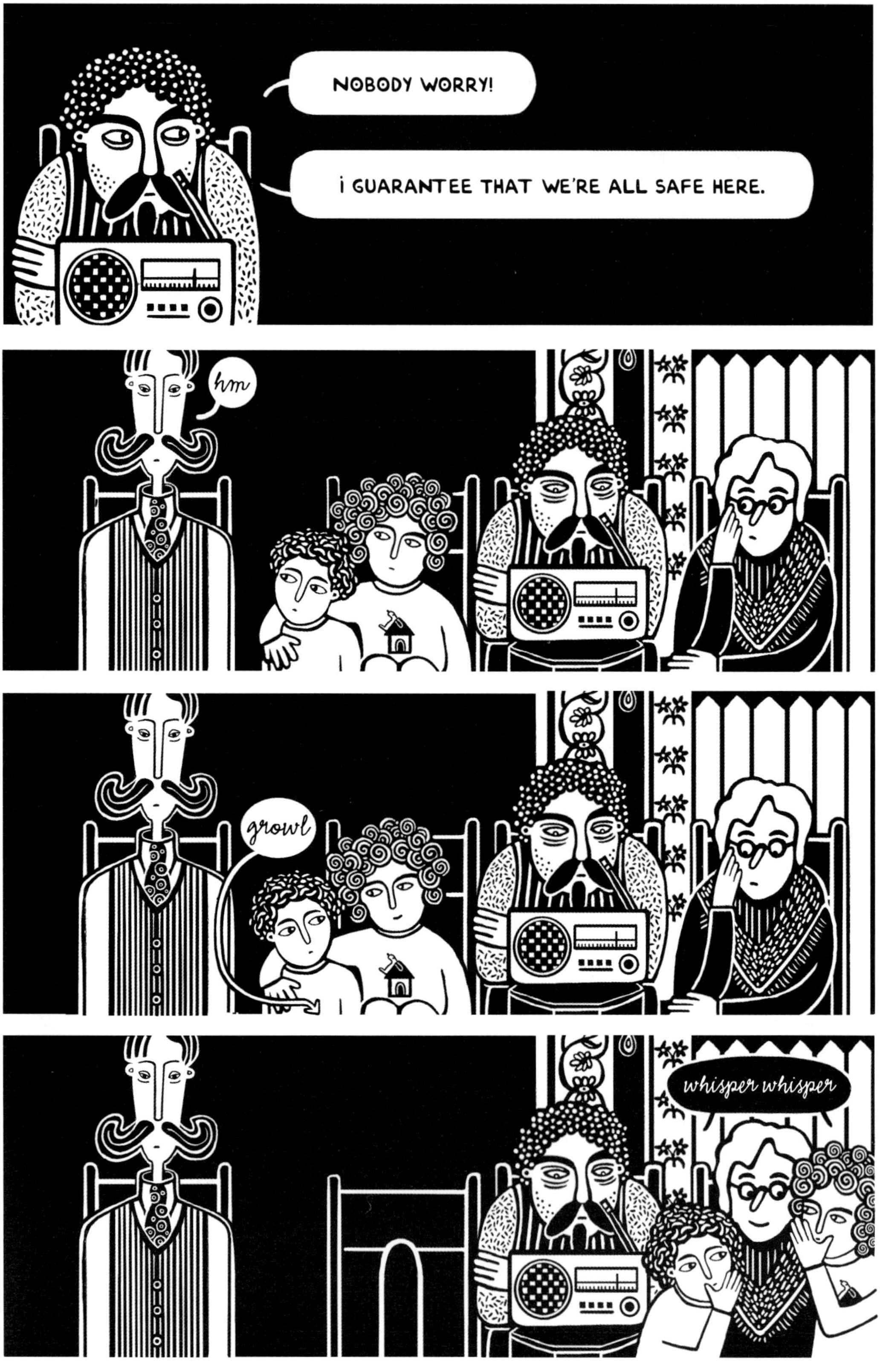
NOBODY WORRY!
I GUARANTEE THAT WE'RE ALL SAFE HERE.
hm
growl
whisper whisper

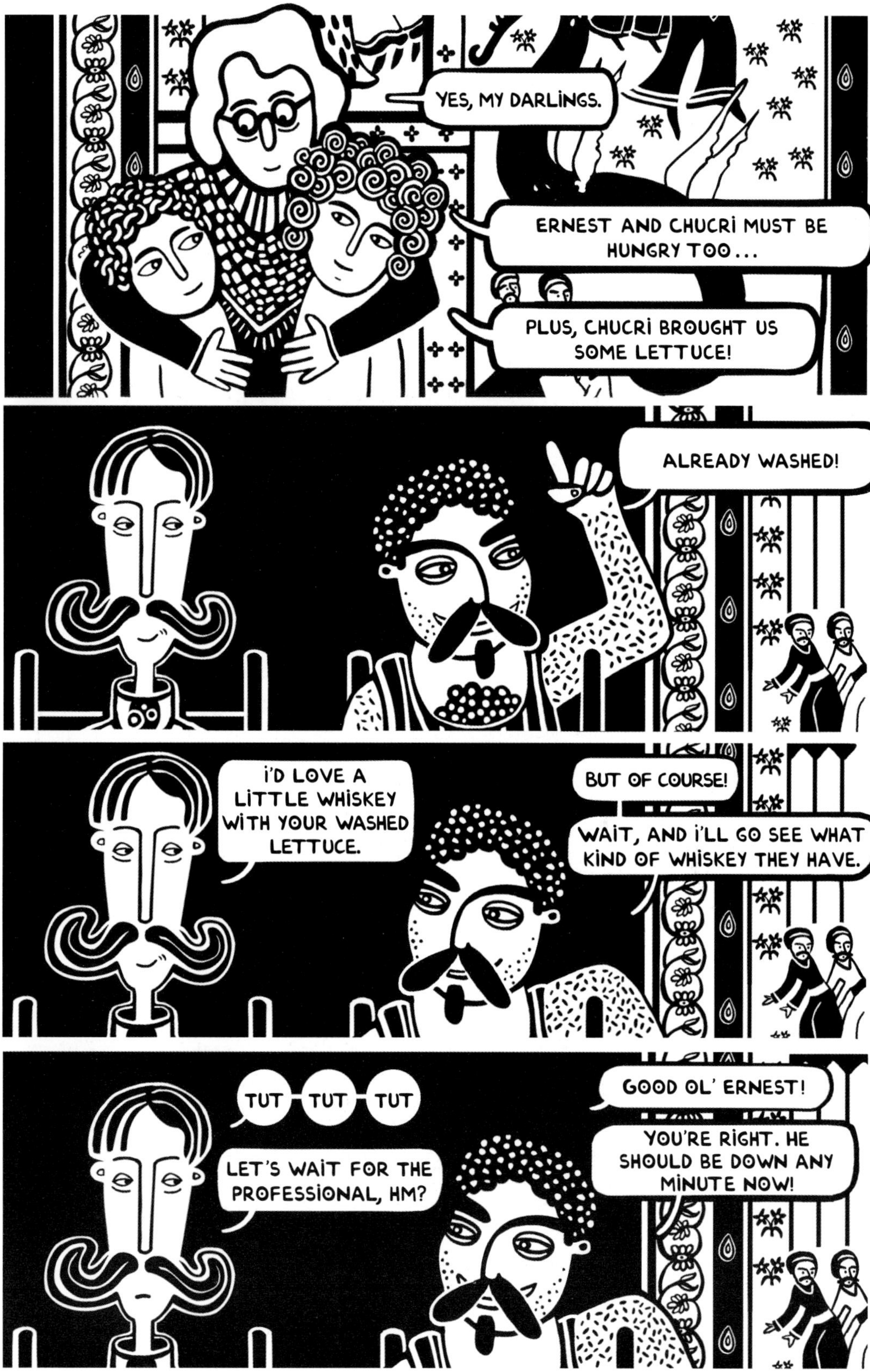
YES, MY DARLINGS.
ERNEST AND CHUCRI MUST BE HUNGRY TOO...
PLUS, CHUCRI BROUGHT US SOME LETTUCE!
ALREADY WASHED!
I'D LOVE A LITTLE WHISKEY WITH YOUR WASHED LETTUCE.
BUT OF COURSE!
WAIT, AND I'LL GO SEE WHAT KIND OF WHISKEY THEY HAVE.
TUT TUT TUT
LET'S WAIT FOR THE PROFESSIONAL, HM?
GOOD OL' ERNEST!
YOU'RE RIGHT. HE SHOULD BE DOWN ANY MINUTE NOW!

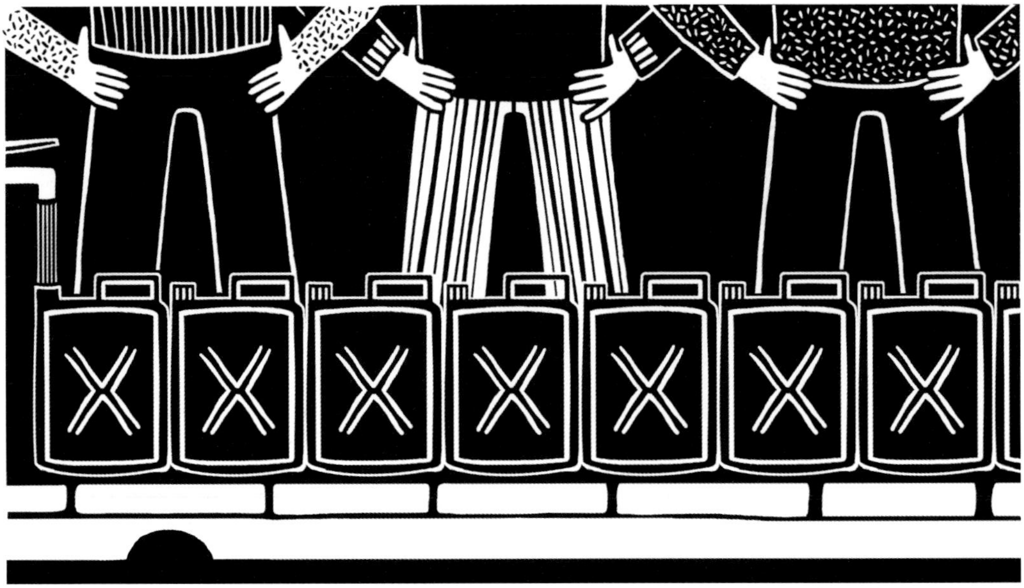

DURING THE WAR, FRUITS AND VEGETABLES WERE IN THEMSELVES A NICE GIFT FOR YOUR NEIGHBOR. AND IF YOU WENT TO THE TROUBLE OF WASHING THEM, WELL, THEY WERE BEYOND VALUE!
CHUCRI WAS THE ONE IN CHARGE OF SUPPLYING US WITH WATER.
HE'D FILL THE TRUNK OF HIS CAR WITH EMPTY JERRY CANS. THEN HE, MY FATHER, AND THE OTHER MEN IN THE NEIGHBORHOOD WOULD GO TO SEE VERA, THE SISTER OF OUR FIFTH-FLOOR NEIGHBOR, MADAME LINDA. VERA LIVED IN A BUILDING WITH AN ARTESIAN WELL.

AFTER FILLING THE BLUE JERRY CANS (THE GREEN WERE RESERVED FOR GASOLINE), THEY POURED THE WATER INTO GLASS AND PLASTIC BOTTLES (THE GLASS ONES WERE WHISKEY BOTTLES MY MOTHER HAD KEPT AND WASHED).

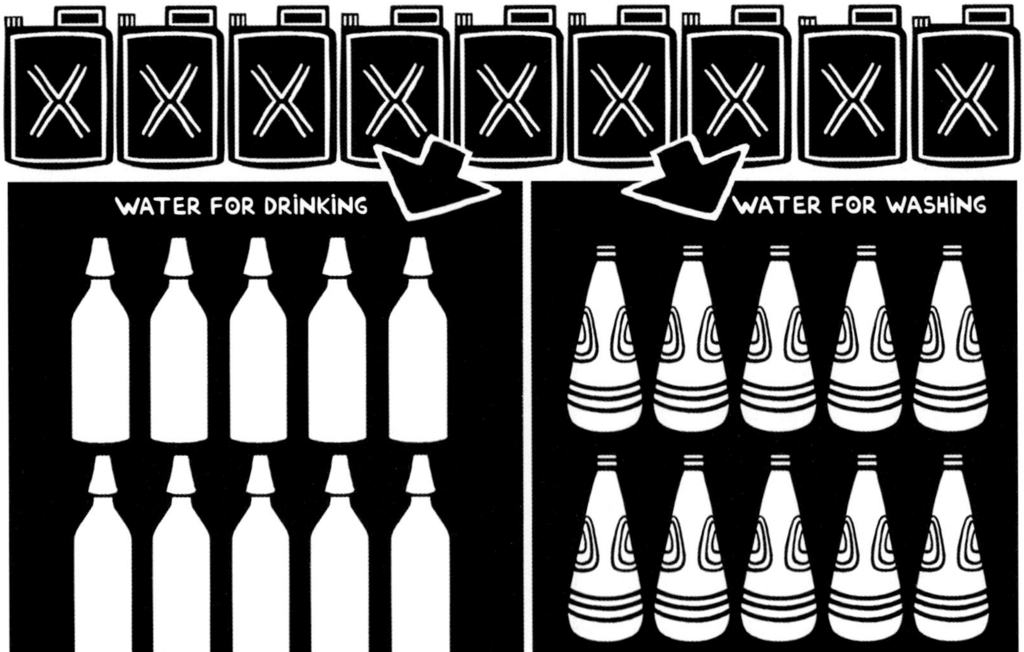
WATER FOR DRINKING
WATER FOR WASHING

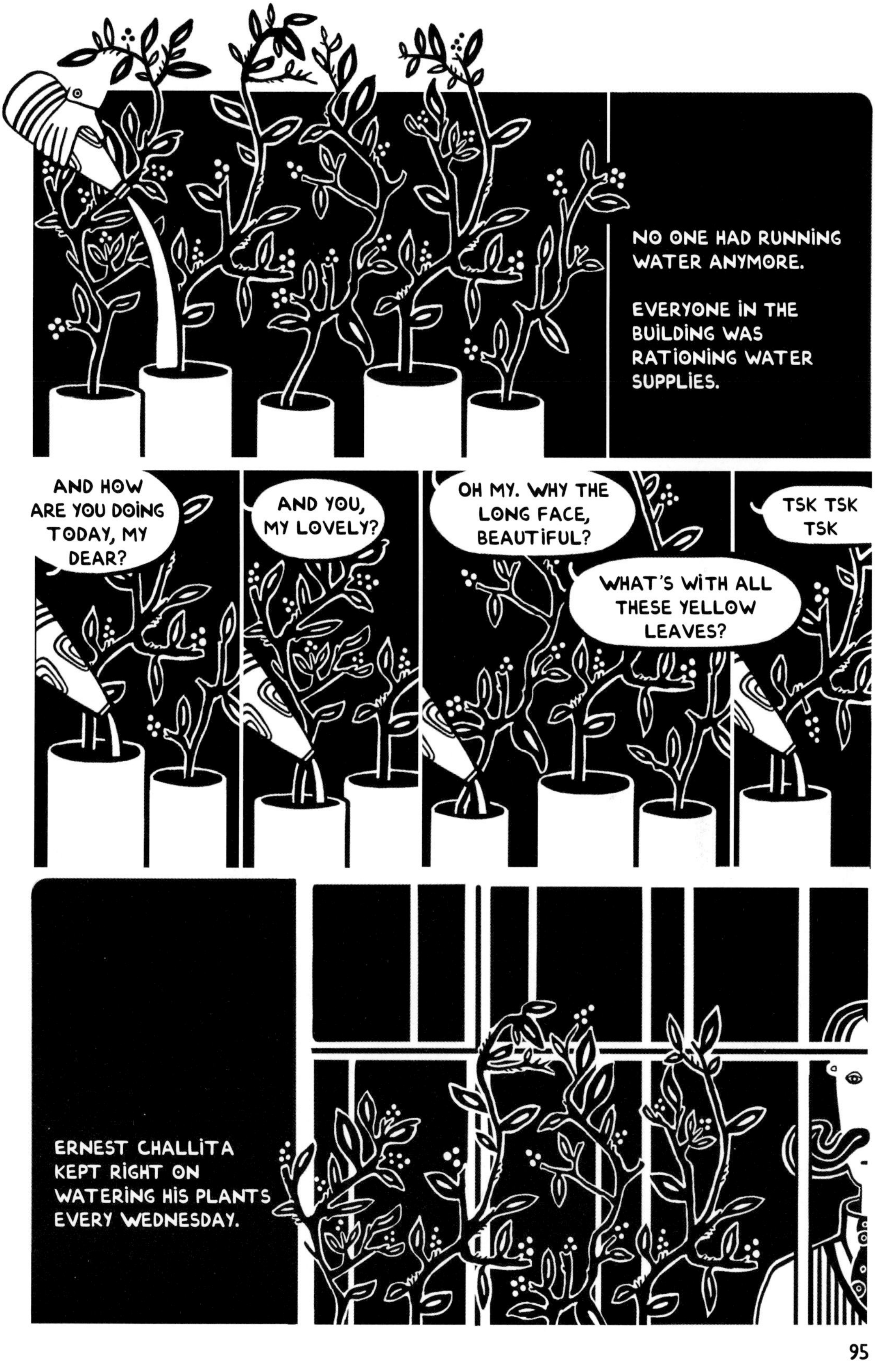
NO ONE HAD RUNNING WATER ANYMORE.
EVERYONE IN THE BUILDING WAS RATIONING WATER SUPPLIES.
AND HOW ARE YOU DOING TODAY, MY DEAR?
AND YOU, MY LOVELY?
OH MY. WHY THE LONG FACE, BEAUTIFUL?
WHAT'S WITH ALL THESE YELLOW LEAVES?
TSK TSK TSK
ERNEST CHALLITA KEPT RIGHT ON WATERING HIS PLANTS EVERY WEDNESDAY.

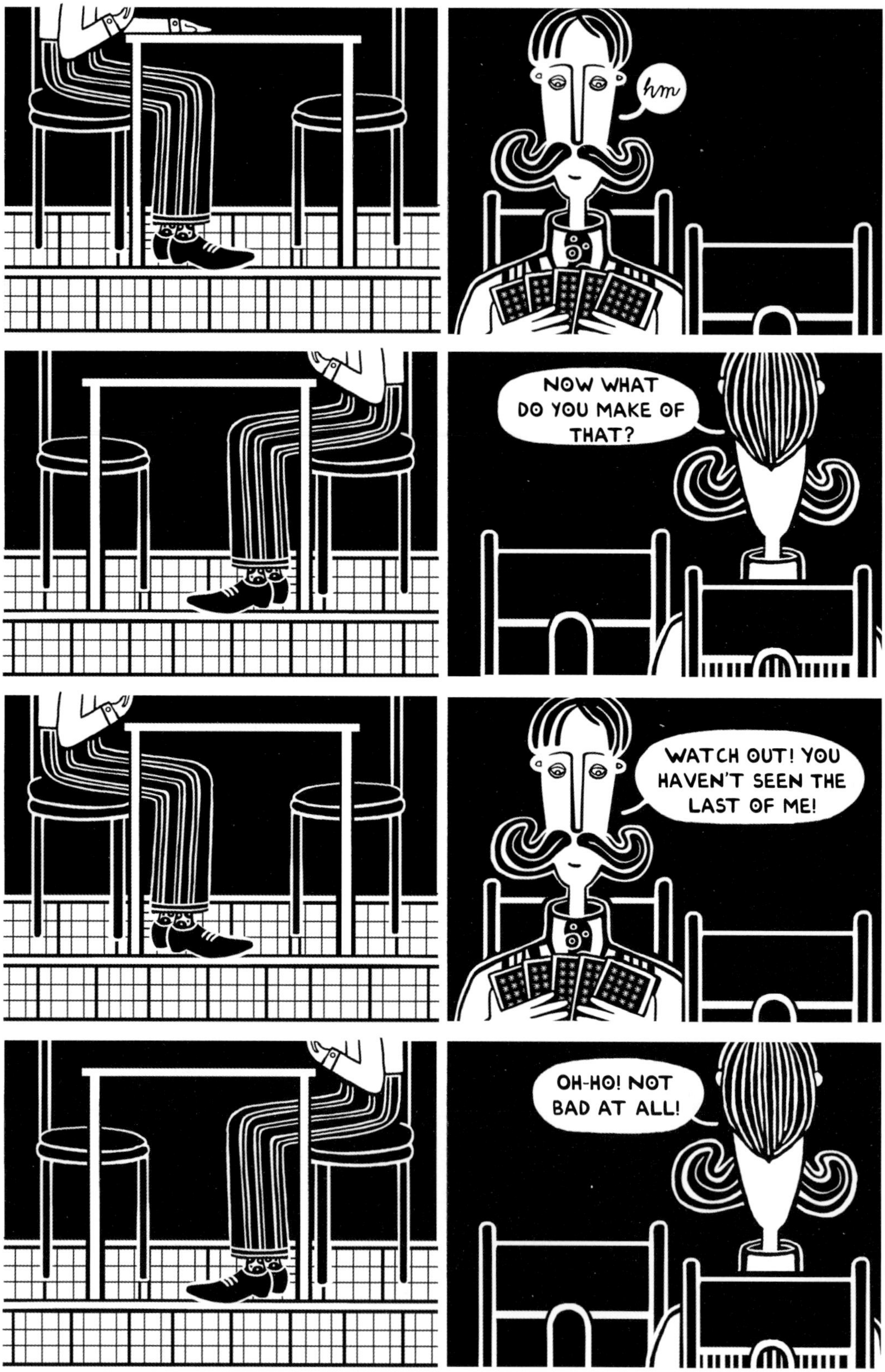
hm
NOW WHAT DO YOU MAKE OF THAT?
WATCH OUT! YOU HAVEN'T SEEN THE LAST OF ME!
OH-HO! NOT BAD AT ALL!

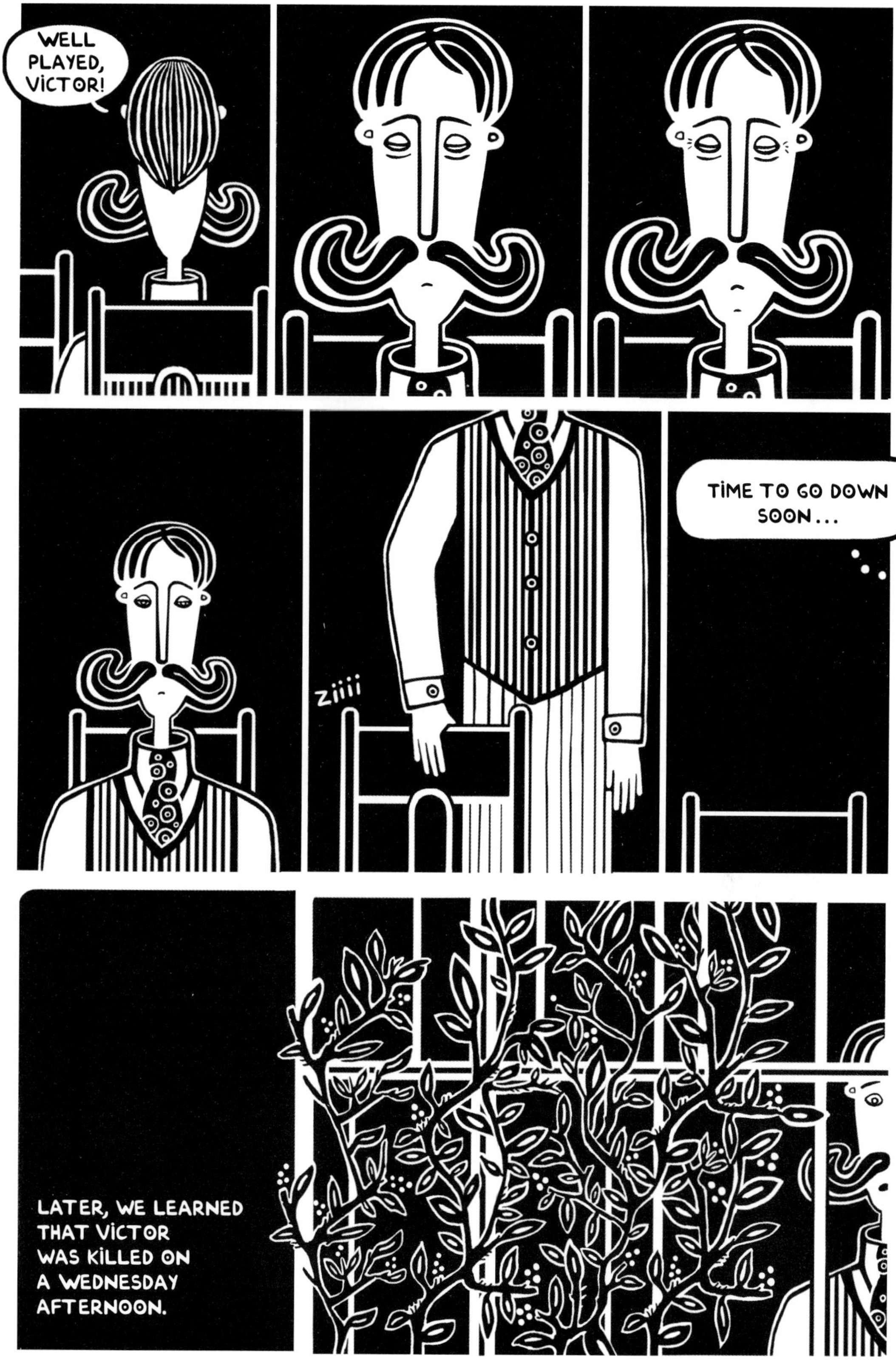
WELL PLAYED, VICTOR!
ZIIII
TIME TO GO DOWN SOON...
LATER, WE LEARNED THAT VICTOR WAS KILLED ON A WEDNESDAY AFTERNOON.

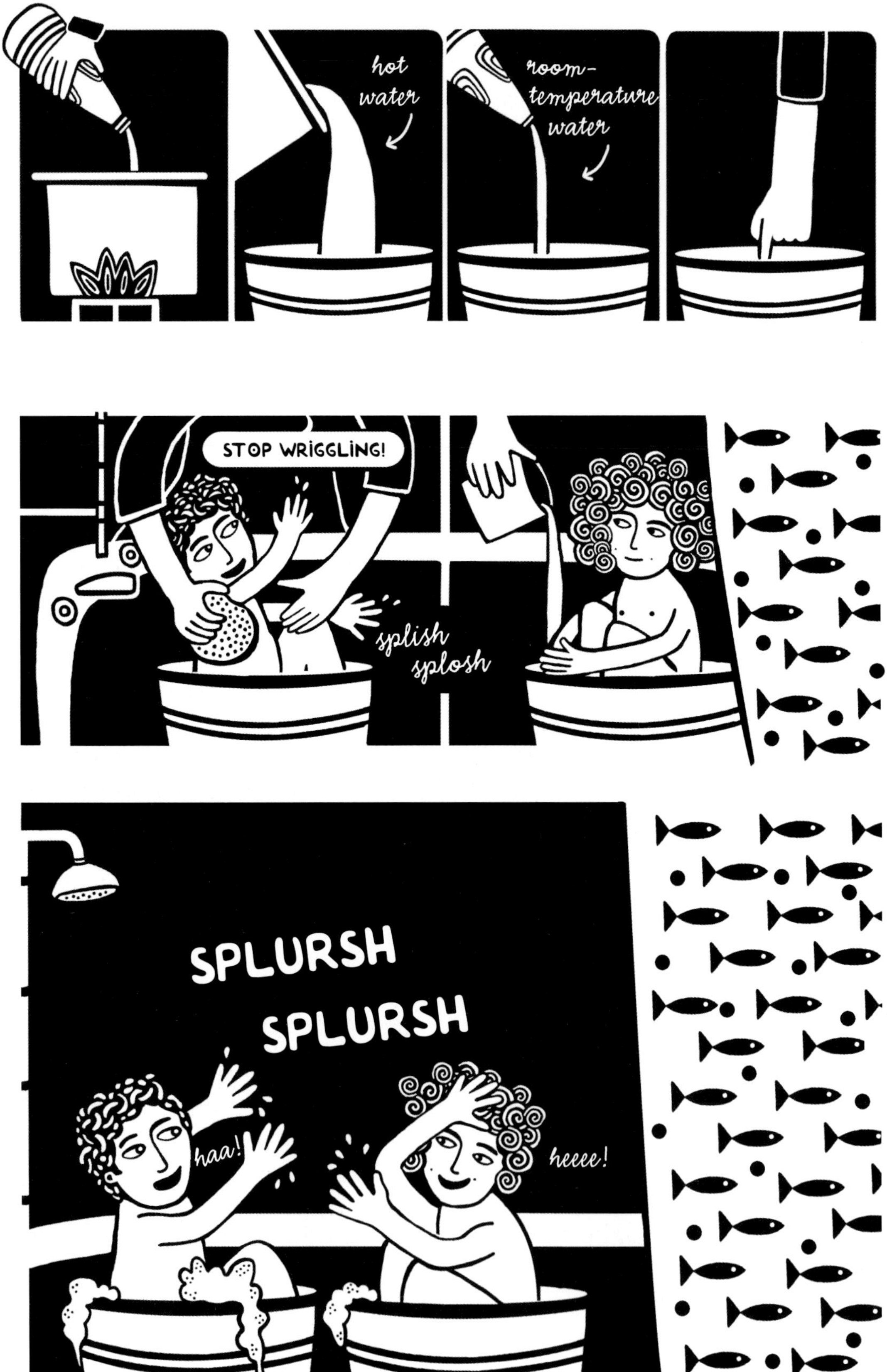
hot water
room-temperature water
STOP WRIGGLING!
splish splosh
SPLURSH
SPLURSH
haa!
heeee!

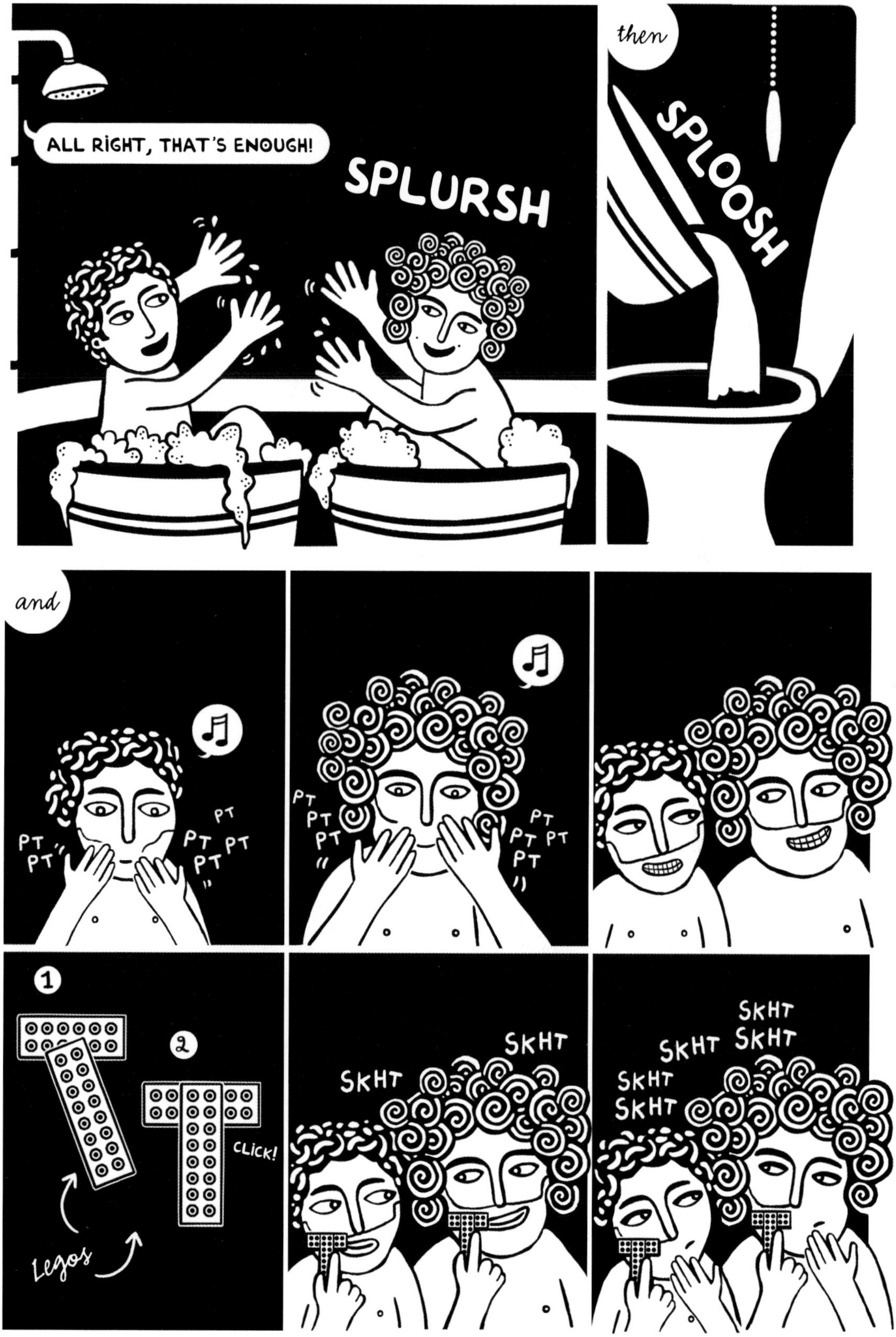
ALL RIGHT, THAT'S ENOUGH!
SPLURSH
then
SPLOOSH
and
PT PT
PT PT PT PT
PT PT PT
PT PT PT PT
1
2
CLICK!
Legos
SKHT
SKHT
SKHT SKHT
SKHT
SKHT SKHT

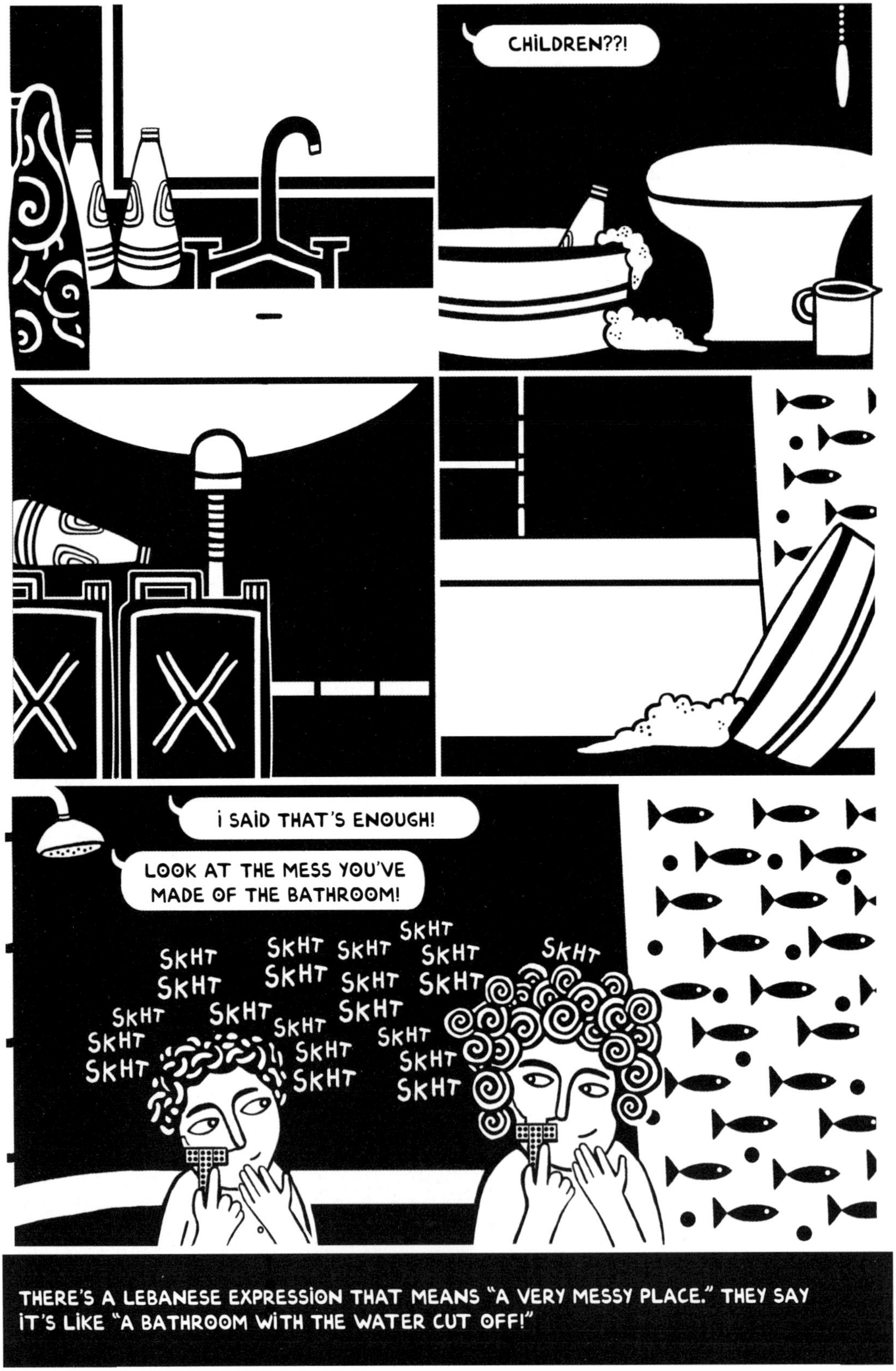
CHILDREN??!
I SAID THAT'S ENOUGH!
LOOK AT THE MESS YOU'VE MADE OF THE BATHROOM!
SKHT SKHT
SKHT SKHT
SKHT SKHT SKHT
SKHT SKHT SKHT
SKHT
SKHT SKHT SKHT
SKHT
SKHT
SKHT SKHT
SKHT SKHT SKHT
THERE'S A LEBANESE EXPRESSION THAT MEANS "A VERY MESSY PLACE." THEY SAY IT'S LIKE "A BATHROOM WITH THE WATER CUT OFF!"

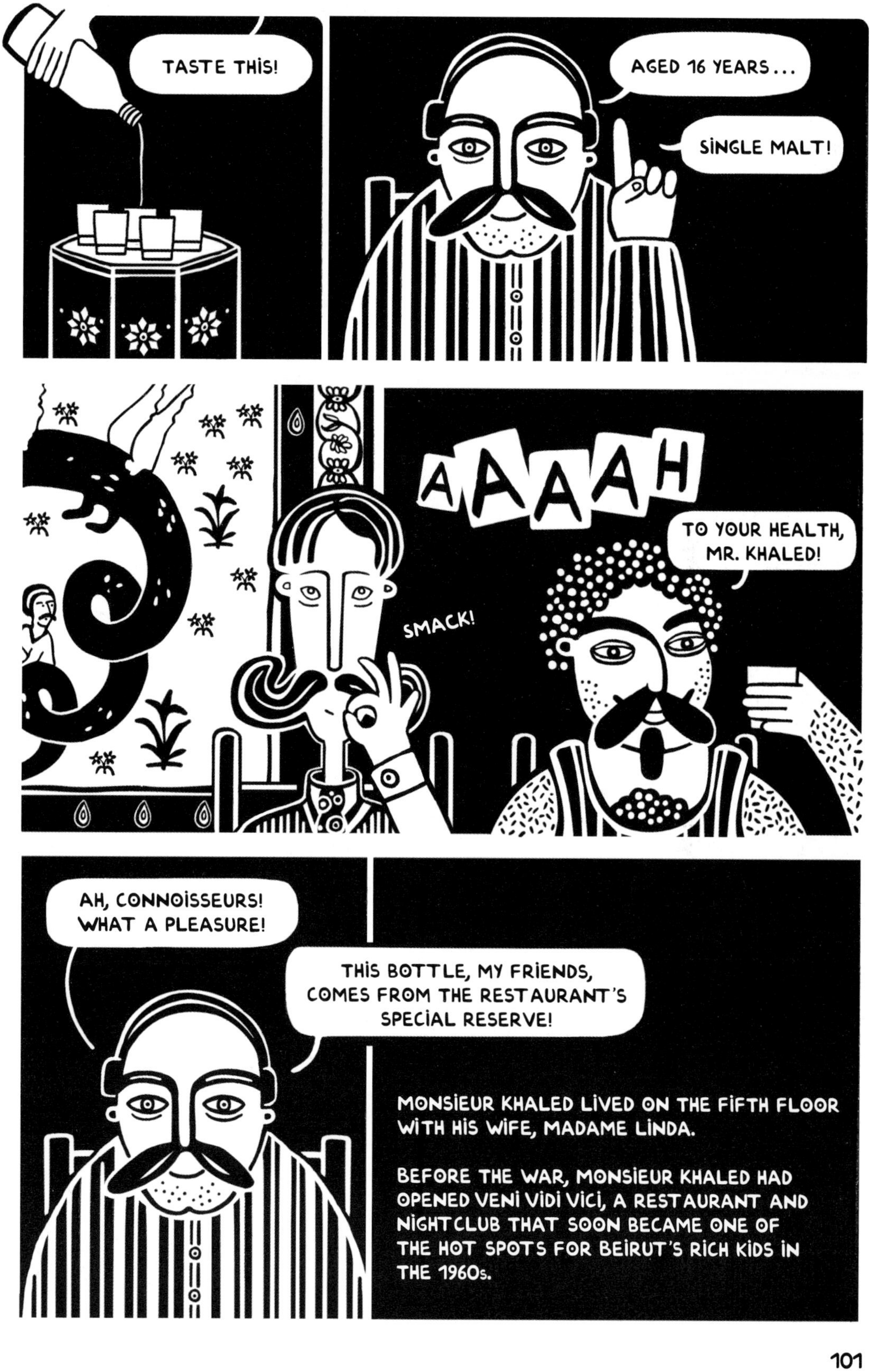
TASTE THIS!
AGED 16 YEARS...
SINGLE MALT!
AAAAH
SMACK!
TO YOUR HEALTH, MR. KHALED!
AH, CONNOISSEURS! WHAT A PLEASURE!
THIS BOTTLE, MY FRIENDS, COMES FROM THE RESTAURANT'S SPECIAL RESERVE!
MONSIEUR KHALED LIVED ON THE FIFTH FLOOR WITH HIS WIFE, MADAME LINDA.
BEFORE THE WAR, MONSIEUR KHALED HAD OPENED VENI VIDI VICI, A RESTAURANT AND NIGHTCLUB THAT SOON BECAME ONE OF THE HOT SPOTS FOR BEIRUT'S RICH KIDS IN THE 1960s.

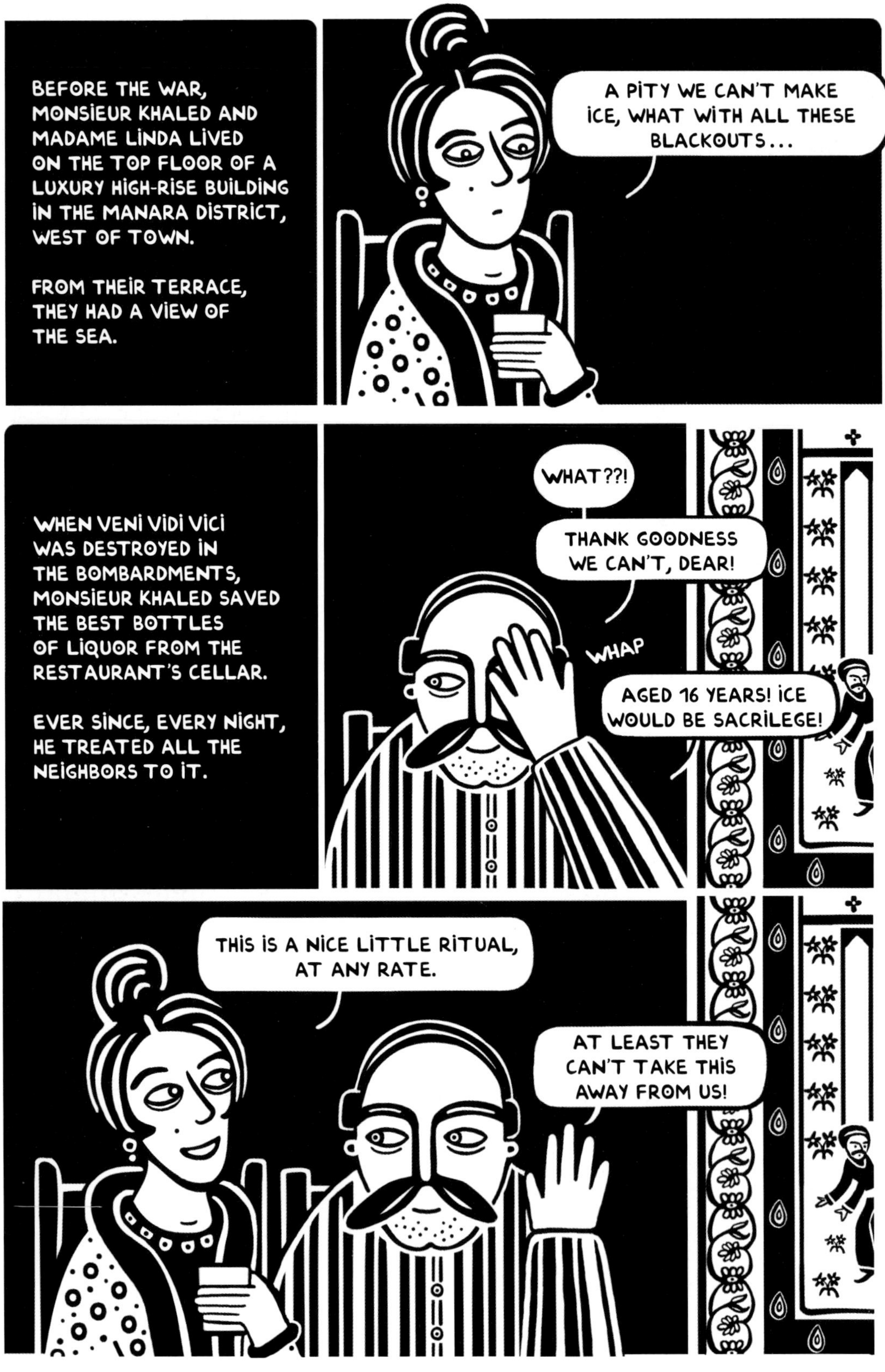
BEFORE THE WAR, MONSIEUR KHALED AND MADAME LINDA LIVED ON THE TOP FLOOR OF A LUXURY HIGH-RISE BUILDING IN THE MANARA DISTRICT, WEST OF TOWN.
FROM THEIR TERRACE, THEY HAD A VIEW OF THE SEA.
A PITY WE CAN'T MAKE ICE, WHAT WITH ALL THESE BLACKOUTS...
WHEN VENI VIDI VICI WAS DESTROYED IN THE BOMBARDMENTS, MONSIEUR KHALED SAVED THE BEST BOTTLES OF LIQUOR FROM THE RESTAURANT'S CELLAR.
EVER SINCE, EVERY NIGHT, HE TREATED ALL THE NEIGHBORS TO IT.
WHAT??!
THANK GOODNESS WE CAN'T, DEAR!
WHAP
AGED 16 YEARS! ICE WOULD BE SACRILEGE!
THIS IS A NICE LITTLE RITUAL, AT ANY RATE.
AT LEAST THEY CAN'T TAKE THIS AWAY FROM US!

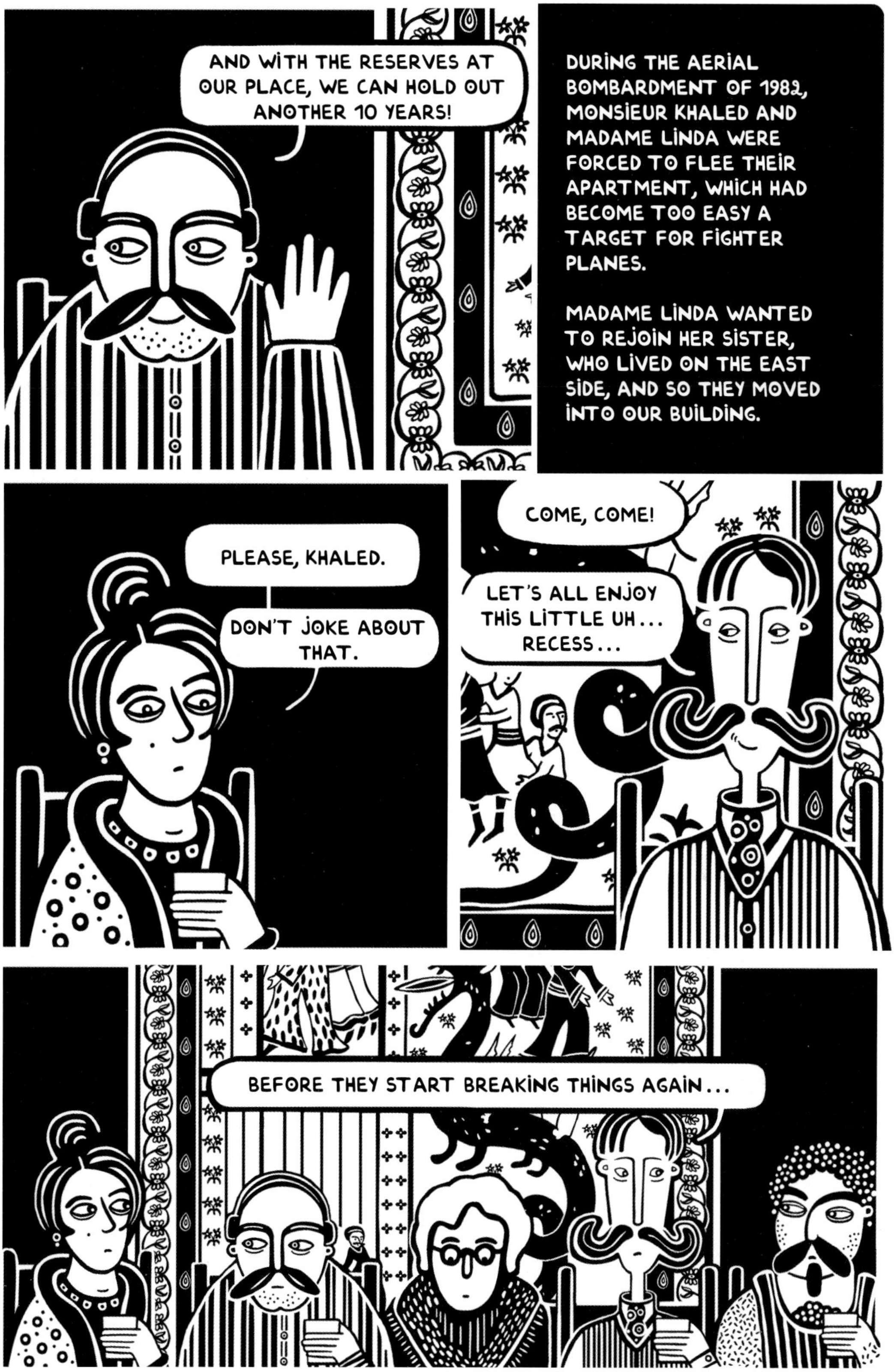
AND WITH THE RESERVES AT OUR PLACE, WE CAN HOLD OUT ANOTHER 10 YEARS!
DURING THE AERIAL BOMBARDMENT OF 1982, MONSIEUR KHALED AND MADAME LINDA WERE FORCED TO FLEE THEIR APARTMENT, WHICH HAD BECOME TOO EASY A TARGET FOR FIGHTER PLANES.
MADAME LINDA WANTED TO REJOIN HER SISTER, WHO LIVED ON THE EAST SIDE, AND SO THEY MOVED INTO OUR BUILDING.
PLEASE, KHALED.
DON'T JOKE ABOUT THAT.
COME, COME!
LET'S ALL ENJOY THIS LITTLE UH... RECESS...
BEFORE THEY START BREAKING THINGS AGAIN...

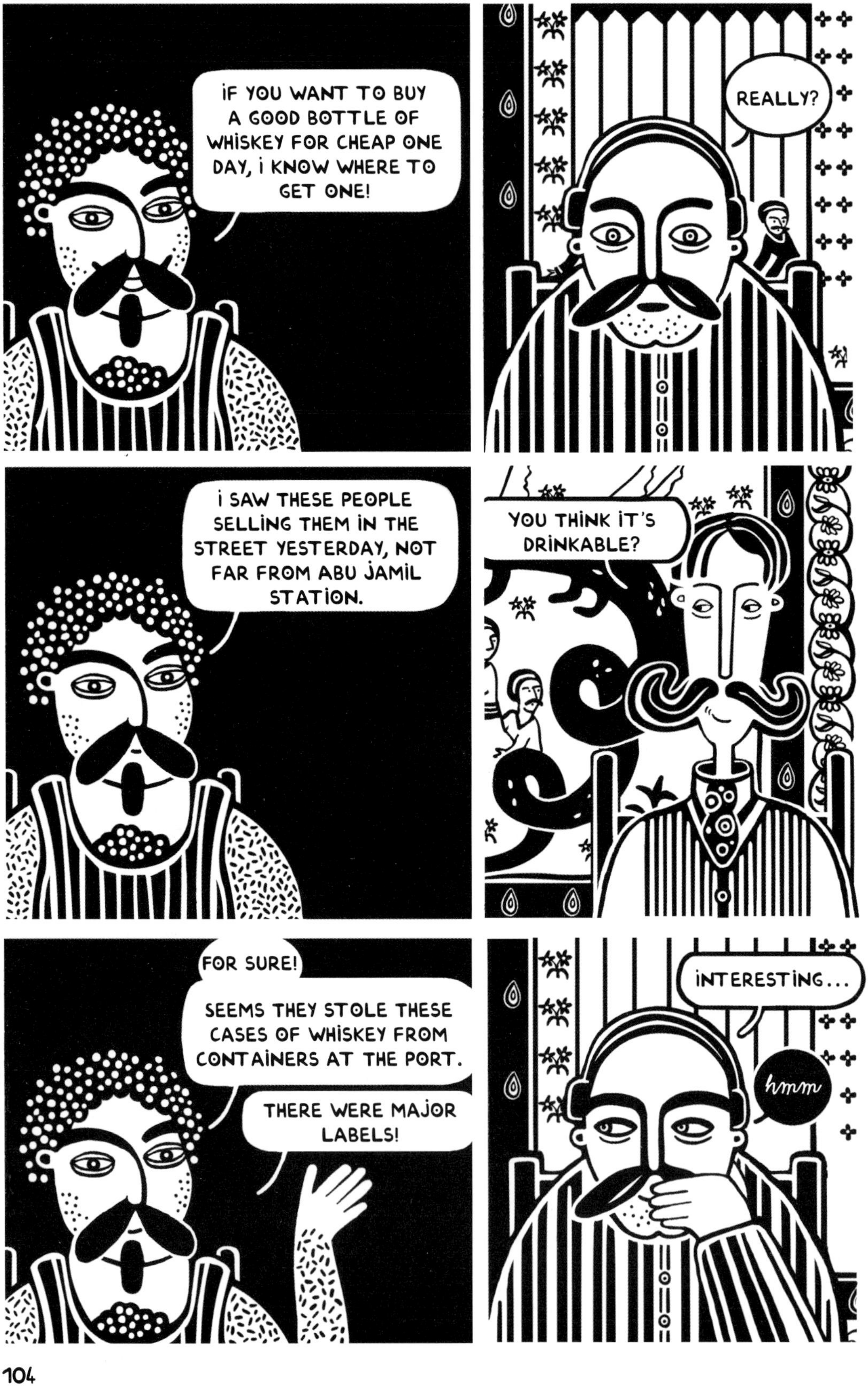
IF YOU WANT TO BUY A GOOD BOTTLE OF WHISKEY FOR CHEAP ONE DAY, I KNOW WHERE TO GET ONE!
REALLY?
I SAW THESE PEOPLE SELLING THEM IN THE STREET YESTERDAY, NOT FAR FROM ABU JAMIL STATION.
YOU THINK IT'S DRINKABLE?
FOR SURE!
SEEMS THEY STOLE THESE CASES OF WHISKEY FROM CONTAINERS AT THE PORT.
THERE WERE MAJOR LABELS!
INTERESTING...
hmm

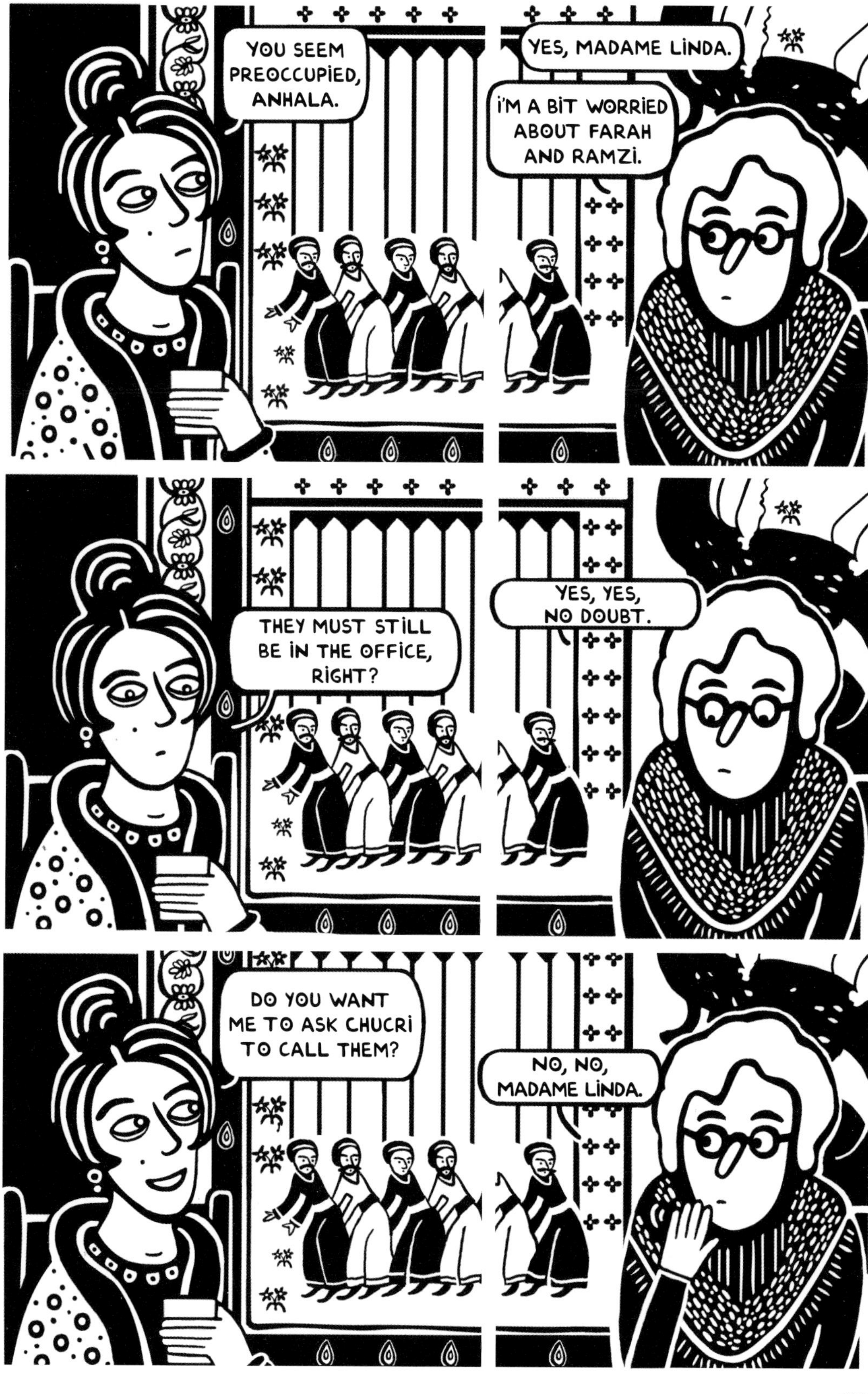
YOU SEEM PREOCCUPIED, ANHALA.
YES, MADAME LINDA.
I'M A BIT WORRIED ABOUT FARAH AND RAMZI.
THEY MUST STILL BE IN THE OFFICE, RIGHT?
YES, YES, NO DOUBT.
DO YOU WANT ME TO ASK CHUCRI TO CALL THEM?
NO, NO, MADAME LINDA.

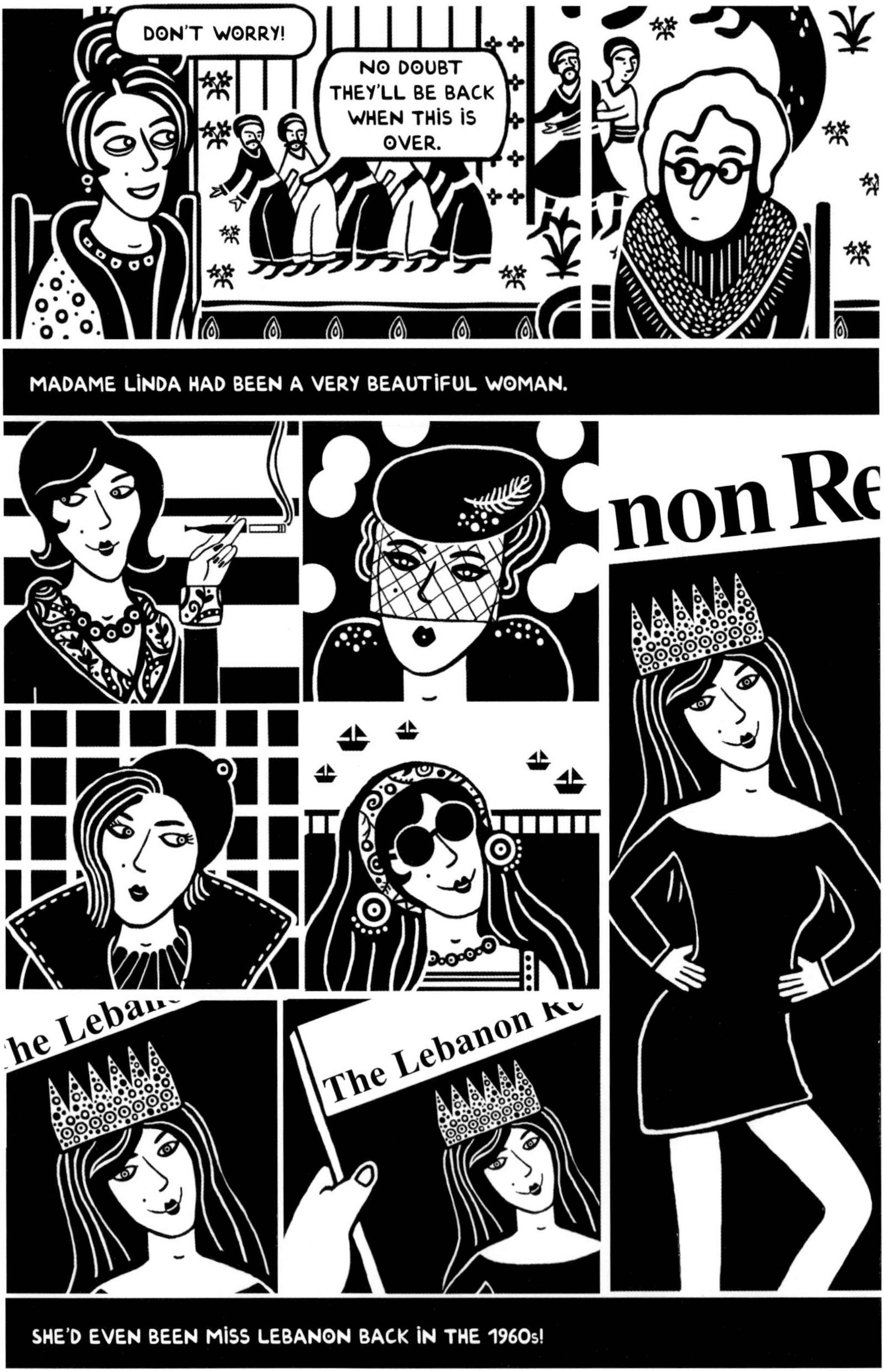
DON'T WORRY!
NO DOUBT THEY'LL BE BACK WHEN THIS IS OVER.
MADAME LINDA HAD BEEN A VERY BEAUTIFUL WOMAN.
The Lebanon
SHE'D EVEN BEEN MISS LEBANON BACK IN THE 1960s!

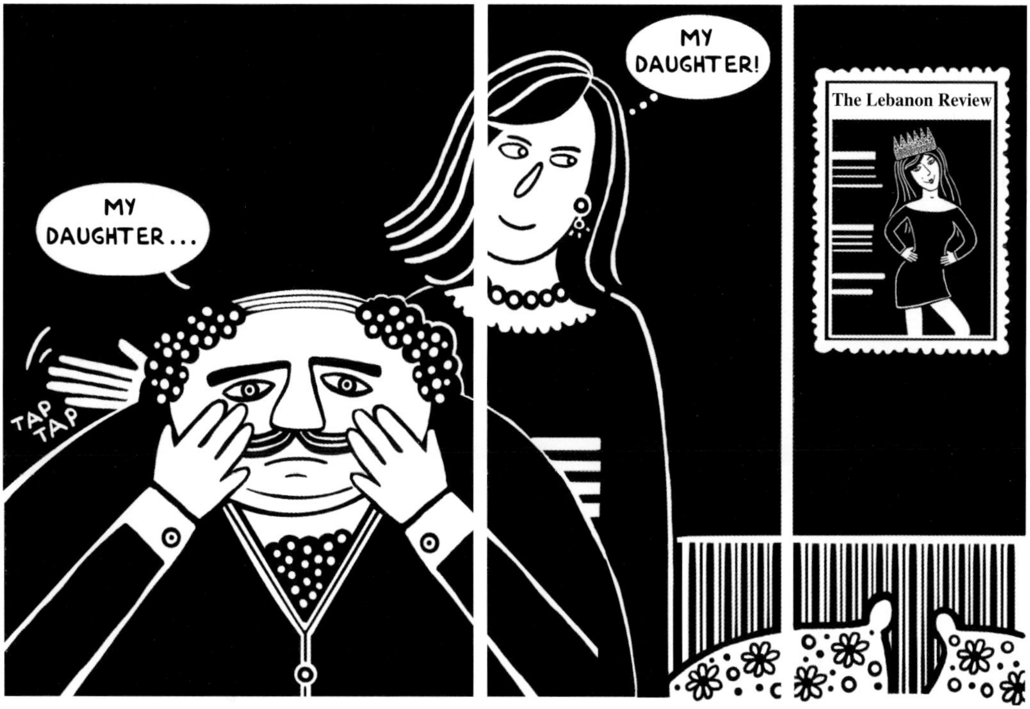
MY DAUGHTER...
TAP TAP
MY DAUGHTER!
The Lebanon Review

THE DAY AFTER SHE WON THE TITLE, THE PHOTO OF HER IN A MINISKIRT ON THE COVER OF THE *LEBANON REVIEW* WAS HER FATHER'S MISERY AND HER MOTHER'S JOY...

AND THEIR NEIGHBORS' DELIGHT.

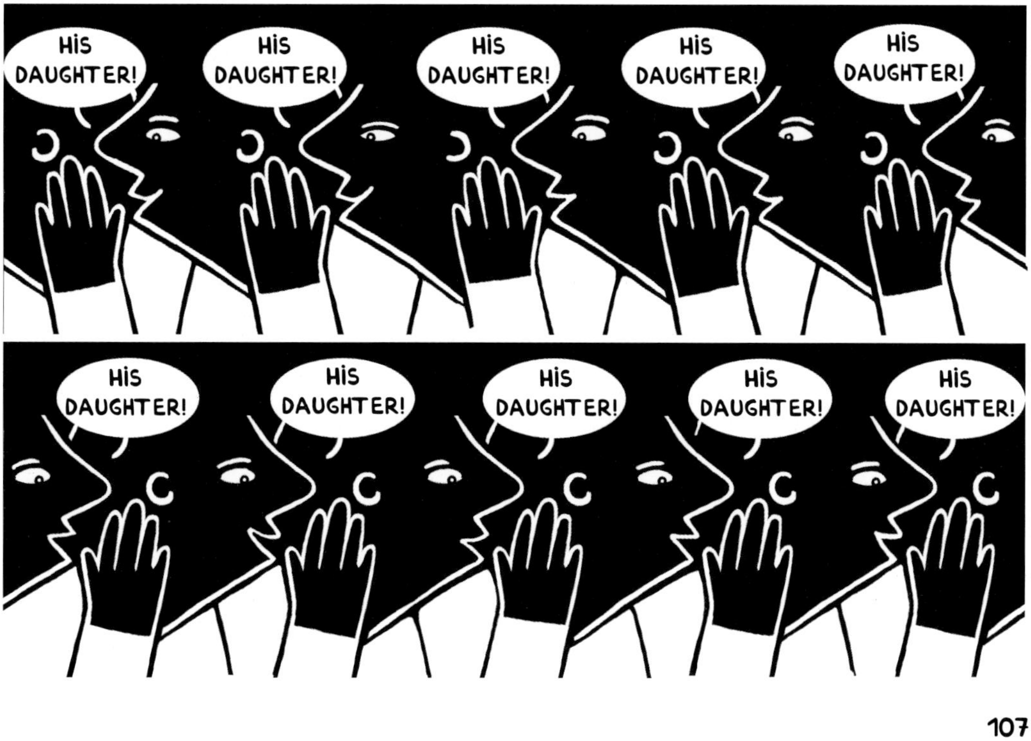
HIS DAUGHTER!
HIS DAUGHTER!
HIS DAUGHTER!
HIS DAUGHTER!
HIS DAUGHTER!
HIS DAUGHTER!
HIS DAUGHTER!
HIS DAUGHTER!
HIS DAUGHTER!
HIS DAUGHTER!

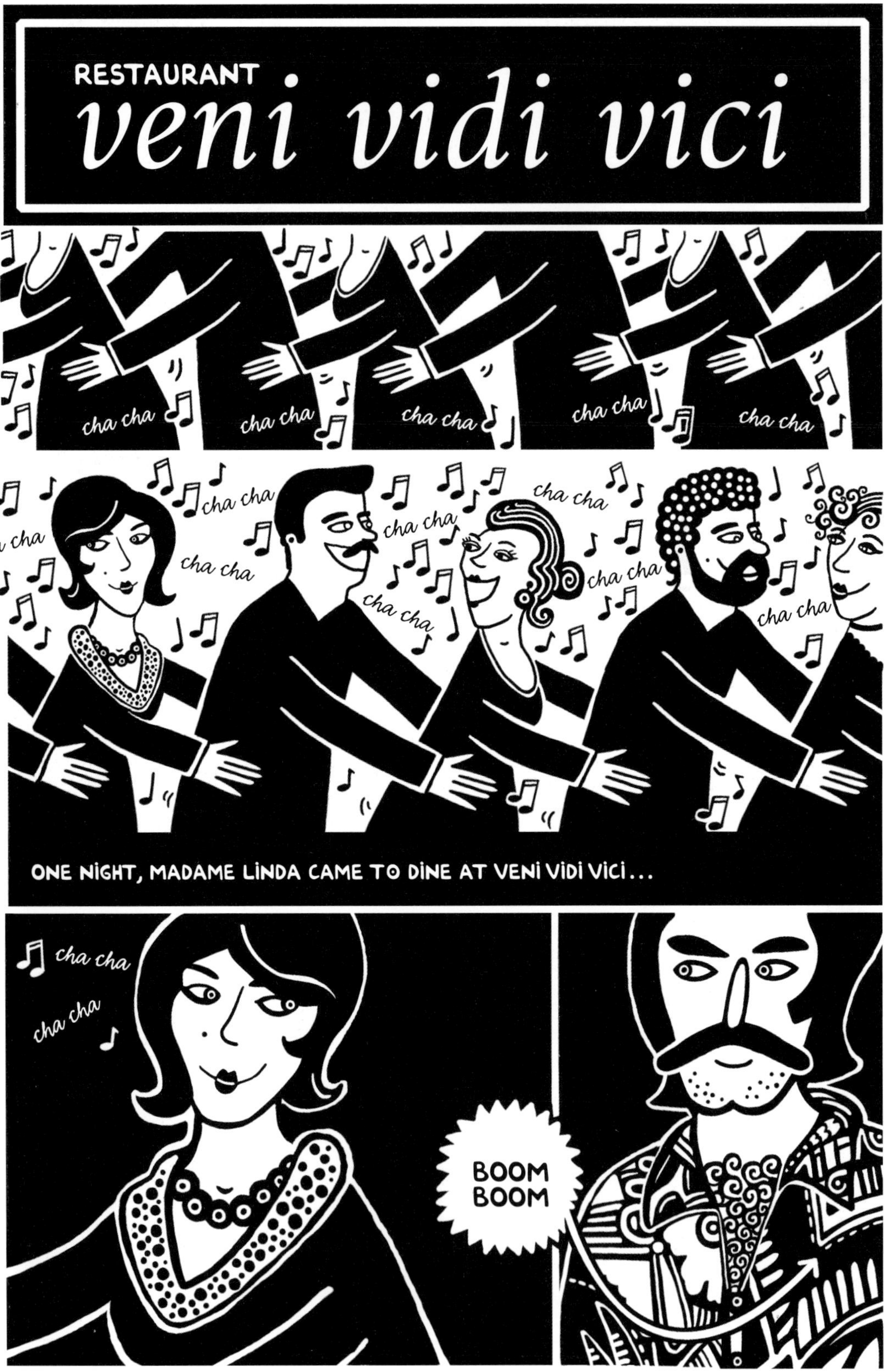

RESTAURANT
veni vidi vici
cha cha
cha cha
cha cha
cha cha
cha cha
cha cha
cha cha
cha cha
cha cha
cha cha
cha cha
cha cha
cha cha
ONE NIGHT, MADAME LINDA CAME TO DINE AT VENI VIDI VICI...
cha cha
cha cha
BOOM BOOM

KHALED SAID HE WAS BORN IN TEXAS.
BUT FOR LINDA'S BEAUTIFUL EYES, HE AGREED TO LIVE HERE.

HE TOLD HER THAT OVER
THERE, THEY HAD A VERY
BEAUTIFUL LIGHTHOUSE,

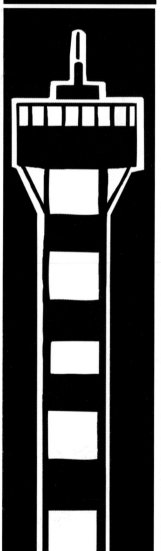

A FERRIS WHEEL, A CLIFF ROAD ALONG THE SEA,
RESTAURANTS, STORES ALL LIT UP,

STREET MERCHANTS, SIDEWALK CAFÉS

AND, ABOVE ALL, THE BEST "MERRY CREAMS" IN THE WORLD.

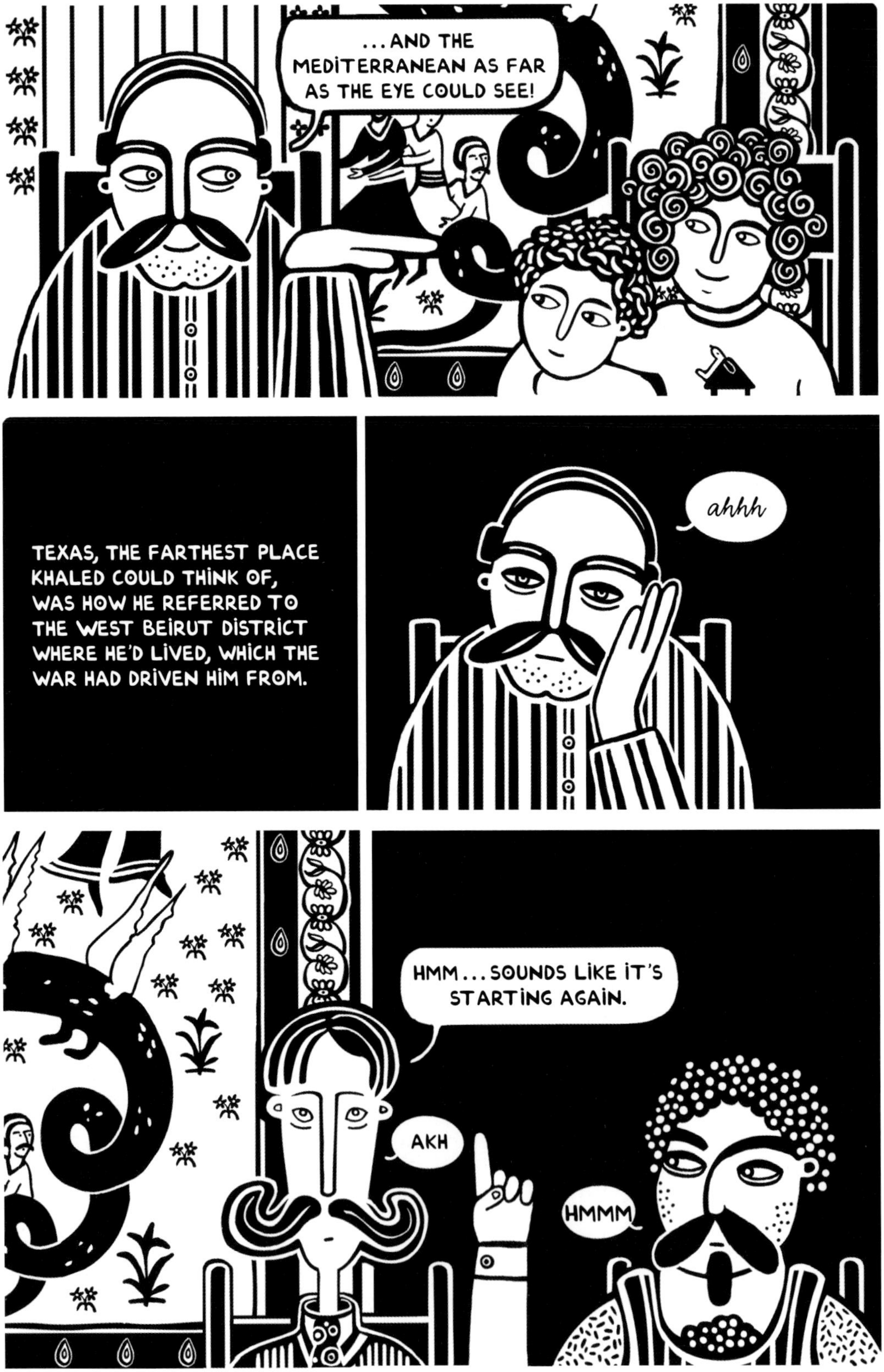
...AND THE MEDITERRANEAN AS FAR AS THE EYE COULD SEE!
TEXAS, THE FARTHEST PLACE KHALED COULD THINK OF, WAS HOW HE REFERRED TO THE WEST BEIRUT DISTRICT WHERE HE'D LIVED, WHICH THE WAR HAD DRIVEN HIM FROM.
ahhh
HMM...SOUNDS LIKE IT'S STARTING AGAIN.
AKH
HMMM

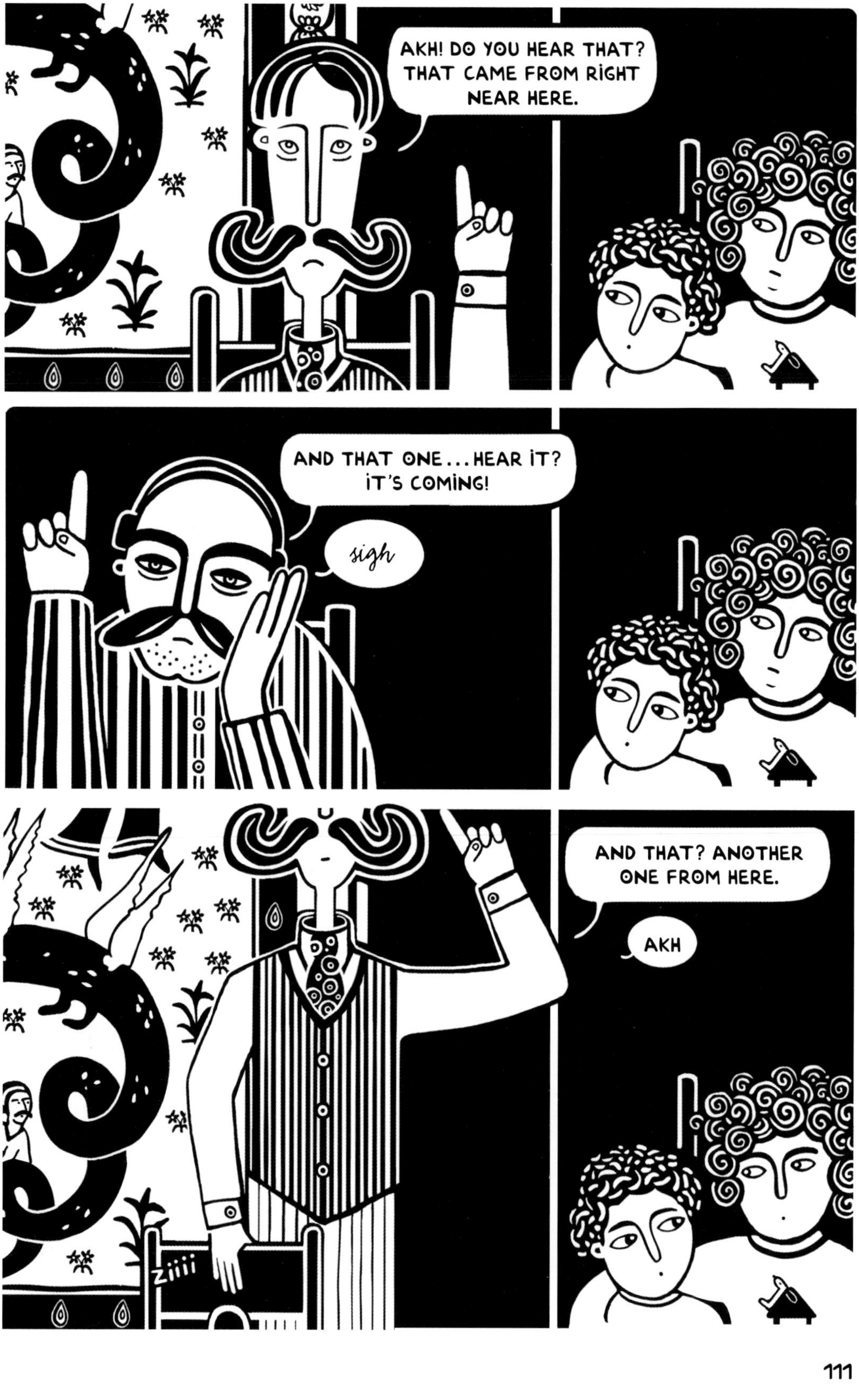
AKH! DO YOU HEAR THAT? THAT CAME FROM RIGHT NEAR HERE.
AND THAT ONE... HEAR IT? IT'S COMING!
sigh
AND THAT? ANOTHER ONE FROM HERE.
AKH
ziiii

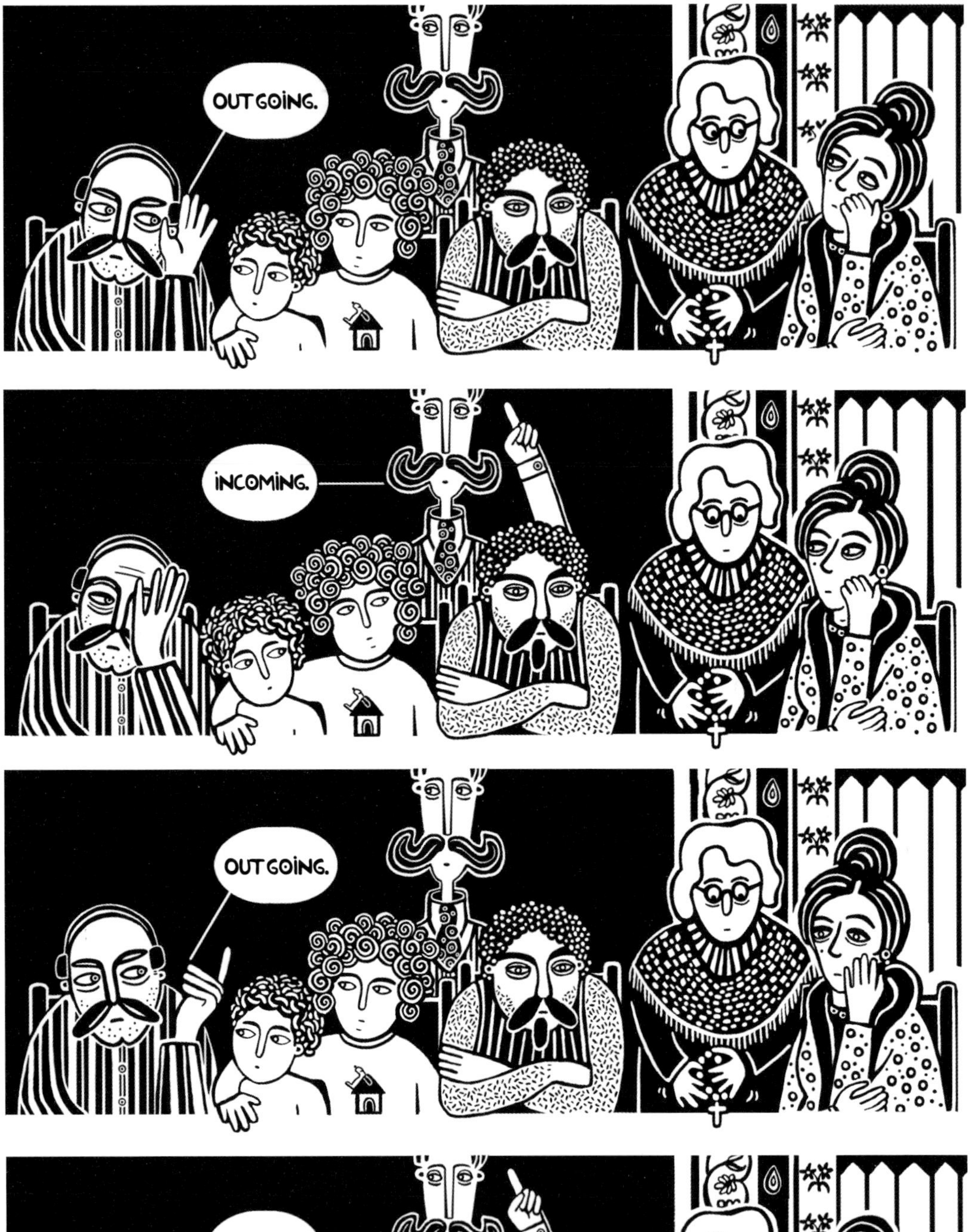
OUTGOING.
INCOMING.
OUTGOING.
INCOMING.

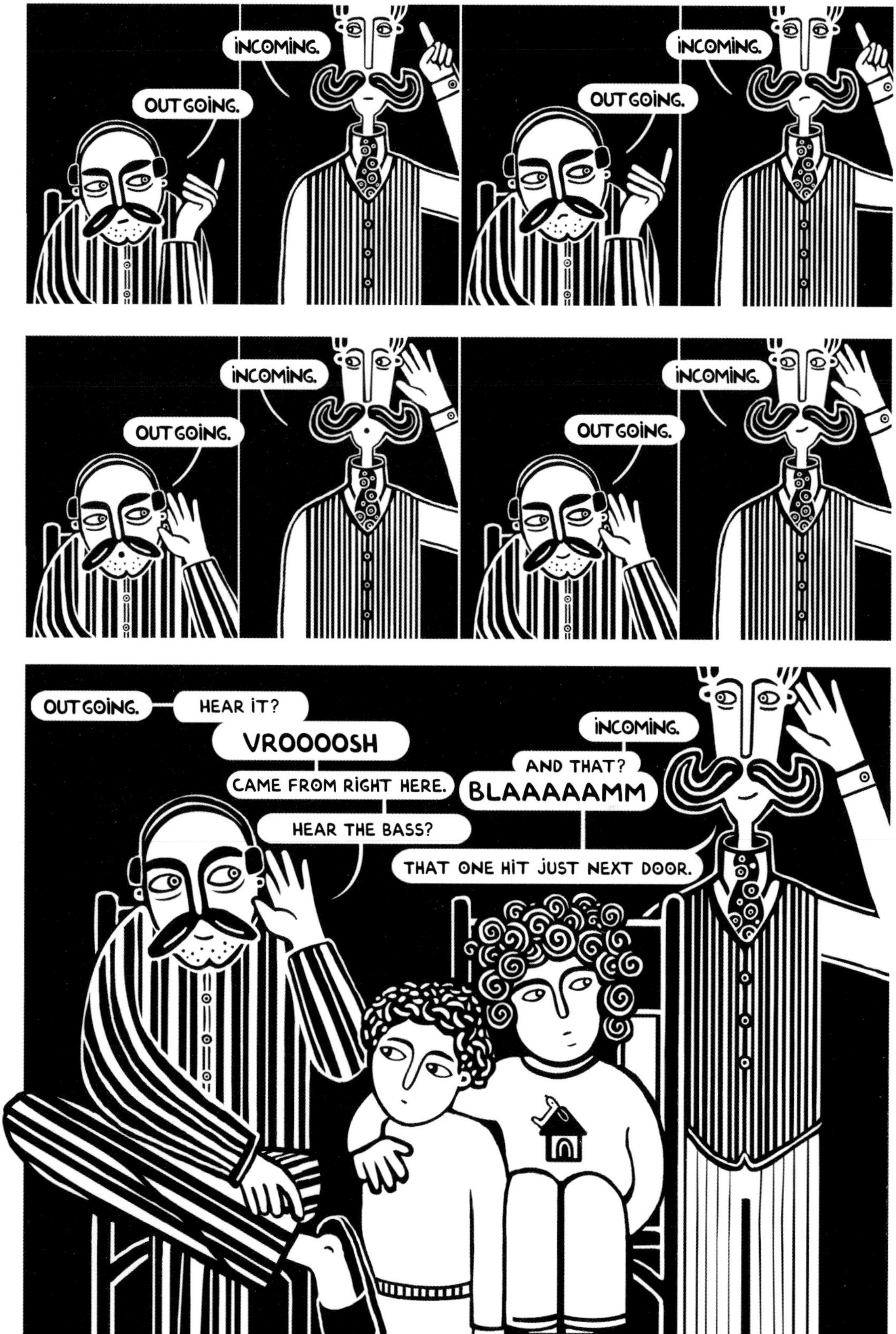
OUTGOING.
INCOMING.
OUTGOING.
INCOMING.
OUTGOING.
INCOMING.
OUTGOING.
INCOMING.
OUTGOING.
HEAR IT?
VROOOOSH
CAME FROM RIGHT HERE.
HEAR THE BASS?
INCOMING.
AND THAT?
BLAAAAAMM
THAT ONE HIT JUST NEXT DOOR.

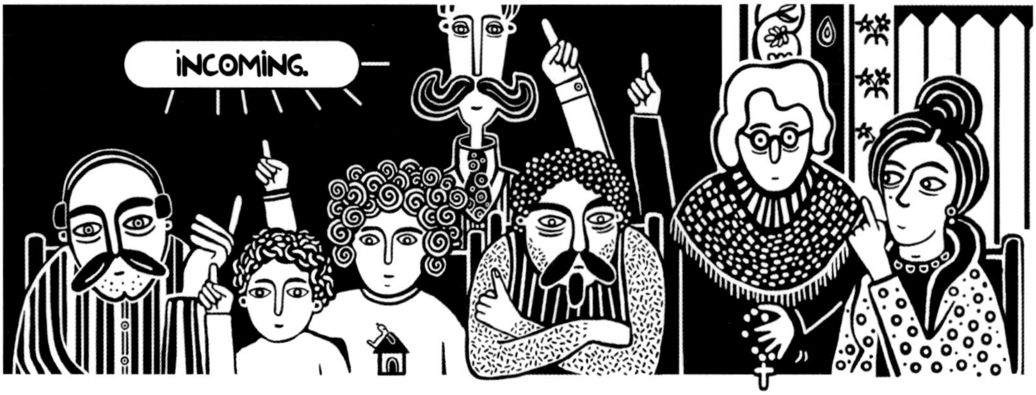
INCOMING.

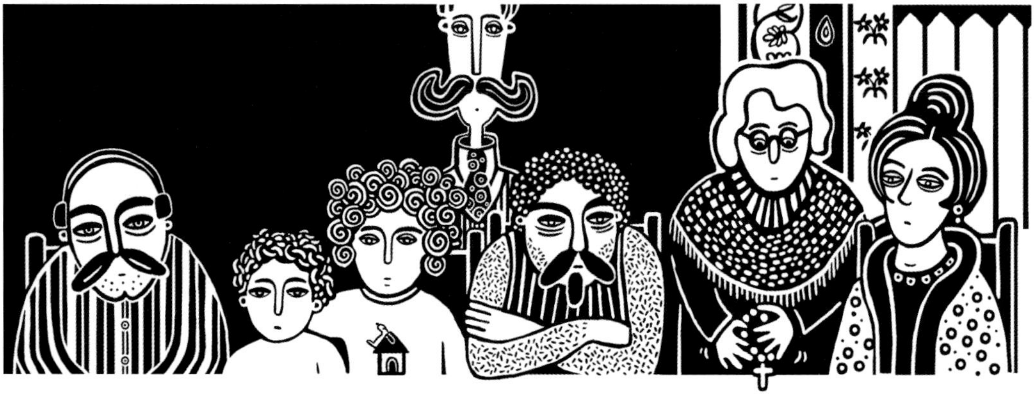

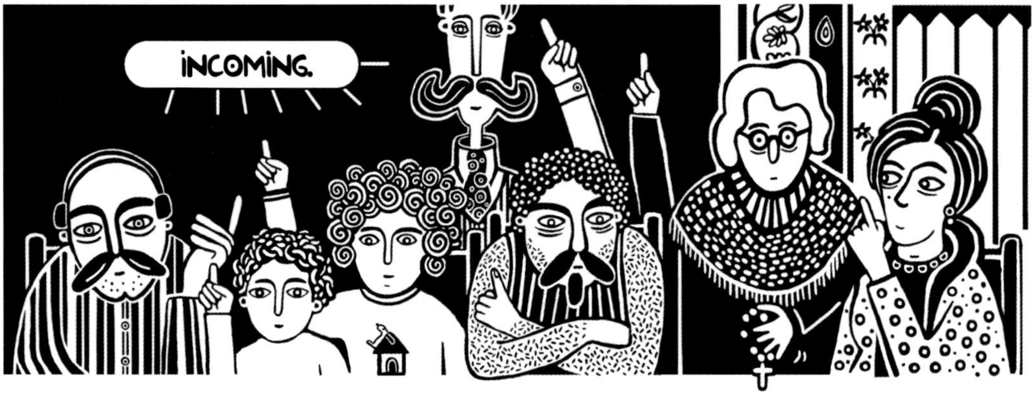
INCOMING.

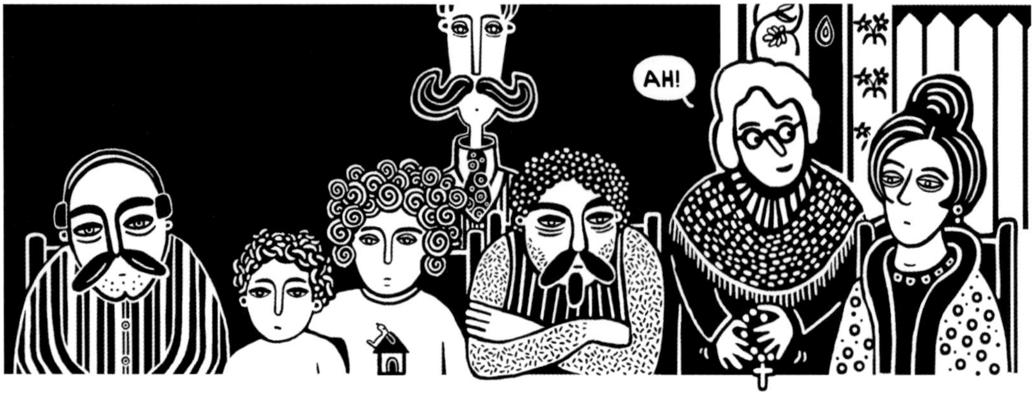
AH!

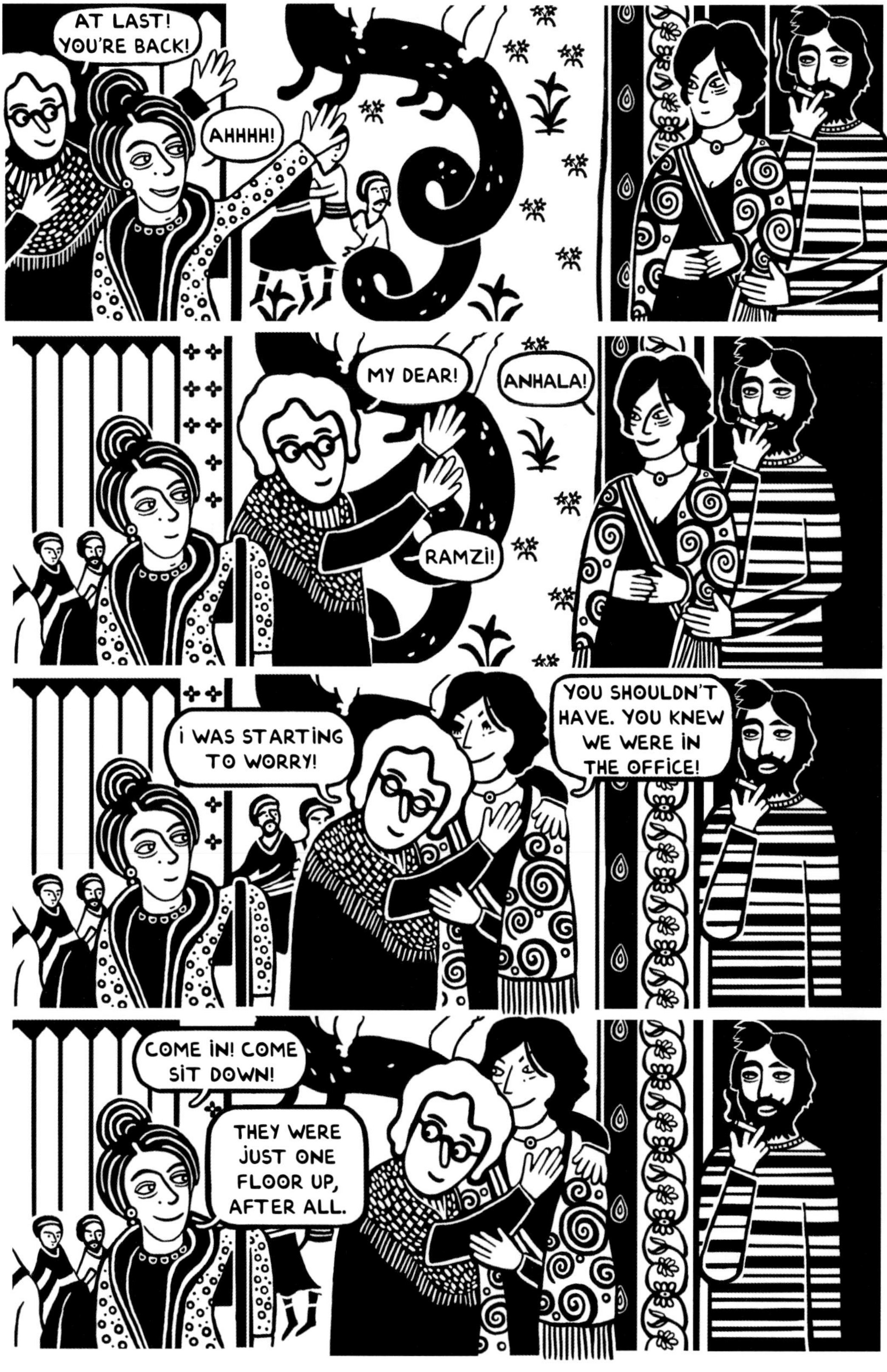
AT LAST! YOU'RE BACK!
AHHHH!
MY DEAR!
ANHALA!
RAMZI!
I WAS STARTING TO WORRY!
YOU SHOULDN'T HAVE. YOU KNEW WE WERE IN THE OFFICE!
COME IN! COME SIT DOWN!
THEY WERE JUST ONE FLOOR UP, AFTER ALL.

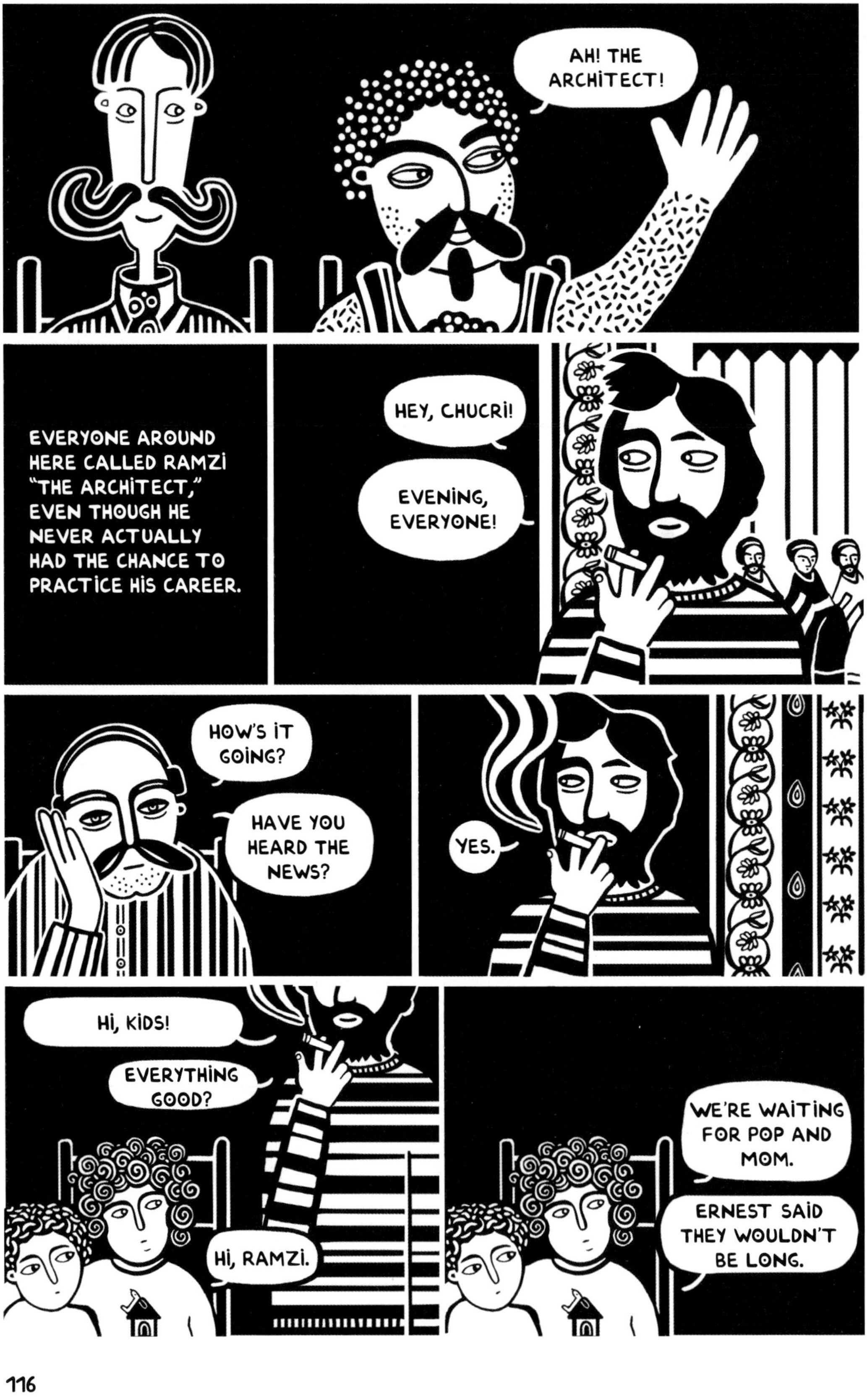
AH! THE ARCHITECT!
EVERYONE AROUND HERE CALLED RAMZI "THE ARCHITECT," EVEN THOUGH HE NEVER ACTUALLY HAD THE CHANCE TO PRACTICE HIS CAREER.
HEY, CHUCRI!
EVENING, EVERYONE!
HOW'S IT GOING?
HAVE YOU HEARD THE NEWS?
YES.
HI, KIDS!
EVERYTHING GOOD?
HI, RAMZI.
WE'RE WAITING FOR POP AND MOM.
ERNEST SAID THEY WOULDN'T BE LONG.

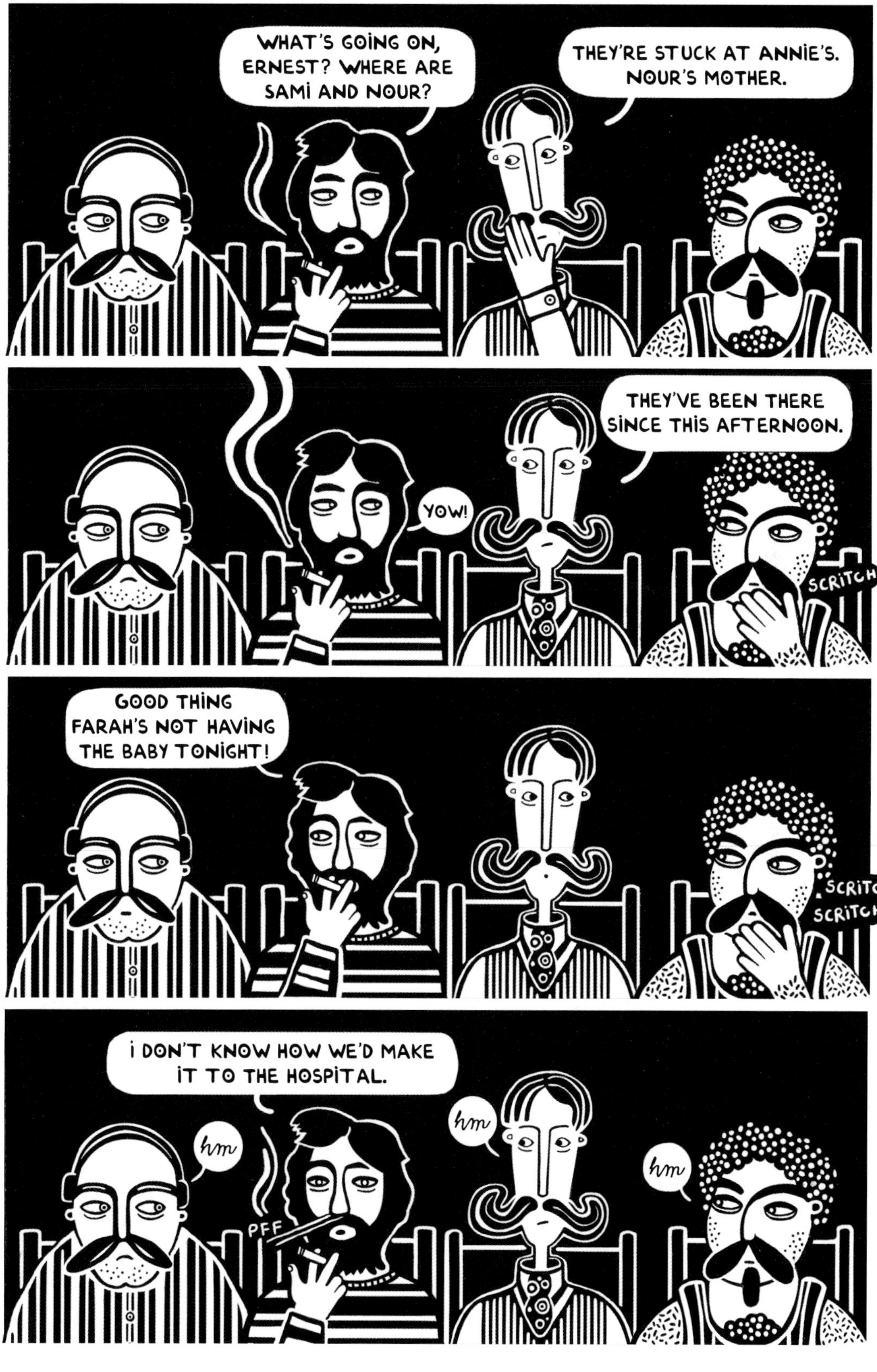
WHAT'S GOING ON, ERNEST? WHERE ARE SAMI AND NOUR?
THEY'RE STUCK AT ANNIE'S. NOUR'S MOTHER.
THEY'VE BEEN THERE SINCE THIS AFTERNOON.
YOW!
SCRITCH
GOOD THING FARAH'S NOT HAVING THE BABY TONIGHT!
SCRITCH
SCRITCH
I DON'T KNOW HOW WE'D MAKE IT TO THE HOSPITAL.
hm
PFF
hm
hm

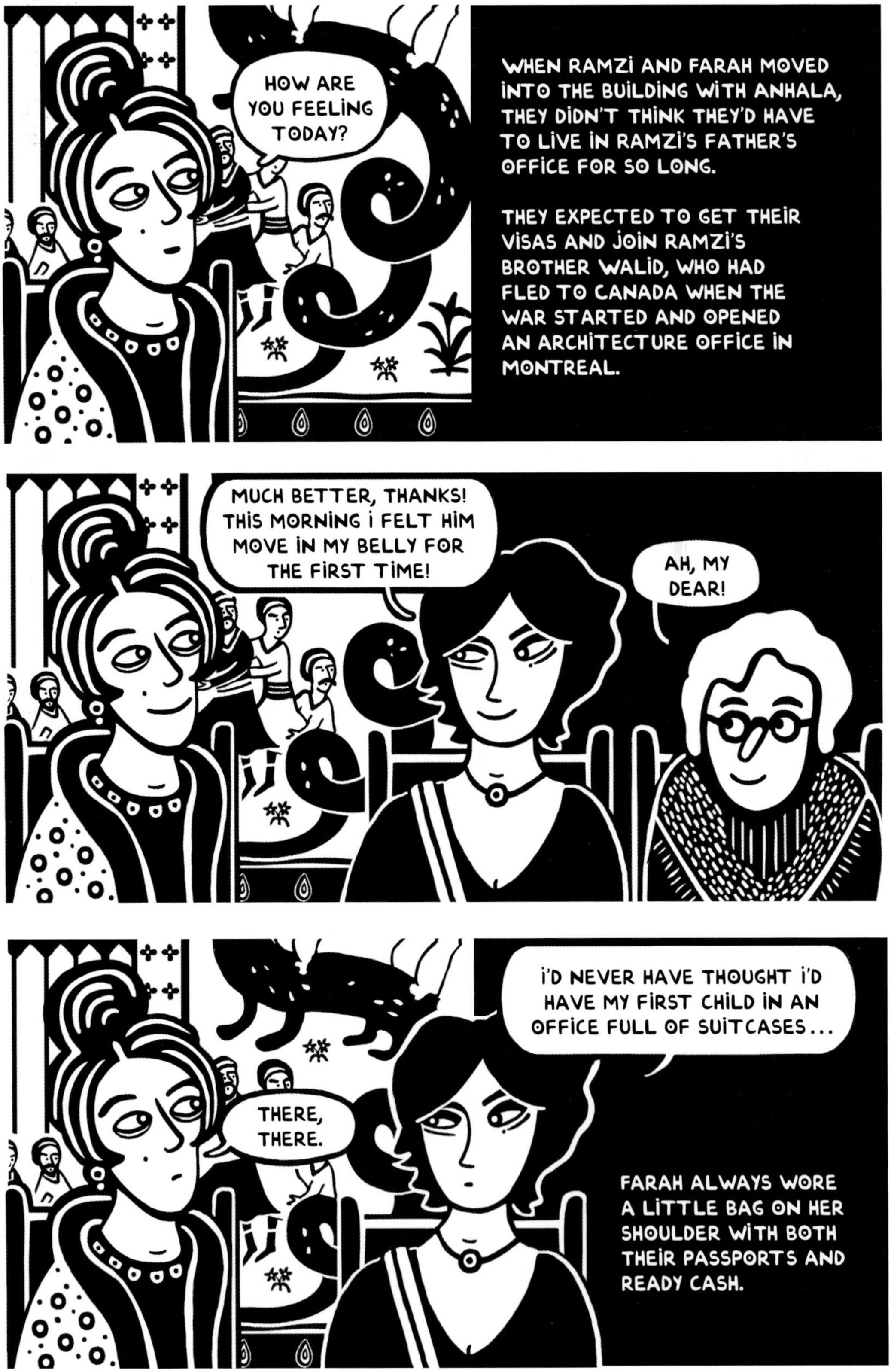
HOW ARE YOU FEELING TODAY?
WHEN RAMZI AND FARAH MOVED INTO THE BUILDING WITH ANHALA, THEY DIDN'T THINK THEY'D HAVE TO LIVE IN RAMZI'S FATHER'S OFFICE FOR SO LONG.
THEY EXPECTED TO GET THEIR VISAS AND JOIN RAMZI'S BROTHER WALID, WHO HAD FLED TO CANADA WHEN THE WAR STARTED AND OPENED AN ARCHITECTURE OFFICE IN MONTREAL.
MUCH BETTER, THANKS! THIS MORNING I FELT HIM MOVE IN MY BELLY FOR THE FIRST TIME!
AH, MY DEAR!
I'D NEVER HAVE THOUGHT I'D HAVE MY FIRST CHILD IN AN OFFICE FULL OF SUITCASES...
THERE, THERE.
FARAH ALWAYS WORE A LITTLE BAG ON HER SHOULDER WITH BOTH THEIR PASSPORTS AND READY CASH.

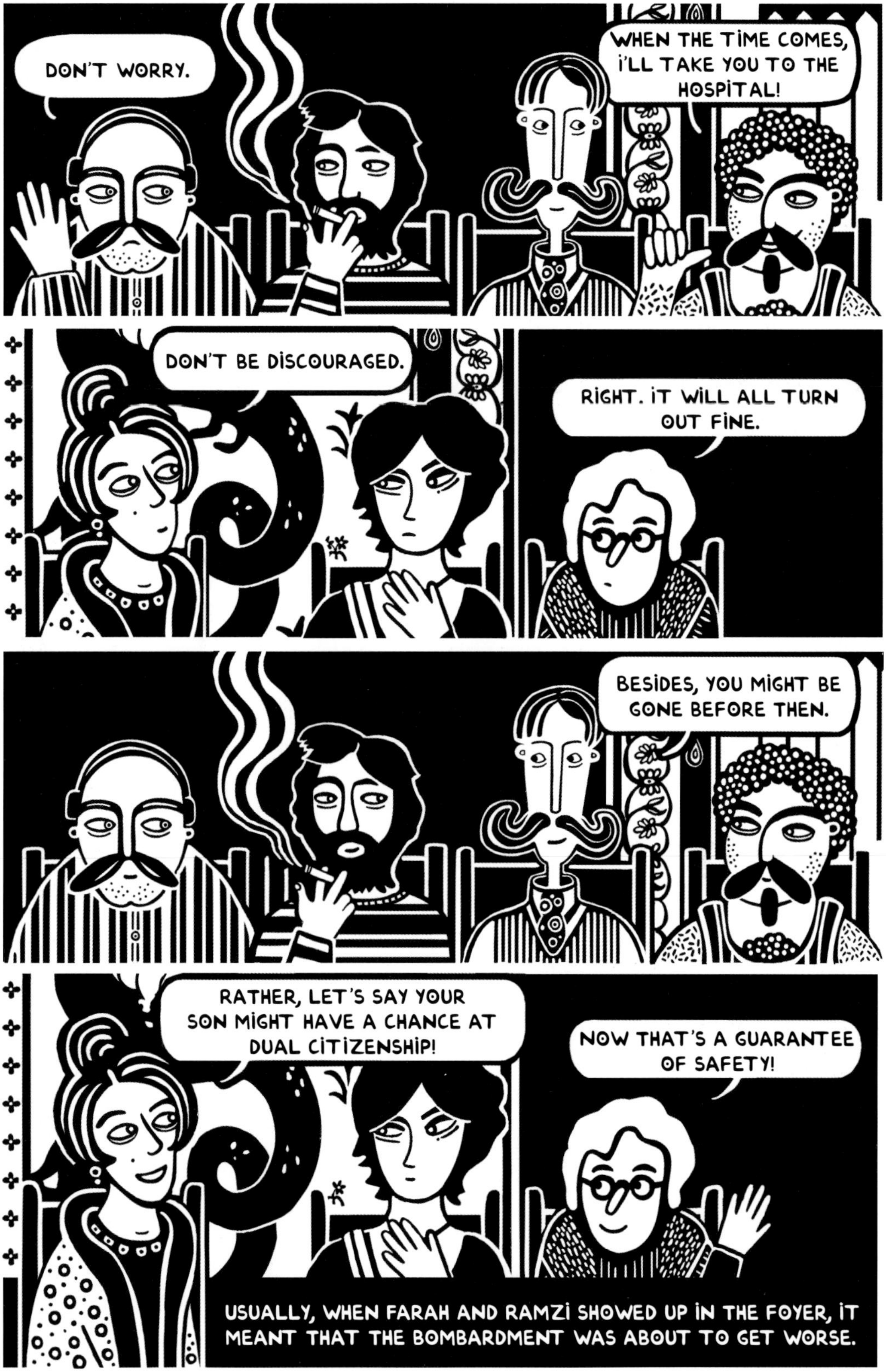
DON'T WORRY.
WHEN THE TIME COMES, I'LL TAKE YOU TO THE HOSPITAL!
DON'T BE DISCOURAGED.
RIGHT. IT WILL ALL TURN OUT FINE.
BESIDES, YOU MIGHT BE GONE BEFORE THEN.
RATHER, LET'S SAY YOUR SON MIGHT HAVE A CHANCE AT DUAL CITIZENSHIP!
NOW THAT'S A GUARANTEE OF SAFETY!
USUALLY, WHEN FARAH AND RAMZI SHOWED UP IN THE FOYER, IT MEANT THAT THE BOMBARDMENT WAS ABOUT TO GET WORSE.

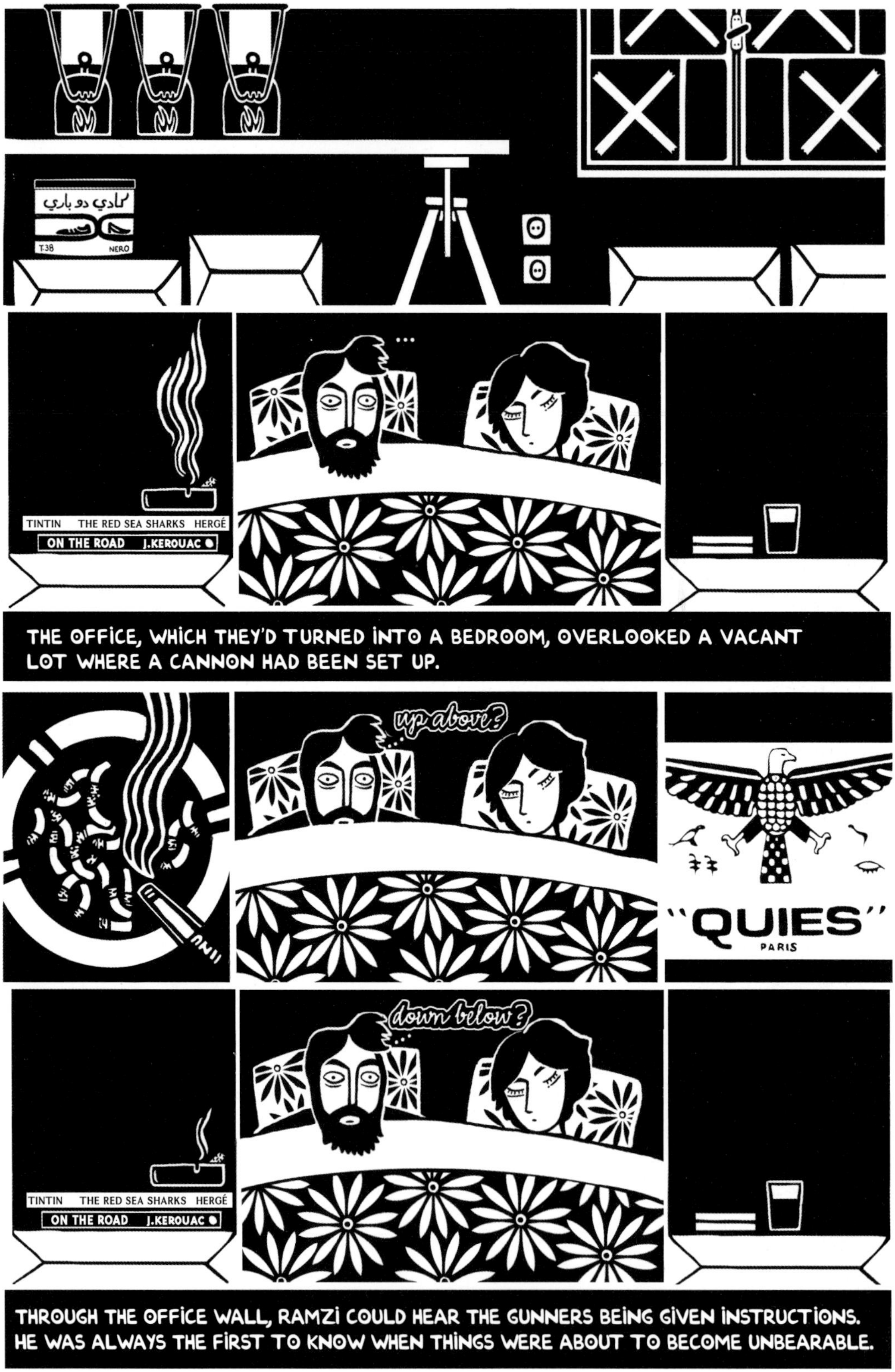
كادي دو باري
T.38
NERO
TINTIN THE RED SEA SHARKS HERGÉ
ON THE ROAD J.KEROUAC
THE OFFICE, WHICH THEY'D TURNED INTO A BEDROOM, OVERLOOKED A VACANT LOT WHERE A CANNON HAD BEEN SET UP.
up above?
"QUIES"
PARIS
TINTIN THE RED SEA SHARKS HERGÉ
ON THE ROAD J.KEROUAC
down below?
THROUGH THE OFFICE WALL, RAMZI COULD HEAR THE GUNNERS BEING GIVEN INSTRUCTIONS.
HE WAS ALWAYS THE FIRST TO KNOW WHEN THINGS WERE ABOUT TO BECOME UNBEARABLE.

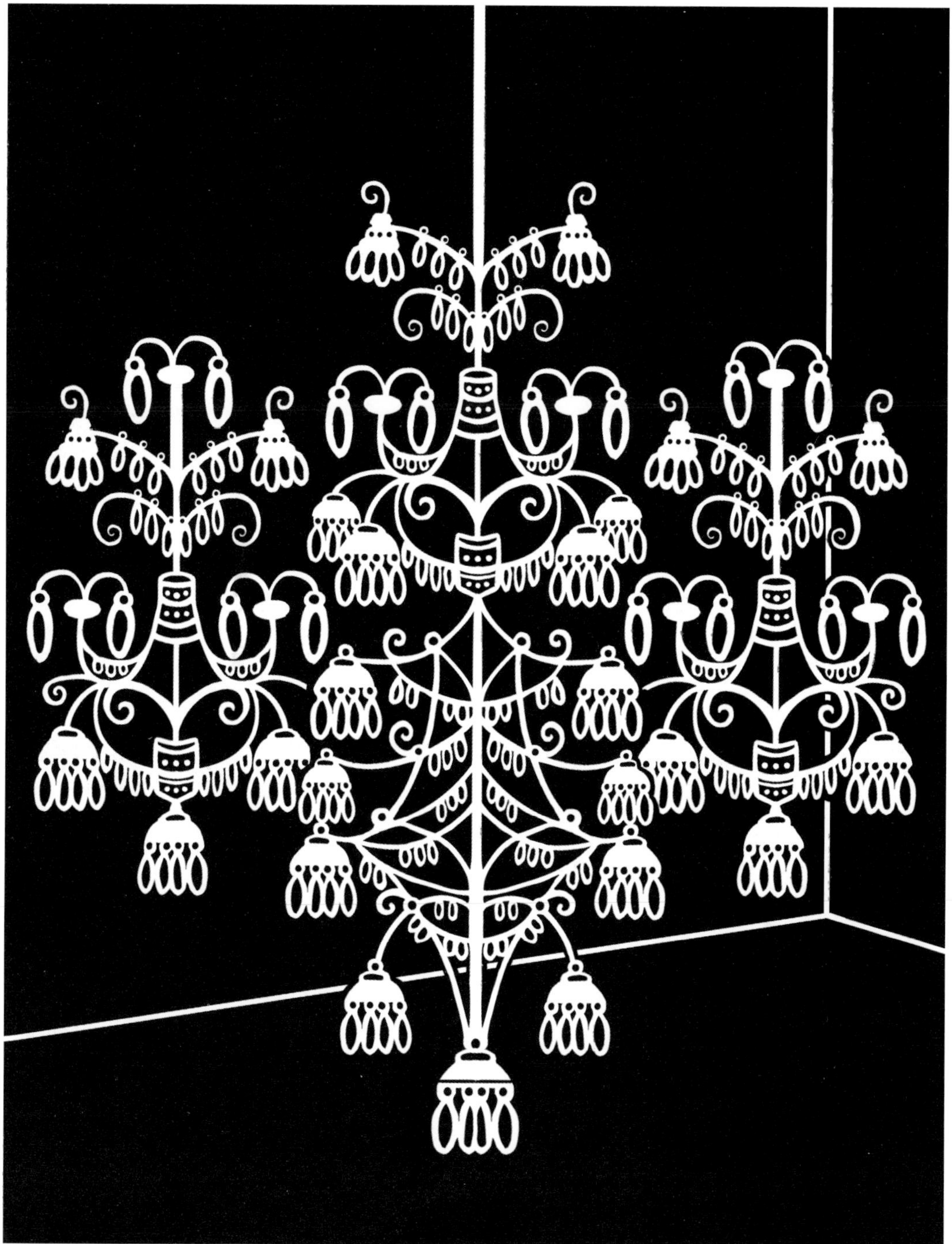

WHERE ANHALA SLEPT, A CRYSTAL CHANDELIER THAT BELONGED TO RAMZI'S FATHER'S CLIENTS HUNG ALMOST TO THE FLOOR.

ALTHOUGH ALL THE BUILDING'S WINDOWS HAD LONG SINCE BURST INTO PIECES, THE CHANDELIER—USELESS BECAUSE THERE WAS NO ELECTRICITY—HAD REMAINED INTACT.

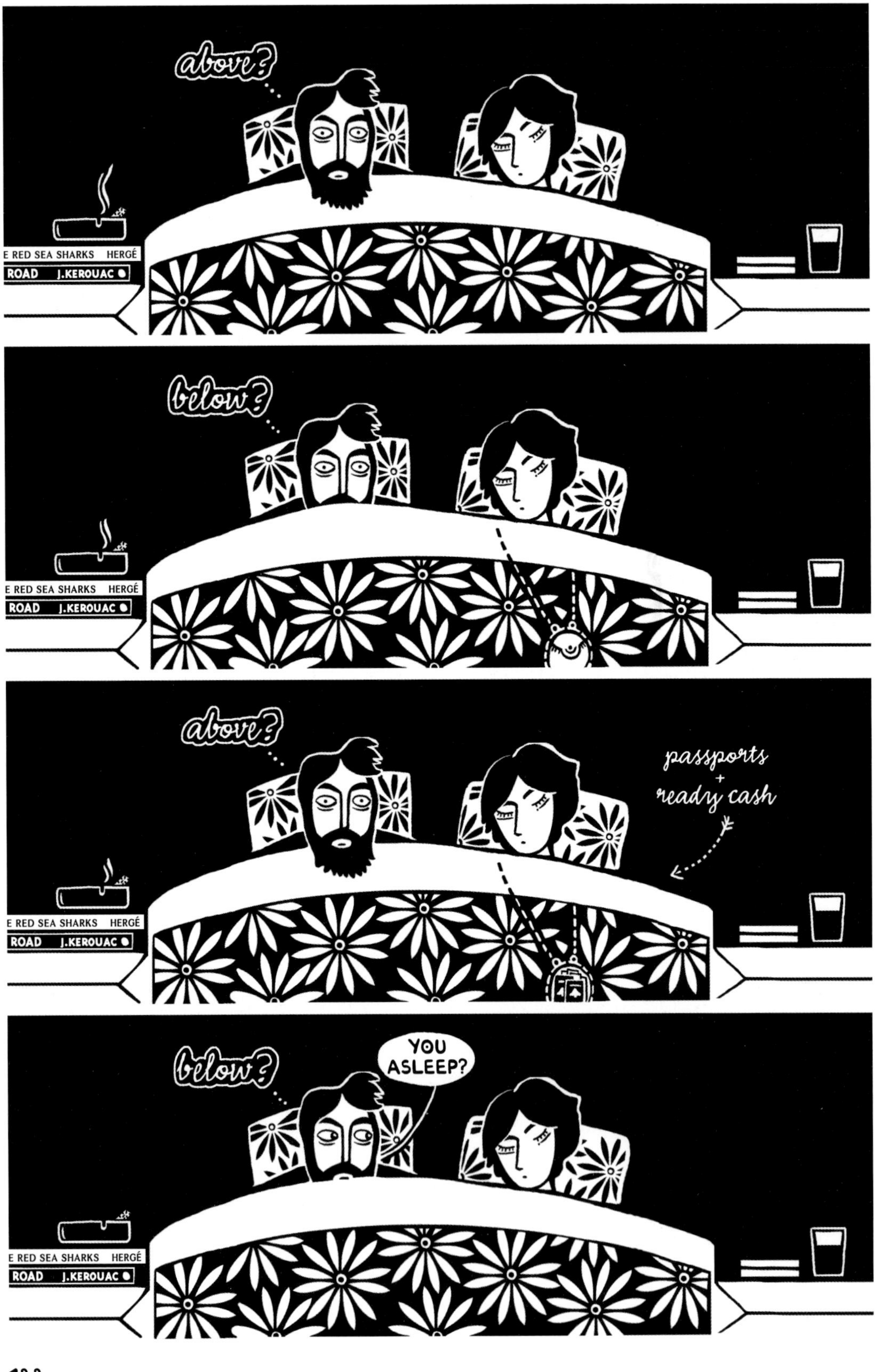

above?
E RED SEA SHARKS HERGÉ
ROAD J.KEROUAC
below?
E RED SEA SHARKS HERGÉ
ROAD J.KEROUAC
above?
passports + ready cash
E RED SEA SHARKS HERGÉ
ROAD J.KEROUAC
below?
YOU ASLEEP?
E RED SEA SHARKS HERGÉ
ROAD J.KEROUAC

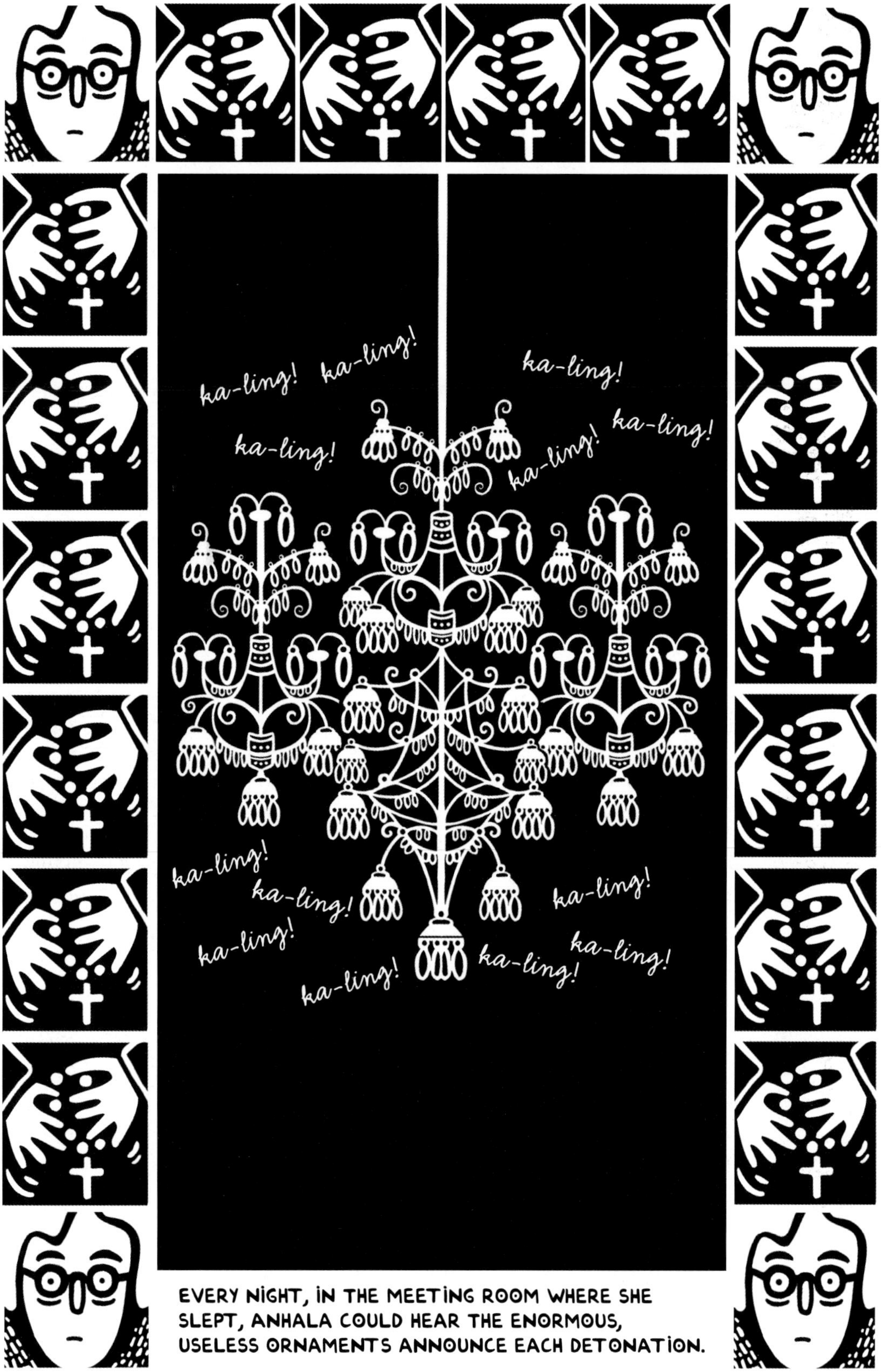
ka-ling! ka-ling!
ka-ling!
ka-ling!
ka-ling! ka-ling!
ka-ling!
ka-ling!
ka-ling!
ka-ling!
ka-ling!
ka-ling!
ka-ling!
EVERY NIGHT, IN THE MEETING ROOM WHERE SHE SLEPT, ANHALA COULD HEAR THE ENORMOUS, USELESS ORNAMENTS ANNOUNCE EACH DETONATION.

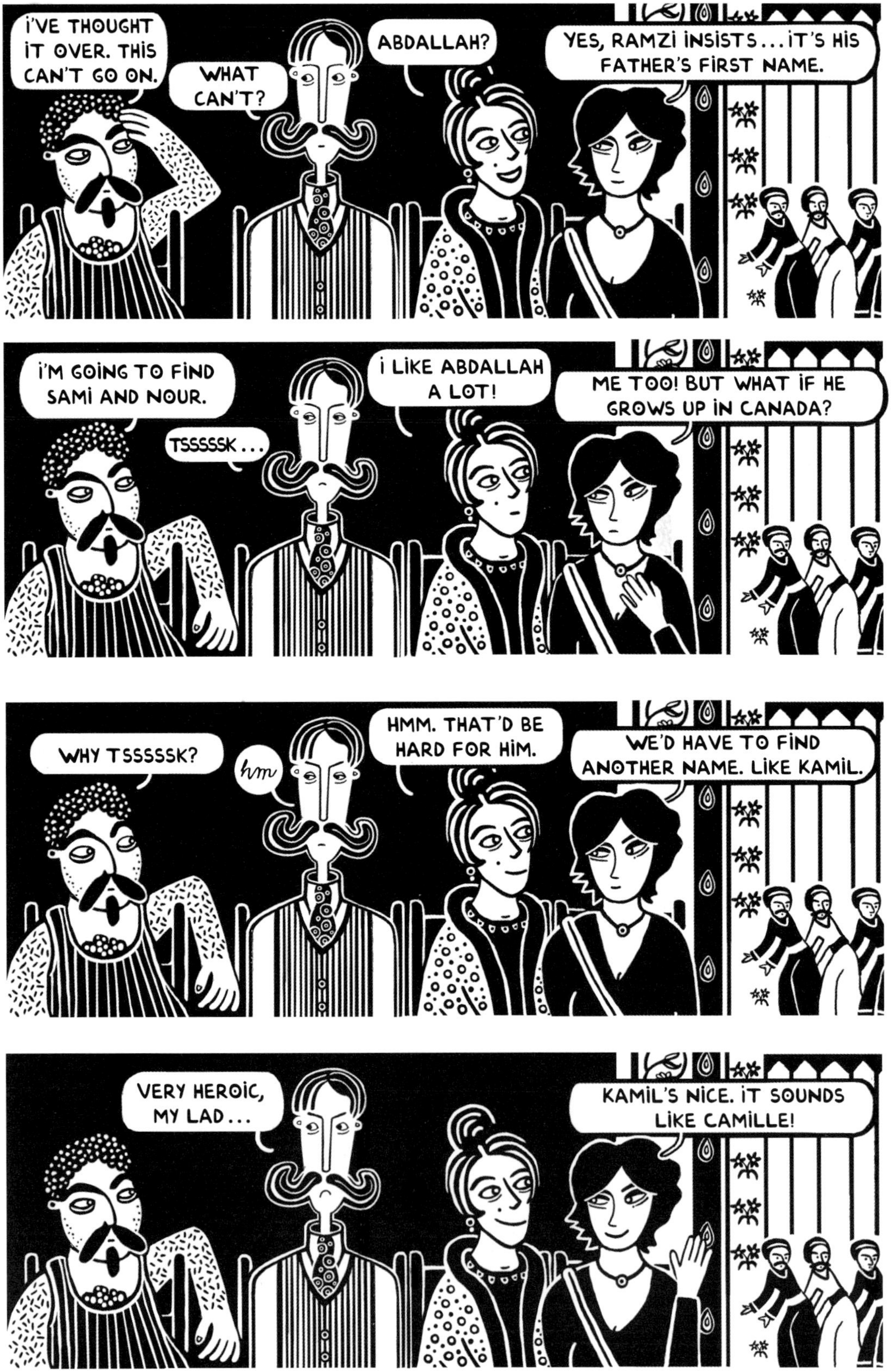
I'VE THOUGHT IT OVER. THIS CAN'T GO ON.
WHAT CAN'T?
ABDALLAH?
YES, RAMZI INSISTS... IT'S HIS FATHER'S FIRST NAME.
I'M GOING TO FIND SAMI AND NOUR.
TSSSSSK...
I LIKE ABDALLAH A LOT!
ME TOO! BUT WHAT IF HE GROWS UP IN CANADA?
WHY TSSSSSK?
hm
HMM. THAT'D BE HARD FOR HIM.
WE'D HAVE TO FIND ANOTHER NAME. LIKE KAMIL.
VERY HEROIC, MY LAD...
KAMIL'S NICE. IT SOUNDS LIKE CAMILLE!

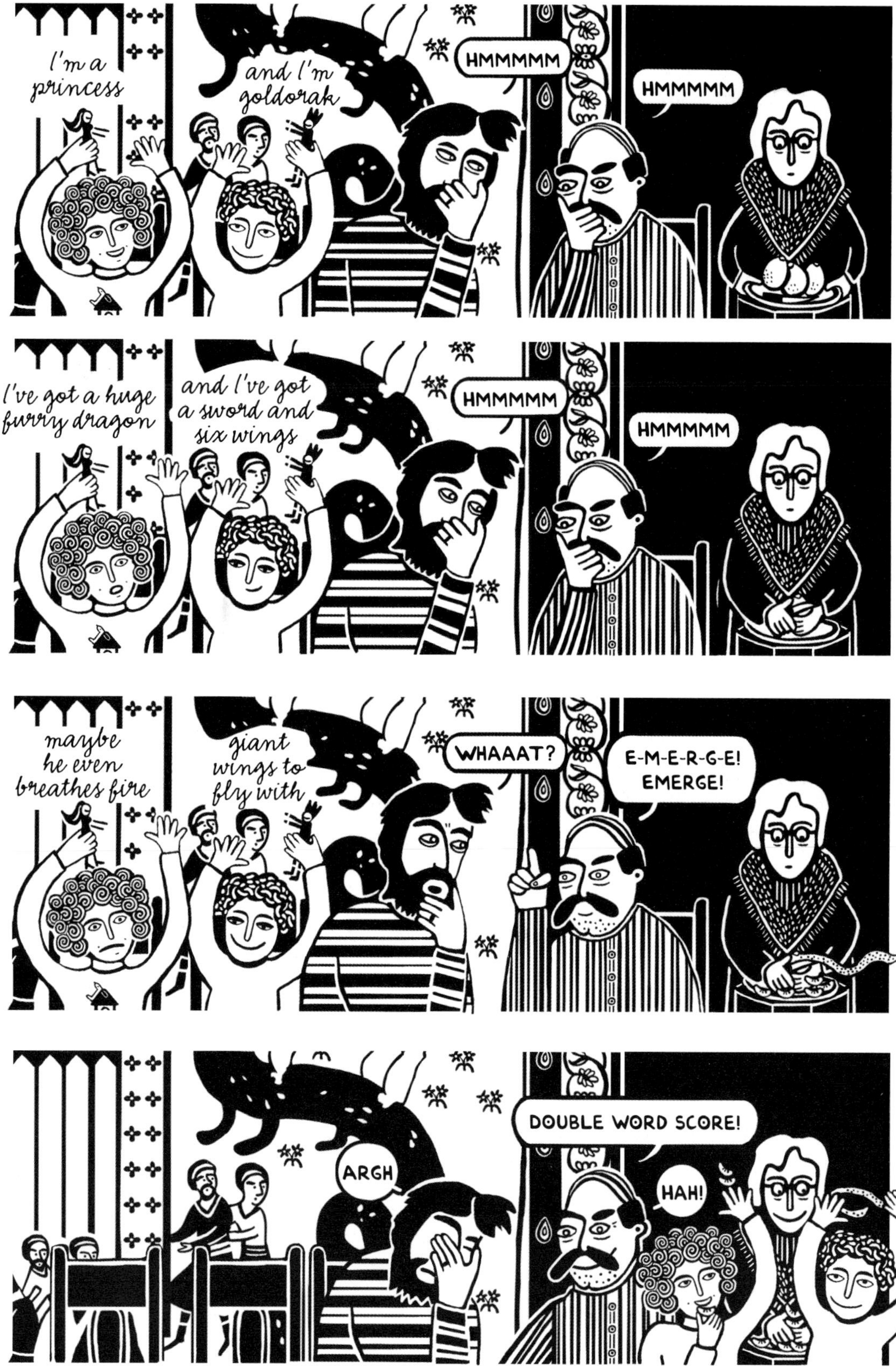
I'm a princess
and I'm goldorak
HMMMMM
HMMMMM
I've got a huge furry dragon
and I've got a sword and six wings
HMMMMM
HMMMMM
maybe he even breathes fire
giant wings to fly with
WHAAAT?
E-M-E-R-G-E! EMERGE!
ARGH
DOUBLE WORD SCORE!
HAH!

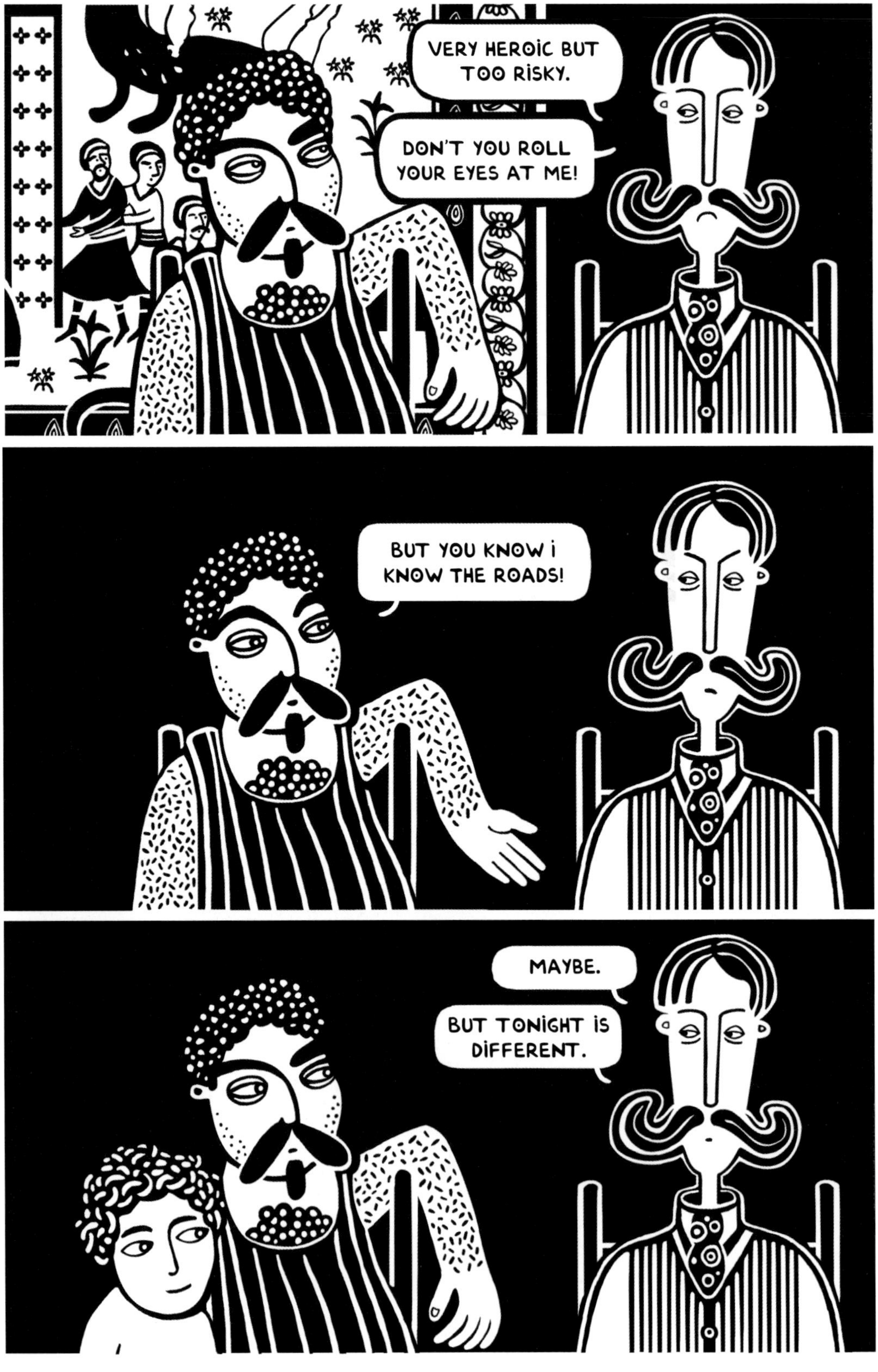
VERY HEROIC BUT TOO RISKY.
DON'T YOU ROLL YOUR EYES AT ME!
BUT YOU KNOW I KNOW THE ROADS!
MAYBE.
BUT TONIGHT IS DIFFERENT.

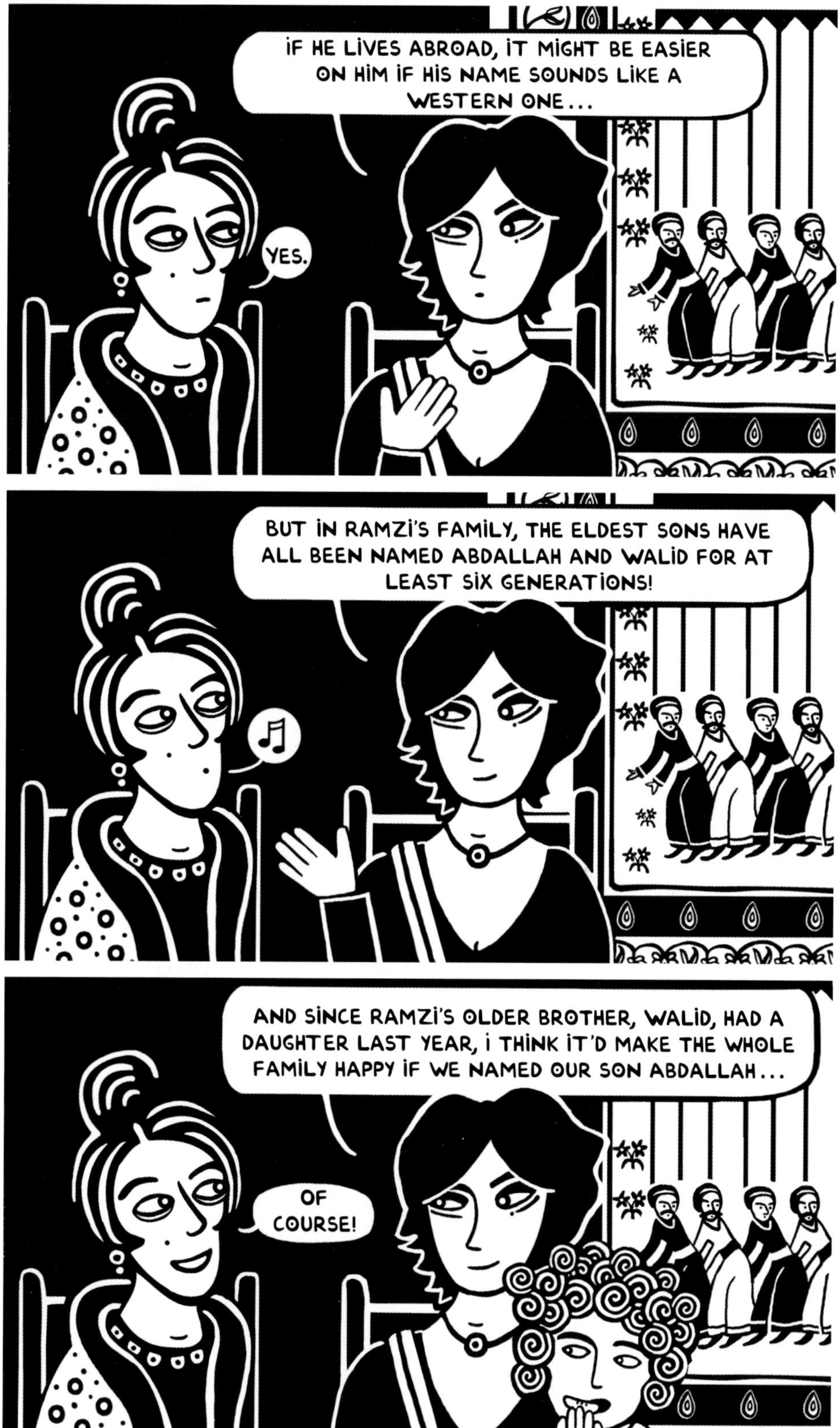
IF HE LIVES ABROAD, IT MIGHT BE EASIER ON HIM IF HIS NAME SOUNDS LIKE A WESTERN ONE...
YES.
BUT IN RAMZI'S FAMILY, THE ELDEST SONS HAVE ALL BEEN NAMED ABDALLAH AND WALID FOR AT LEAST SIX GENERATIONS!
♫
AND SINCE RAMZI'S OLDER BROTHER, WALID, HAD A DAUGHTER LAST YEAR, I THINK IT'D MAKE THE WHOLE FAMILY HAPPY IF WE NAMED OUR SON ABDALLAH...
OF COURSE!

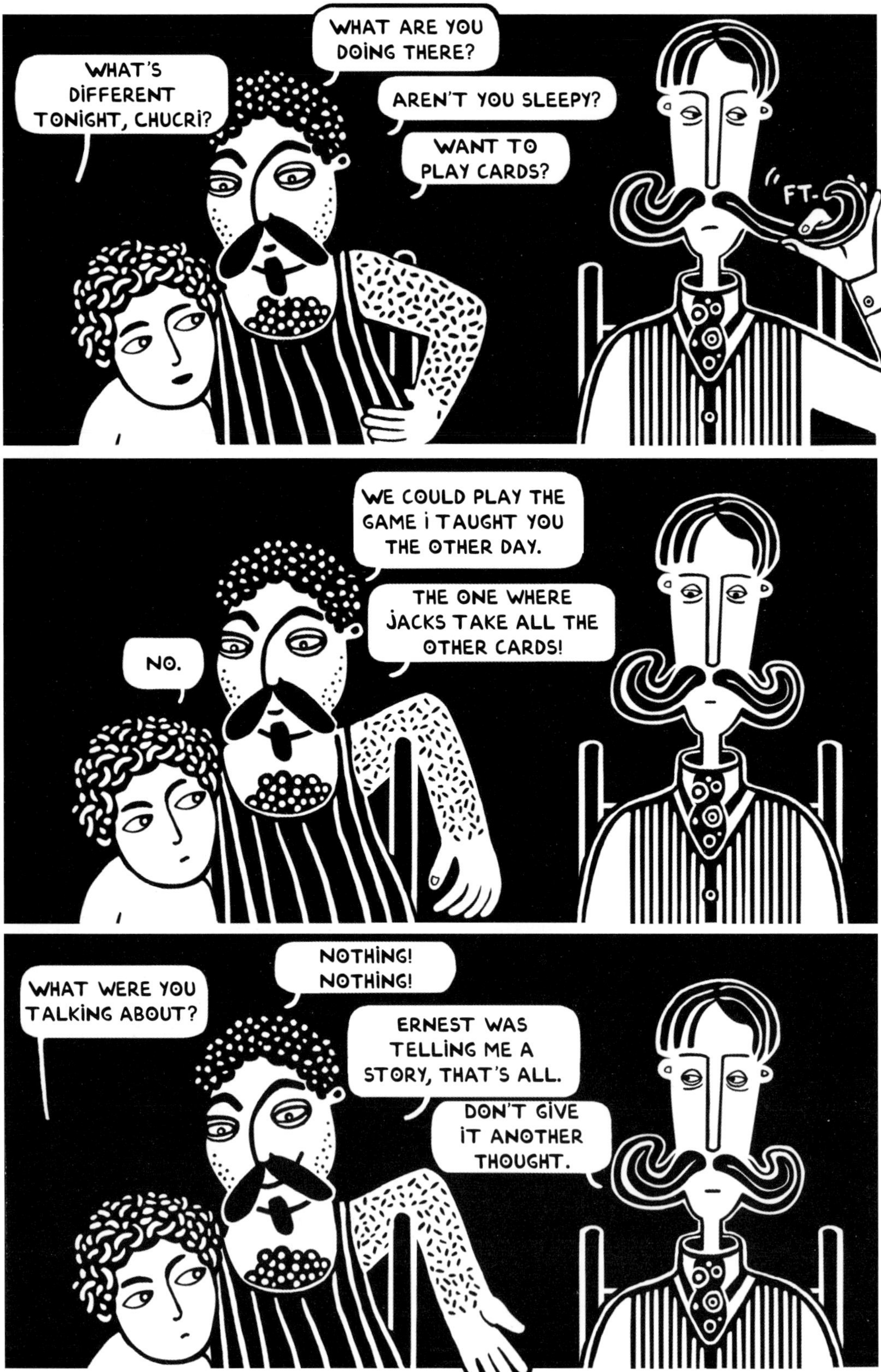

WHAT'S DIFFERENT TONIGHT, CHUCRI?
WHAT ARE YOU DOING THERE?
AREN'T YOU SLEEPY?
WANT TO PLAY CARDS?
FT-
WE COULD PLAY THE GAME I TAUGHT YOU THE OTHER DAY.
THE ONE WHERE JACKS TAKE ALL THE OTHER CARDS!
NO.
WHAT WERE YOU TALKING ABOUT?
NOTHING! NOTHING!
ERNEST WAS TELLING ME A STORY, THAT'S ALL.
DON'T GIVE IT ANOTHER THOUGHT.

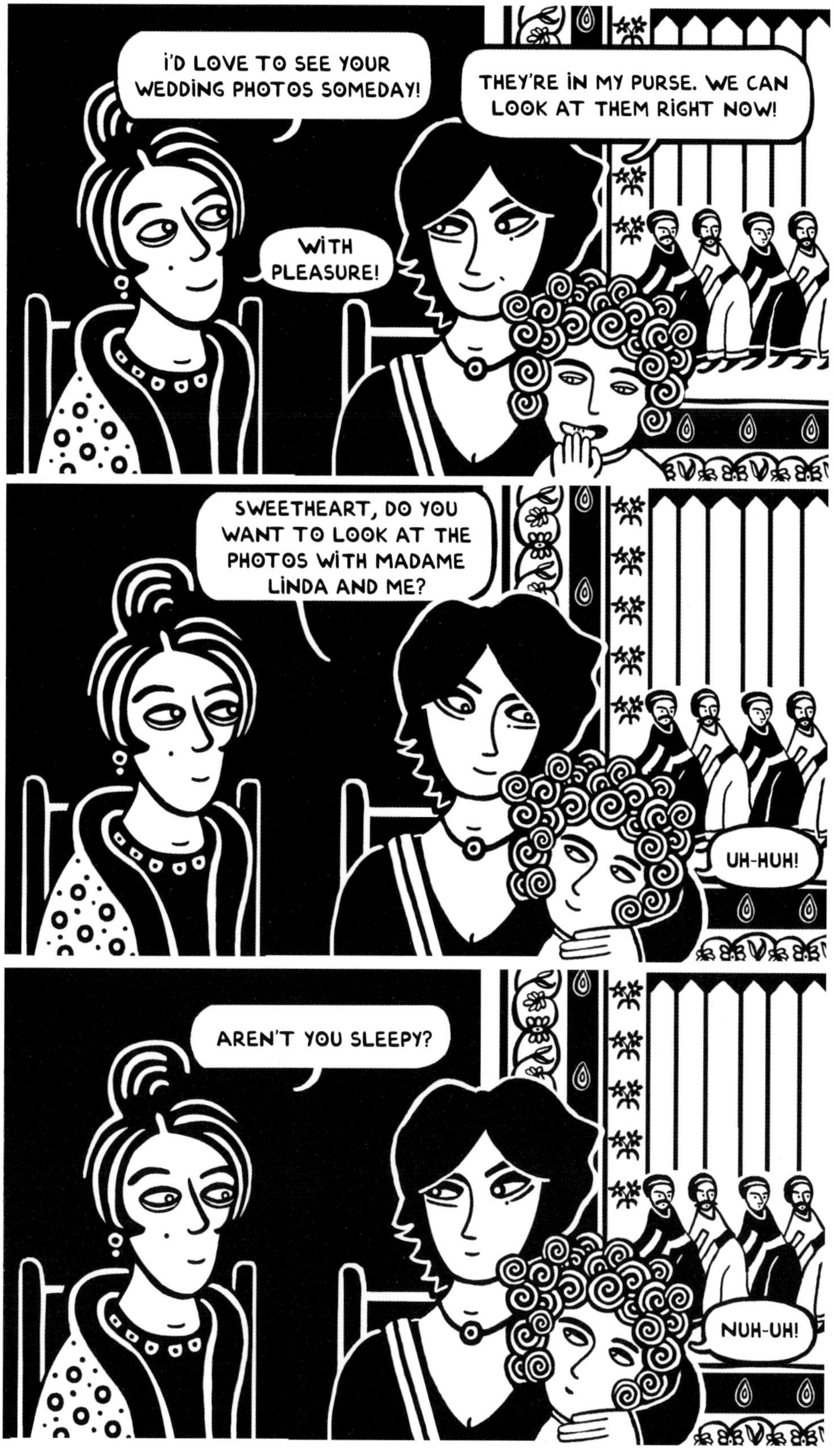
I'D LOVE TO SEE YOUR WEDDING PHOTOS SOMEDAY!
THEY'RE IN MY PURSE. WE CAN LOOK AT THEM RIGHT NOW!
WITH PLEASURE!
SWEETHEART, DO YOU WANT TO LOOK AT THE PHOTOS WITH MADAME LINDA AND ME?
UH-HUH!
AREN'T YOU SLEEPY?
NUH-UH!

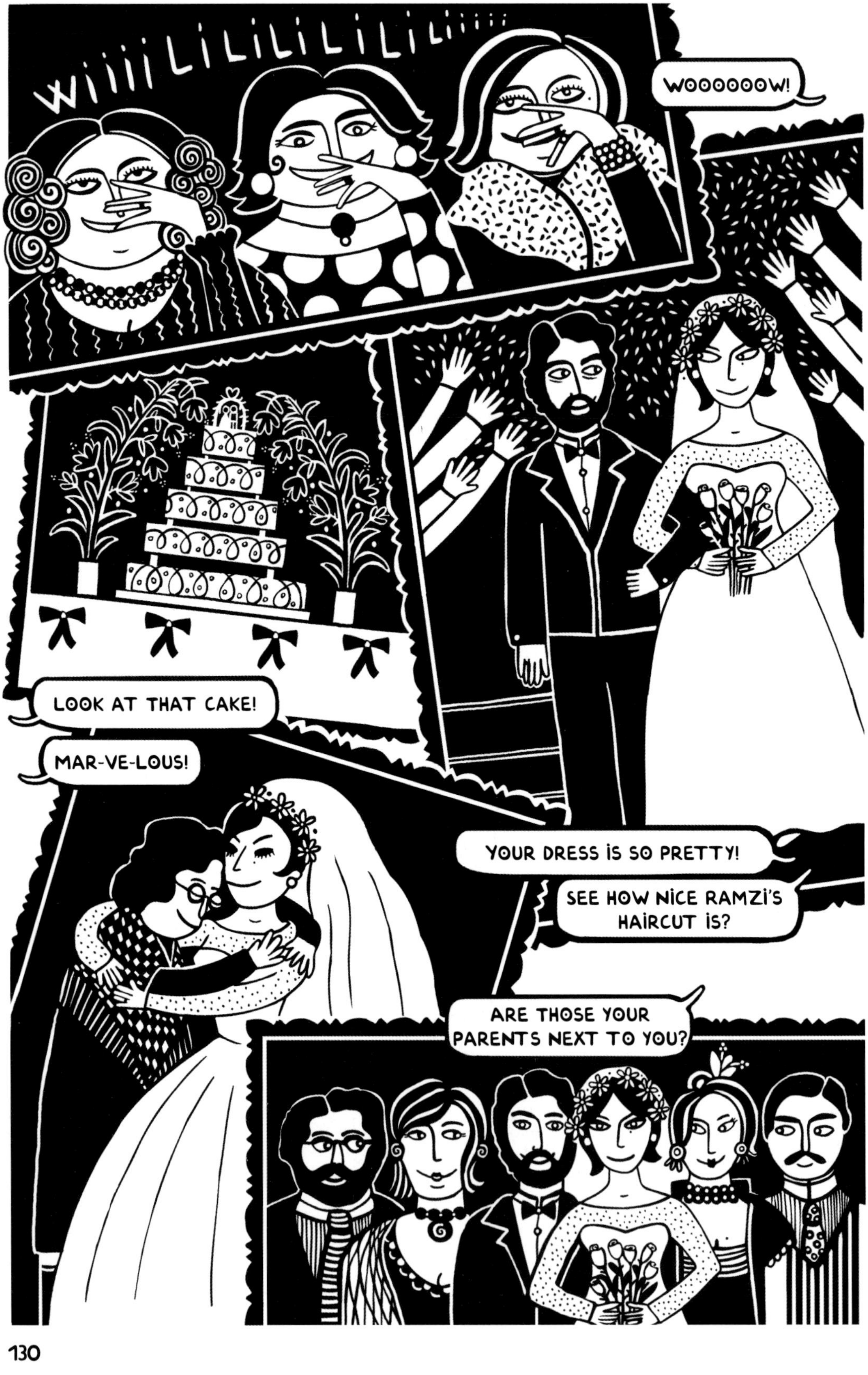
WiiiiLiLiLiLiLiiiiii
WOOOOOOW!
LOOK AT THAT CAKE!
MAR-VE-LOUS!
YOUR DRESS IS SO PRETTY!
SEE HOW NICE RAMZI'S HAIRCUT IS?
ARE THOSE YOUR PARENTS NEXT TO YOU?

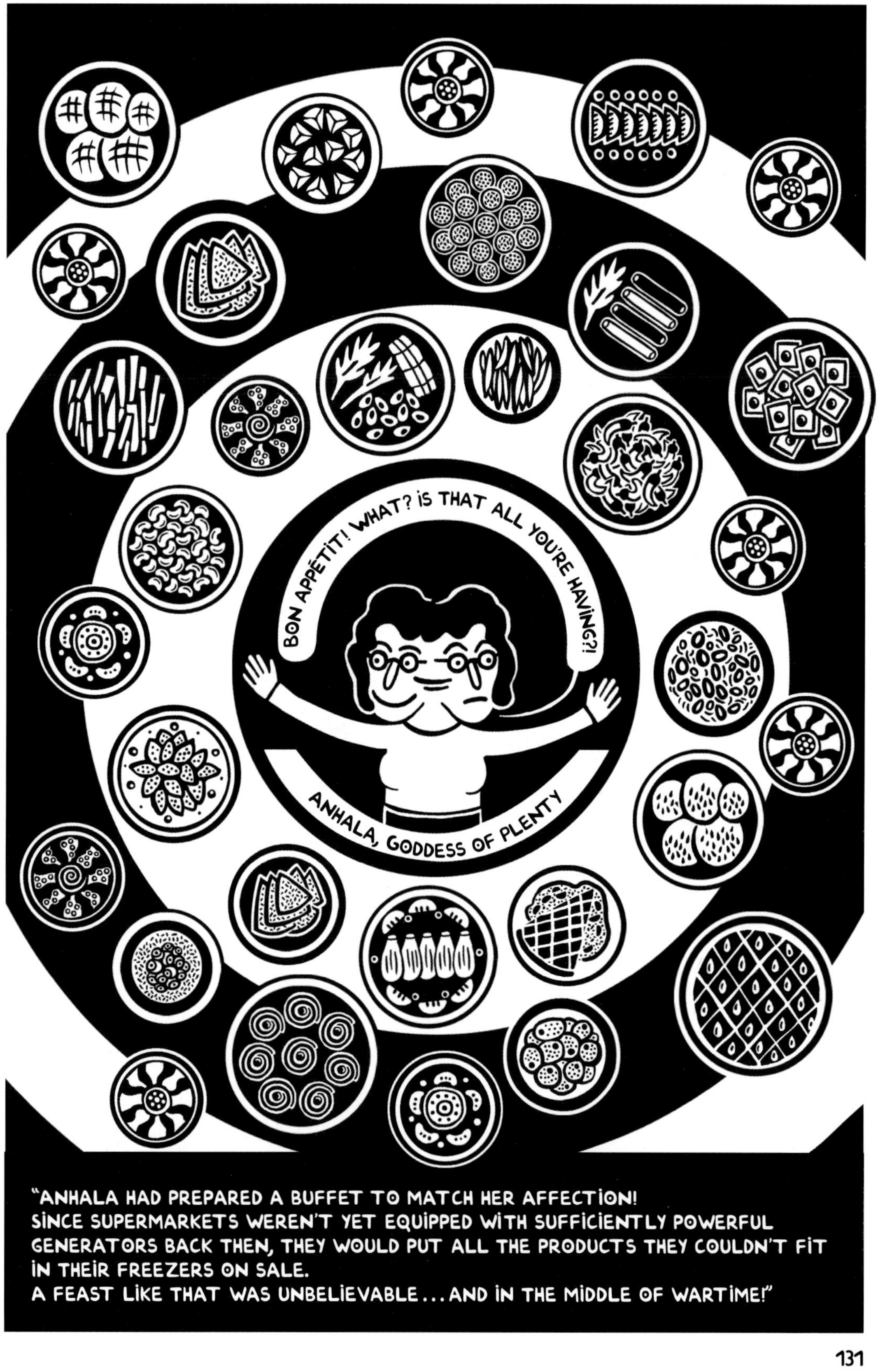
BON APPÉTIT! WHAT? IS THAT ALL YOU'RE HAVING?!
ANHALA, GODDESS OF PLENTY

"ANHALA HAD PREPARED A BUFFET TO MATCH HER AFFECTION!
SINCE SUPERMARKETS WEREN'T YET EQUIPPED WITH SUFFICIENTLY POWERFUL GENERATORS BACK THEN, THEY WOULD PUT ALL THE PRODUCTS THEY COULDN'T FIT IN THEIR FREEZERS ON SALE.
A FEAST LIKE THAT WAS UNBELIEVABLE ... AND IN THE MIDDLE OF WARTIME!"

"MAMA INSISTED WE HAVE MY DRESS MADE BY THE EMINENT DESIGNER COUSSA, WHO'D DESIGNED HER OWN WEDDING DRESS. BACK THEN IT WAS HIM, THAT IS. NOW HIS SON HAD TAKEN OVER THE STUDIO.
NEXT, JEAN, THE SHOEMAKER ON GHANDOUR EL-SAAD STREET, DESIGNED WHITE SHOES WITH BUTTON STRAPS THAT MATCHED MY DRESS. HE STUDIED IN ITALY, YOU KNOW! ON THE WEDDING DAY, FOUAD, THE STYLIST AT THE MA BELLE SALON, CAME TO THE HOUSE TO DO MY HAIR.
I WAS TREATED LIKE A REAL PRINCESS!"

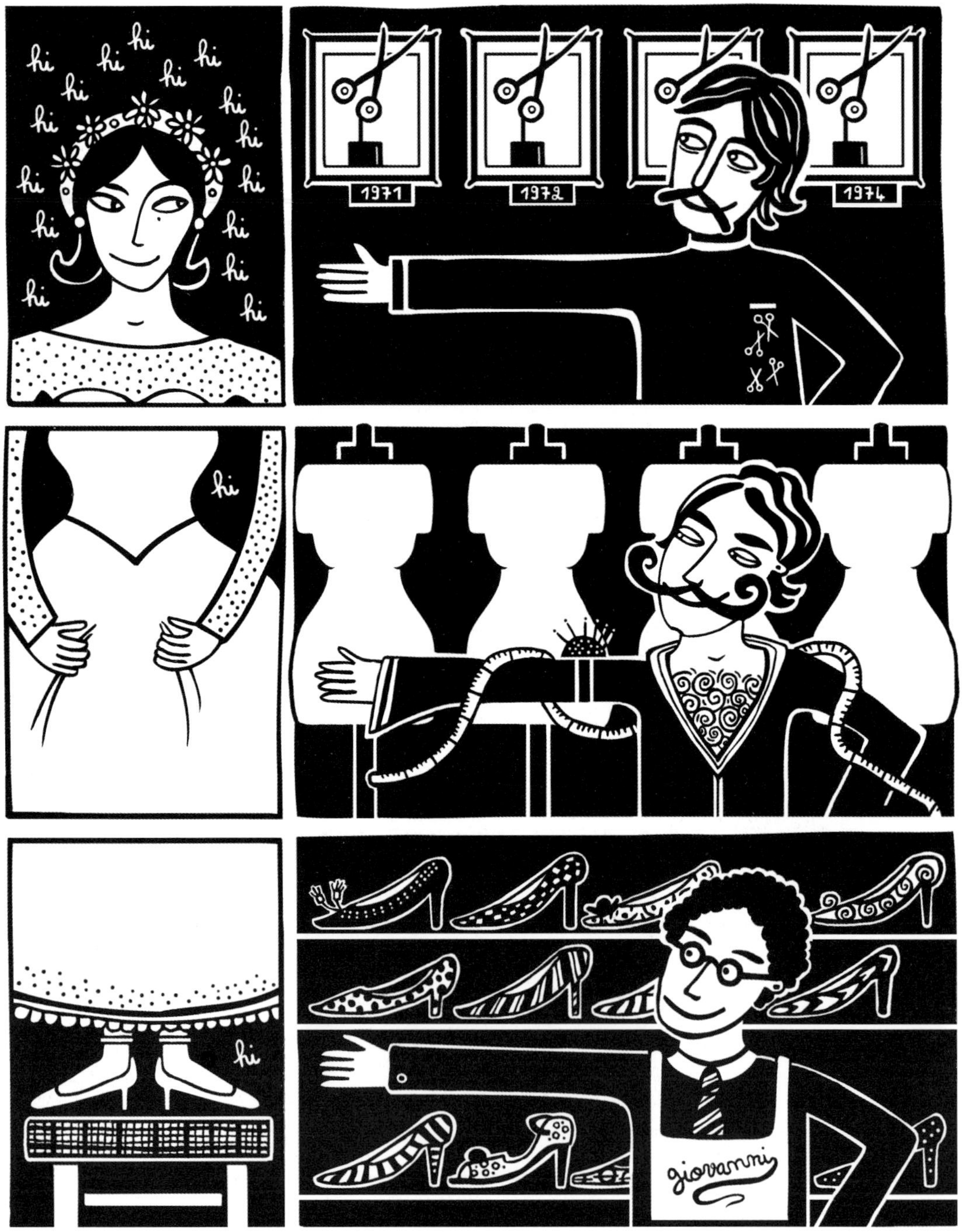
hi
hi
hi
hi
hi
hi
hi
hi
hi
hi
hi
hi
hi
hi
hi
hi
1971
1972
1974
hi
hi
giovanni

"MAMA ABSOLUTELY INSISTED ON ACTING AS IF EVERYTHING WERE NORMAL— WHEN SHE WAS THE ONE WHO'D RALLIED EVERYONE!
JAMAL, THE BEAUTICIAN AT MA BELLE, CAME TO DO MY MAKEUP. HIS YOUNGER SISTER PATRICIA CAME WITH HIM, WITH HER TWEEZER KIT AND OTHER INSTRUMENTS OF TORTURE...
AND SAMIA, WHO'D TAKEN CARE OF MAMA'S NAILS FOREVER, GAVE ME A MEMORABLE MANICURE AND PEDICURE, IN MY ROOM AT MY PARENTS' HOUSE!"

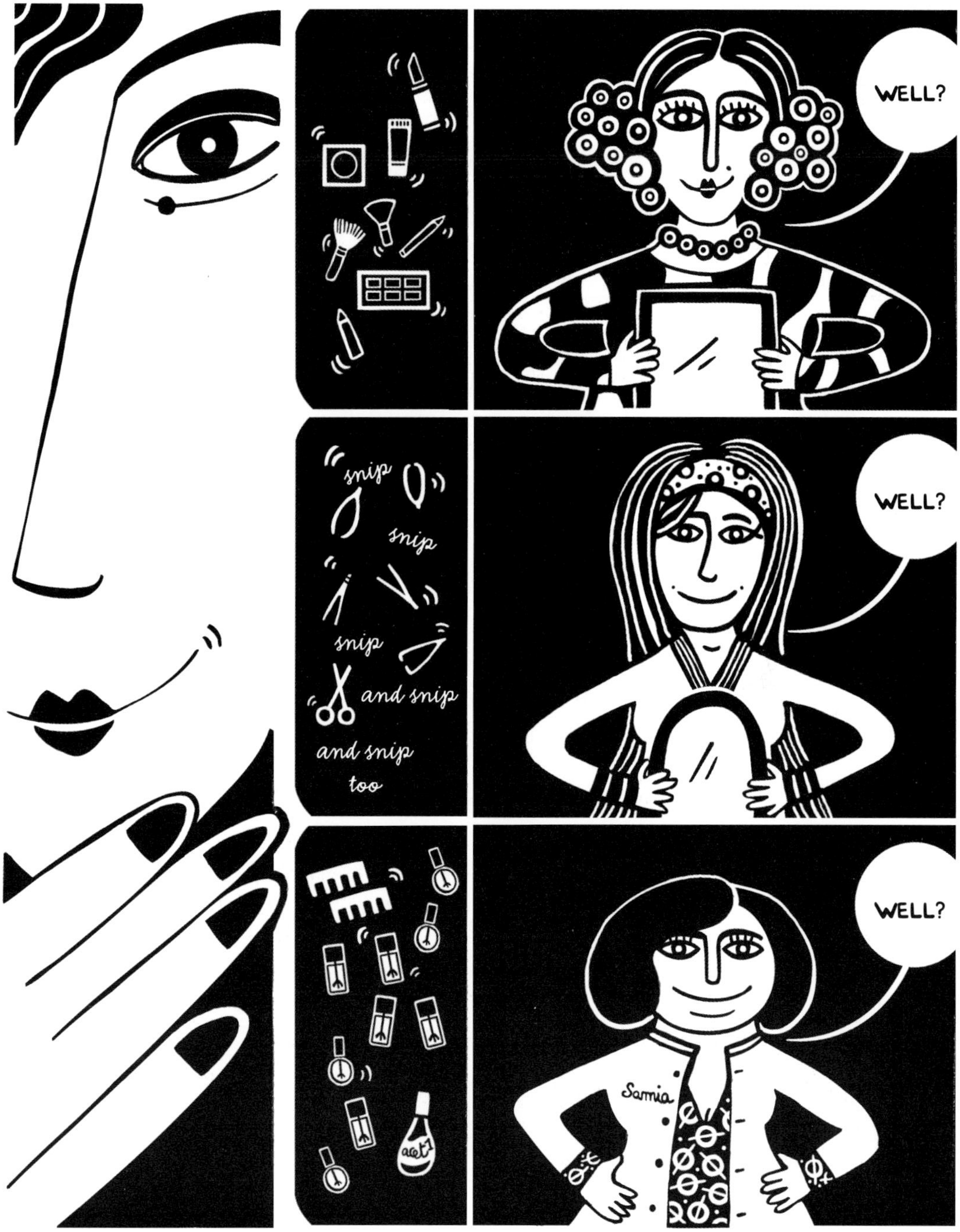
WELL?
snip
snip
snip
and snip
and snip too
WELL?
WELL?
Samia

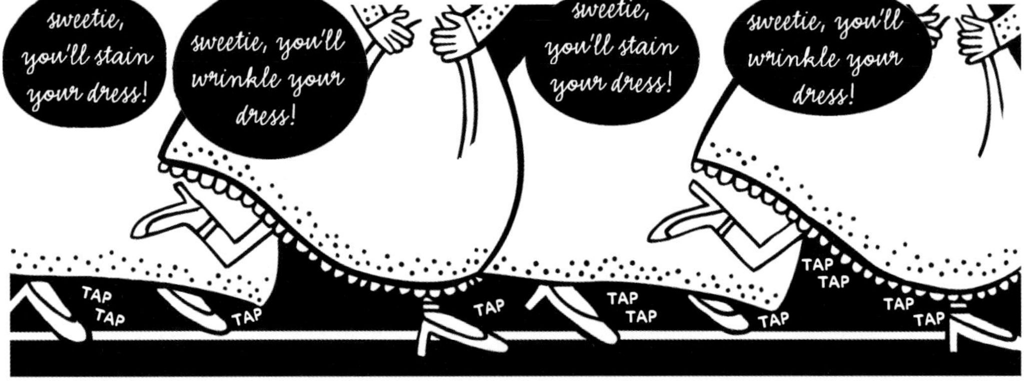
sweetie, you'll stain your dress!
sweetie, you'll wrinkle your dress!
sweetie, you'll stain your dress!
sweetie, you'll wrinkle your dress!
TAP TAP
TAP
TAP
TAP TAP
TAP TAP
TAP
TAP TAP

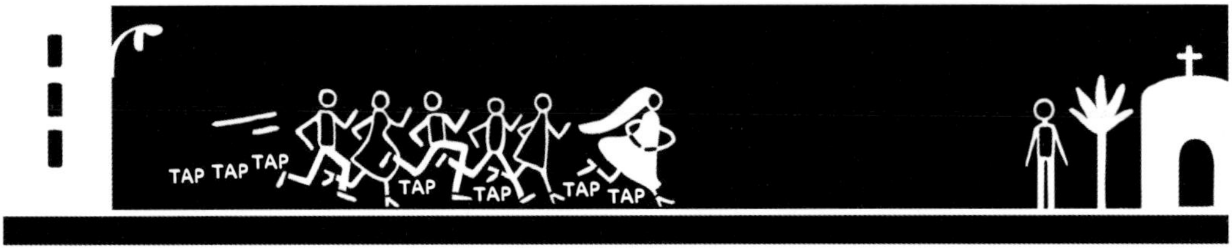
TAP TAP TAP
TAP
TAP
TAP TAP

"I DON'T REMEMBER THE RELIGIOUS CEREMONY VERY WELL ANYMORE.
SINCE RAMZI WAS A MARONITE, WE WERE MARRIED ACCORDING TO THE MARONITE RITE. QUITE PRACTICAL, IN THE END!
FIRST OF ALL: BECAUSE THERE WAS A MARONITE CHURCH RIGHT ACROSS FROM MY PARENTS' HOUSE.
NEXT: BECAUSE THE CEREMONY WAS SHORTER THAN THE ORTHODOX ONE.
IT REASSURED ALL THE GUESTS TO KNOW WE WOULDN'T SPEND MUCH TIME OUTSIDE THE HOUSE!

I REMEMBER THAT TO AVOID THE SNIPER, WE HAD TO RUN FROM MY PARENTS' HOUSE TO THE CHURCH AND THEN FROM THE CHURCH BACK TO MY PARENTS.

MAMA WAS SO STRESSED OUT BY THE CROSSING BACK AND FORTH THAT SHE STARTED FIXATING ON MY DRESS!"

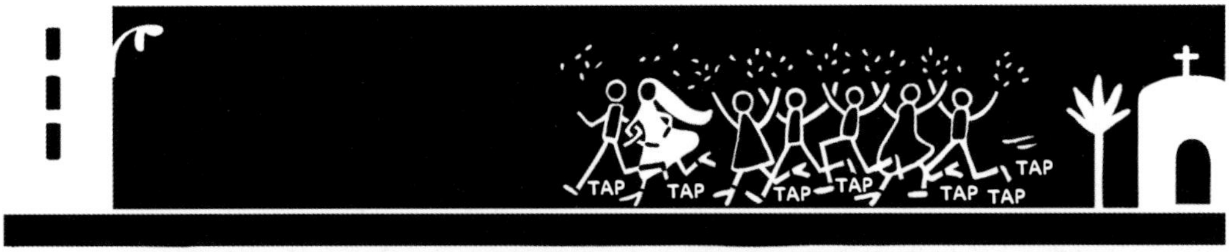
TAP
TAP
TAP
TAP
TAP TAP
TAP

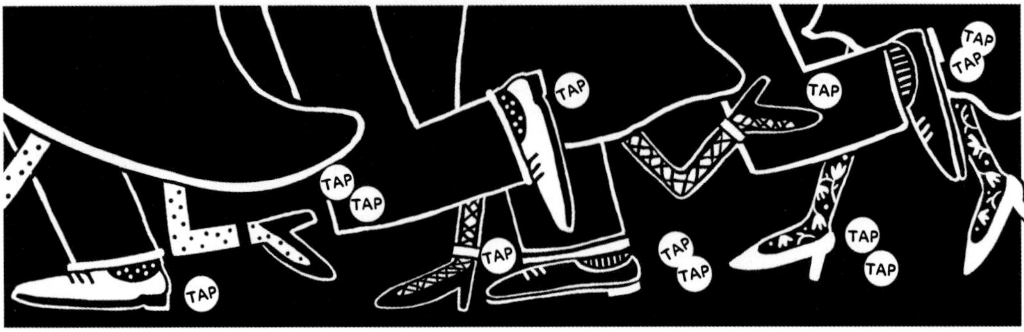
TAP TAP
TAP
TAP
TAP TAP
TAP
TAP TAP
TAP TAP
TAP

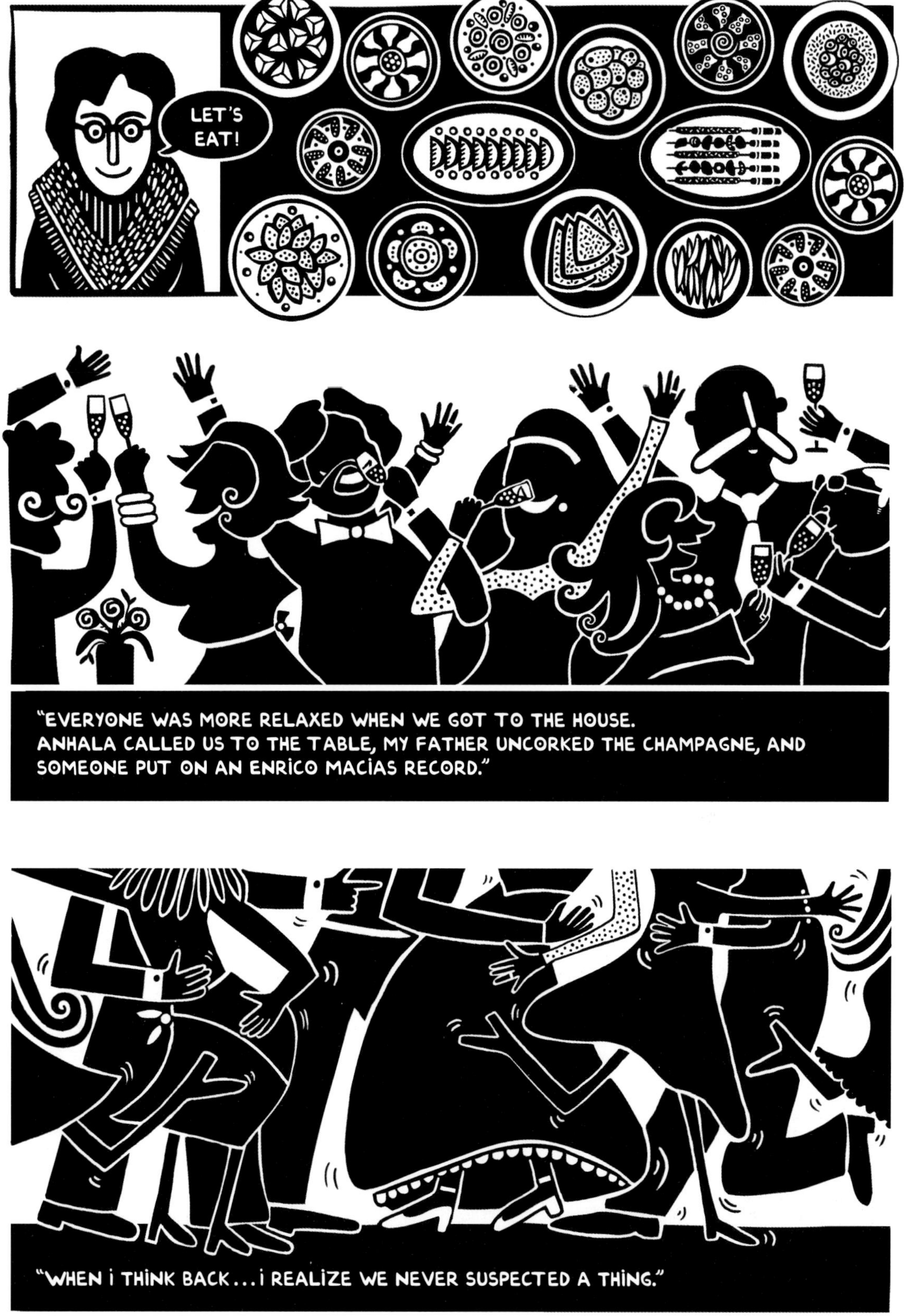
LET'S EAT!
"EVERYONE WAS MORE RELAXED WHEN WE GOT TO THE HOUSE. ANHALA CALLED US TO THE TABLE, MY FATHER UNCORKED THE CHAMPAGNE, AND SOMEONE PUT ON AN ENRICO MACIAS RECORD."
"WHEN I THINK BACK... I REALIZE WE NEVER SUSPECTED A THING."

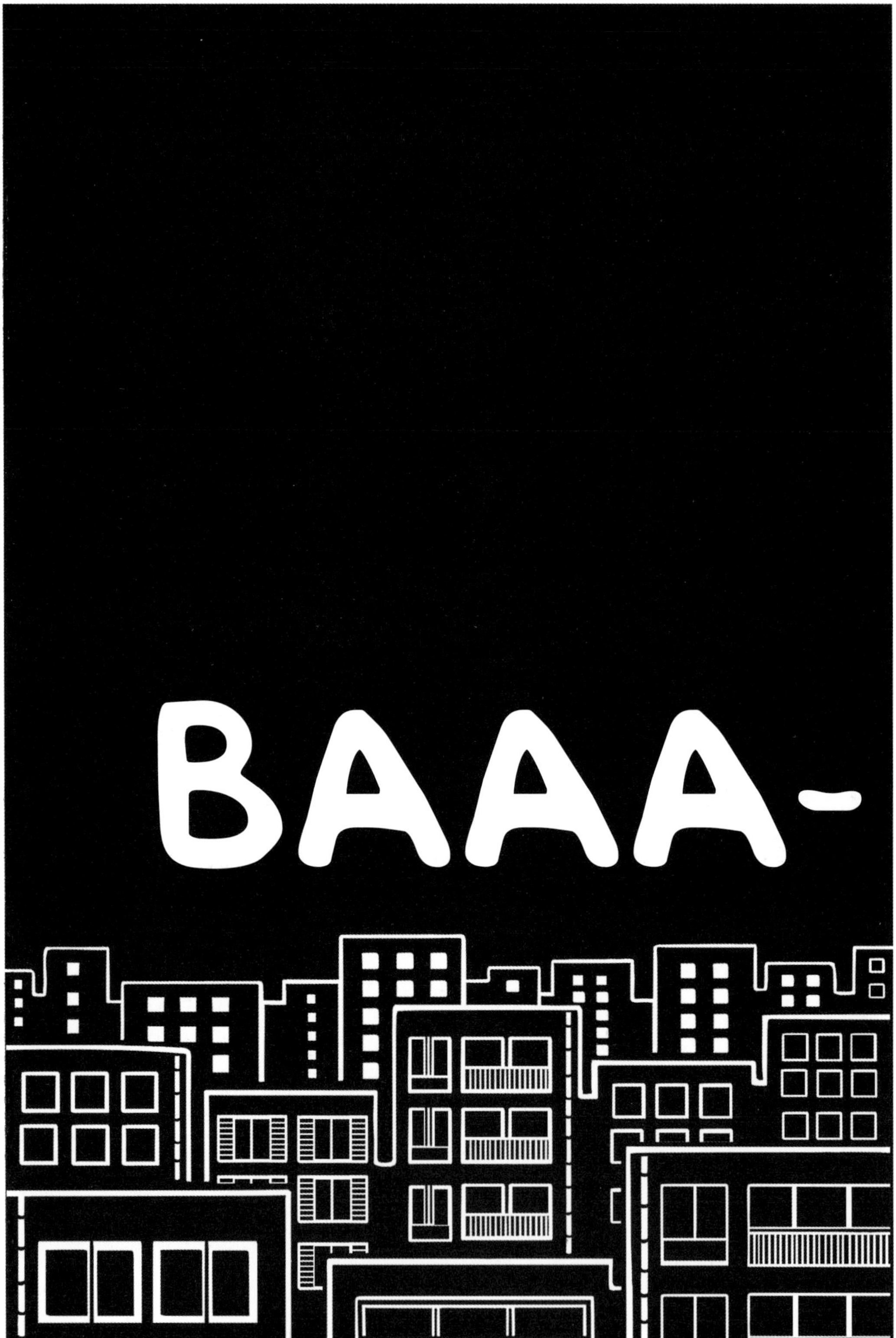
BAAA-

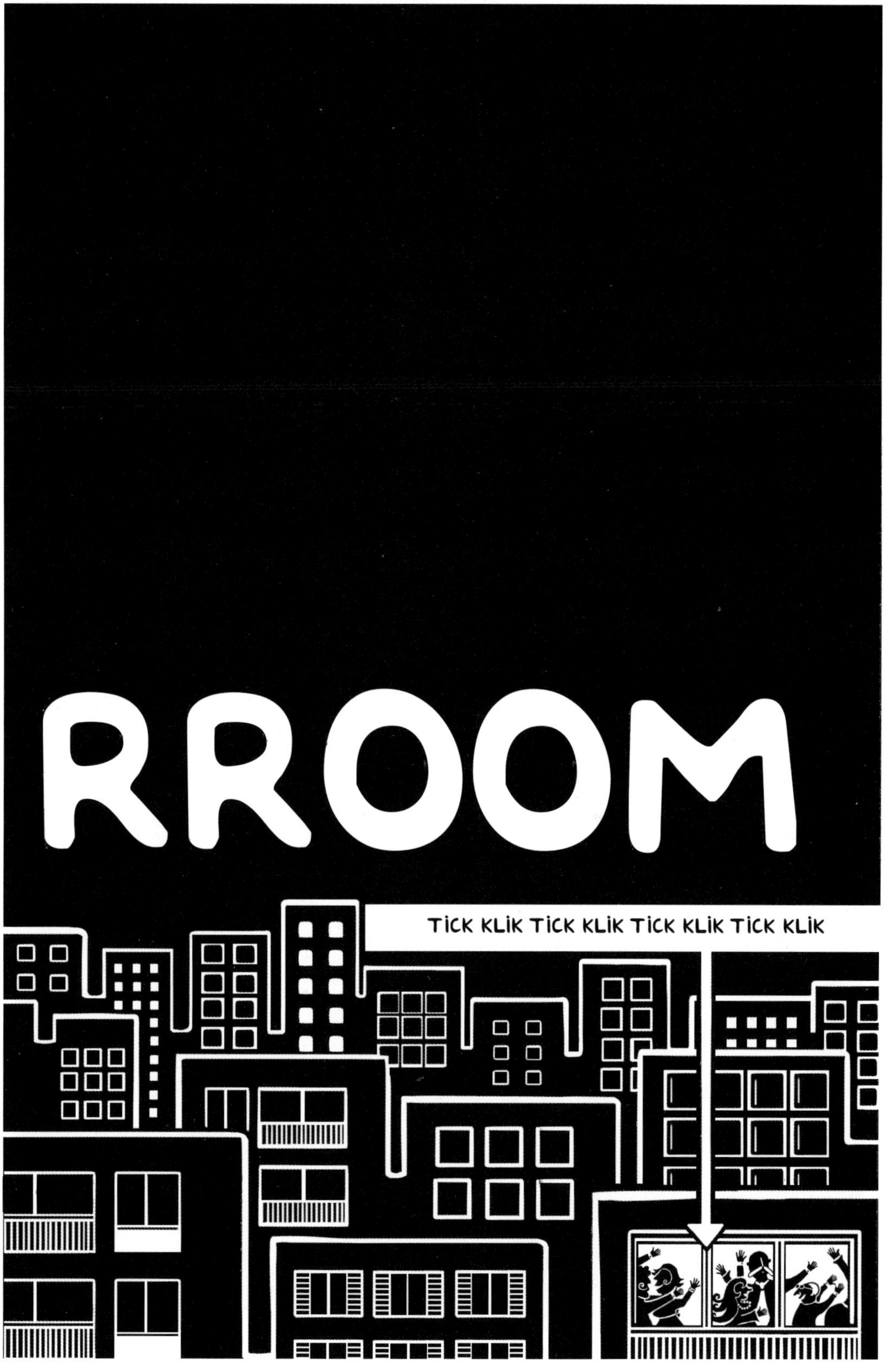
RROOM
TICK KLIK TICK KLIK TICK KLIK TICK KLIK

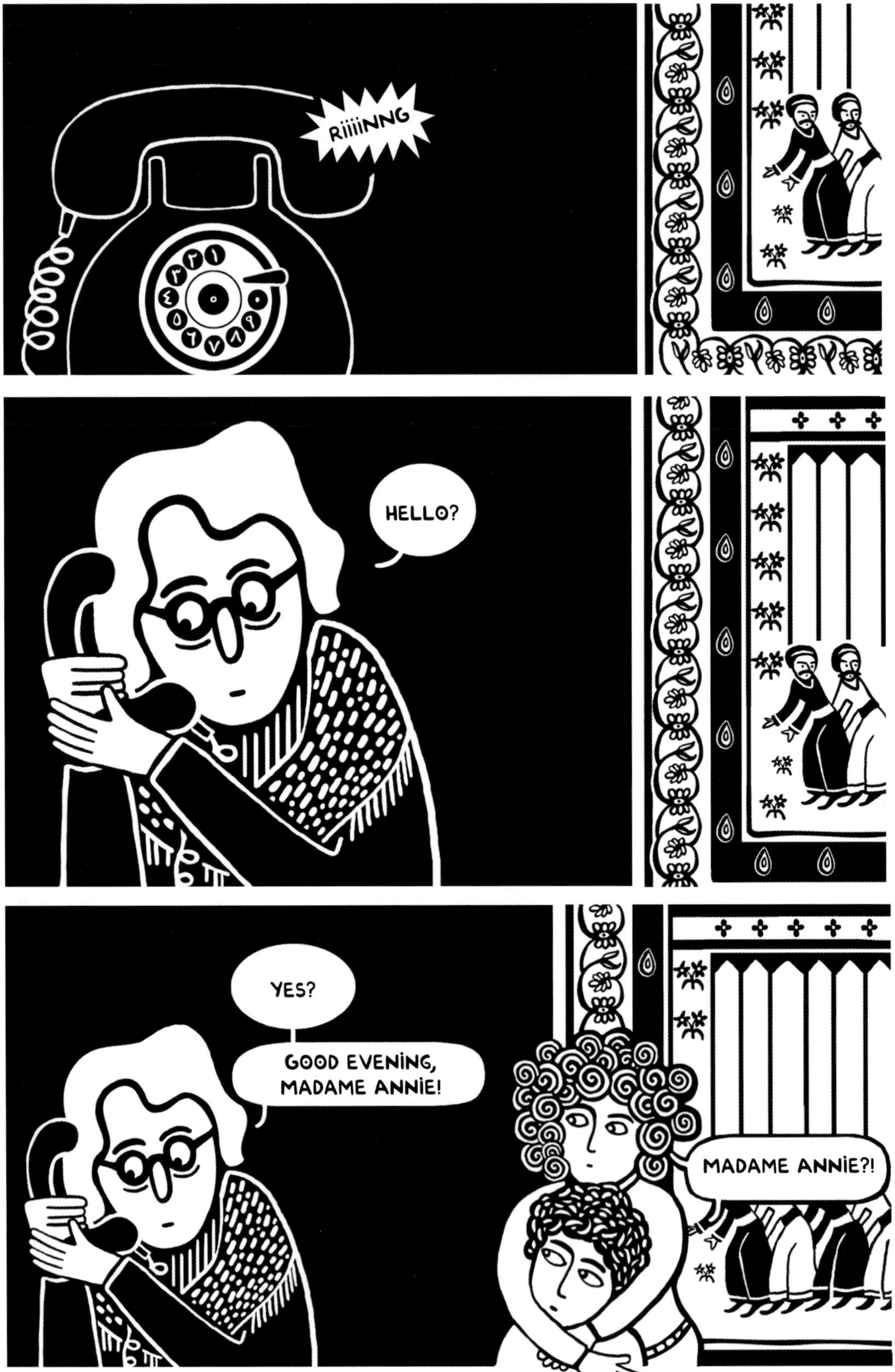
RiiiiNNG
HELLO?
YES?
GOOD EVENiNG, MADAME ANNiE!
MADAME ANNiE?!

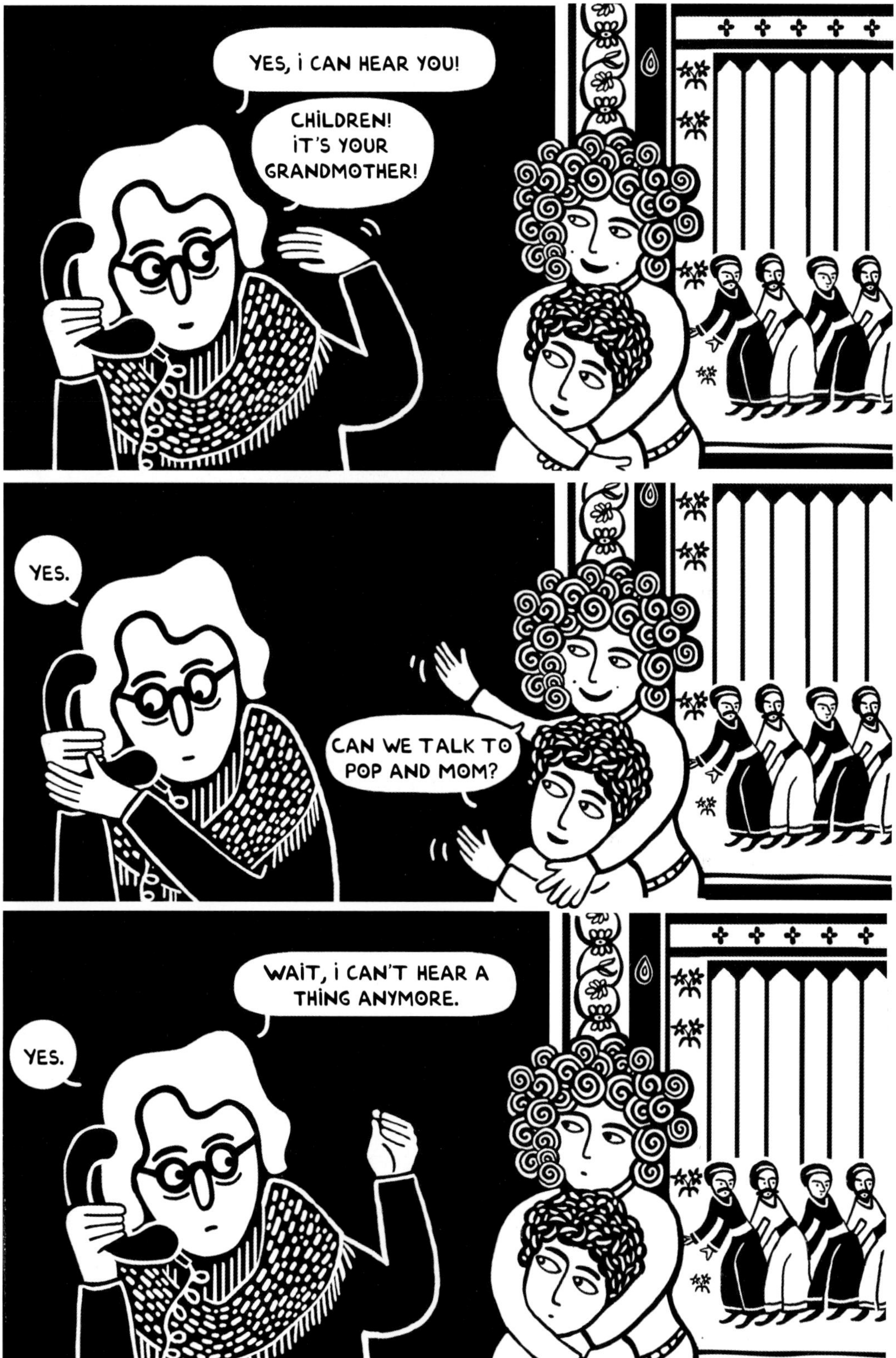
YES, I CAN HEAR YOU!
CHILDREN! IT'S YOUR GRANDMOTHER!
YES.
CAN WE TALK TO POP AND MOM?
WAIT, I CAN'T HEAR A THING ANYMORE.
YES.

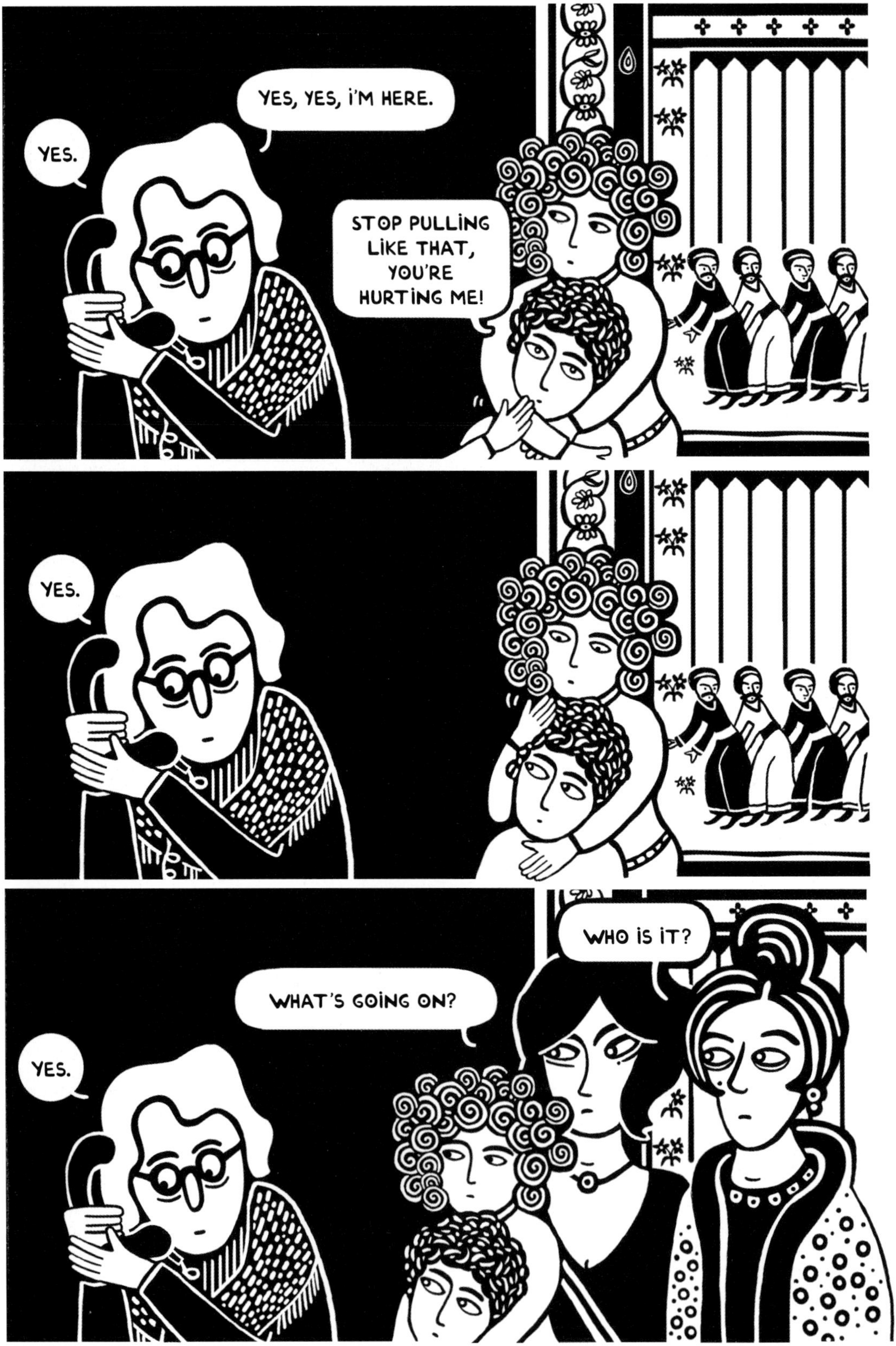
YES.
YES, YES, I'M HERE.
STOP PULLING LIKE THAT, YOU'RE HURTING ME!
YES.
YES.
WHAT'S GOING ON?
WHO IS IT?

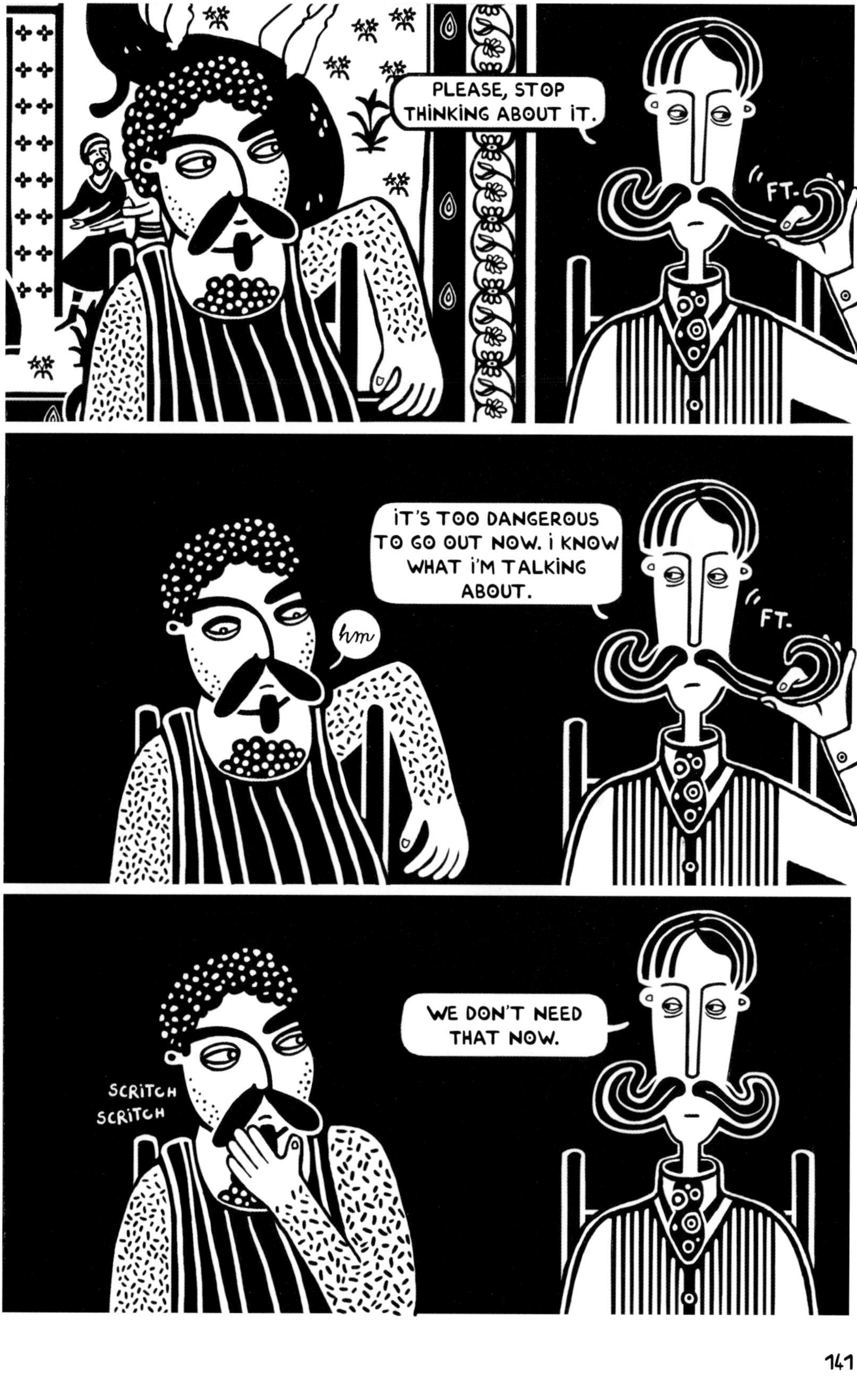
PLEASE, STOP THINKING ABOUT IT.
FT-
IT'S TOO DANGEROUS TO GO OUT NOW. I KNOW WHAT I'M TALKING ABOUT.
FT.
hm
WE DON'T NEED THAT NOW.
SCRITCH SCRITCH

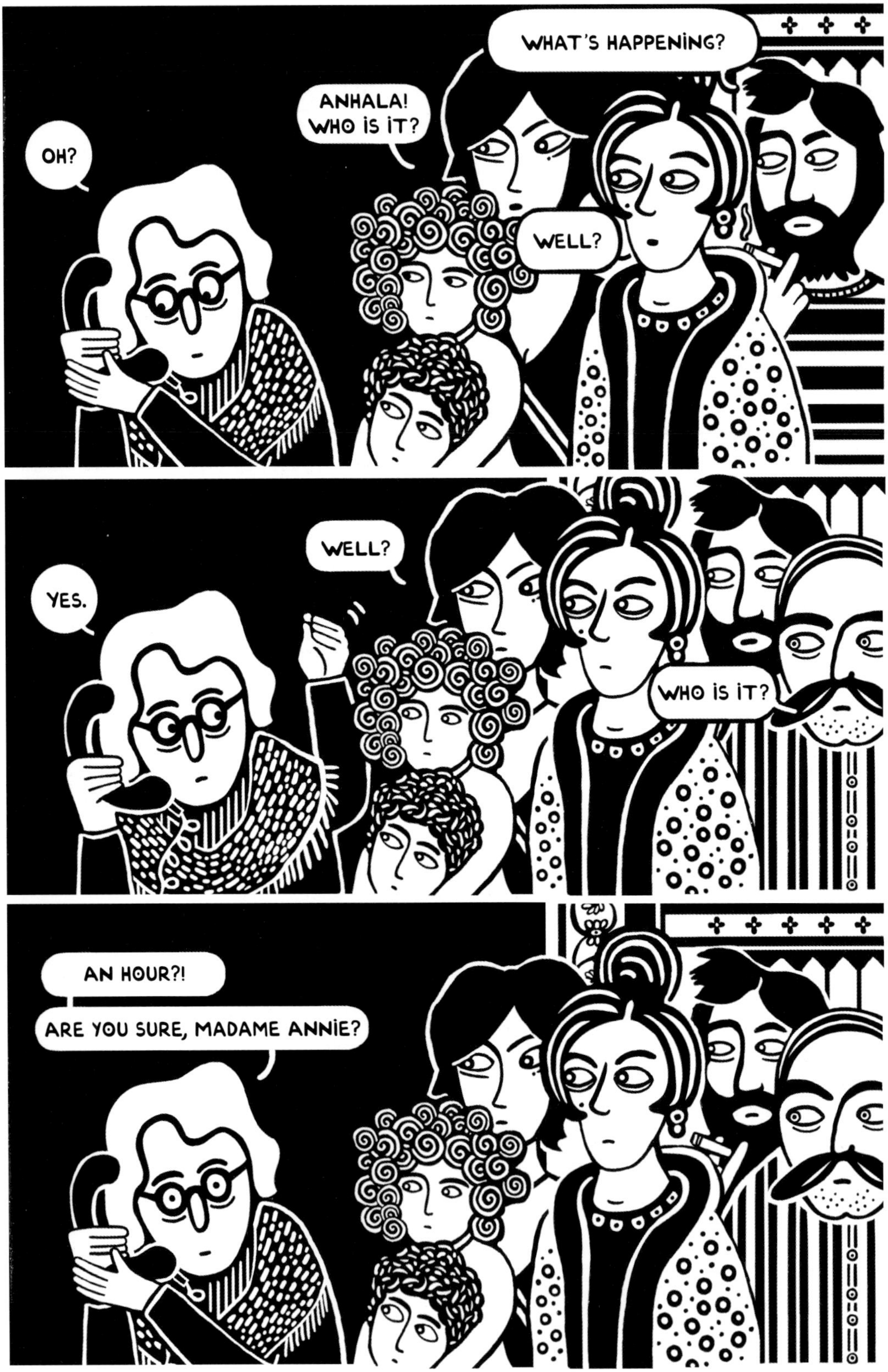

OH?
ANHALA! WHO IS IT?
WHAT'S HAPPENING?
WELL?
YES.
WELL?
WHO IS IT?
AN HOUR?!
ARE YOU SURE, MADAME ANNIE?

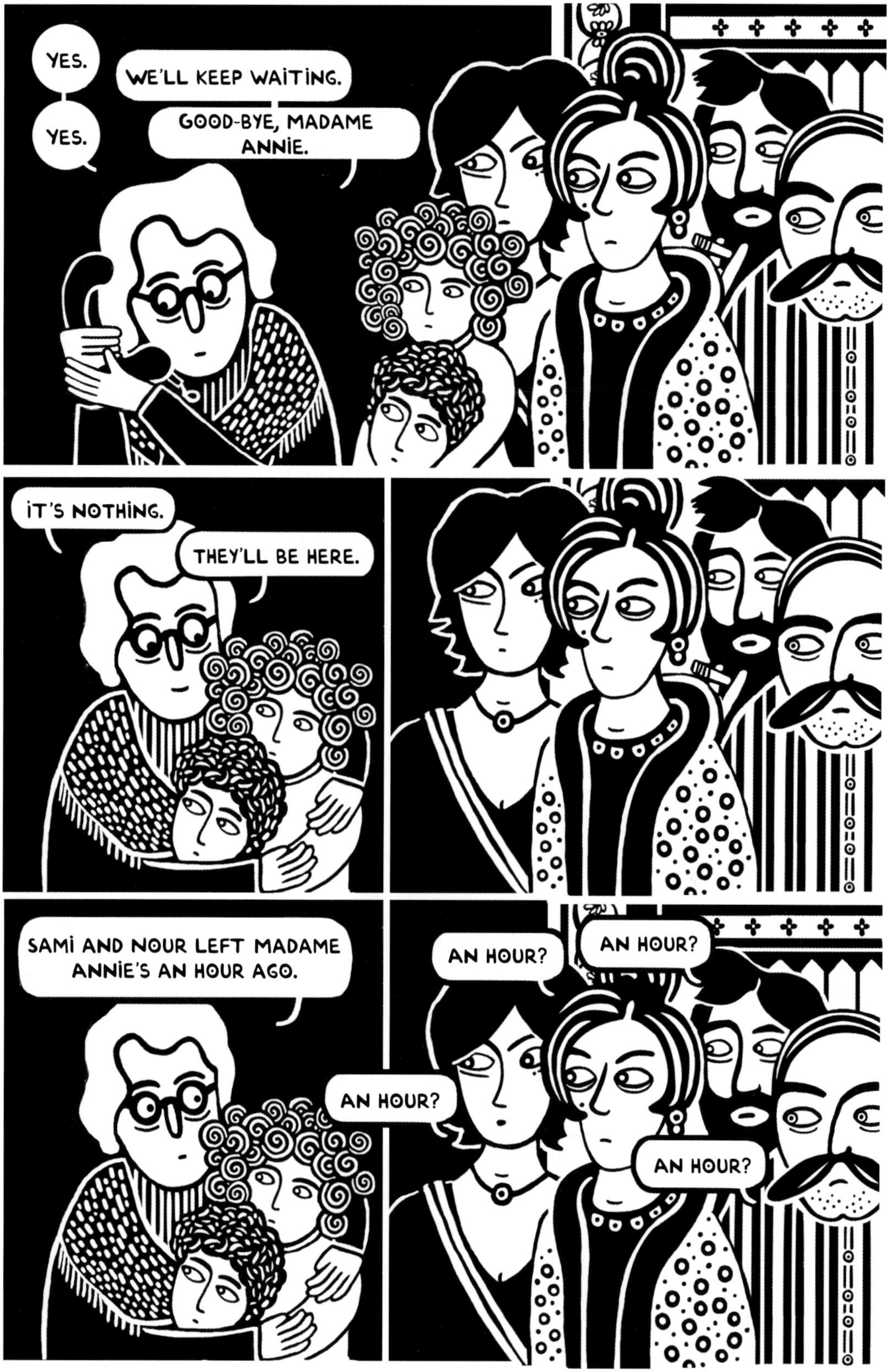
YES.
YES.
WE'LL KEEP WAITING.
GOOD-BYE, MADAME ANNIE.
IT'S NOTHING.
THEY'LL BE HERE.
SAMI AND NOUR LEFT MADAME ANNIE'S AN HOUR AGO.
AN HOUR?
AN HOUR?
AN HOUR?
AN HOUR?

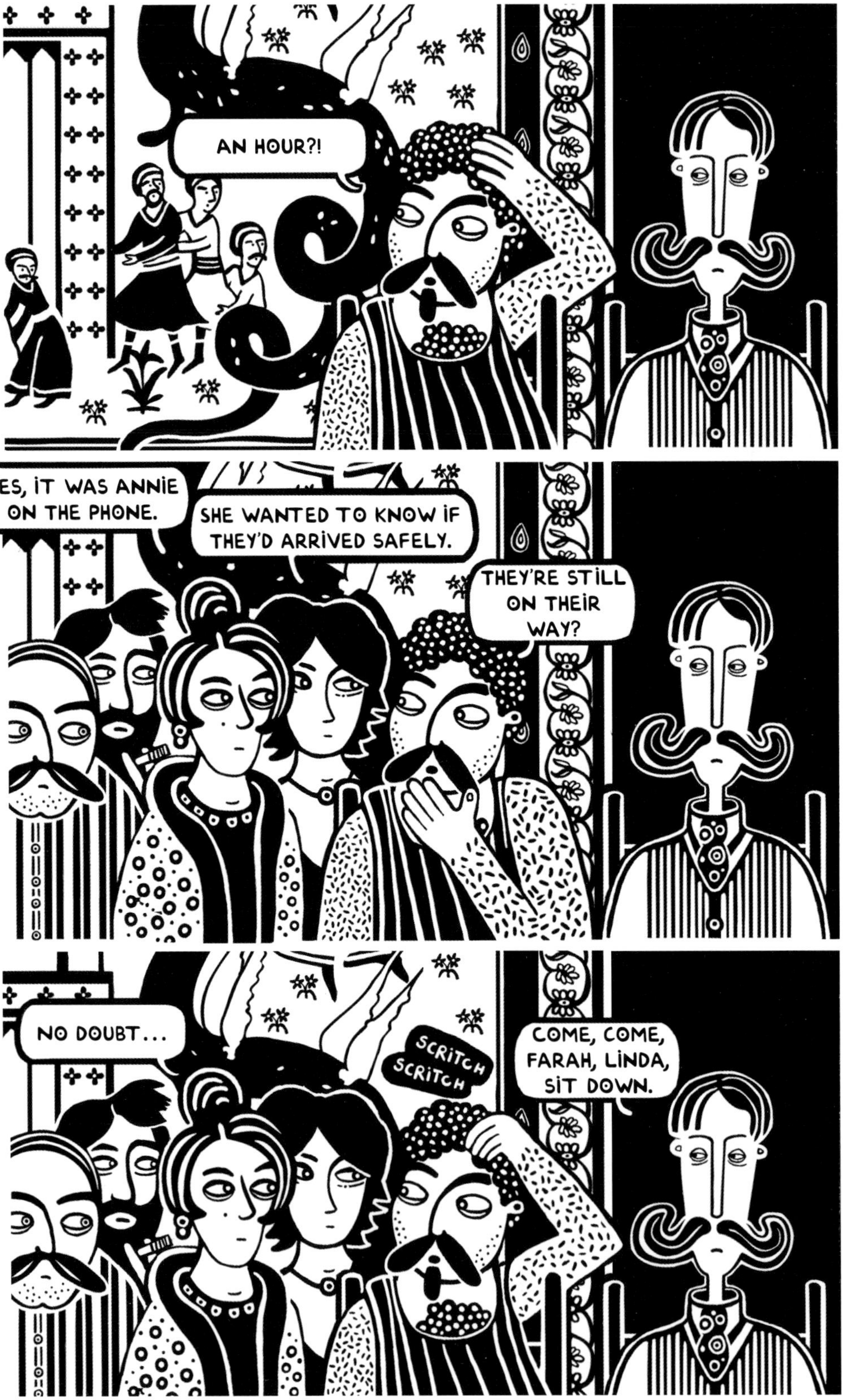
AN HOUR?!
YES, IT WAS ANNIE ON THE PHONE.
SHE WANTED TO KNOW IF THEY'D ARRIVED SAFELY.
THEY'RE STILL ON THEIR WAY?
NO DOUBT...
SCRITCH SCRITCH
COME, COME, FARAH, LINDA, SIT DOWN.

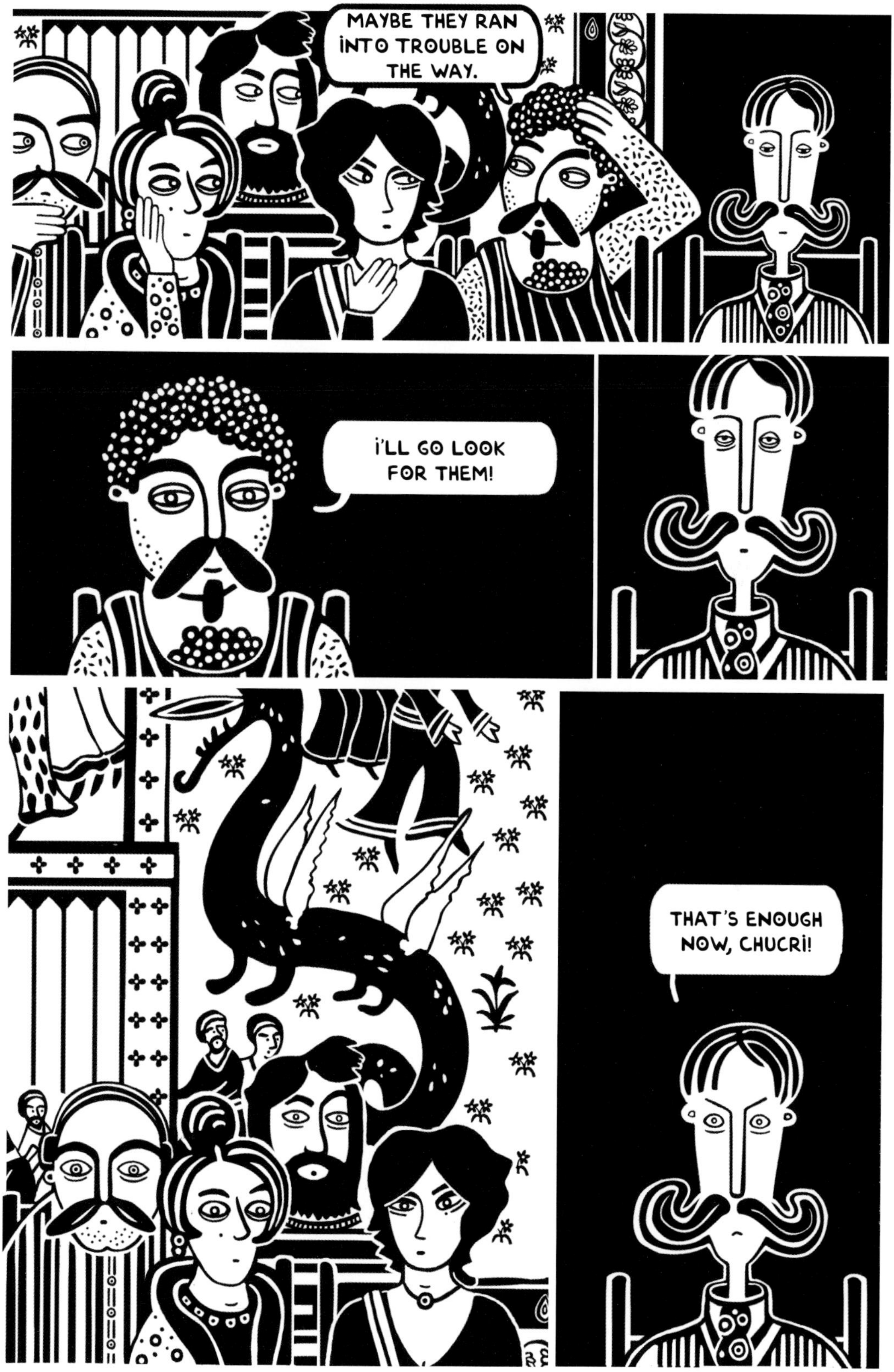
MAYBE THEY RAN INTO TROUBLE ON THE WAY.
I'LL GO LOOK FOR THEM!
THAT'S ENOUGH NOW, CHUCRI!

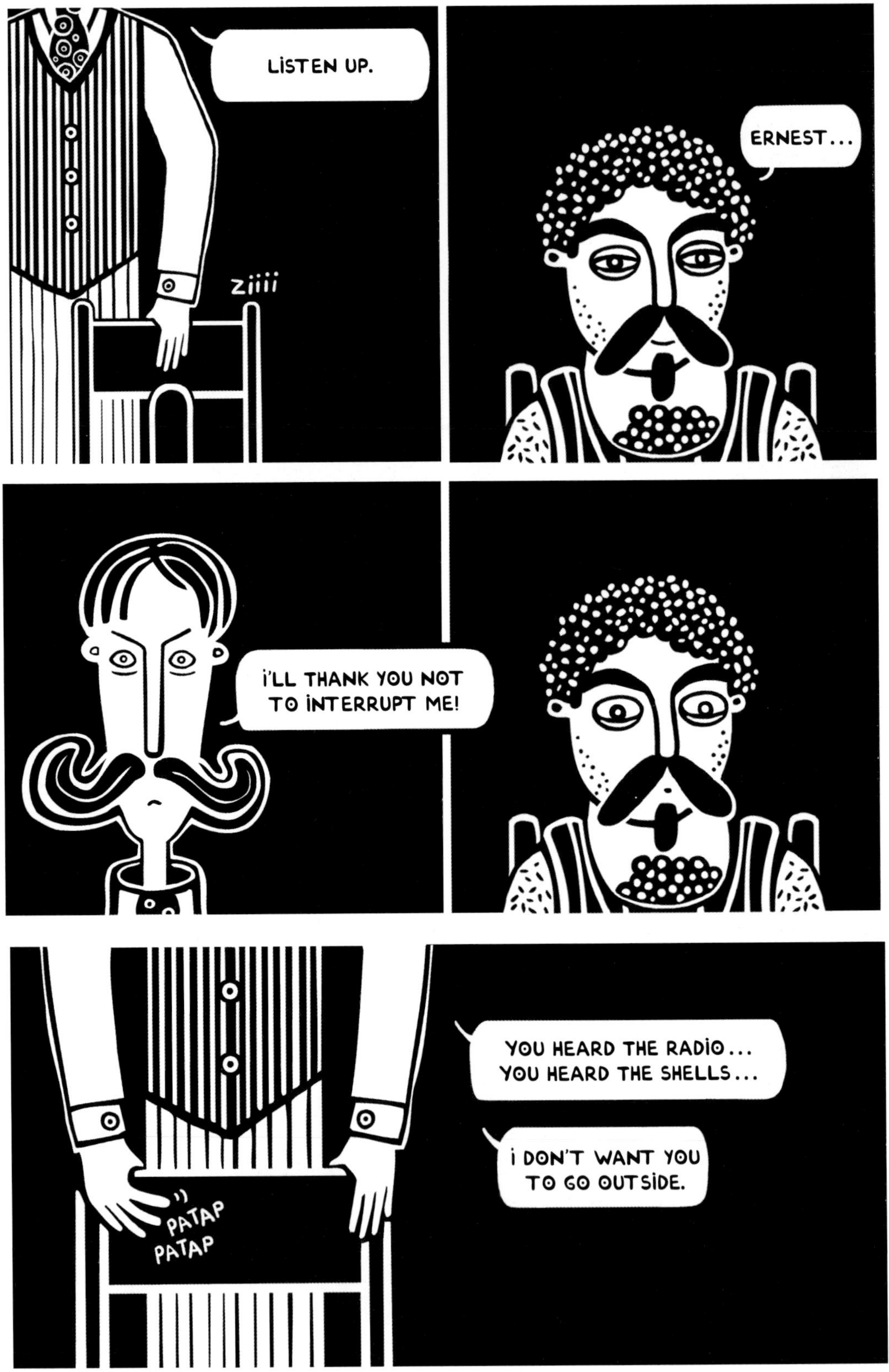
LISTEN UP.
ZIIII
ERNEST...
I'LL THANK YOU NOT TO INTERRUPT ME!
YOU HEARD THE RADIO... YOU HEARD THE SHELLS...
I DON'T WANT YOU TO GO OUTSIDE.
PATAP PATAP

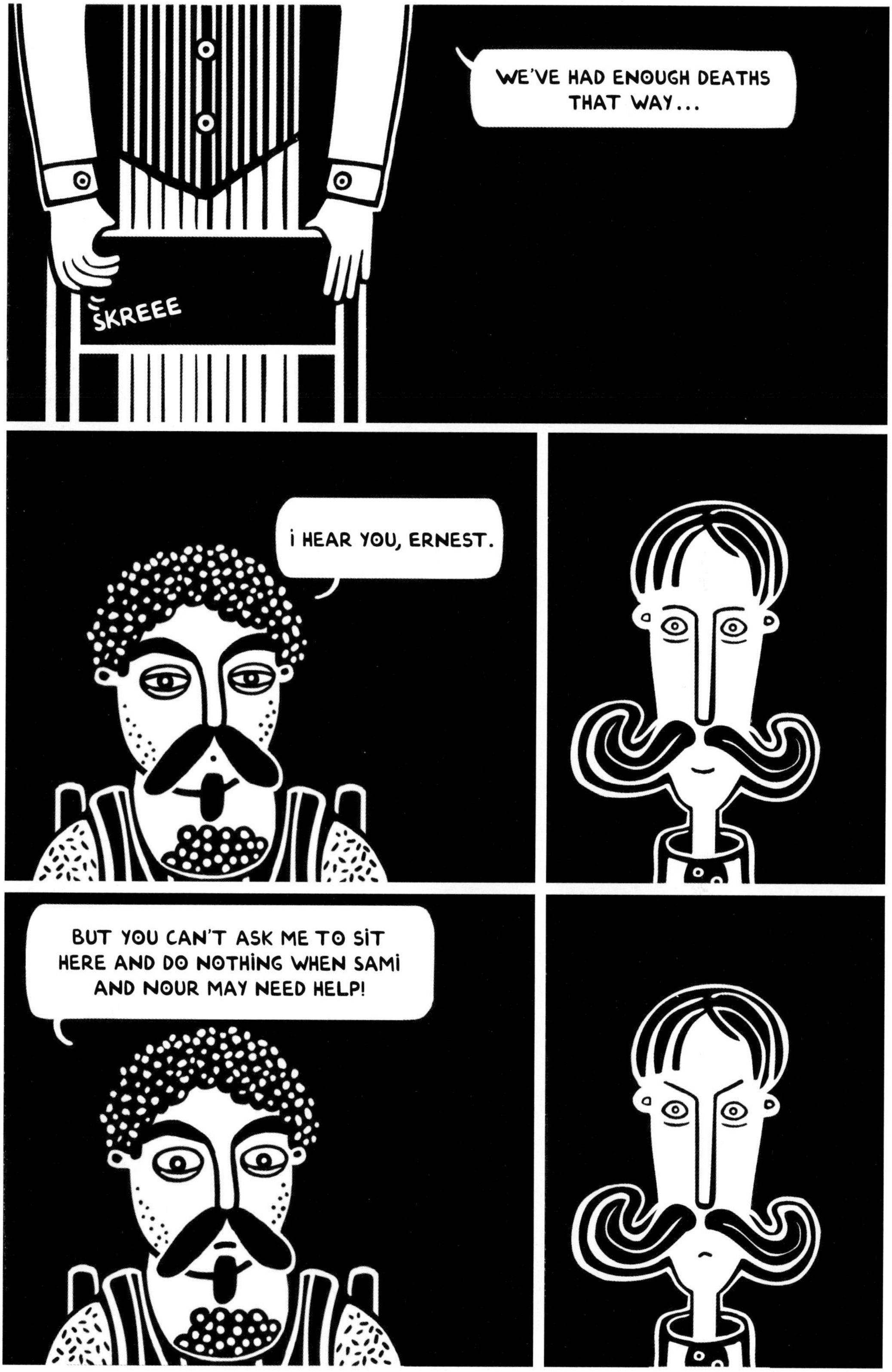
SKREEE
WE'VE HAD ENOUGH DEATHS THAT WAY...
i HEAR YOU, ERNEST.
BUT YOU CAN'T ASK ME TO SiT HERE AND DO NOTHiNG WHEN SAMi AND NOUR MAY NEED HELP!

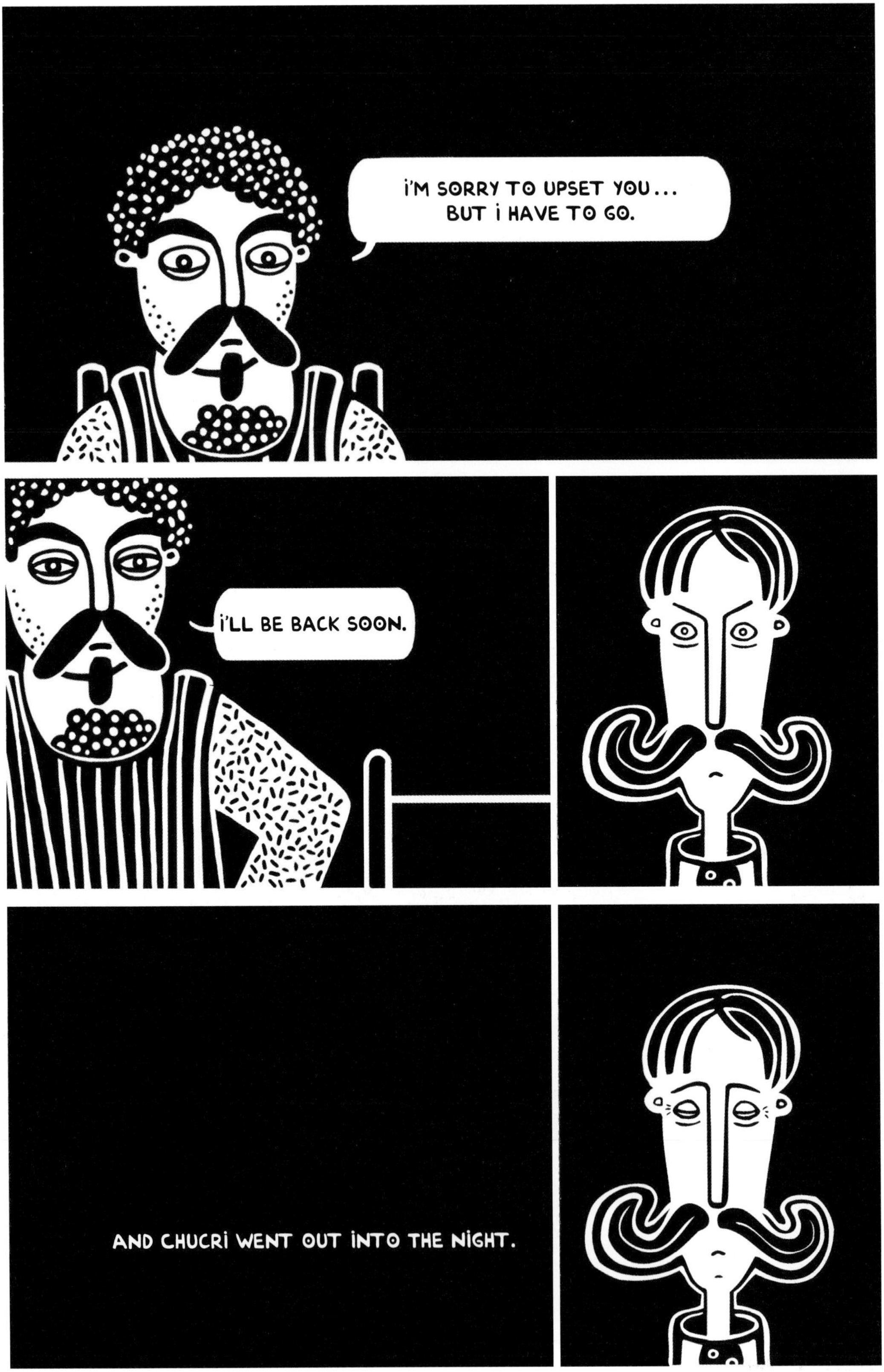
i'M SORRY TO UPSET YOU...
BUT i HAVE TO GO.
i'LL BE BACK SOON.
AND CHUCRi WENT OUT iNTO THE NiGHT.

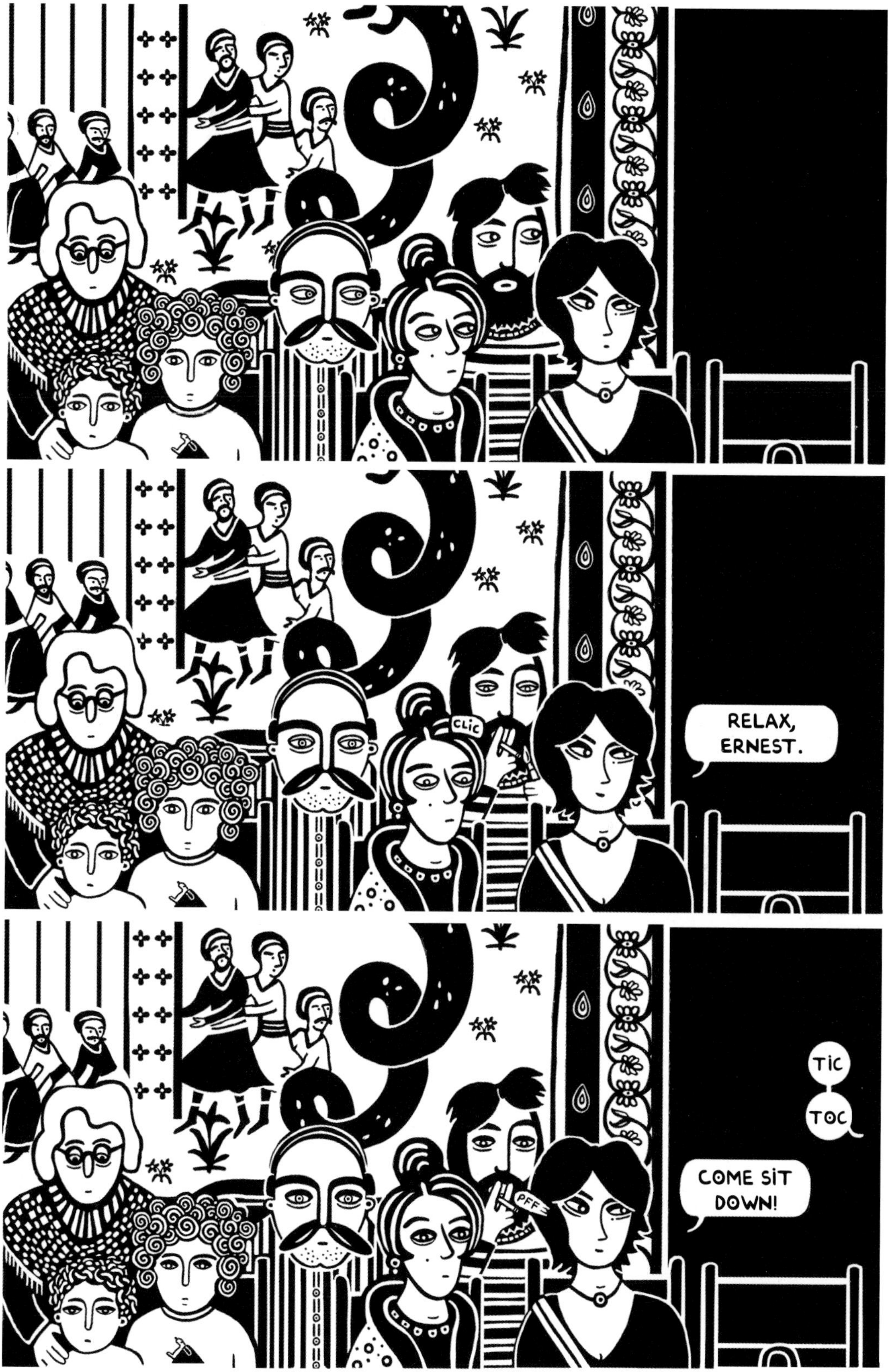
CLIC
RELAX, ERNEST.
TIC
TOC
PFF
COME SIT DOWN!

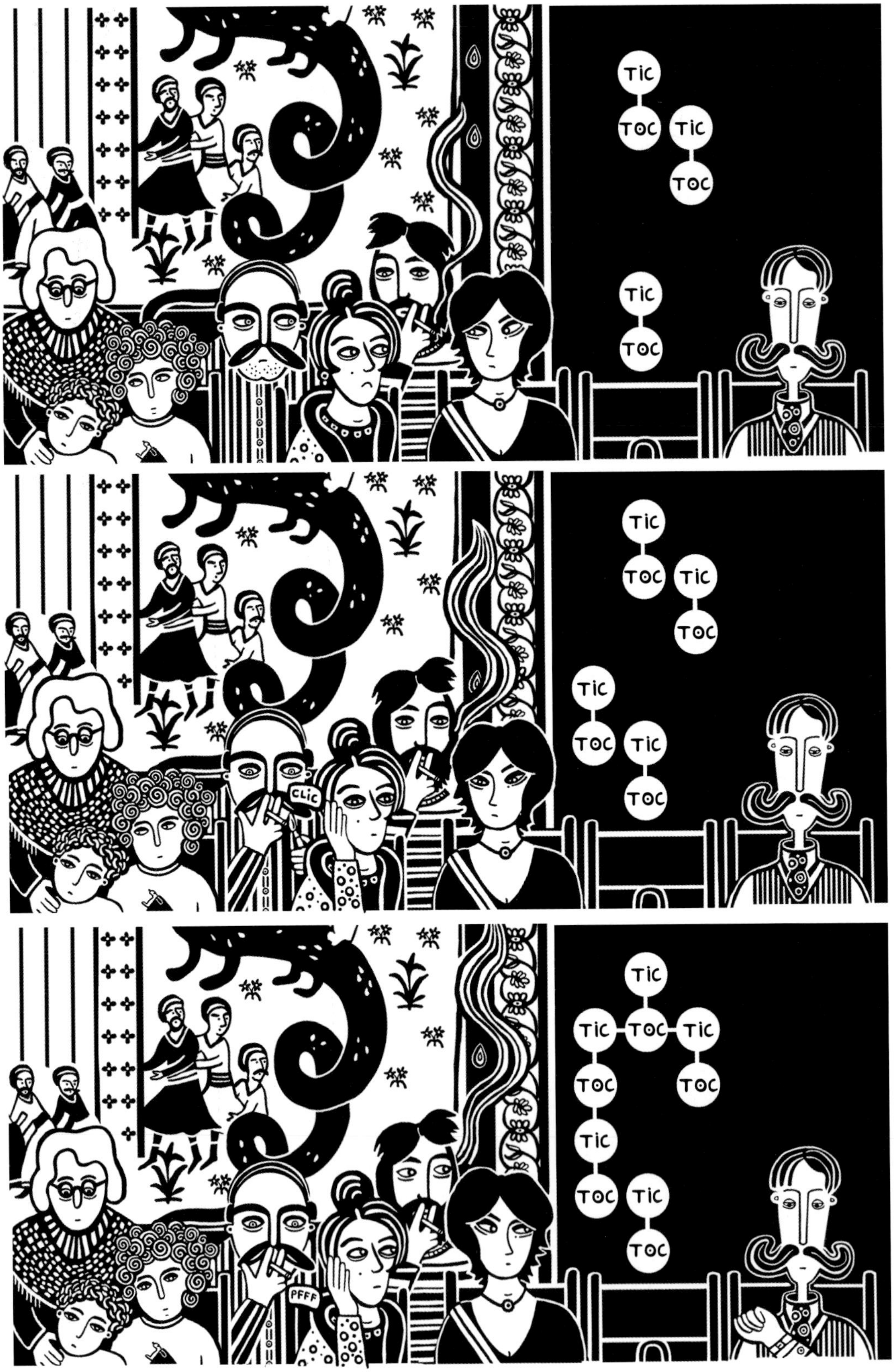
TIC
TOC
TIC
TOC
TIC
TOC
TIC
TOC
TIC
TOC
CLIC
TIC
TOC
TIC
TOC
TIC
TOC
TIC
TOC
TIC
TOC
TIC
TOC
TIC
TOC
PFFF

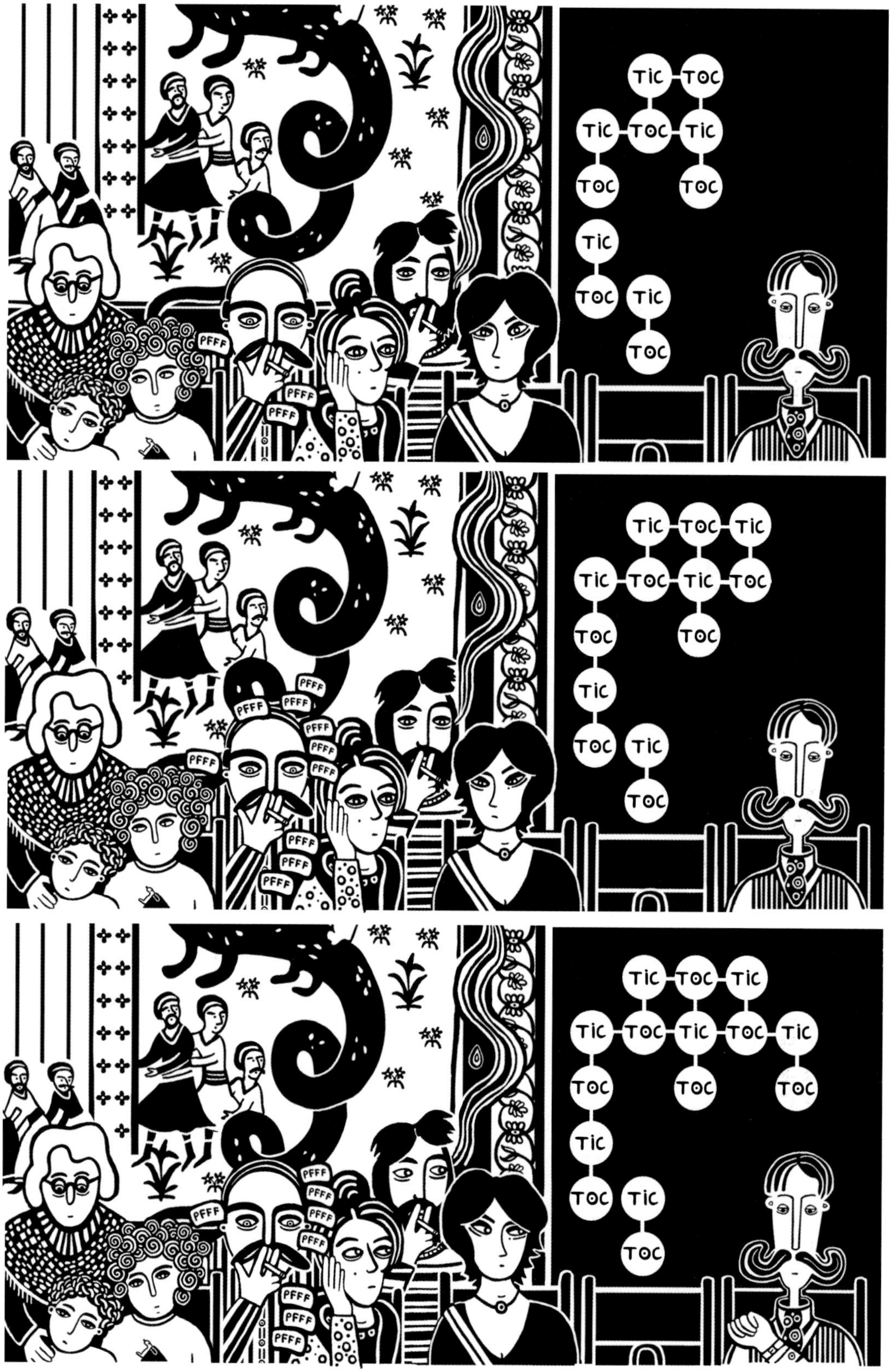
PFFF
PFFF
PFFF
TIC TOC
TIC TOC TIC
TOC TOC
TIC
TOC TIC
TOC
PFFF
PFFF
PFFF
PFFF
PFFF
PFFF
PFFF
PFFF
PFFF
PFFF
TIC TOC TIC
TIC TOC TIC TOC
TOC TOC
TIC
TOC TIC
TOC
PFFF
PFFF
PFFF
PFFF
PFFF
PFFF
PFFF
PFFF
TIC TOC TIC
TIC TOC TIC TOC TIC
TOC TOC TOC
TIC
TOC TIC
TOC

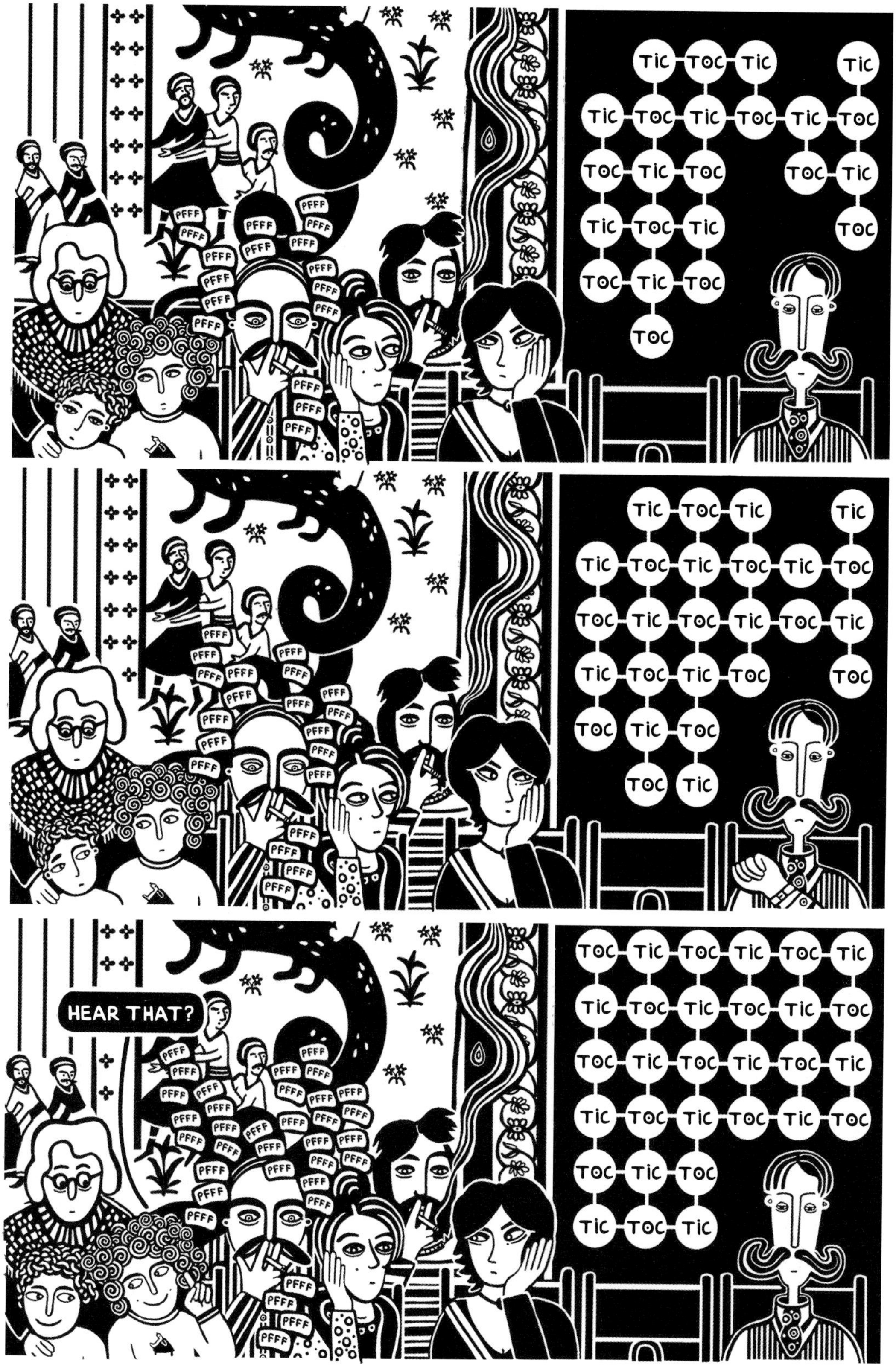
PFFF
TIC TOC TIC TIC
TIC TOC TIC TOC TIC TOC
TOC TIC TOC TOC TIC
TIC TOC TIC TOC
TOC TIC TOC
TOC
PFFF
TIC TOC TIC TIC
TIC TOC TIC TOC TIC TOC
TOC TIC TOC TIC TOC TIC
TIC TOC TIC TOC TOC
TOC TIC TOC
TOC TIC
HEAR THAT?
PFFF
TOC TIC TOC TIC TOC TIC
TIC TOC TIC TOC TIC TOC
TOC TIC TOC TIC TOC TIC
TIC TOC TIC TOC TIC TOC
TOC TIC TOC
TIC TOC TIC

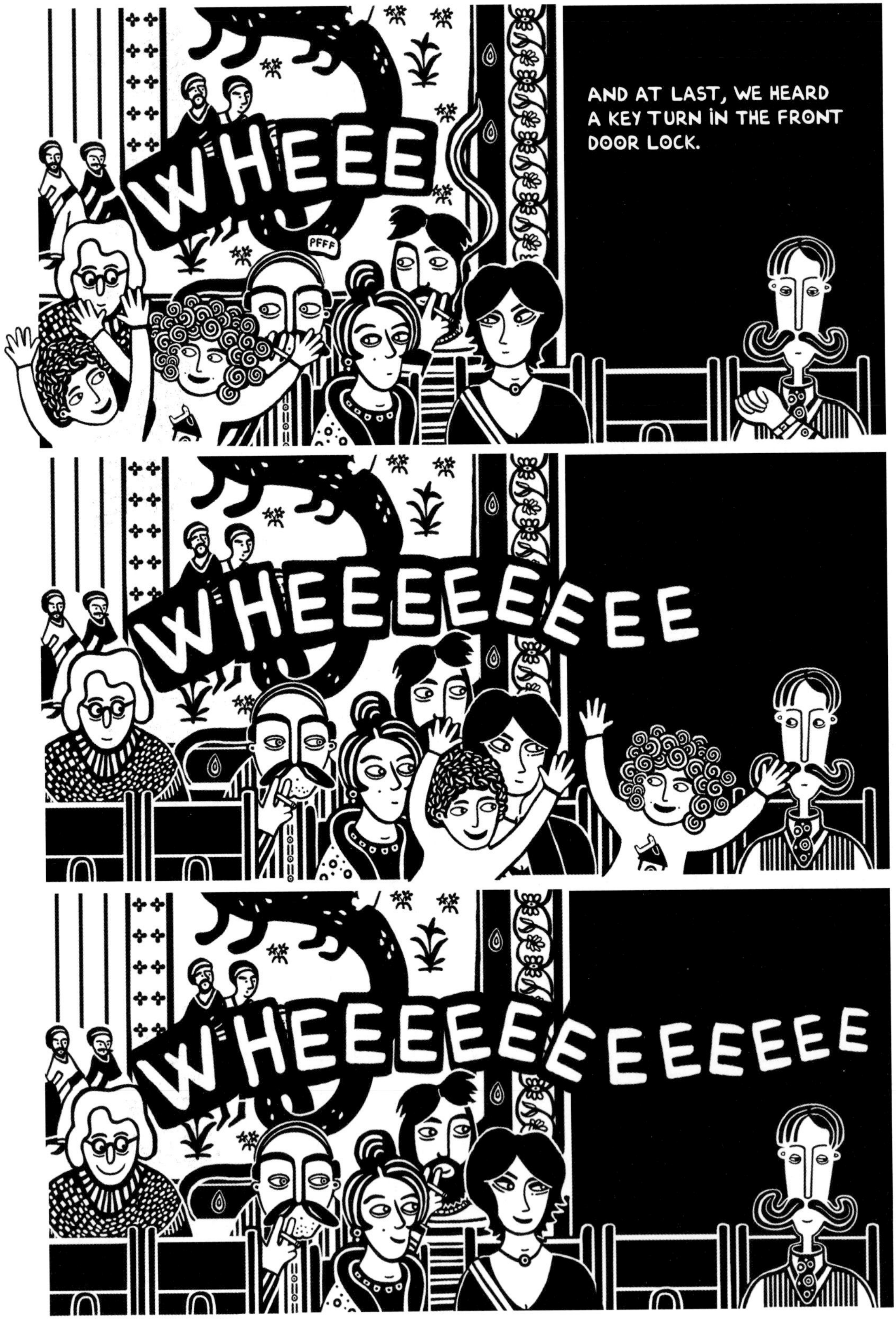
AND AT LAST, WE HEARD A KEY TURN IN THE FRONT DOOR LOCK.
WHEEE
PFFF
WHEEEEEEEE
WHEEEEEEEEEEEE

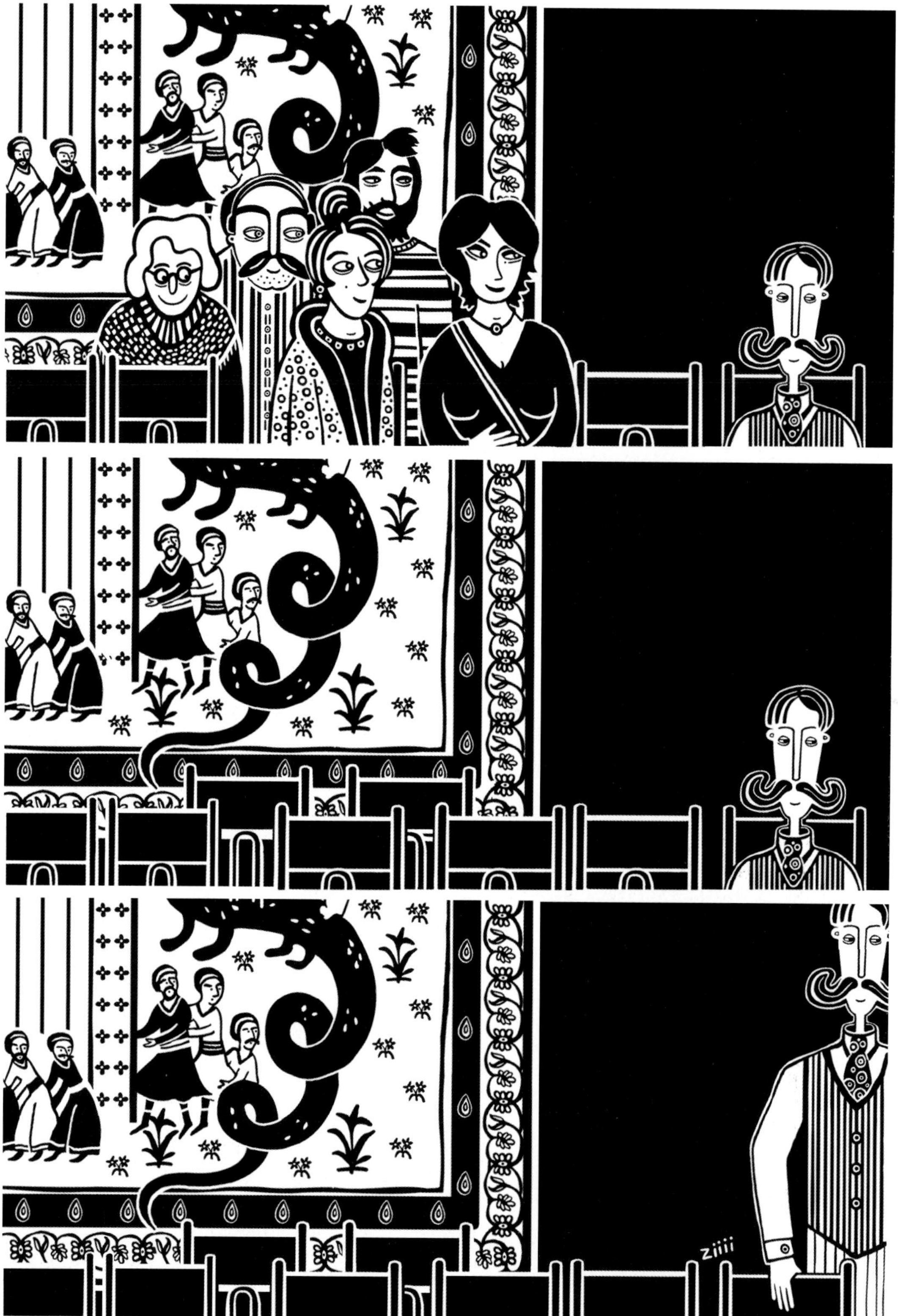
ziiii

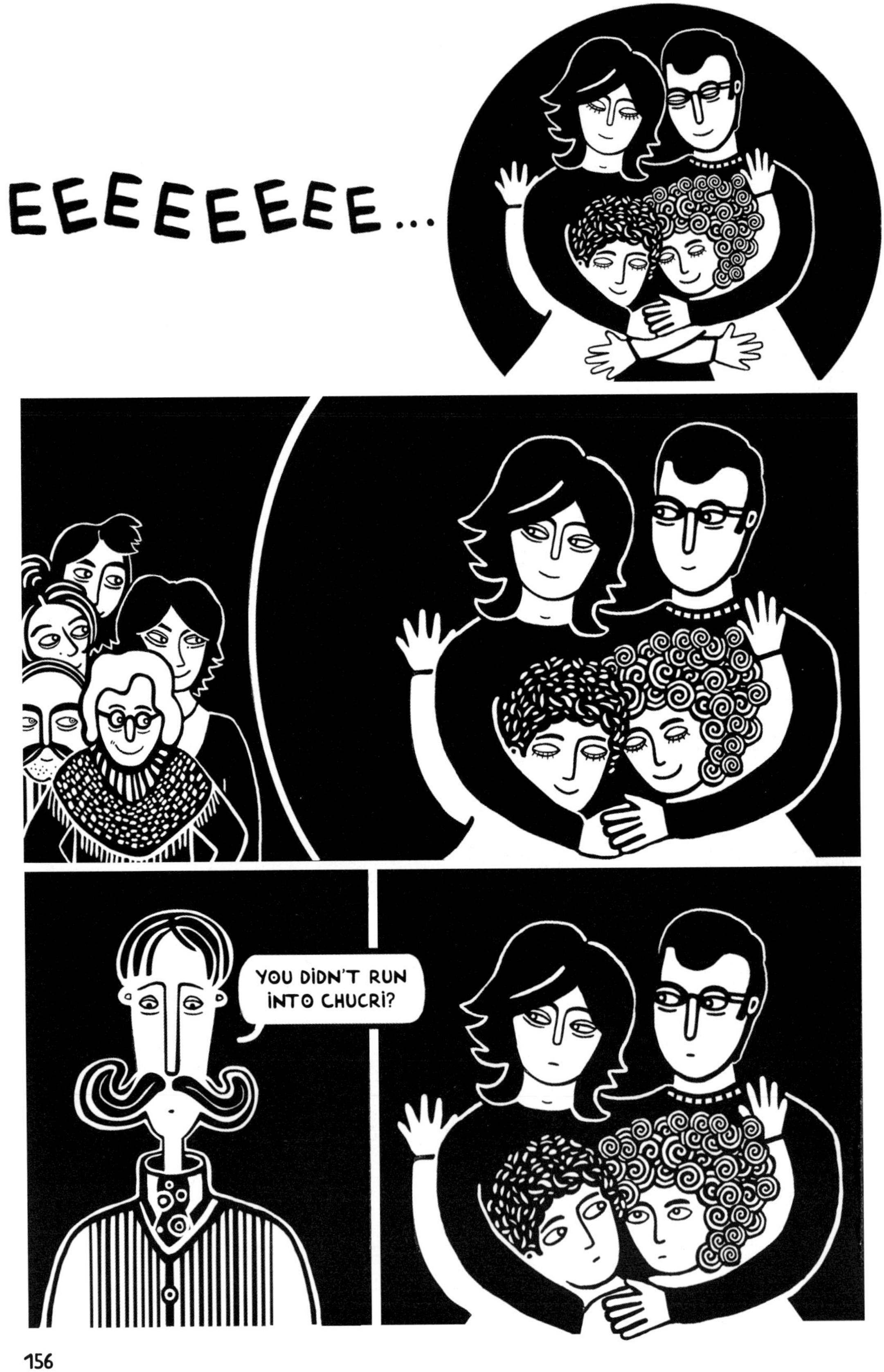
EEEEEEEE...
YOU DIDN'T RUN INTO CHUCRI?

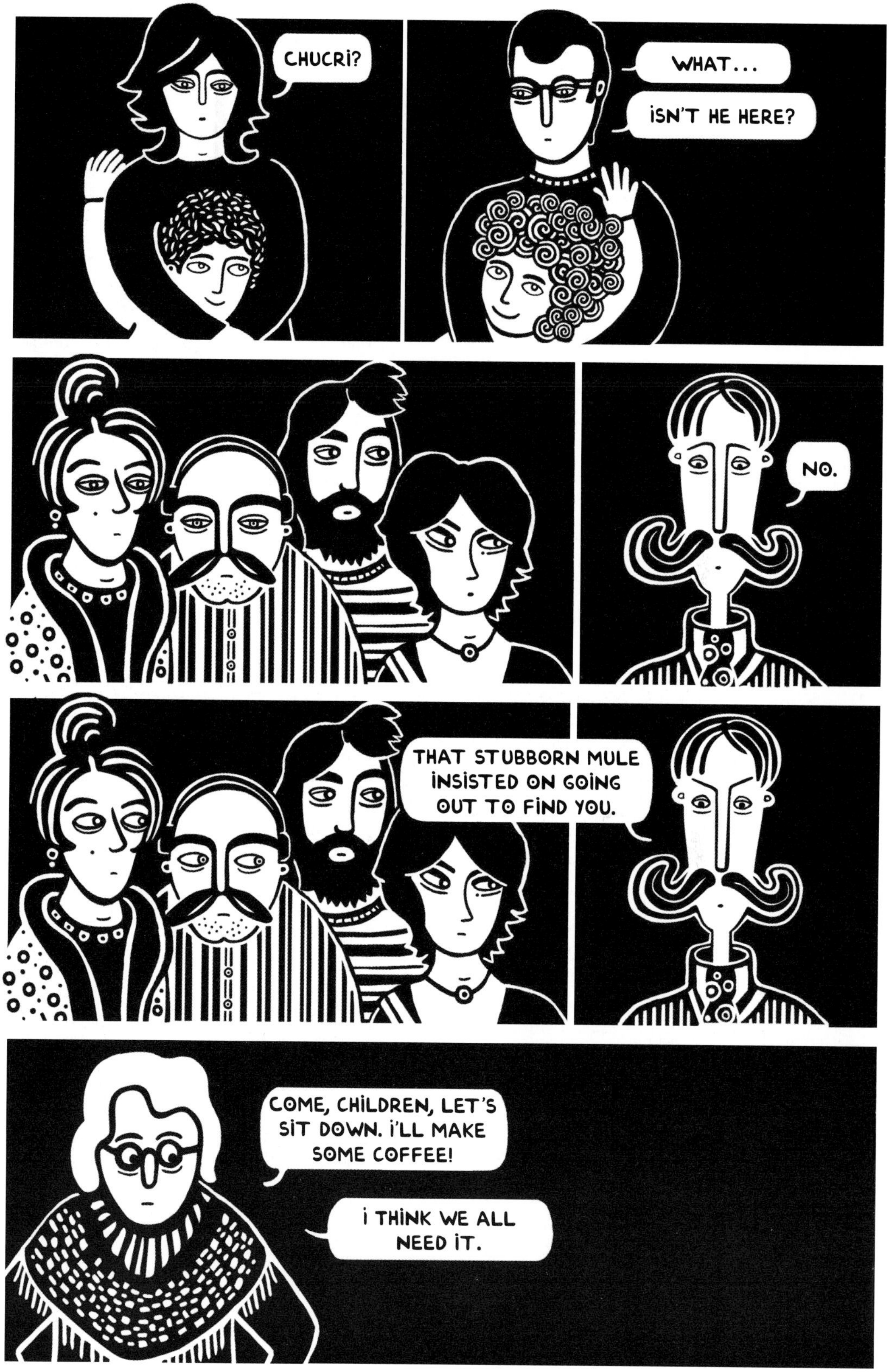
CHUCRI?
WHAT...
ISN'T HE HERE?
NO.
THAT STUBBORN MULE INSISTED ON GOING OUT TO FIND YOU.
COME, CHILDREN, LET'S SIT DOWN. I'LL MAKE SOME COFFEE!
I THINK WE ALL NEED IT.

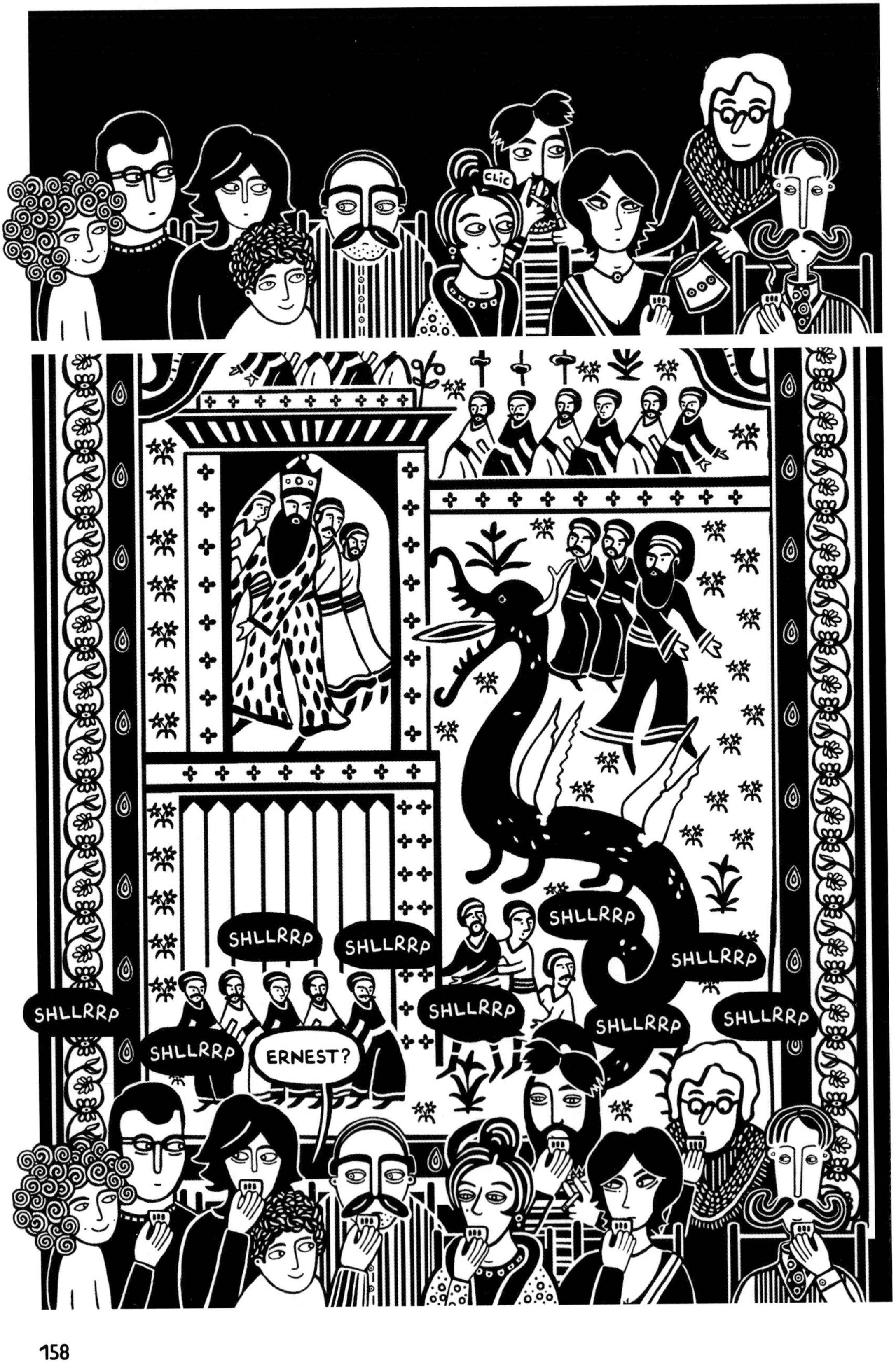
CLIC
SHLLRRP
SHLLRRP
SHLLRRP
SHLLRRP
SHLLRRP
SHLLRRP
SHLLRRP
SHLLRRP
SHLLRRP
ERNEST?

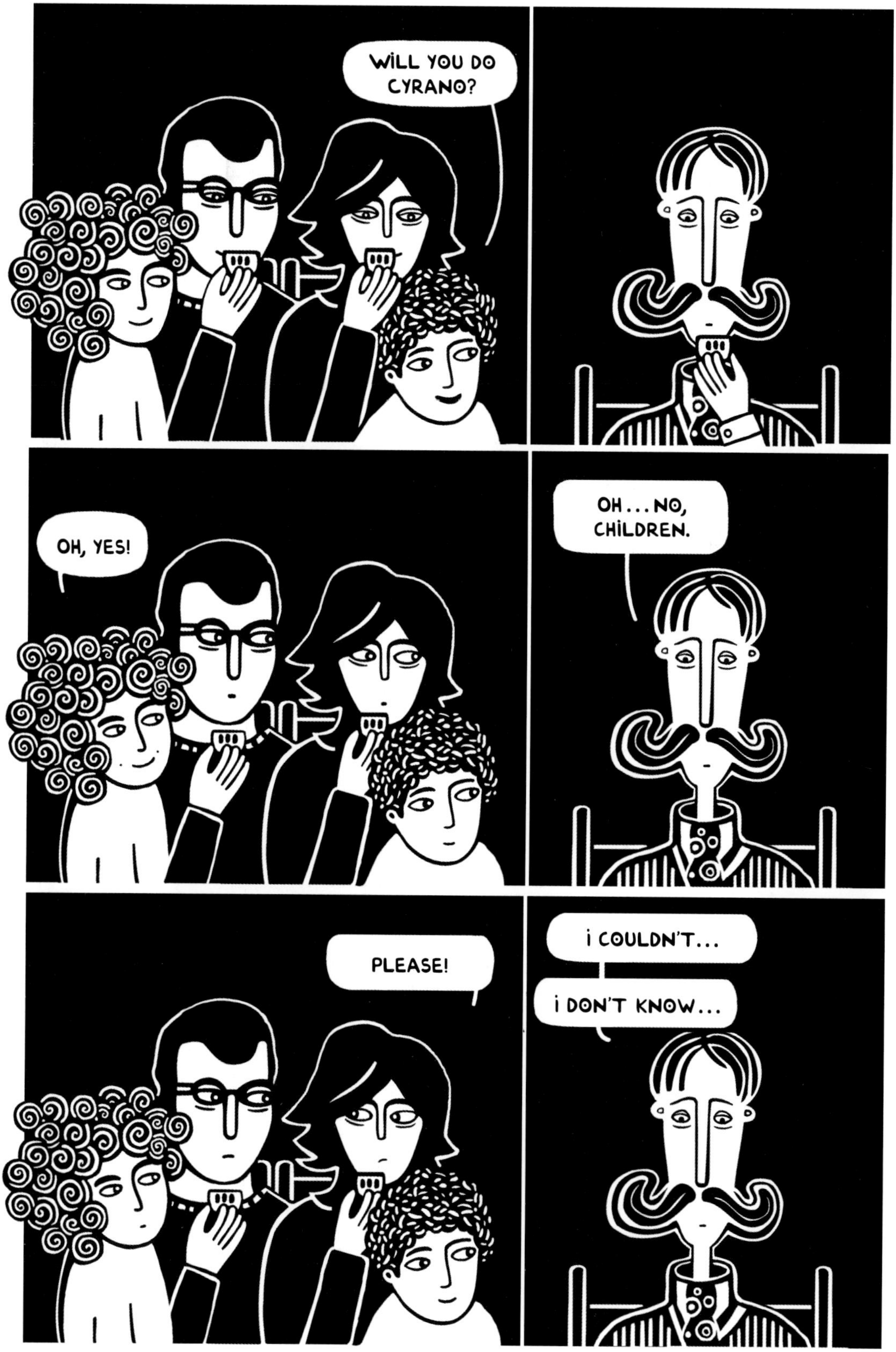
WILL YOU DO CYRANO?
OH, YES!
OH... NO, CHILDREN.
PLEASE!
I COULDN'T...
I DON'T KNOW...

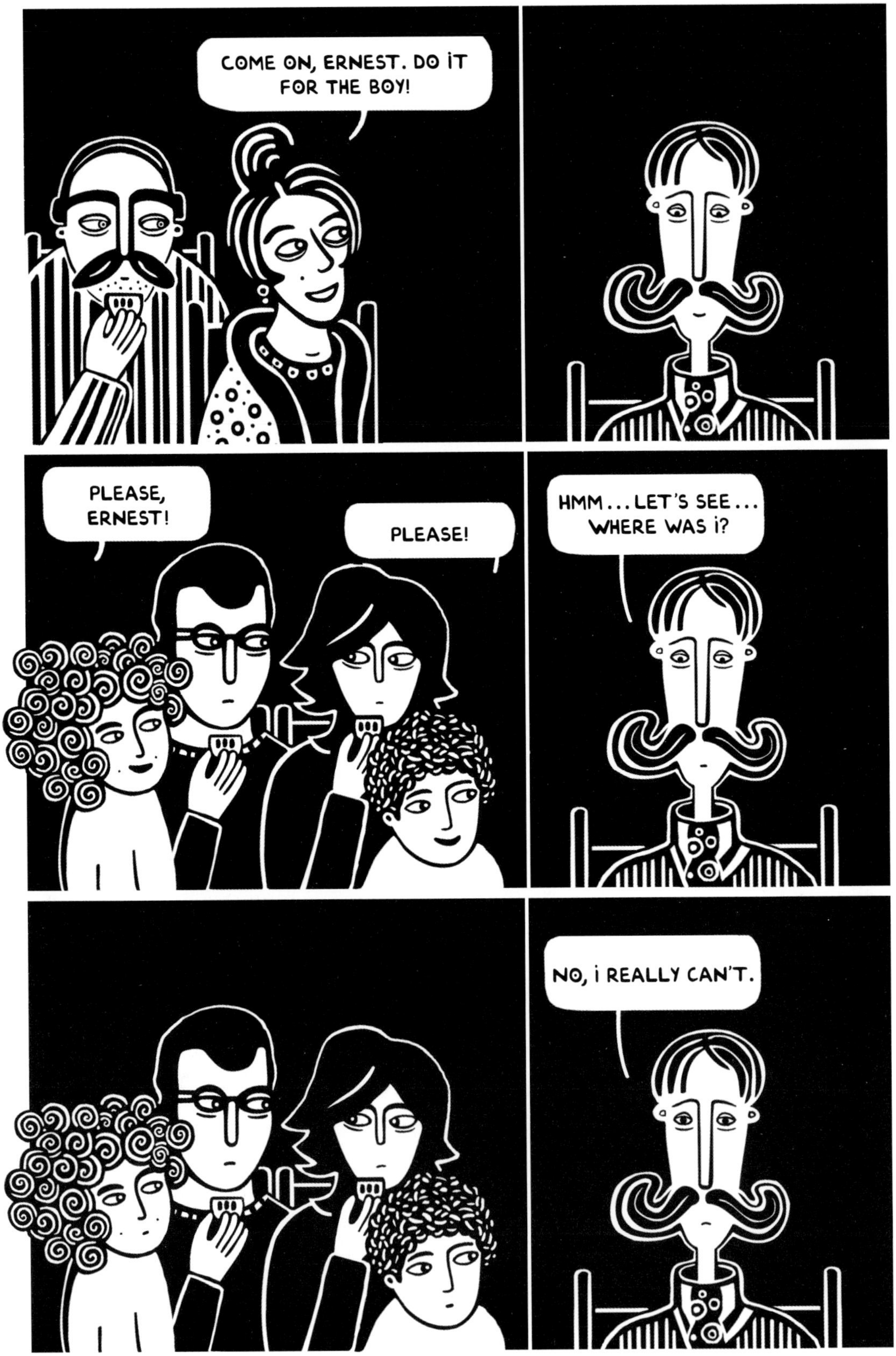
COME ON, ERNEST. DO IT FOR THE BOY!
PLEASE, ERNEST!
PLEASE!
HMM... LET'S SEE... WHERE WAS I?
NO, I REALLY CAN'T.

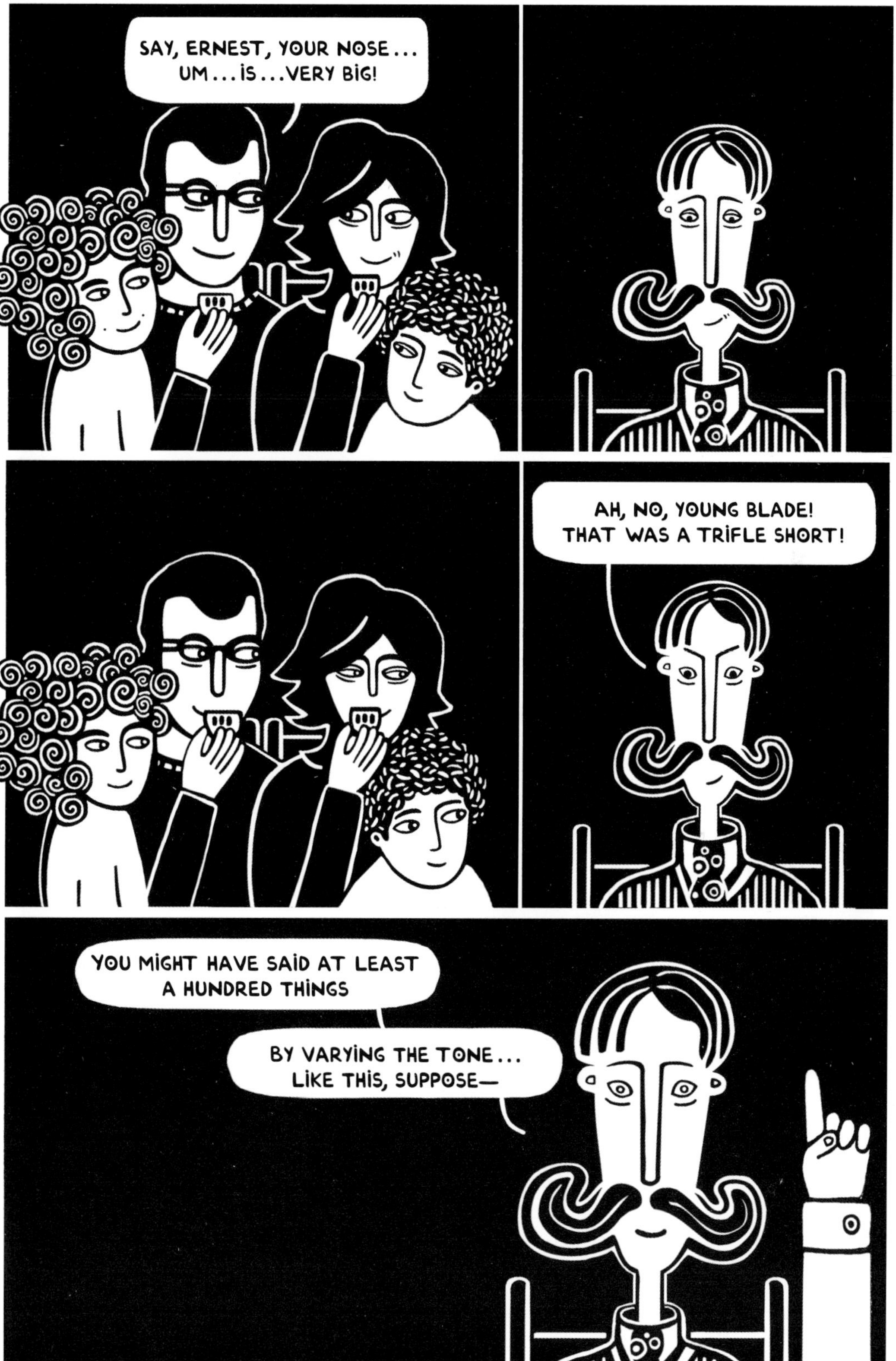
SAY, ERNEST, YOUR NOSE... UM...IS...VERY BIG!
AH, NO, YOUNG BLADE! THAT WAS A TRIFLE SHORT!
YOU MIGHT HAVE SAID AT LEAST A HUNDRED THINGS
BY VARYING THE TONE... LIKE THIS, SUPPOSE—

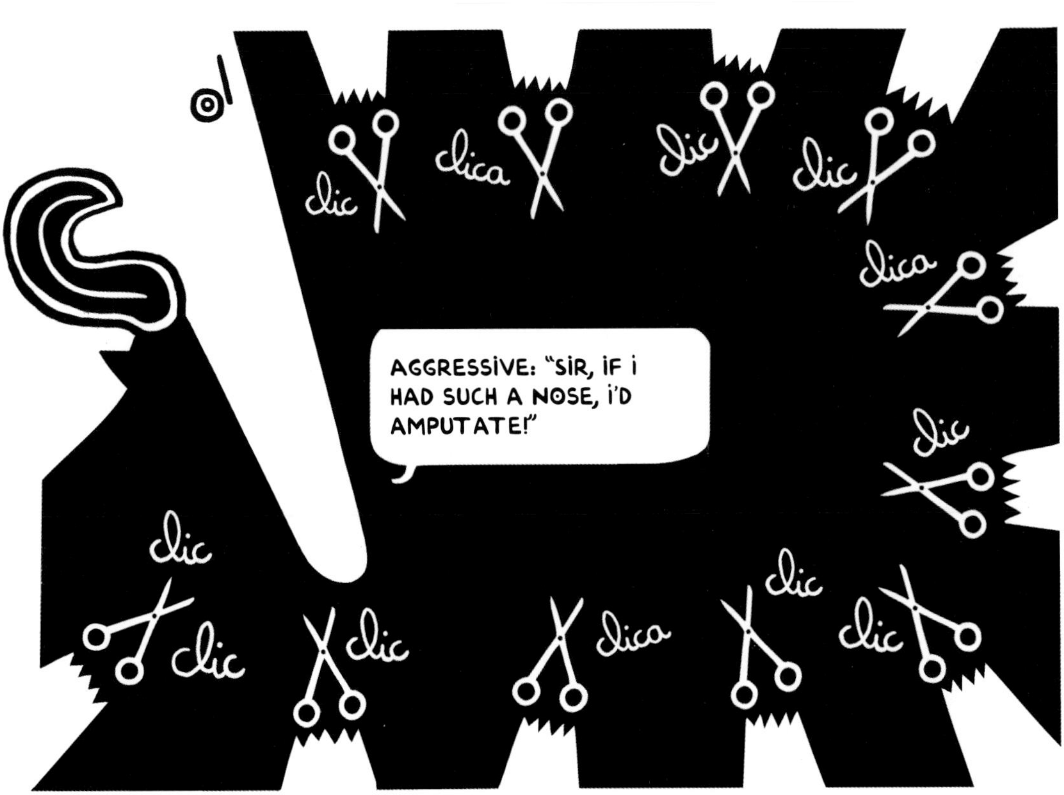
clic
clica
clic
clic
clica
AGGRESSIVE: "SIR, IF I HAD SUCH A NOSE, I'D AMPUTATE!"
clic
clic
clic
clic
clica
clic
clic

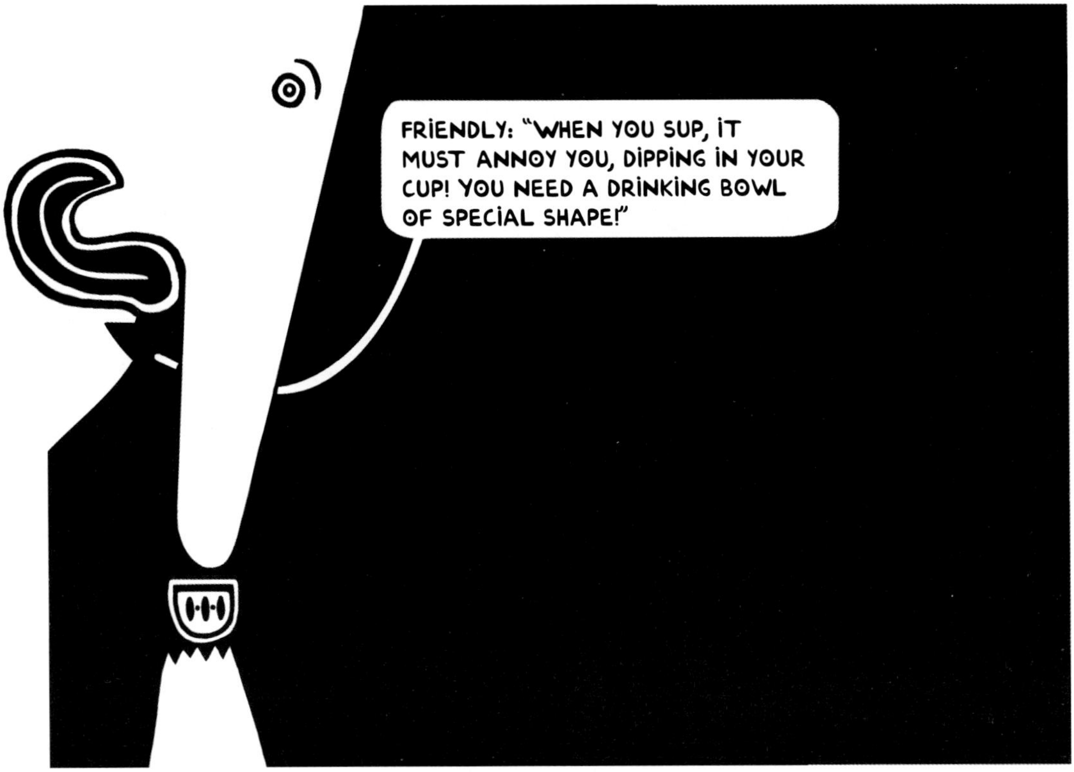
FRIENDLY: "WHEN YOU SUP, IT MUST ANNOY YOU, DIPPING IN YOUR CUP! YOU NEED A DRINKING BOWL OF SPECIAL SHAPE!"

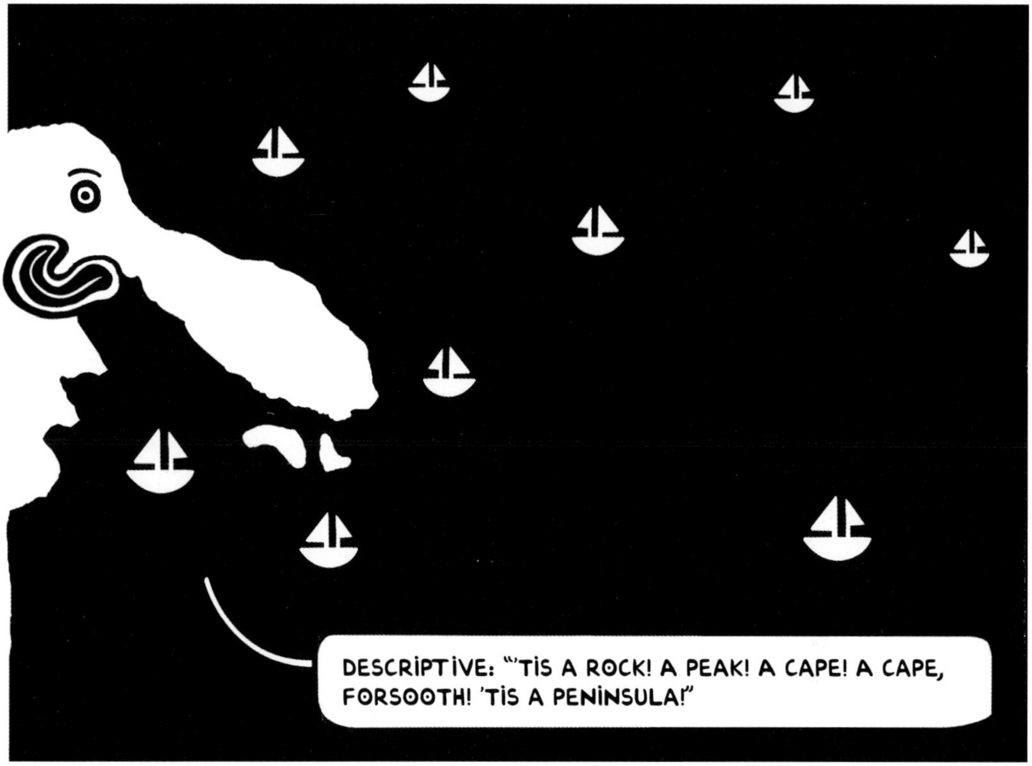
DESCRIPTIVE: "'TIS A ROCK! A PEAK! A CAPE! A CAPE, FORSOOTH! 'TIS A PENINSULA!"

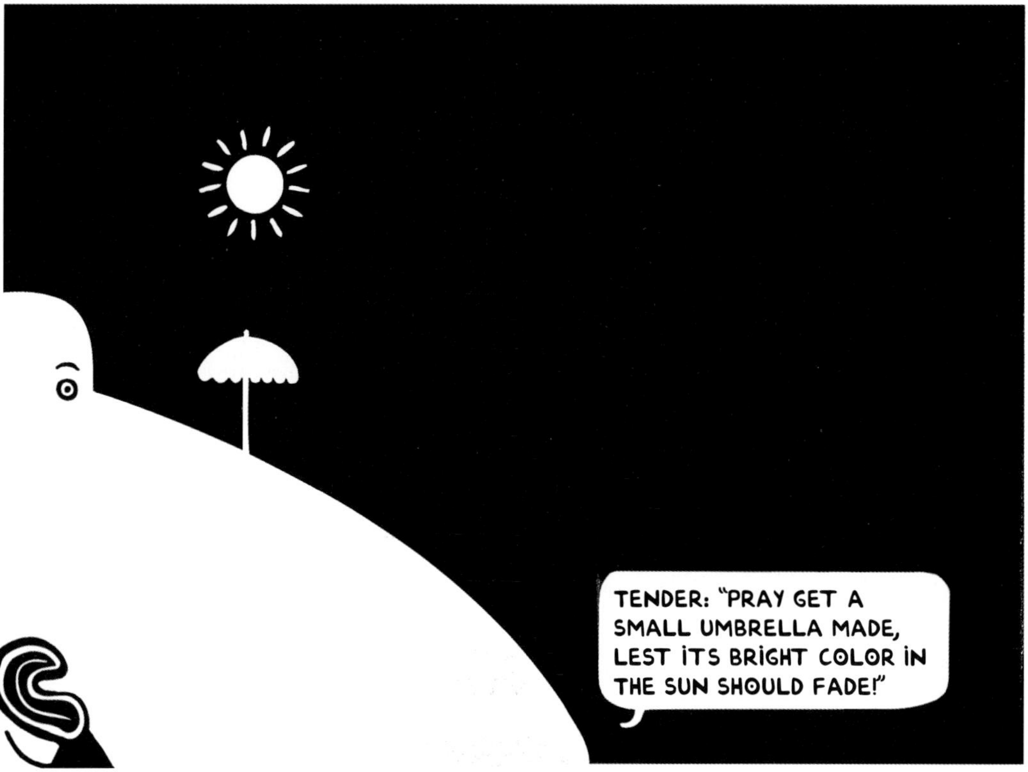
TENDER: "PRAY GET A SMALL UMBRELLA MADE, LEST ITS BRIGHT COLOR IN THE SUN SHOULD FADE!"

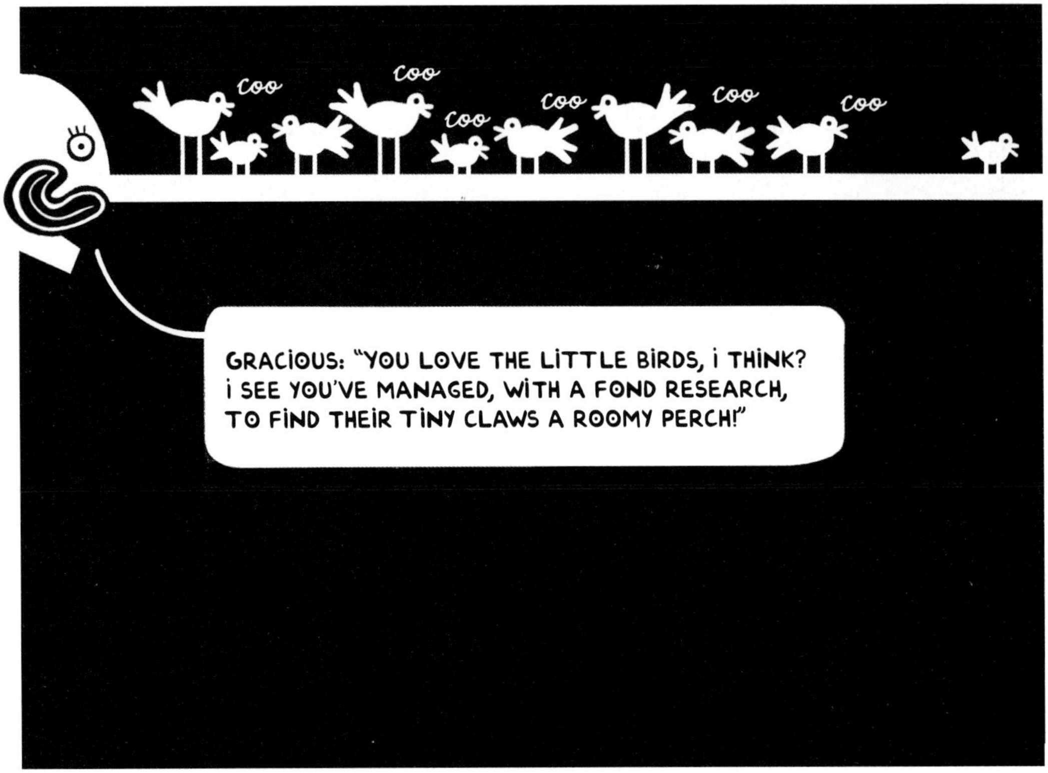
COO
COO
COO
COO
COO
COO
GRACIOUS: "YOU LOVE THE LITTLE BIRDS, I THINK? I SEE YOU'VE MANAGED, WITH A FOND RESEARCH, TO FIND THEIR TINY CLAWS A ROOMY PERCH!"

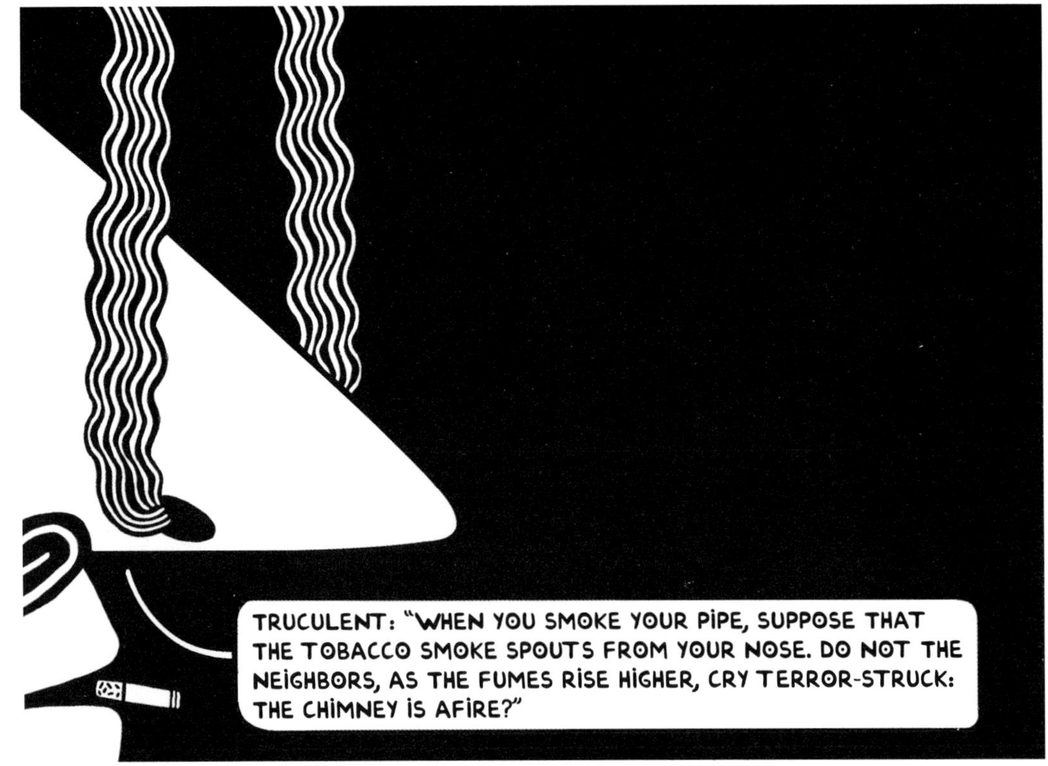
TRUCULENT: "WHEN YOU SMOKE YOUR PIPE, SUPPOSE THAT THE TOBACCO SMOKE SPOUTS FROM YOUR NOSE. DO NOT THE NEIGHBORS, AS THE FUMES RISE HIGHER, CRY TERROR-STRUCK: THE CHIMNEY IS AFIRE?"

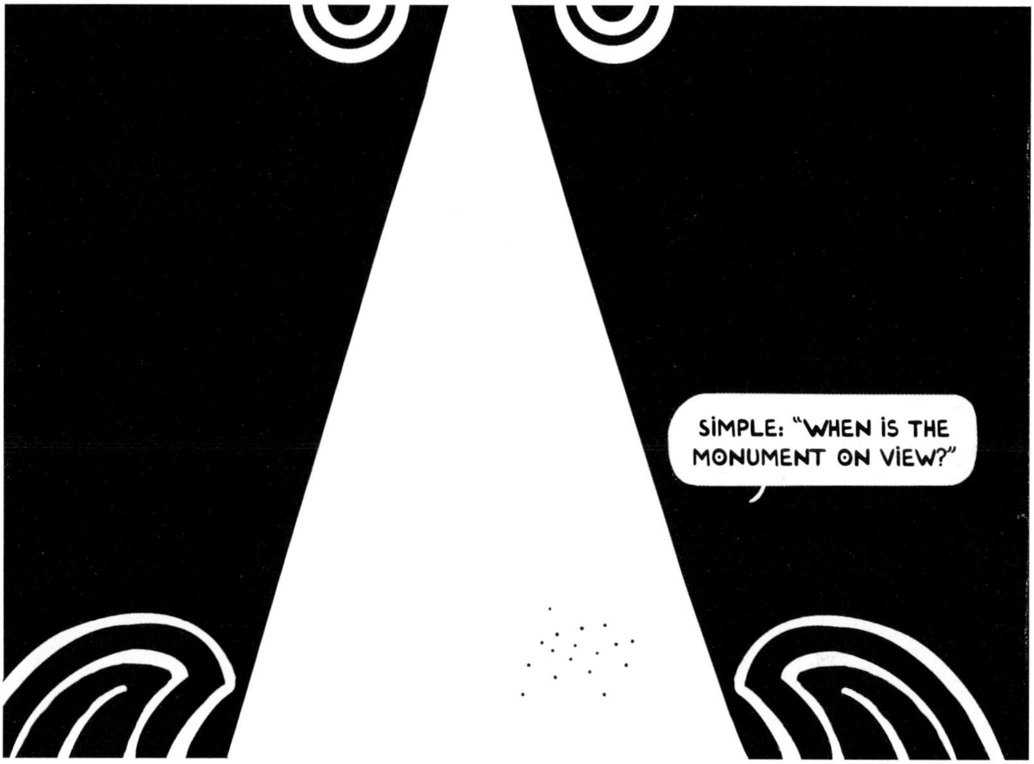
SIMPLE: "WHEN IS THE MONUMENT ON VIEW?"

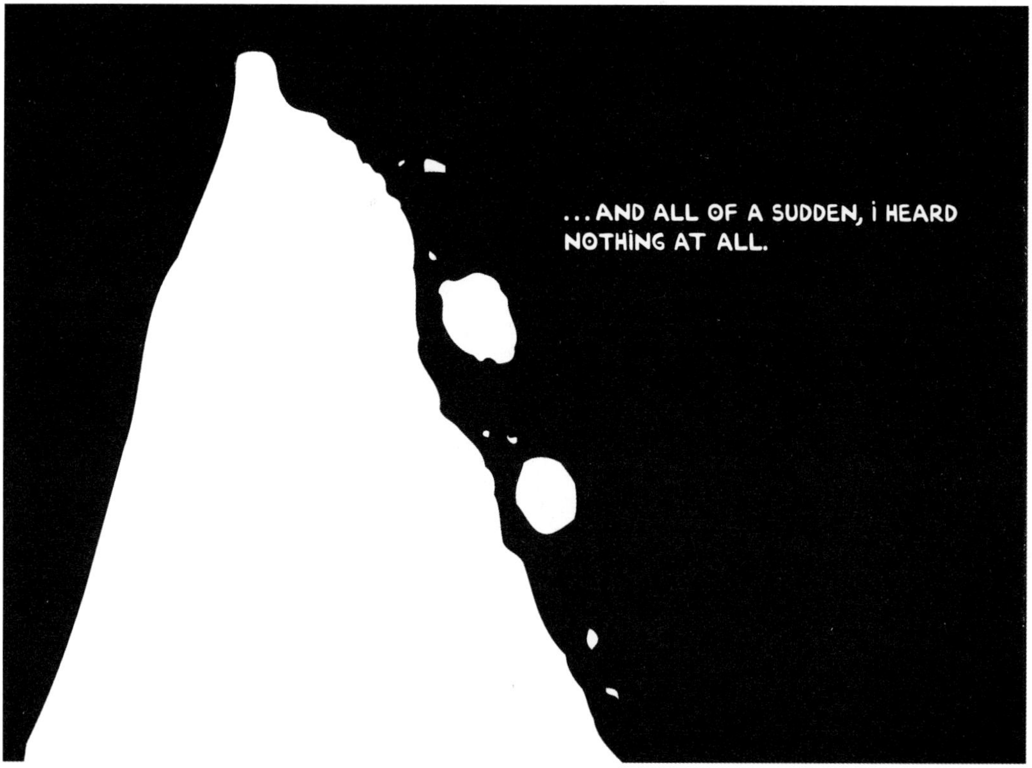
...AND ALL OF A SUDDEN, I HEARD NOTHING AT ALL.

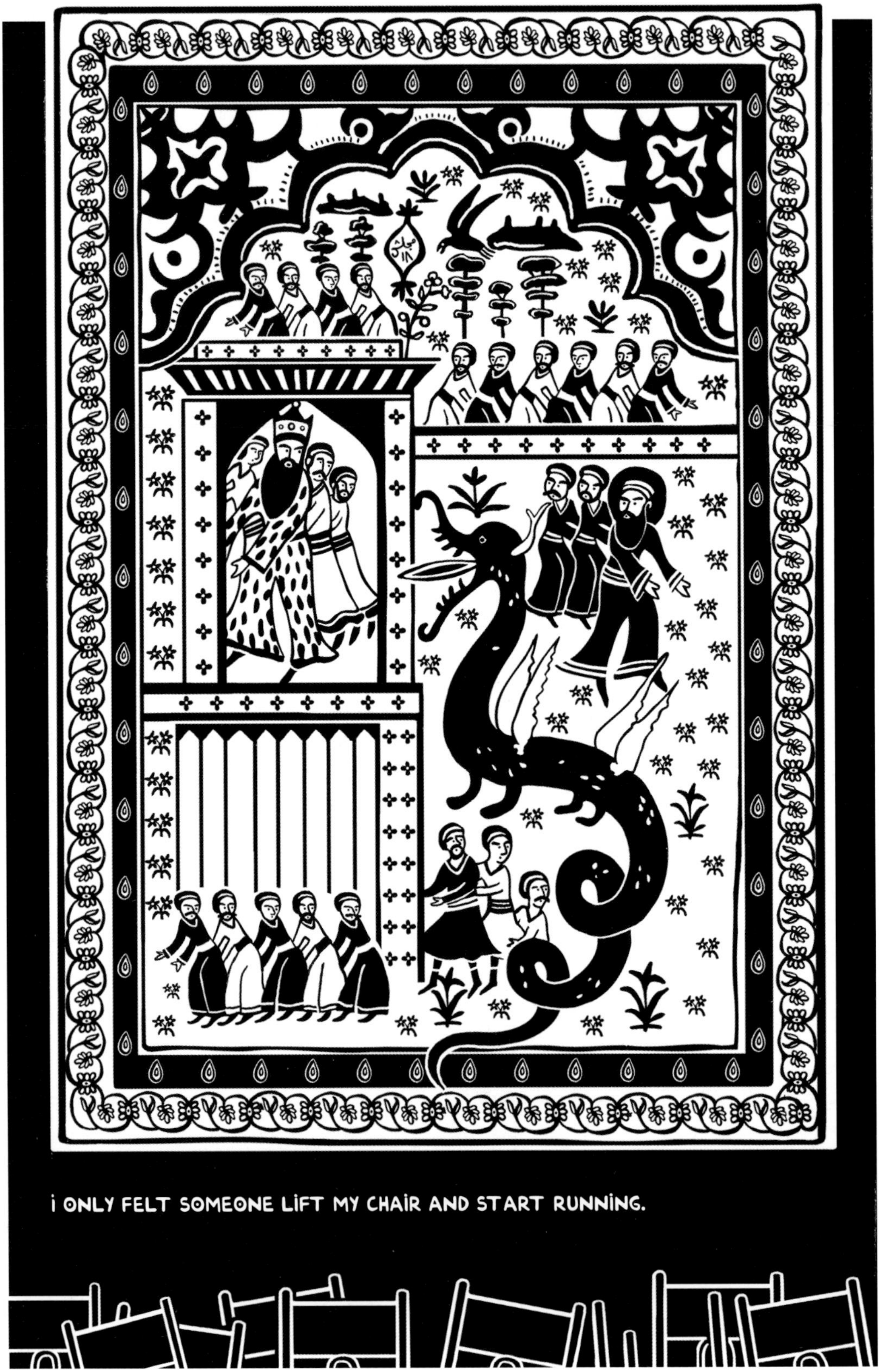
I ONLY FELT SOMEONE LIFT MY CHAIR AND START RUNNING.

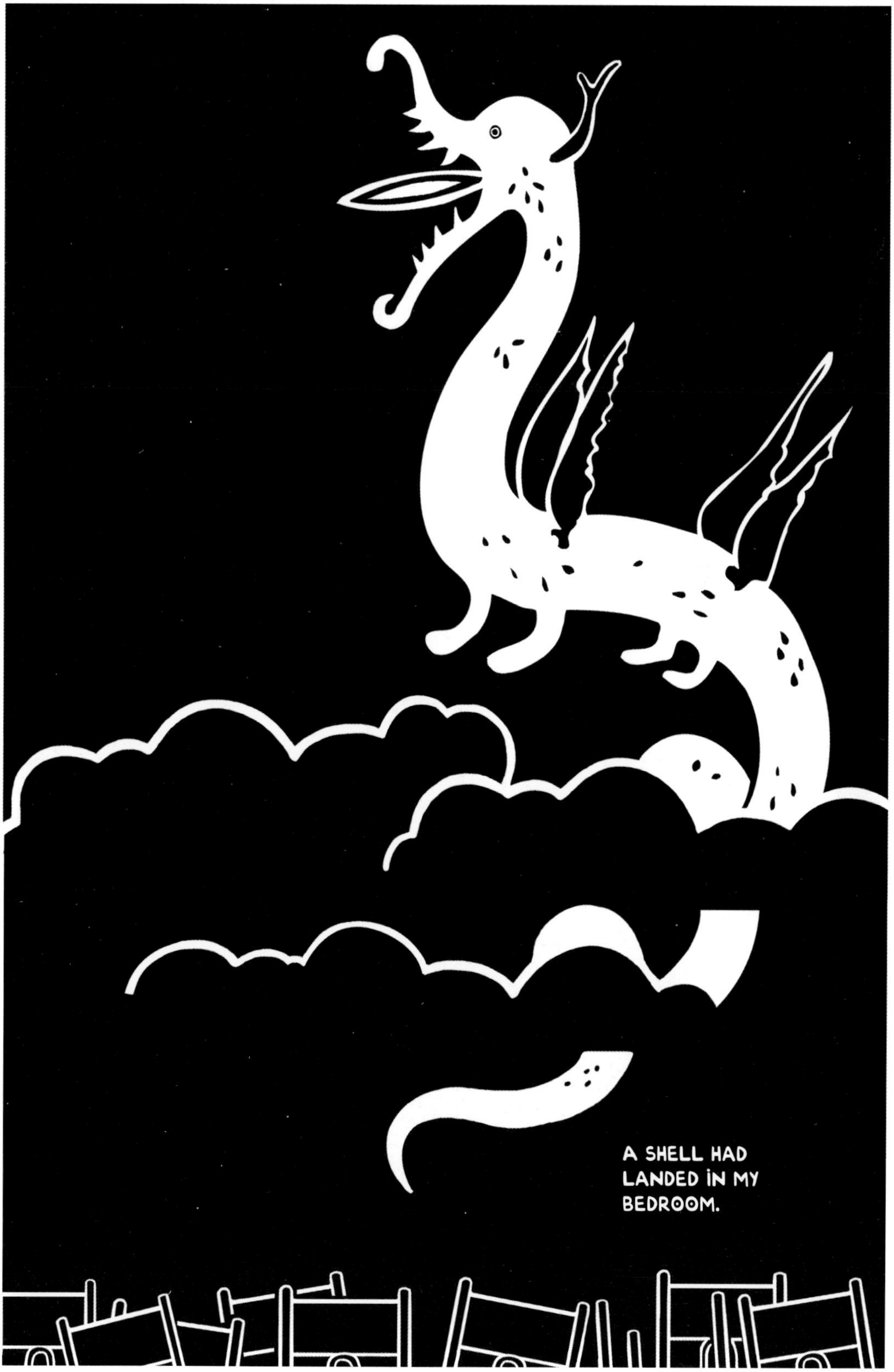
A SHELL HAD LANDED IN MY BEDROOM.

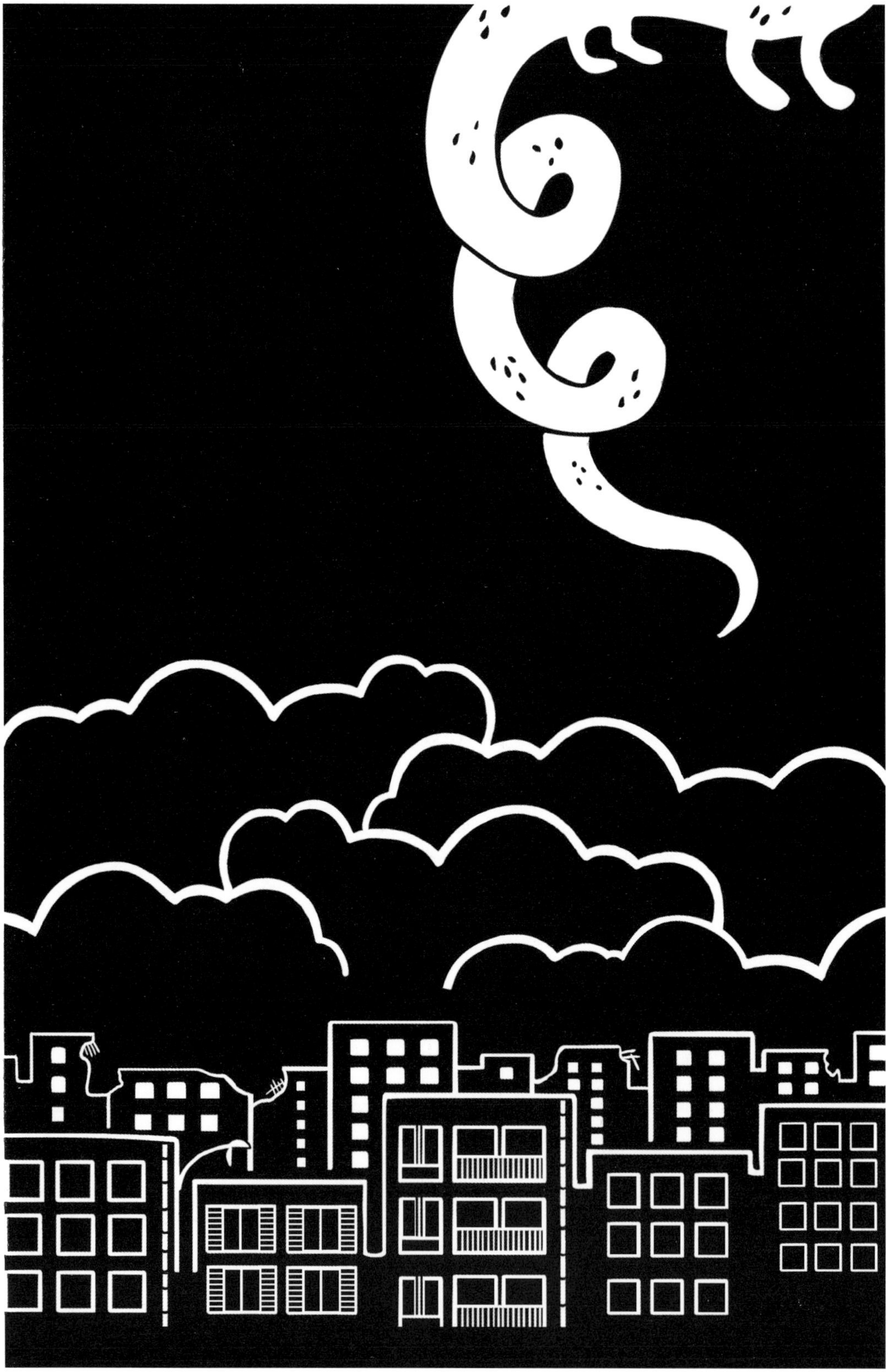

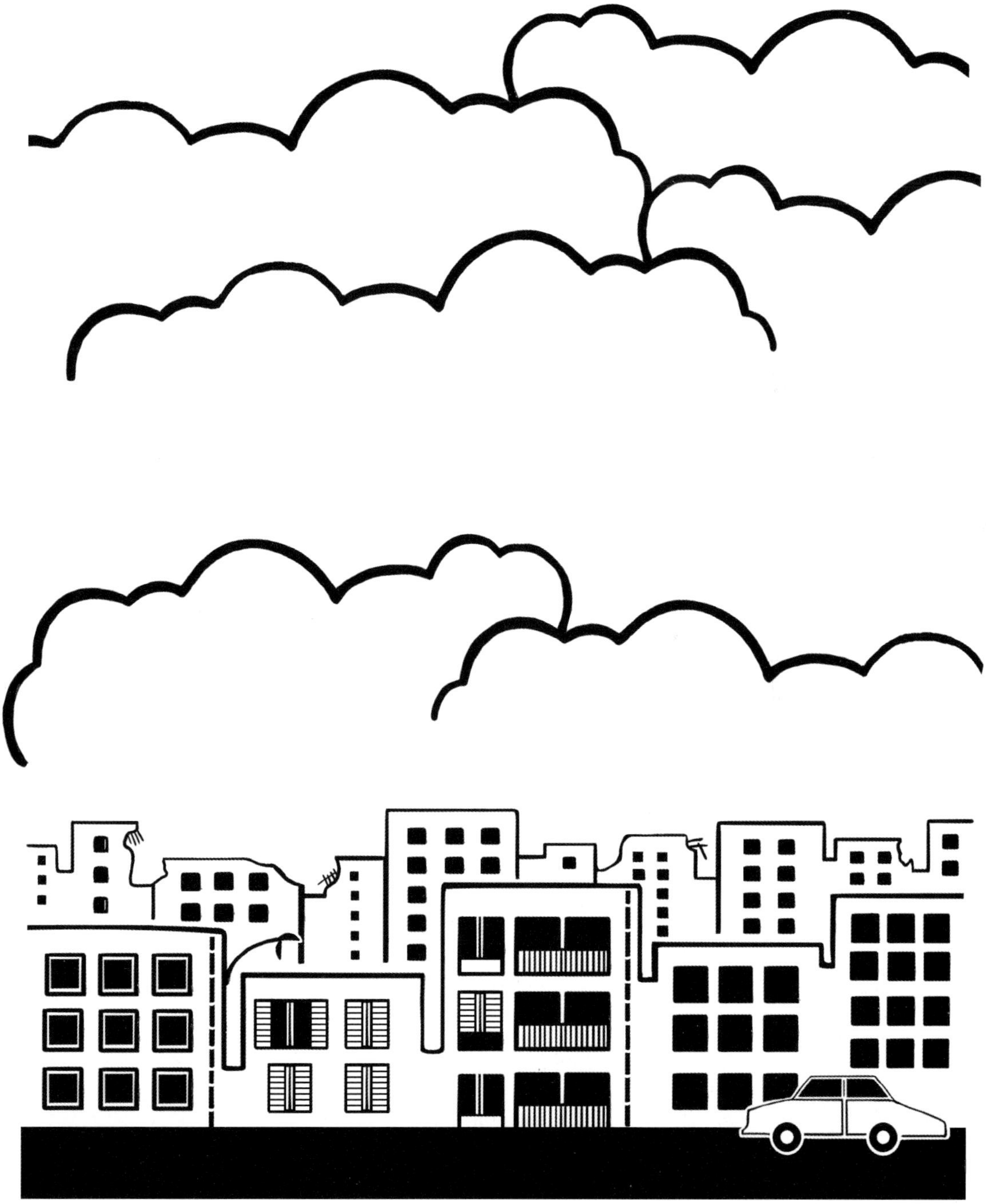

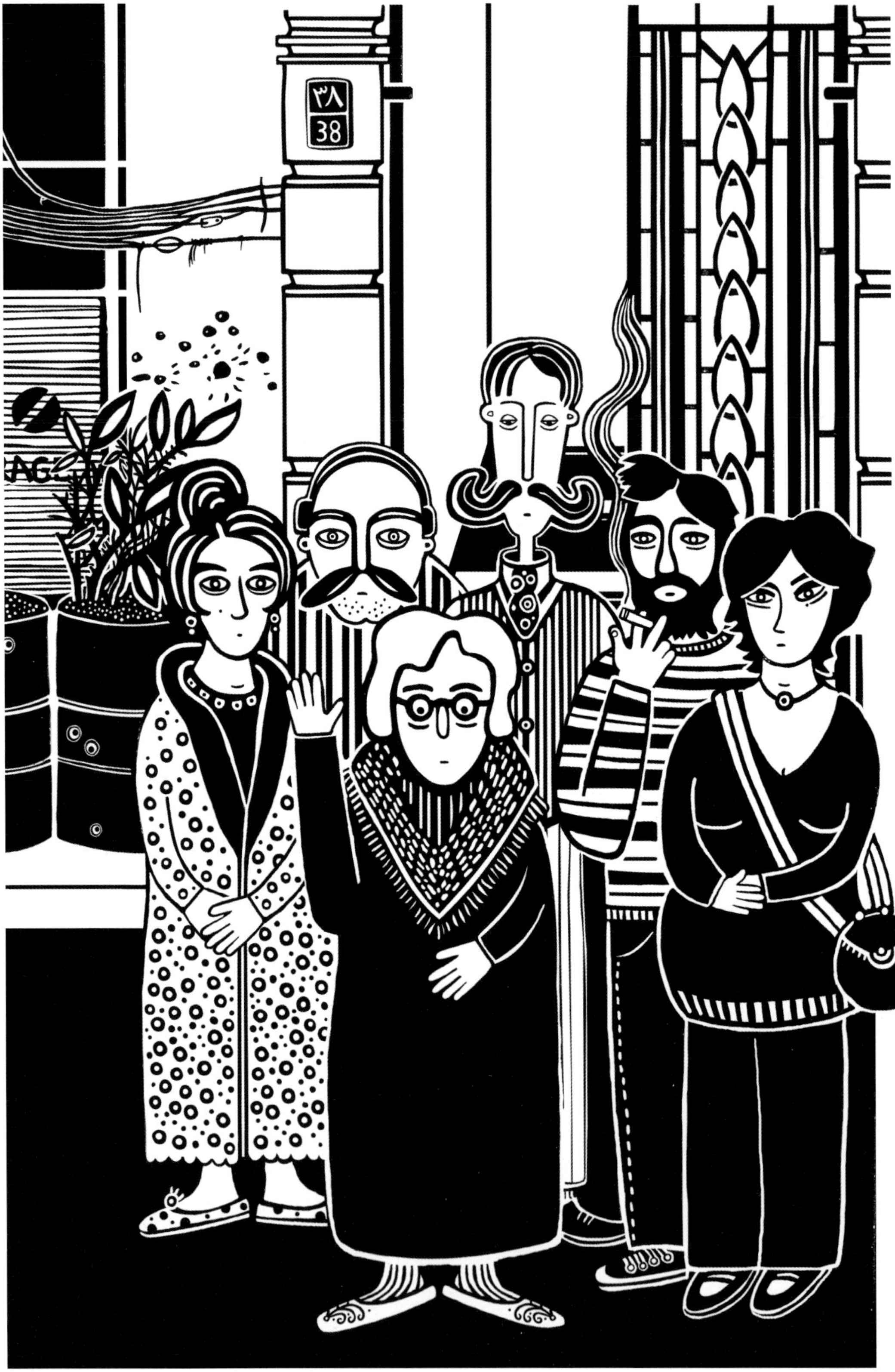
۳۸
38

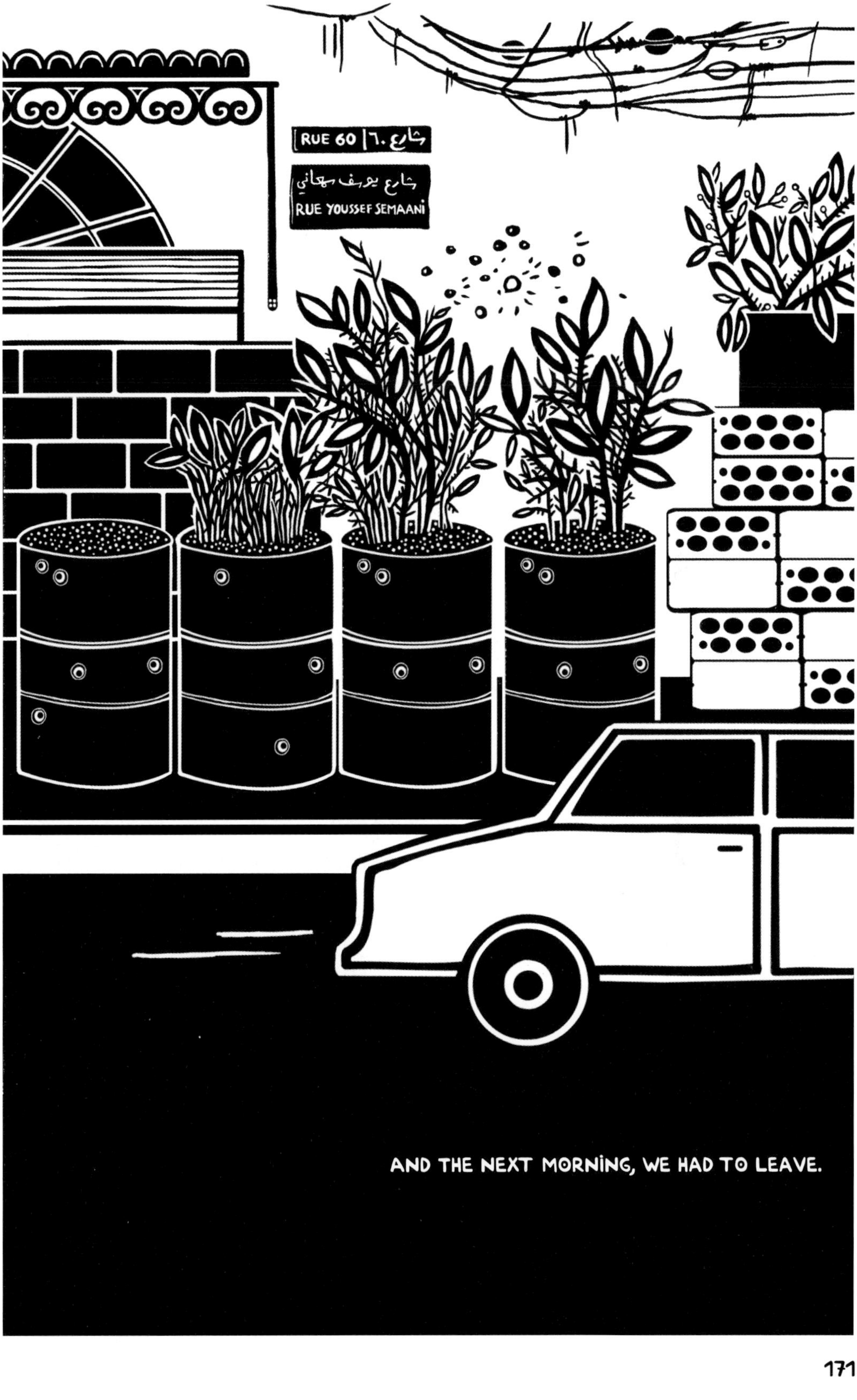
RUE 60 | شارع ٦٠
شارع يوسف سمعاني
RUE YOUSSEF SEMAANI
AND THE NEXT MORNING, WE HAD TO LEAVE.

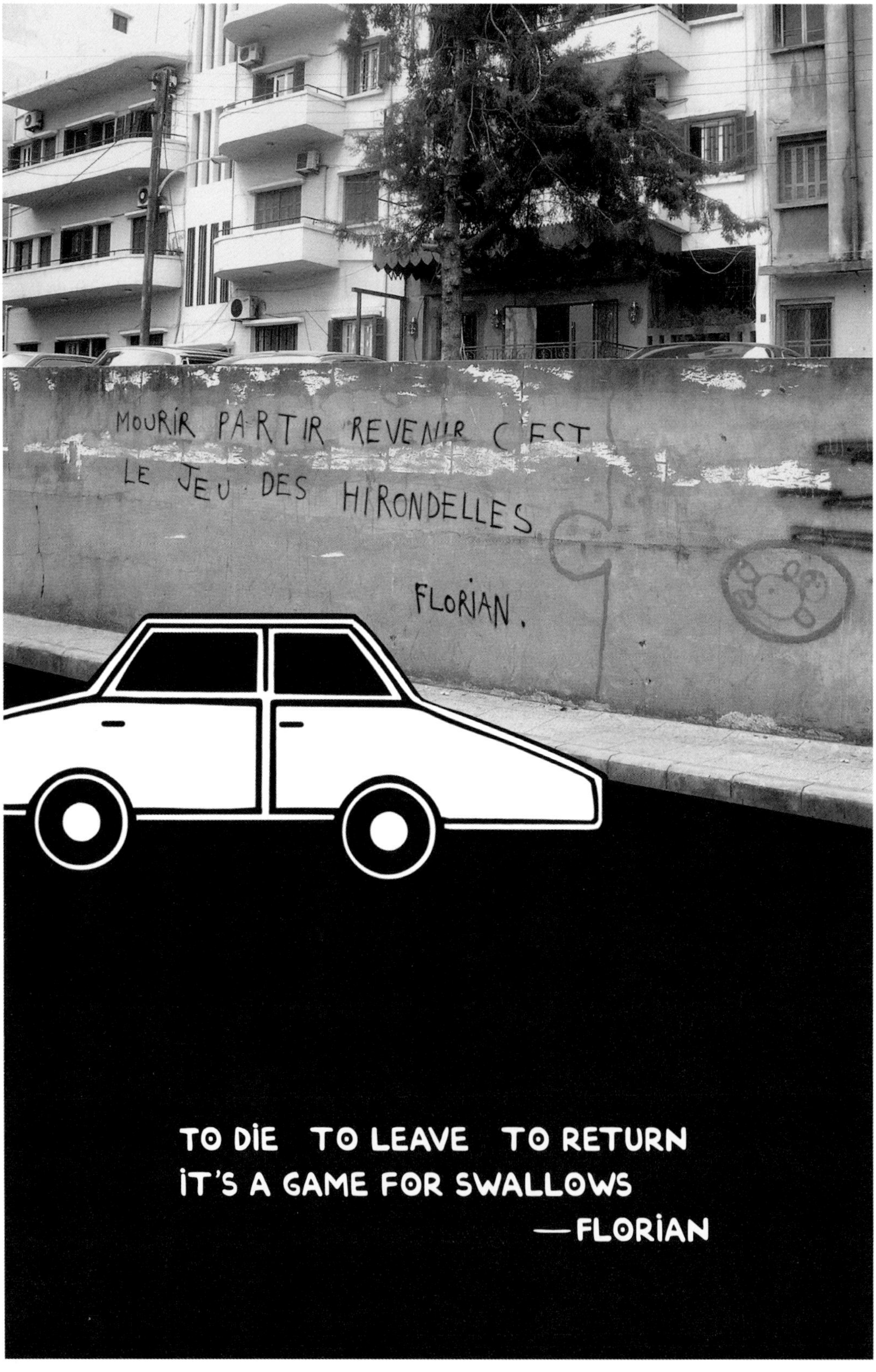
MOURIR PARTIR REVENIR C'EST
LE JEU DES HIRONDELLES
FLORIAN.
TO DIE TO LEAVE TO RETURN
IT'S A GAME FOR SWALLOWS
—FLORIAN

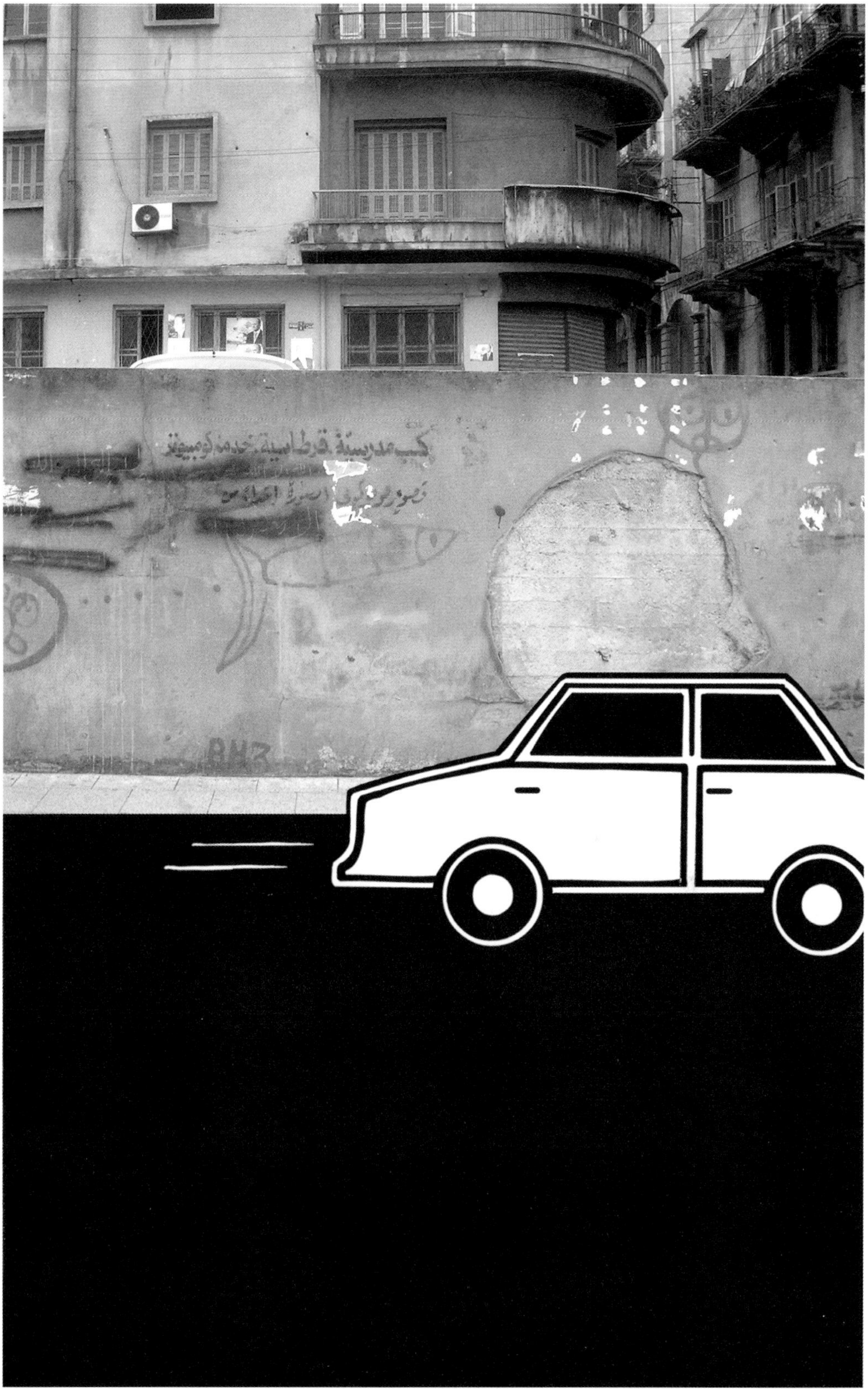

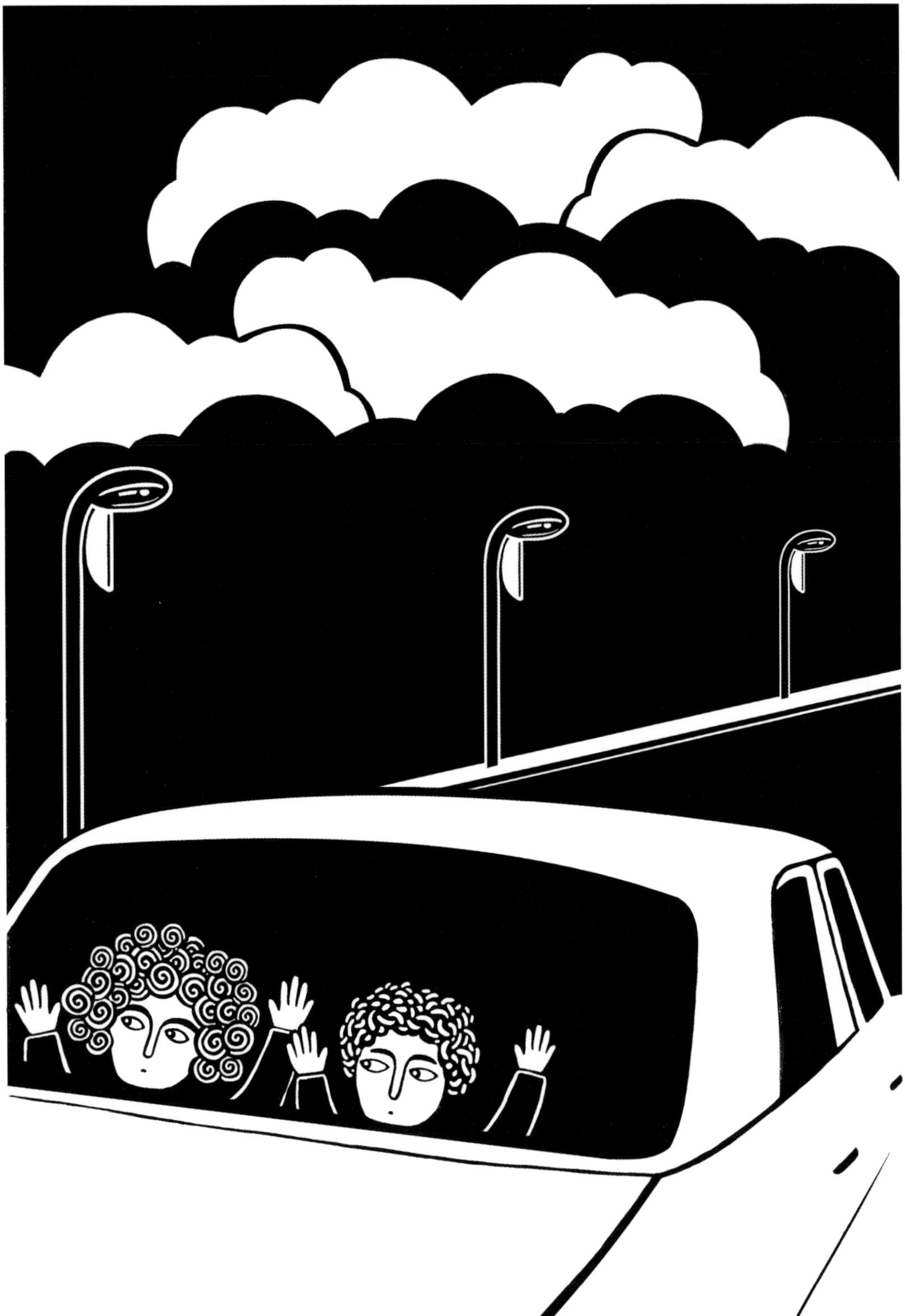

A WEEK LATER, MY PARENTS WENT BACK TO OUR APARTMENT TO GATHER A FEW THINGS.

THE BUILDING WAS EMPTY.

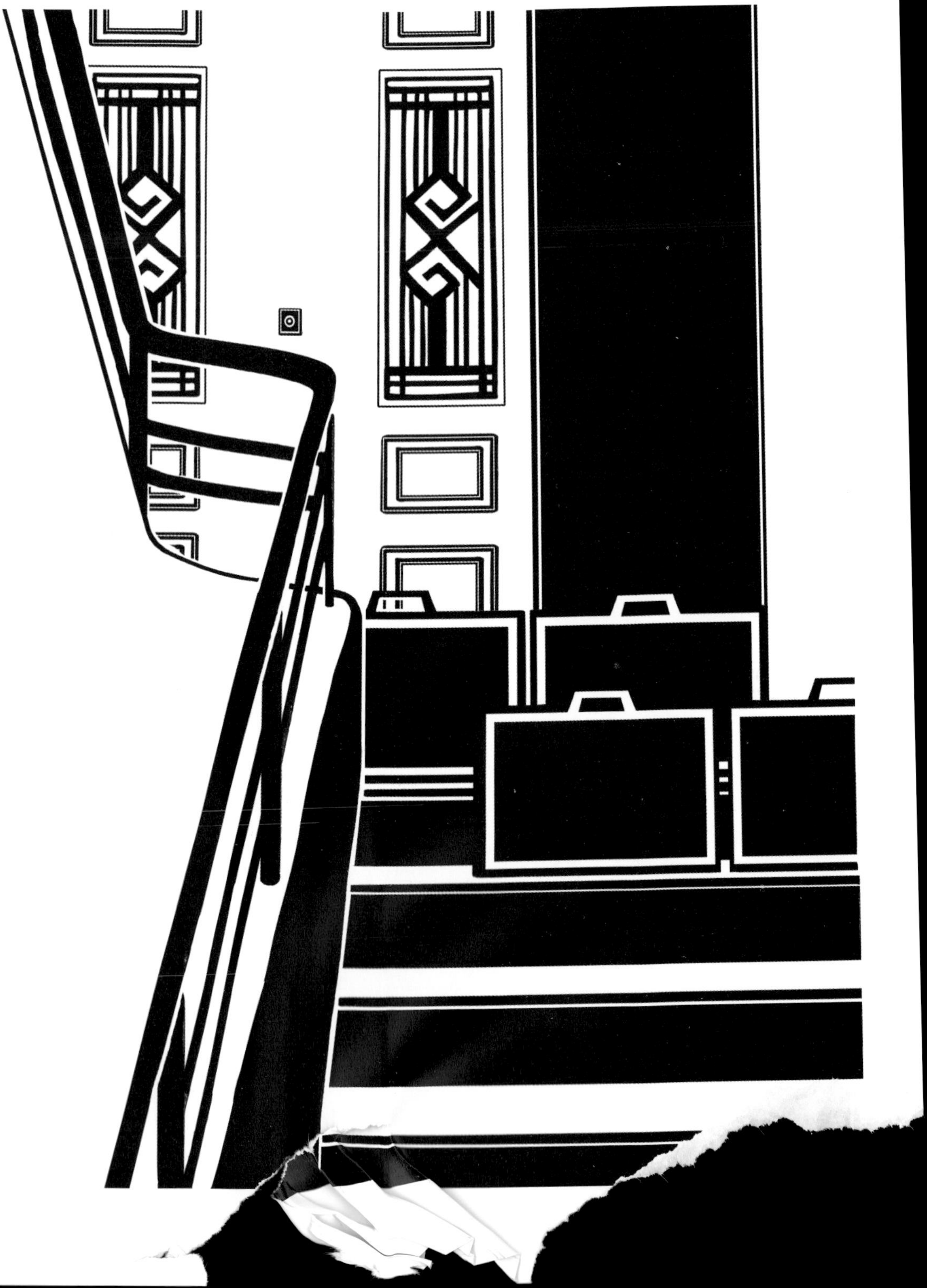

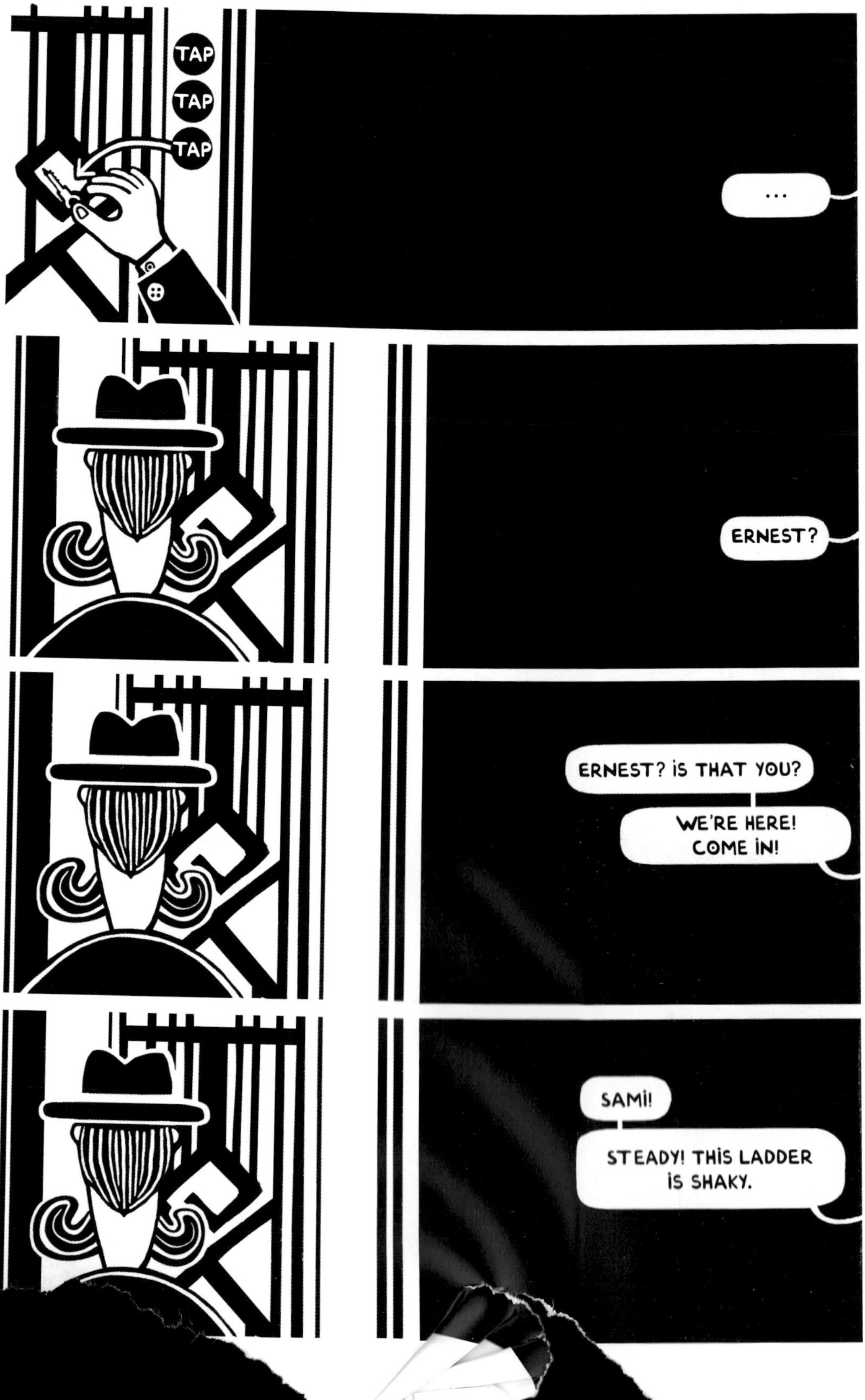
TAP
TAP
TAP
...
ERNEST?
ERNEST? IS THAT YOU?
WE'RE HERE! COME IN!
SAMI!
STEADY! THIS LADDER IS SHAKY.

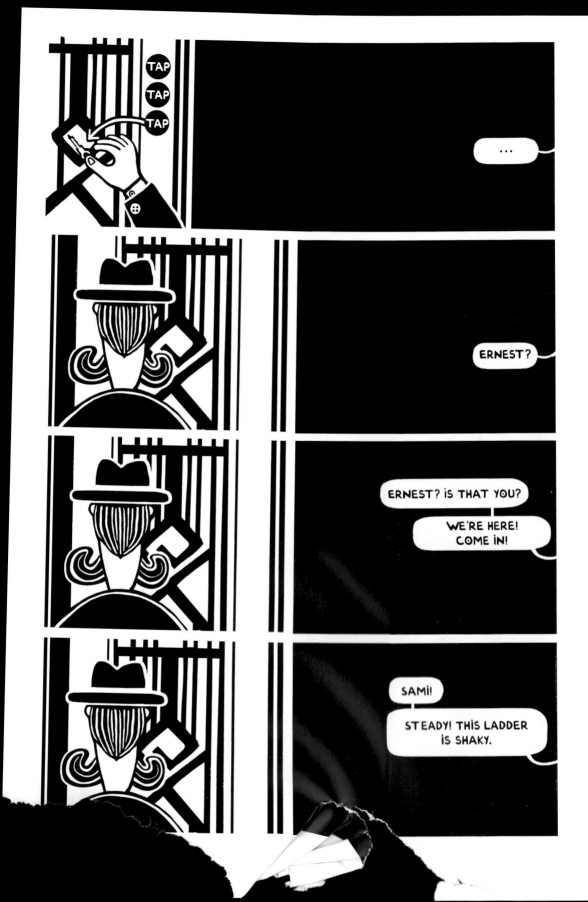

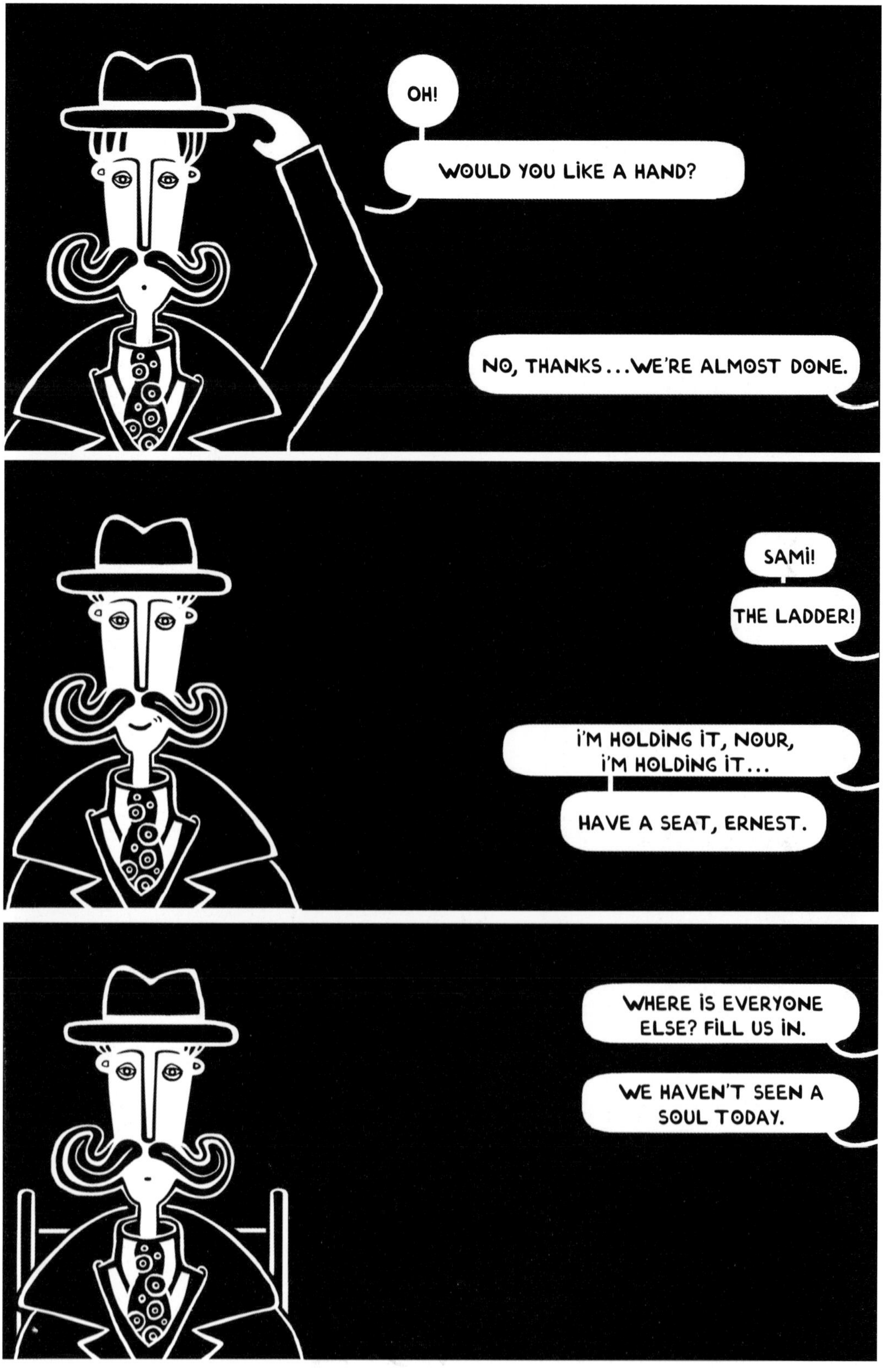

OH!
WOULD YOU LIKE A HAND?
NO, THANKS...WE'RE ALMOST DONE.
SAMI!
THE LADDER!
I'M HOLDING IT, NOUR, I'M HOLDING IT...
HAVE A SEAT, ERNEST.
WHERE IS EVERYONE ELSE? FILL US IN.
WE HAVEN'T SEEN A SOUL TODAY.

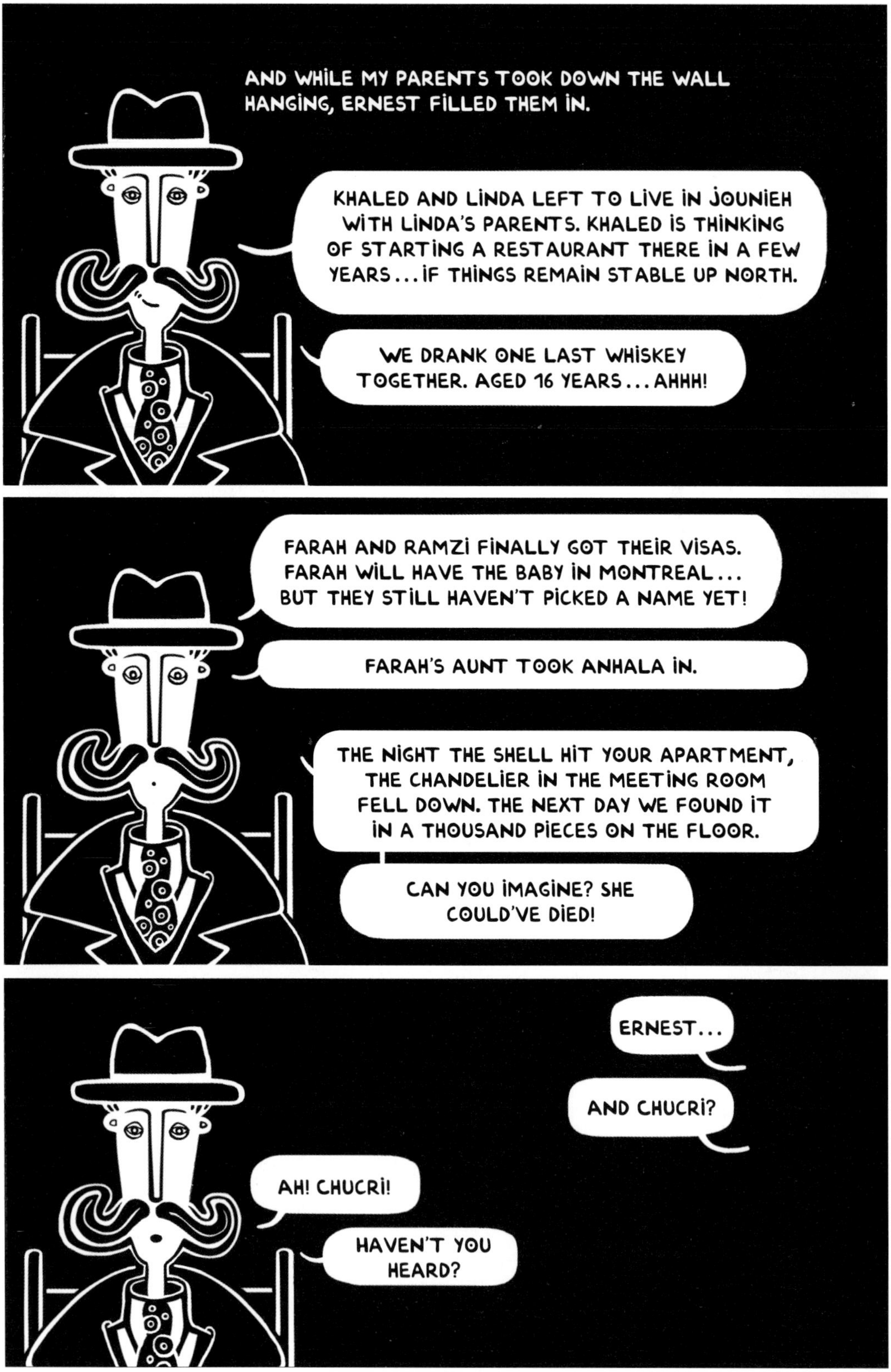
AND WHILE MY PARENTS TOOK DOWN THE WALL HANGING, ERNEST FILLED THEM IN.
KHALED AND LINDA LEFT TO LIVE IN JOUNIEH WITH LINDA'S PARENTS. KHALED IS THINKING OF STARTING A RESTAURANT THERE IN A FEW YEARS... IF THINGS REMAIN STABLE UP NORTH.
WE DRANK ONE LAST WHISKEY TOGETHER. AGED 16 YEARS... AHHH!
FARAH AND RAMZI FINALLY GOT THEIR VISAS. FARAH WILL HAVE THE BABY IN MONTREAL... BUT THEY STILL HAVEN'T PICKED A NAME YET!
FARAH'S AUNT TOOK ANHALA IN.
THE NIGHT THE SHELL HIT YOUR APARTMENT, THE CHANDELIER IN THE MEETING ROOM FELL DOWN. THE NEXT DAY WE FOUND IT IN A THOUSAND PIECES ON THE FLOOR.
CAN YOU IMAGINE? SHE COULD'VE DIED!
ERNEST...
AND CHUCRI?
AH! CHUCRI!
HAVEN'T YOU HEARD?

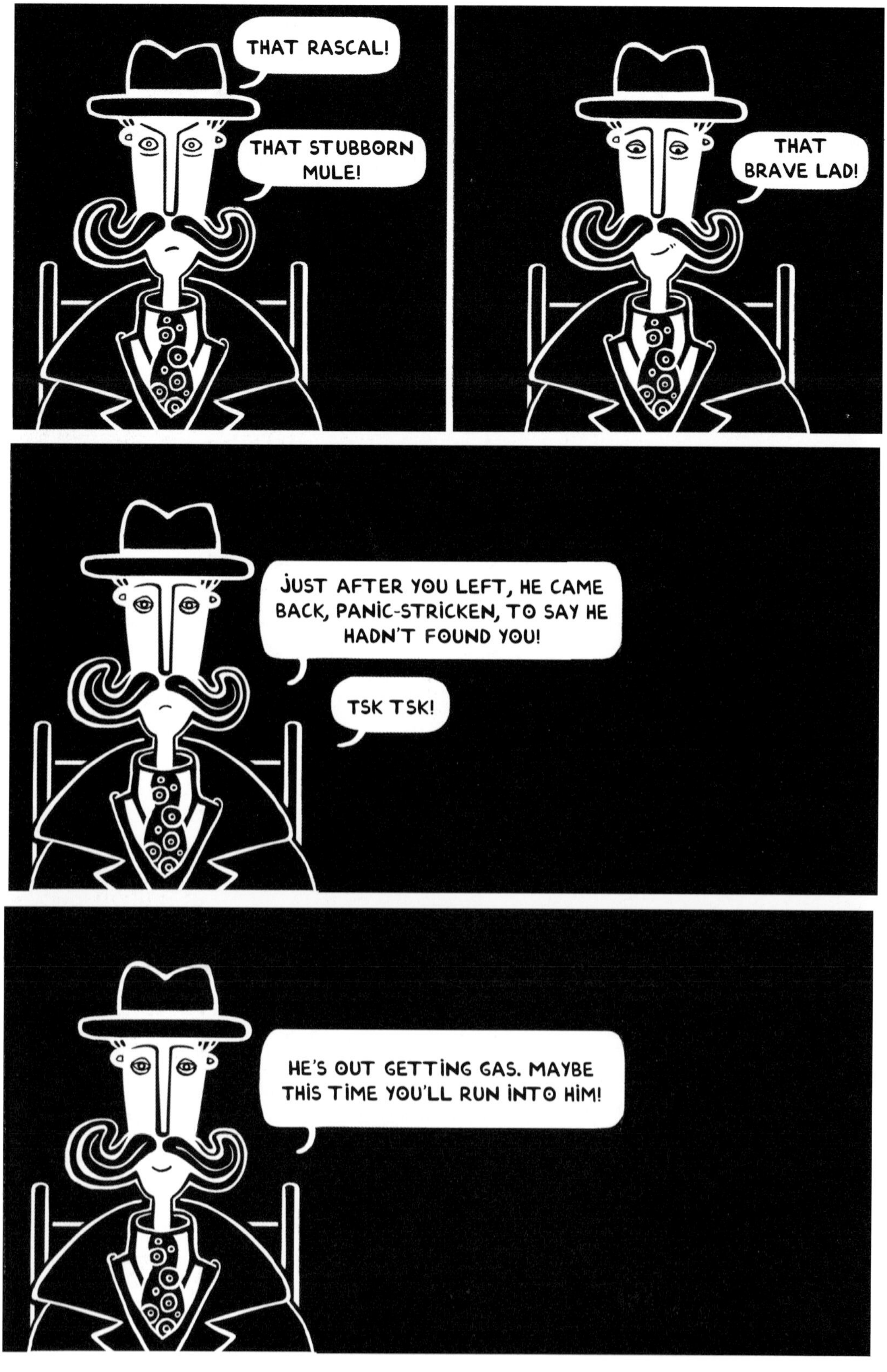
THAT RASCAL!
THAT STUBBORN MULE!
THAT BRAVE LAD!
JUST AFTER YOU LEFT, HE CAME BACK, PANIC-STRICKEN, TO SAY HE HADN'T FOUND YOU!
TSK TSK!
HE'S OUT GETTING GAS. MAYBE THIS TIME YOU'LL RUN INTO HIM!

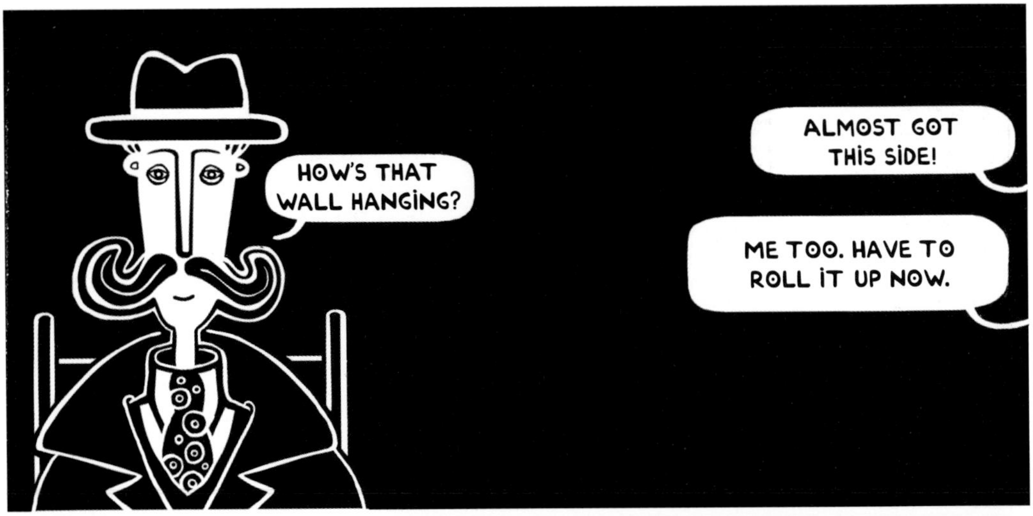
HOW'S THAT WALL HANGING?
ALMOST GOT THIS SIDE!
ME TOO. HAVE TO ROLL IT UP NOW.

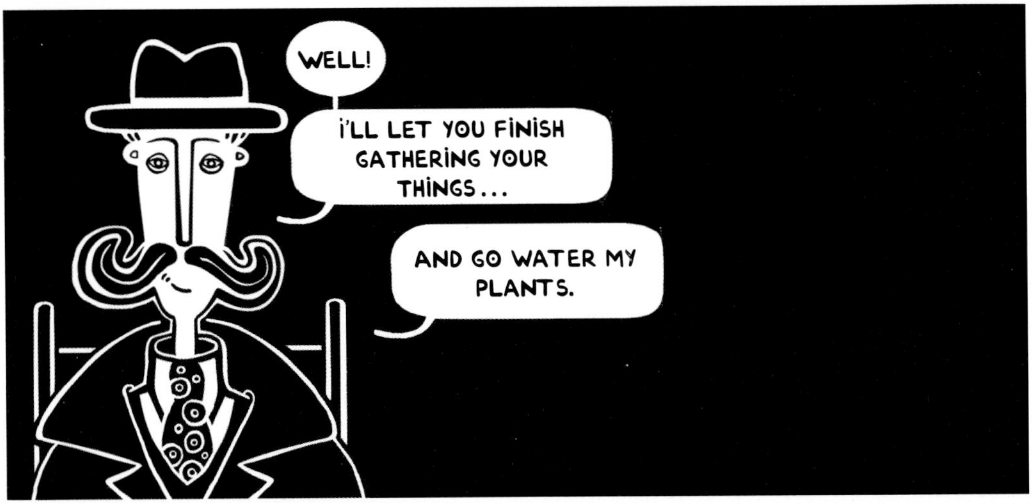
WELL!
I'LL LET YOU FINISH GATHERING YOUR THINGS...
AND GO WATER MY PLANTS.

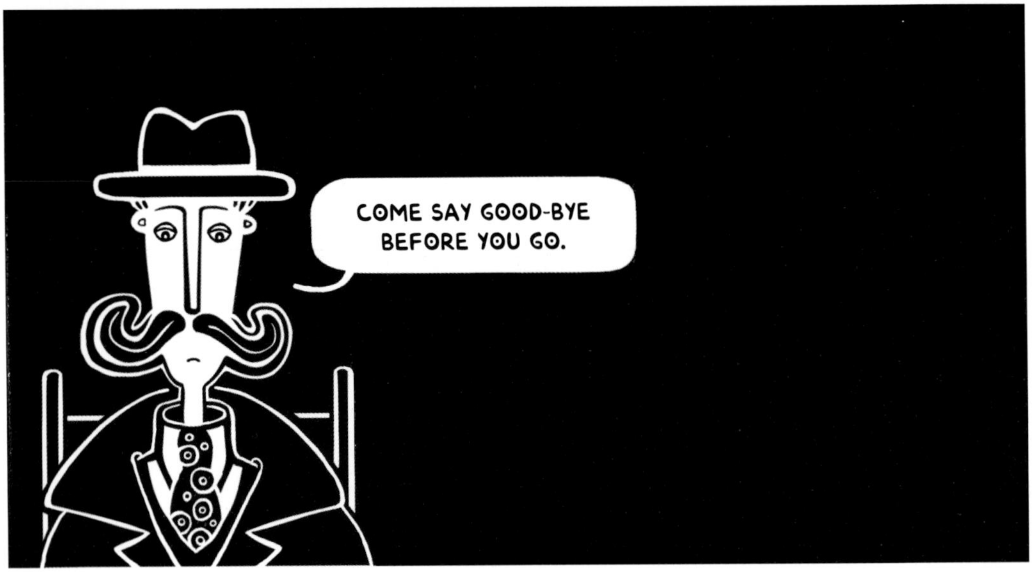
COME SAY GOOD-BYE BEFORE YOU GO.

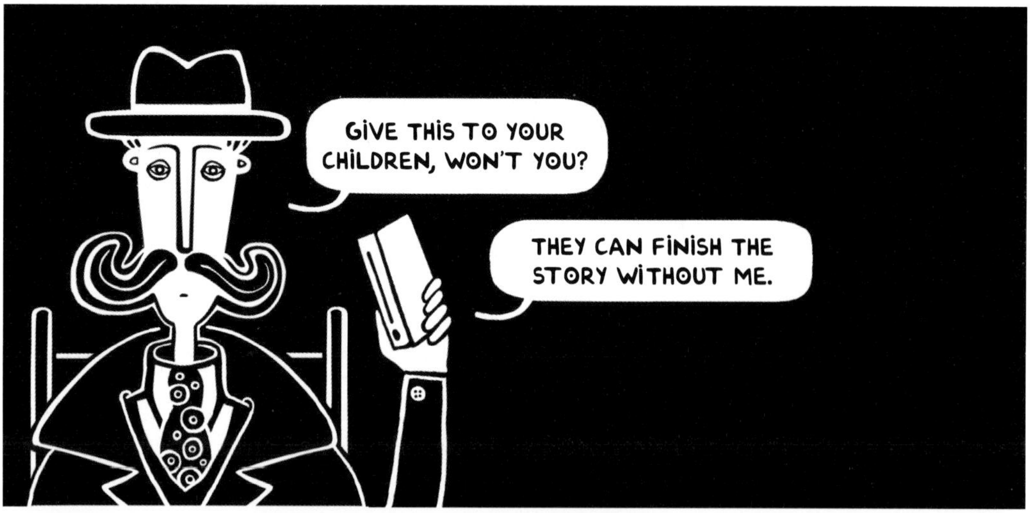
GIVE THIS TO YOUR CHILDREN, WON'T YOU?
THEY CAN FINISH THE STORY WITHOUT ME.

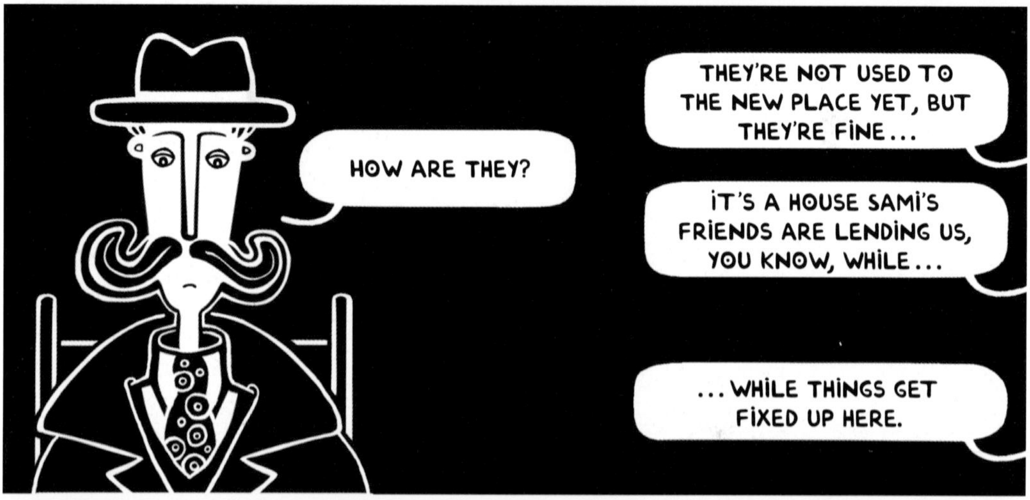
HOW ARE THEY?
THEY'RE NOT USED TO THE NEW PLACE YET, BUT THEY'RE FINE...
IT'S A HOUSE SAMI'S FRIENDS ARE LENDING US, YOU KNOW, WHILE...
...WHILE THINGS GET FIXED UP HERE.

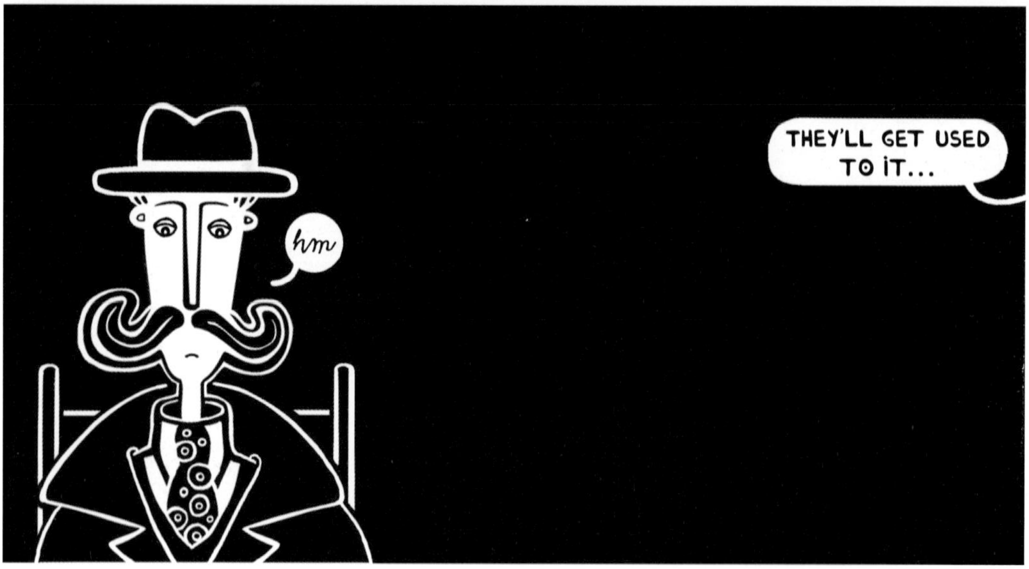
THEY'LL GET USED TO IT...
hm

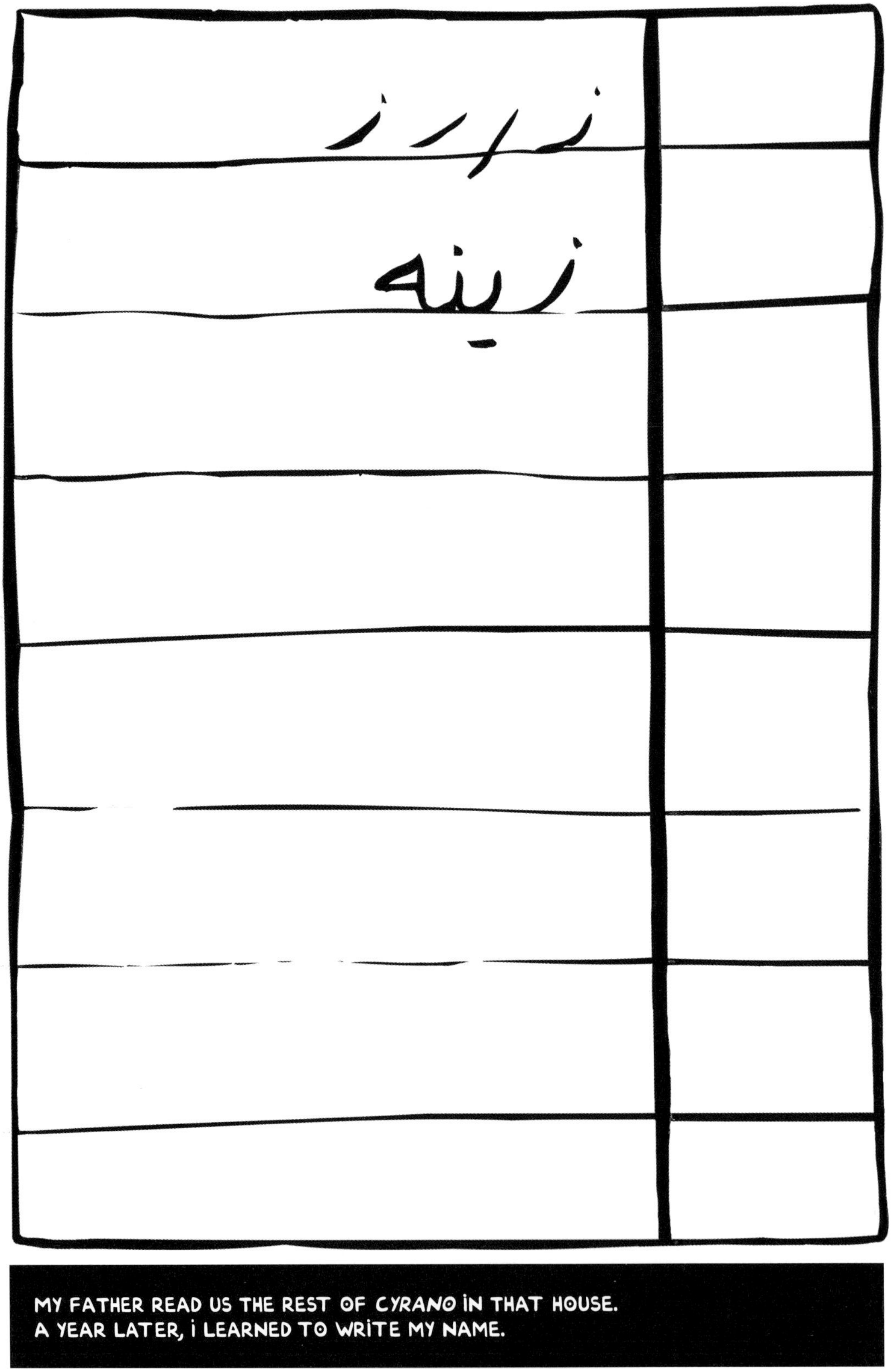

ز ر ر ز
زينه
MY FATHER READ US THE REST OF *CYRANO* IN THAT HOUSE.
A YEAR LATER, I LEARNED TO WRITE MY NAME.

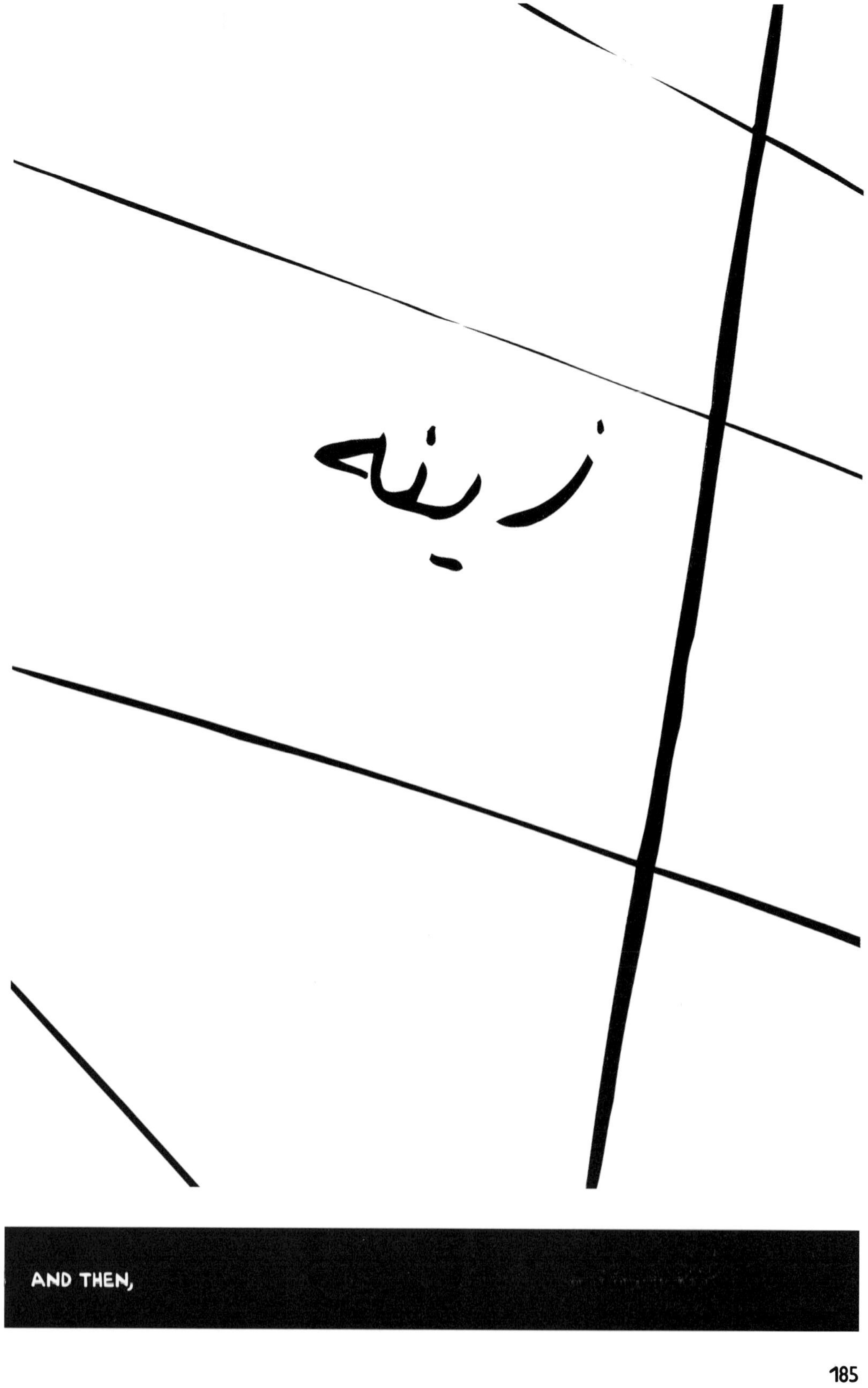
زینه
AND THEN,

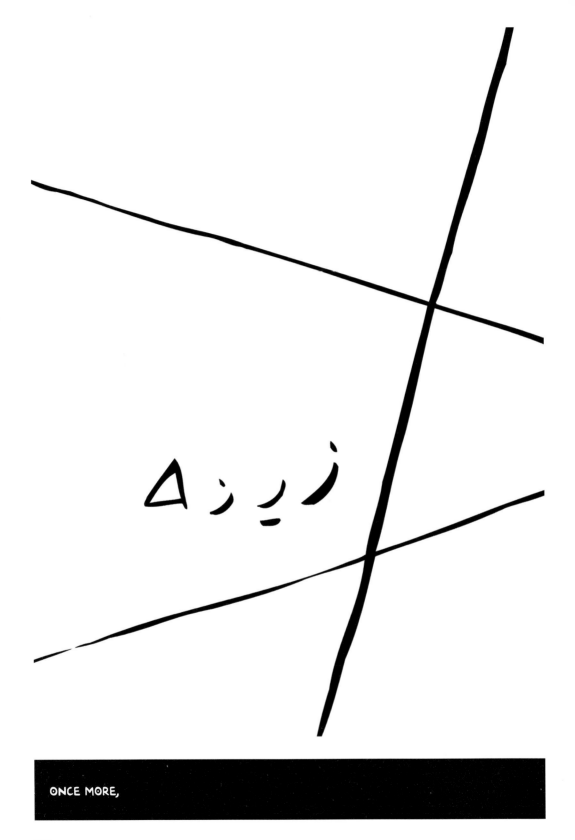

ONCE MORE,

WE HAD

TO LEAVE.

TiC

TOC

TiC

TOC

Paris, February 2020

It's been a second,
a minute,
days,
even years
since I made
this book.

In the meantime, a detail has come back to mind.

When I was a child, I was told,
"The French filmed your grandmama."

My grandmother is a very beautiful woman,
and in my little girl's imagination,
I came up with
an image of her
as a movie star.

Blowout,
boa,
pearl necklace,
cigarette holder,
bedroom eyes . . .

In short, something a bit glamorous and twirly . . .

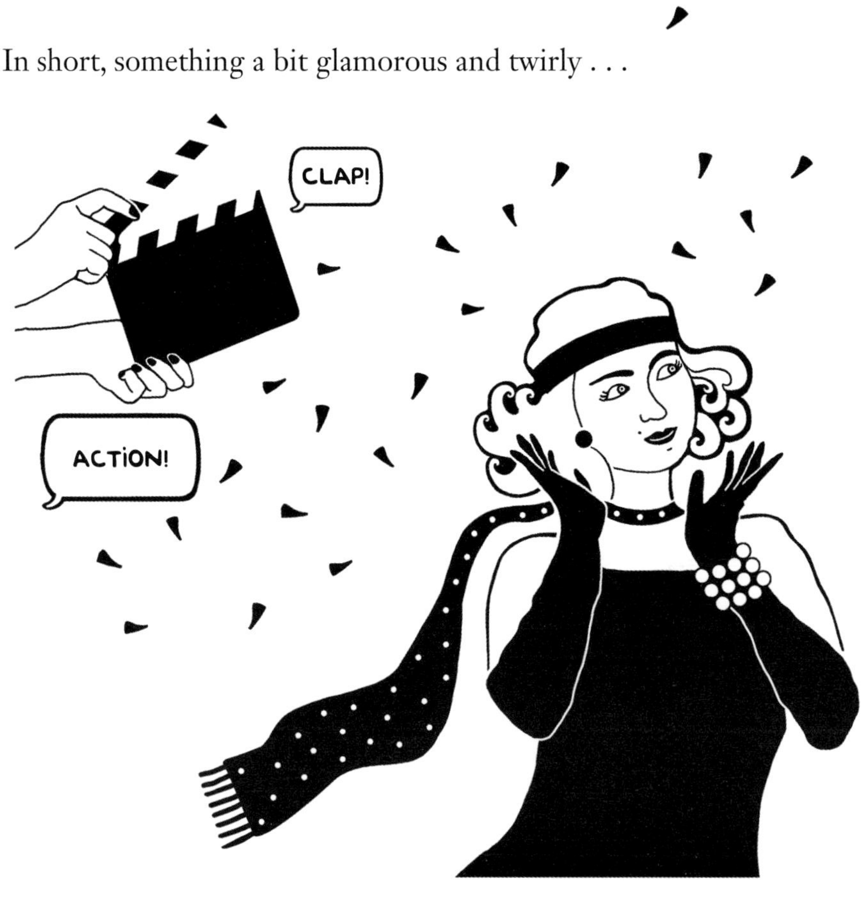
CLAP!
ACTION!

Light years away, at any rate,
from the footage I found in 2006
on the INA website.*

I must have needed a dash of dreams to put up with
the present.

It was a while before I realized
"The French filmed your grandmother"
meant that footage.
That "The French filmed your grandmother"
meant the woman with fearful eyes
whose reticence forced a smile for the camera,
whispering in her pink sweater,
which must've been scratchy:

I THINK
WE'RE SORT OF
MAYBE
MORE OR LESS
SAFE HERE
?

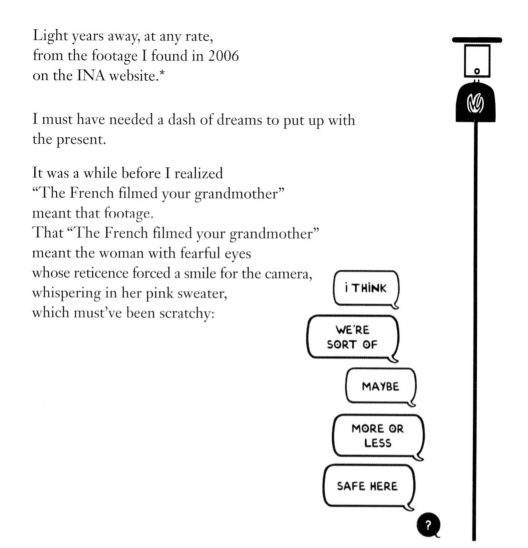

. . . at the very moment when the roar of a fallen shell resounded not so far away.

There was this thing she'd do with her shoulders,
as if to pull her head back between them,
and also an expression
I knew so well,
for conveying what she would never
put into words:
"See what has become of us?"

*Institut national de l'audiovisuel (the National Audiovisual Institute of France)

My grandmama would never talk to me about the war.
It was as if her memories stopped
on April 13, 1975.

But when it came to Beirut in the '60s,
her stories were endless.
She and my grandfather had
sown their wild oats
and seen the world.

Lucky children of that carefree era
of the "Switzerland of the Middle East"
that orphaned my generation,
they can be seen partying in every photo.

Was that because they were always partying?
Or because back then
the only photos people took were at parties?

At any rate, they loved each other.
Cheek to cheek,
under paper streamers,
from Buenos Aires to Ulaanbaatar.

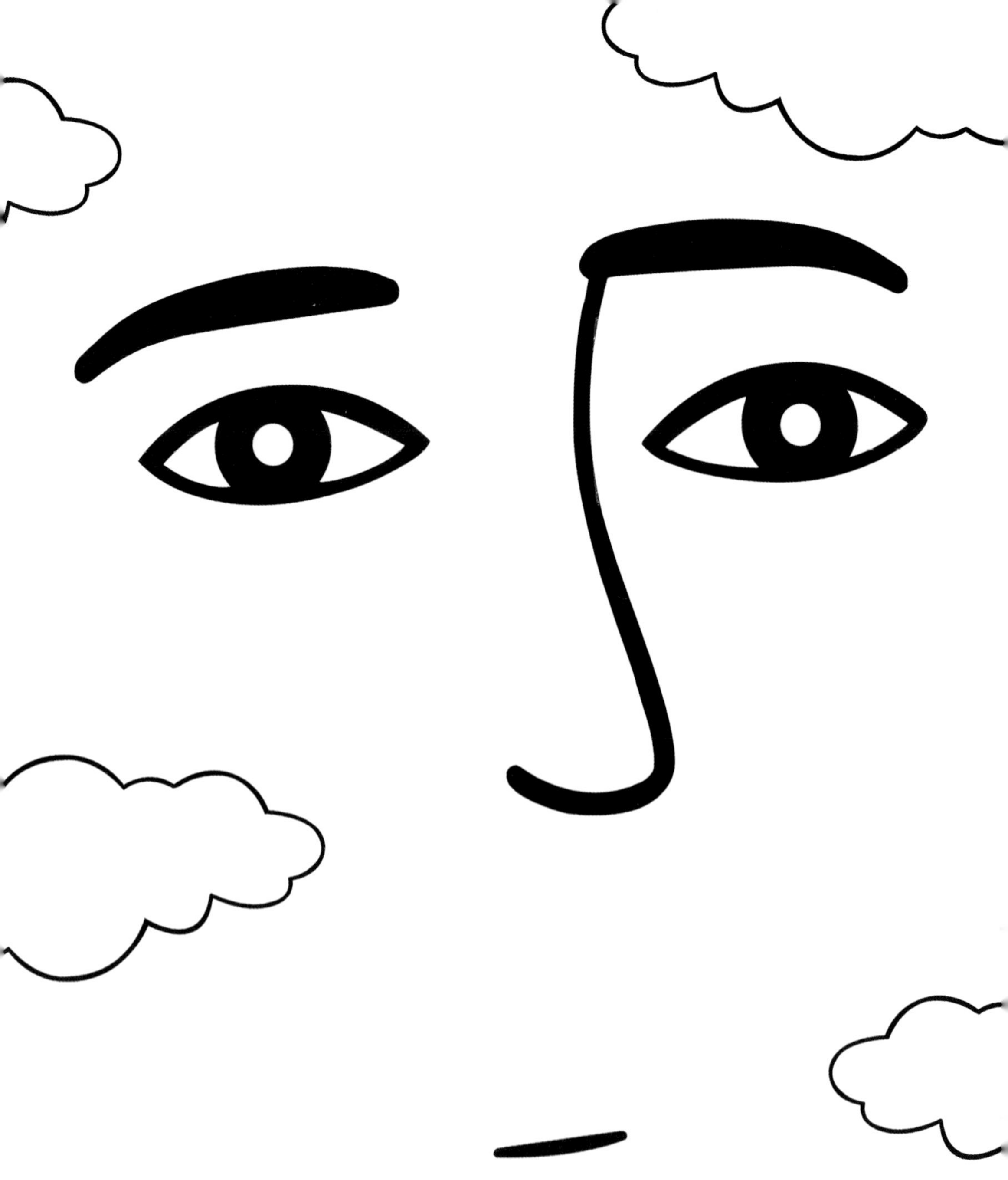

Watching her face fill my computer screen
in that 1984 footage from Channel 2 news,
I thought that instead of telling me her stories,
she had, unbeknownst to her, paved the way for an exploration
of our collective memory thirty-two years later.

My grandmama has since lost my grandfather.
Soon afterward, she lost her memory.

For real, this time.

She doesn't really know if I live in Beirut or Paris anymore.

Or if I'm working

or if I have a boyfriend.

Children, maybe?

She knows my name.

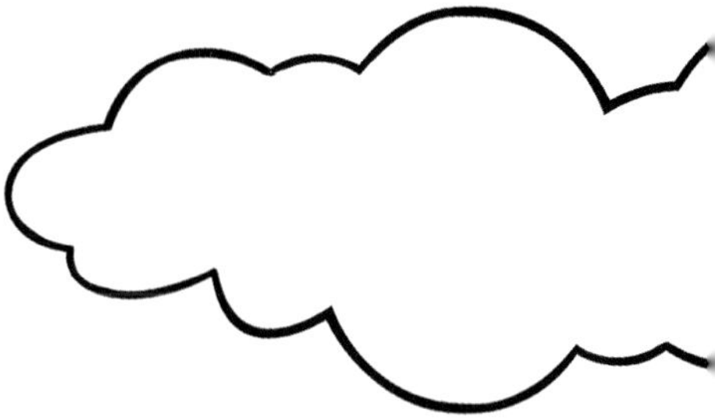

She knows who I am, gets her bearings:
I'm "the brunette" among my blonde cousins.

She knows I'm my parents' daughter

and my brother's sister.

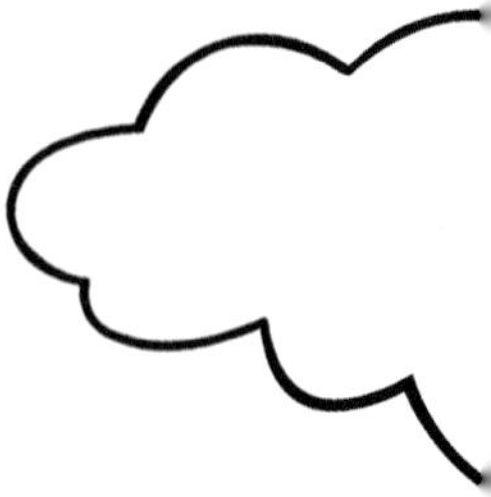

That's about it.

When I go to see her, I get the same strange
feeling as when I'm in an airplane
flying to Beirut—
to be exact, in the last few minutes
before landing.

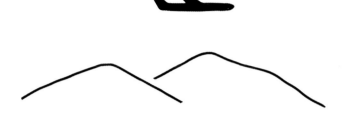

I see the city from above,
the urban density,
the coast.

I guess at the rest.

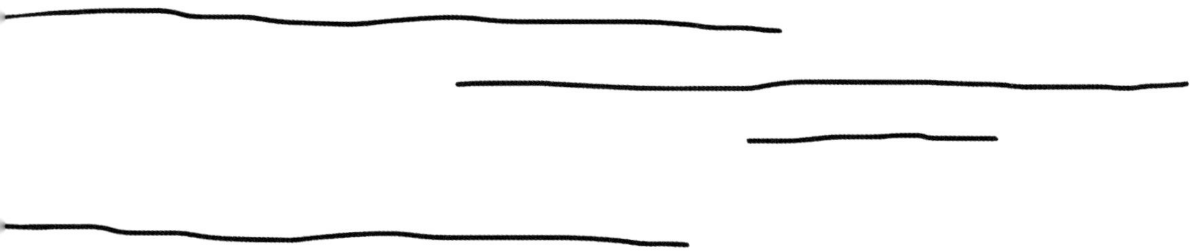

And I wonder: "Will she recognize me?"

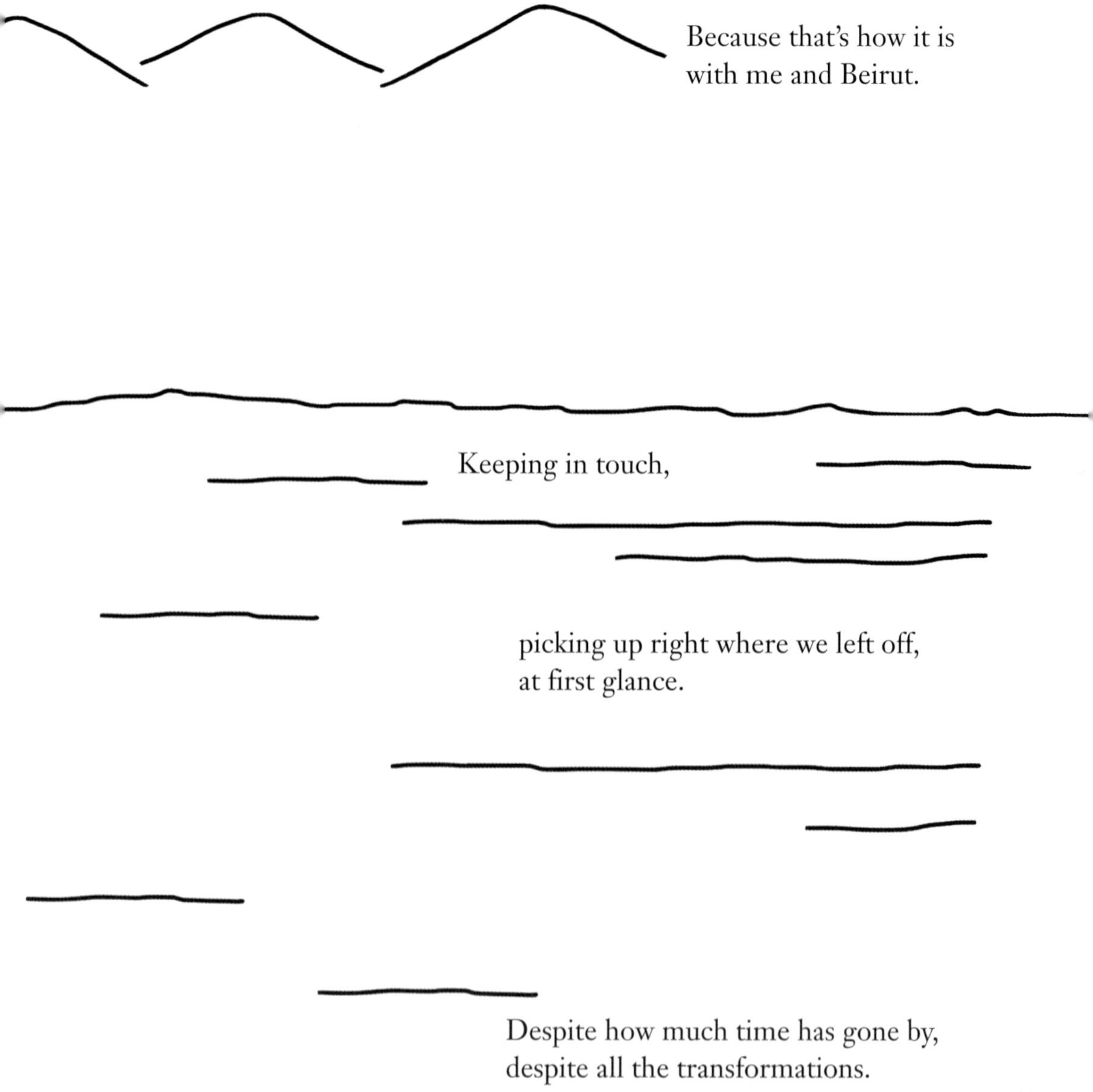
Because that's how it is
with me and Beirut.
Keeping in touch,
picking up right where we left off,
at first glance.
Despite how much time has gone by,
despite all the transformations.

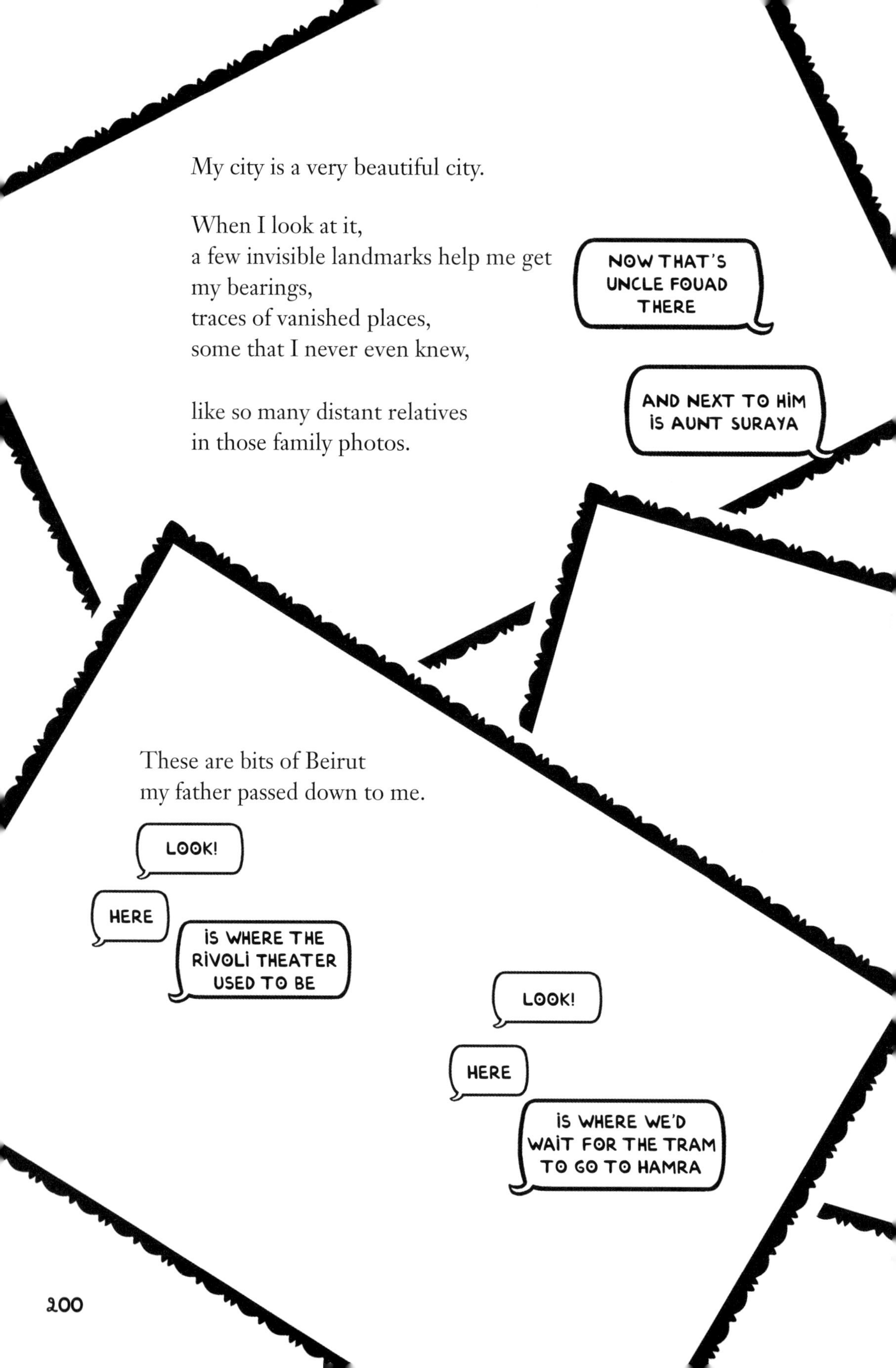
My city is a very beautiful city.
When I look at it,
a few invisible landmarks help me get
my bearings,
traces of vanished places,
some that I never even knew,
like so many distant relatives
in those family photos.
NOW THAT'S UNCLE FOUAD THERE
AND NEXT TO HIM IS AUNT SURAYA
These are bits of Beirut
my father passed down to me.
LOOK!
HERE
IS WHERE THE RIVOLI THEATER USED TO BE
LOOK!
HERE
IS WHERE WE'D WAIT FOR THE TRAM TO GO TO HAMRA

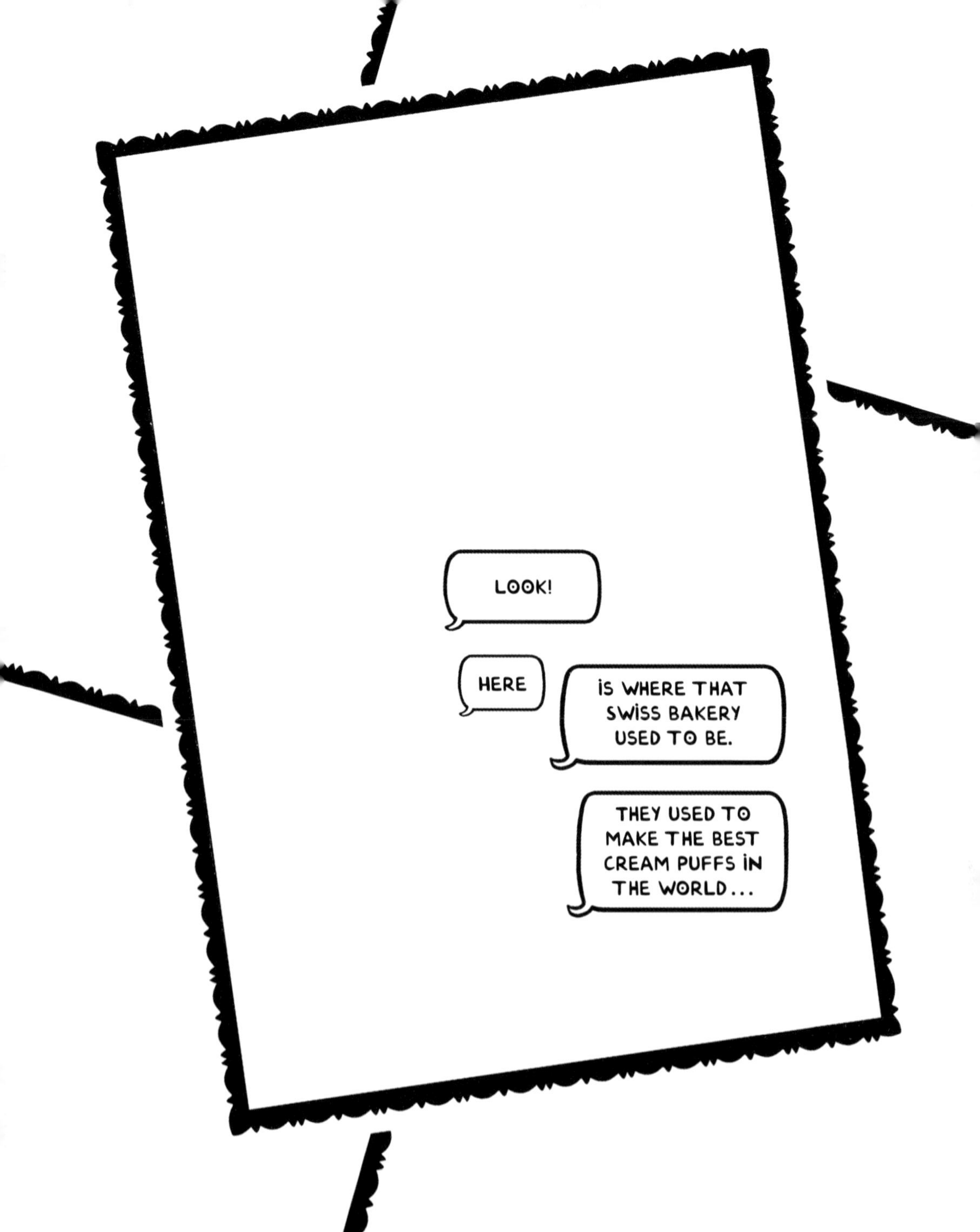
LOOK!
HERE
IS WHERE THAT SWISS BAKERY USED TO BE.
THEY USED TO MAKE THE BEST CREAM PUFFS IN THE WORLD...

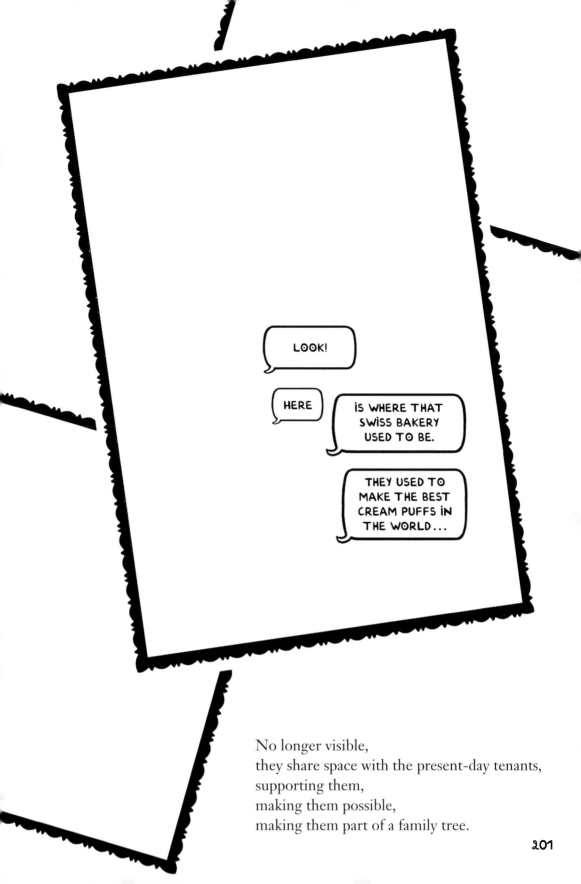

No longer visible,
they share space with the present-day tenants,
supporting them,
making them possible,
making them part of a family tree.

Among these milestones
are a few words
that Florian
graffitied on a wall between my home

and what used to be the "other side."

A poetic sentinel
in a city that's done its best
to wipe out every last trace
of recent history

these few fragile words

MOURIR PARTIR

LE JEU DES

REVENIR C'EST

HIRONDELLES

in blue paint on a cinder block wall
survived for several decades.

And then, the wall was torn down.

To die, to leave, to return
It's a game for swallows

I spent a long time looking
for the "Florian"
who wrote those words.
By turns, he's
taken on various
faces and
figures.

Imaginary transformations.

At first, he was almost
Jean-Pierre Claris de Florian,
the 18th-century writer of fables.
I've combed through
his works looking for a swallow.

In vain.

Then he was
a young Frenchman come to Lebanon
in the late '80s
to work construction,
rebuilding
schools and hospitals.

This second Florian
had written me
before we met up
in Paris.
His letter was handwritten
in blue ink,
as if to encourage me
to compare the writing
on the wall
with that of the letter.

Faced with my joy
and my incredulity
at having found him so soon
after my book came out,
this Florian confessed
that more than anything, he only wanted
to be that
Florian.

And then, one night, my heart skipped a beat.

I was watching François Truffaut's
Love on the Run
when I clearly heard,
in the title song
written by Alain Souchon,
these words:
"To leave, to return, to be on the move, it's a game for swallows."

Getting warmer.

That song—
Florian
must've known it.
Had he transformed
the lyrics
of Souchon
to adapt them
to Lebanese reality?

And who was he?

Last year,
he was embodied by
a French gendarme
posted to Beirut
in the early 2000s.
Someone had seen him
reading my book,
standing in a bookstore
in the 9th arrondissement
of Paris.
Supposedly, moved, he told
the bearded bookseller:

"I'm the one who did that graffiti."

That Florian was stocky
and wearing a jacket.
Skimpy clues
that I hastened
to pass on
to the French Embassy
in Lebanon.

No gendarme
who'd served
during those years
had gone by Florian
for his first name
or last . . .

A pseudonym, then?

Another dead end.

And a few months ago, Paul Matar,
former director
of the Monnot Theater,
right behind
where the wall had been,
told me:

"Hey, I know your Florian!"

At last.

This fifth iteration
of a single man
grown ever more
ghostly
was "a tall
(he'd insisted, very tall)
guy,"
a dancer
with a
Belgian
company
who'd come to give
a performance
in the late '80s
at the theater.

His first name was Florian.

That's all there was to it.

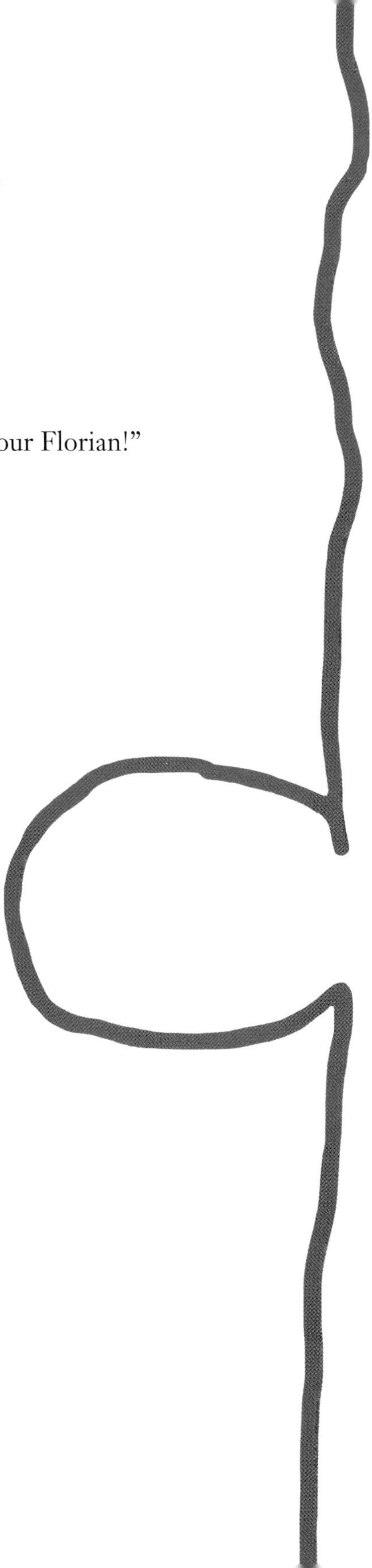

No, wait—something more. Something incredible.

From his backpack
Paul took out
a framed drawing.
It wasn't signed,
but there was no doubt
it was by Florian.

I decided to believe him.

Later on, I recalled another detail.

One day, I'd gotten
an email from a stranger
telling me
he'd been a student
at Saint Joseph University,
a stone's throw from "Florian's wall,"
which he walked by every morning
to get to class.

He was too young to have
known the war,
but after reading my book,
he said,
he'd paid special attention
to graffiti
such that one day,
noticing the words
had been slowly
fading away,
he decided to go over them,
letter by letter,
in spray paint.

I imagined the silence
of his hand
going over a few words
painted on a wall . . .

I imagined
that young man from behind,
everything around him
under construction:
cranes,
jackhammers,
cement mixers,
excavators . . .

It doesn't matter who Florian was.

In a country
where history lessons
in school textbooks
stop,
like my grandmother's
memories,
on April 13, 1975,
he played a part in passing on
a fragment of our memory.

Today, the walls of Beirut are silent no more.

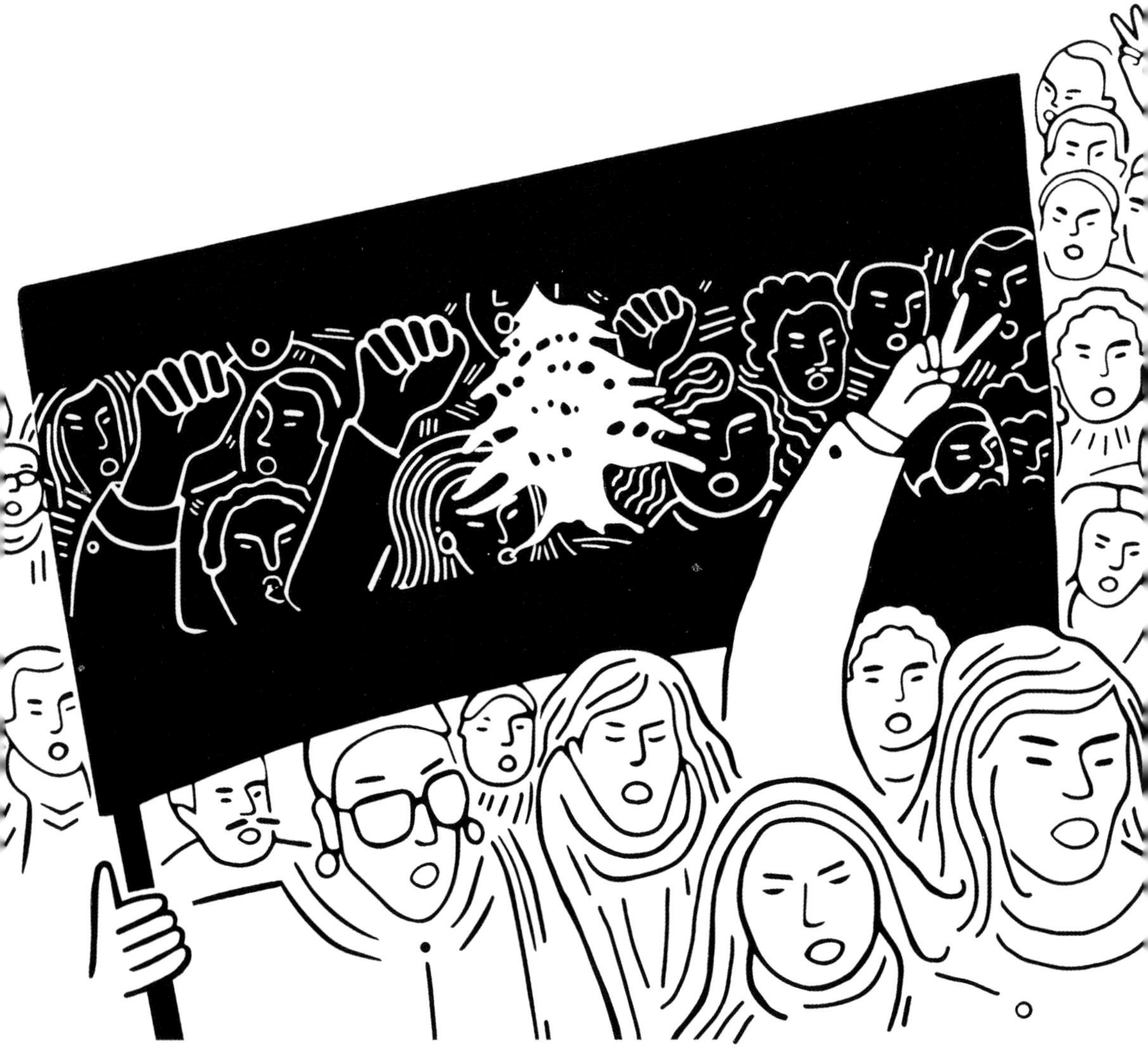

Since October 17, 2019,
words are out in the streets once more,
exchanged in public squares,
painted on banners
and on walls.

The once-confiscated public space
has, bit by bit, been reappropriated
by its citizens.

Our territories,
checkered by war
and the politics of rebuilding,
are, yard by yard,
reoccupied.

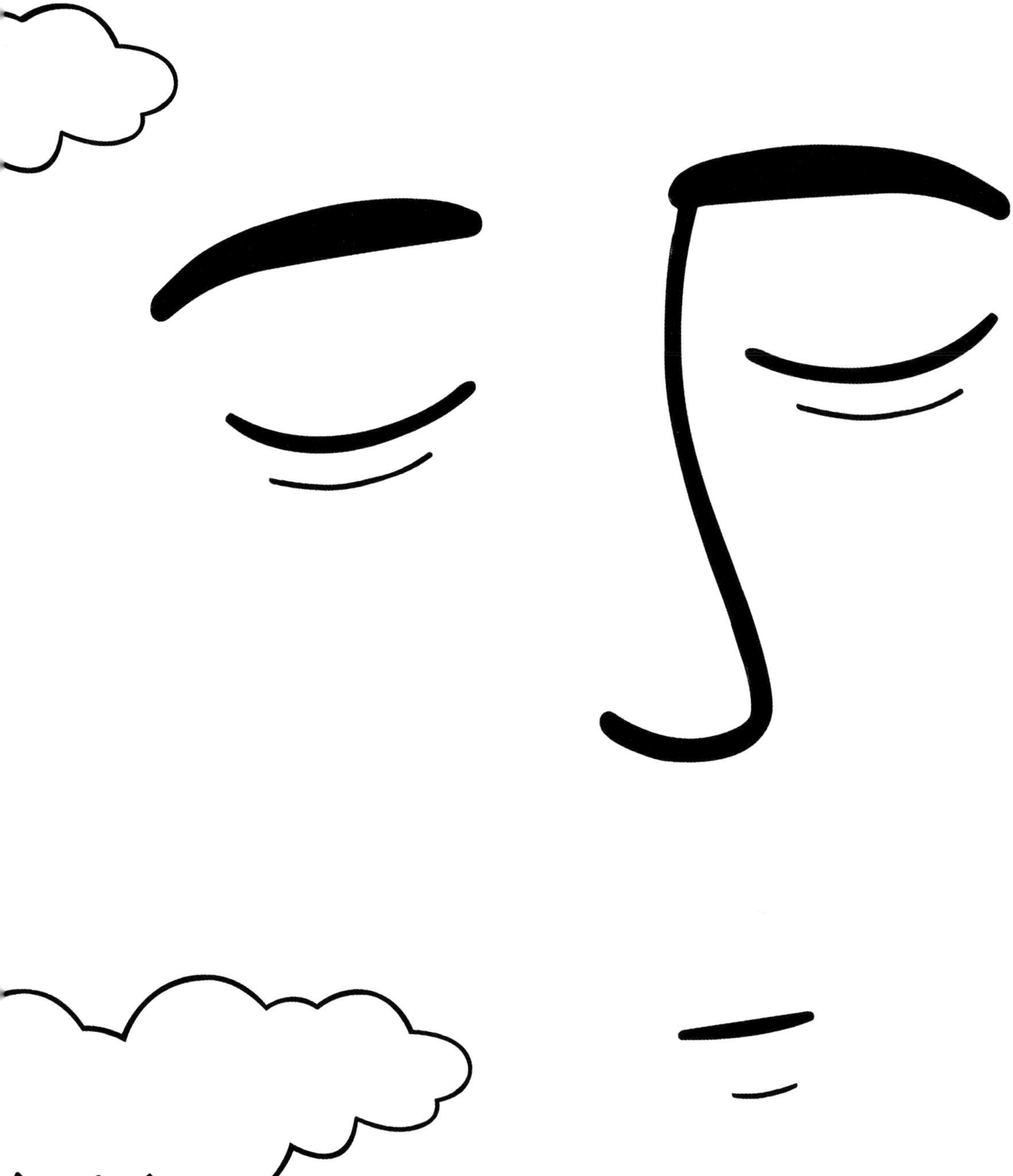

As for my grandmama,
she speaks less and less.
After a few minutes
of conversation,
her gaze settles
on her crossword puzzle.

I watch her write
with trembling hand
letters
in the little white
boxes.

Sometimes she goes outside the lines.

I study her face—
Earth seen from above—
when she finally
falls asleep,

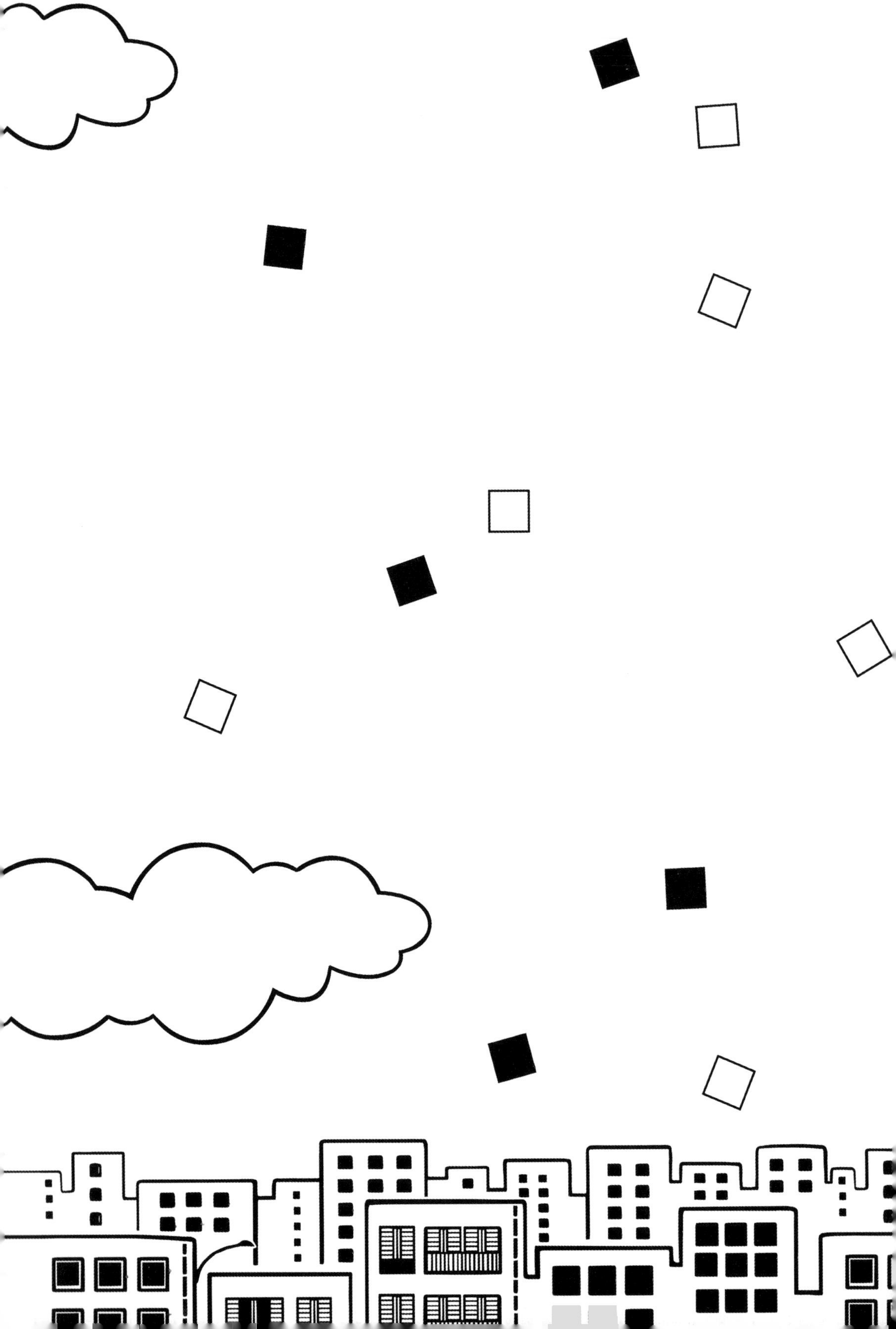

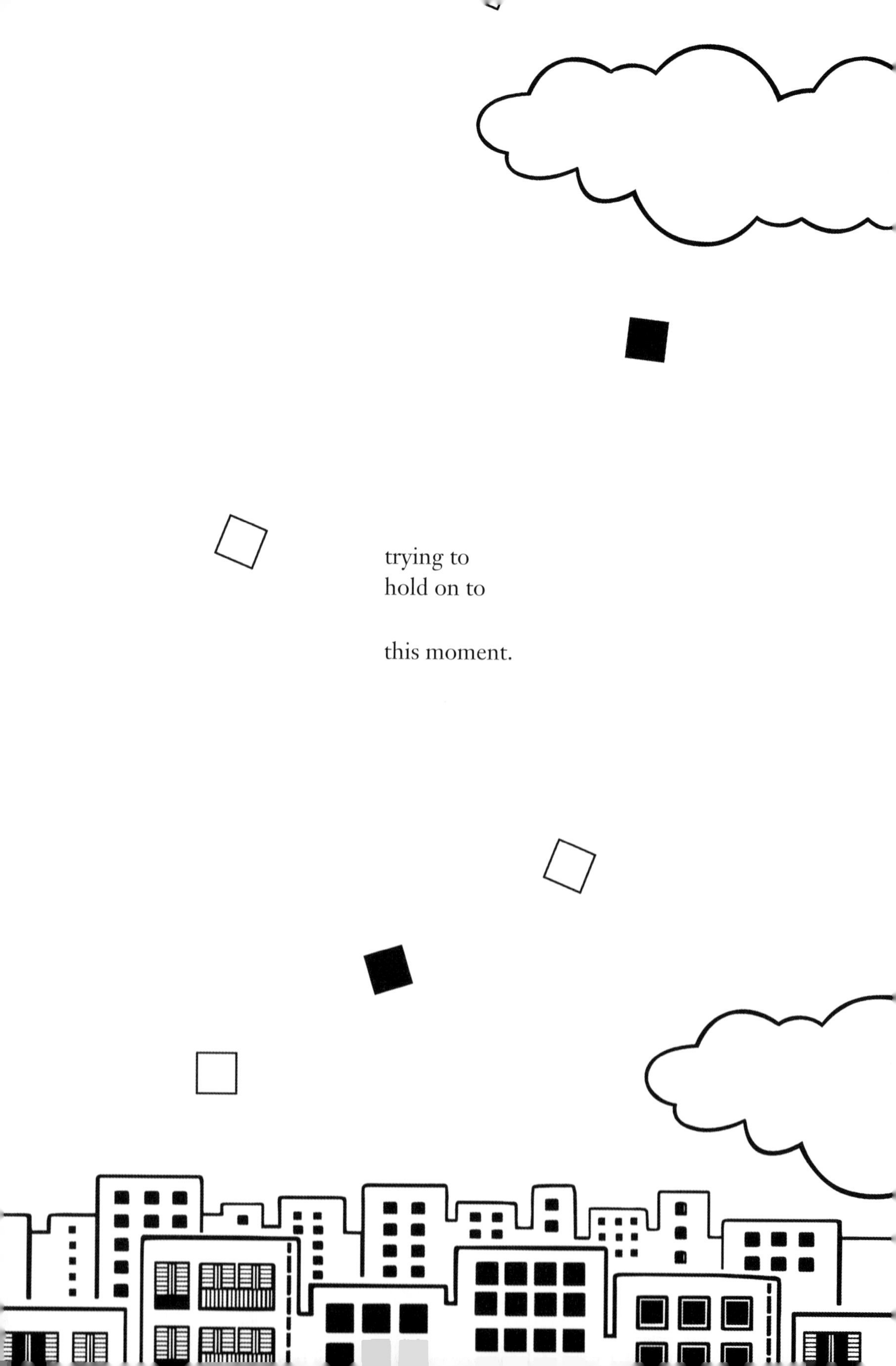

trying to
hold on to

this moment.

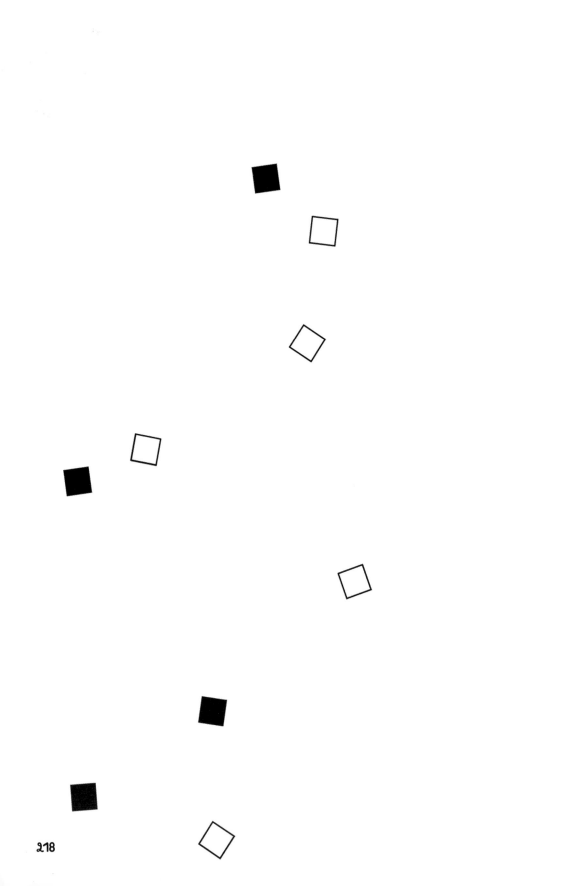

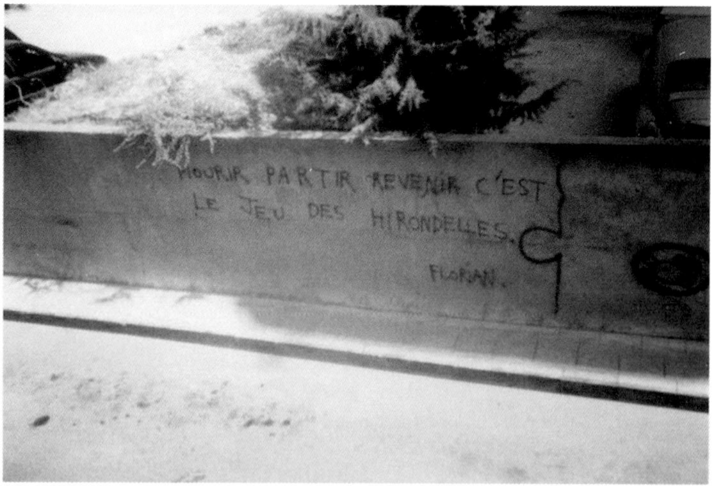
MOURIR PARTIR REVENIR C'EST
LE JEU DES HIRONDELLES.
FLORIAN.

2001

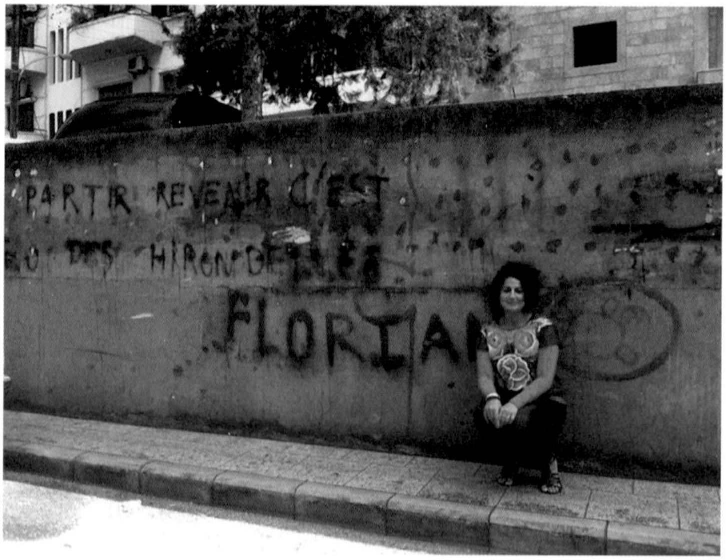
PARTIR REVENIR C'EST

2011

TO VIEW THE FOOTAGE AT THE INA ARCHIVE, VISIT
https://www.ina.fr/video/CAB8400185401
/histoire-d-une-rue-sur-le-passagedu-musee-video.html

FOR PAP AND MAM
FOR PHILIPPE

FOR ERNEST

ABOUT THE AUTHOR

Zeina Abirached was born in Beirut in 1981 in the middle of the civil war and was ten years old when it finally ended. She currently travels between Beirut and Paris. She studied graphic arts and commercial design at the Lebanese Academy of Fine Arts (ALBA) and in 2002 was awarded the top prize at the International Comic Book Festival in Beirut for her first graphic novel, *[Beyrouth] Catharsis*. She moved to Paris in 2004, where she attended the National School of Decorative Arts. In 2006, she began to publish graphic works in French with the publisher Cambourakis.

A Game for Swallows: To Die, To Leave, To Return (2012), the English-language edition of her graphic memoir *Mourir partir revenir, le jeu des hirondelles* (Cambourakis, 2007), received acclaim including the distinction of Batchelder Honor Book and places on the ALA Notable Children's Books and the USBBY Outstanding International Books lists. *I Remember Beirut* (2014), the English-language edition of her graphic memoir *Je me souviens (Beyrouth)* (Cambourakis, 2008), earned similar recognition including a Junior Library Guild Selection and places on the Notable Books for a Global Society and YALSA Great Graphic Novels for Teens lists.

Abirached's more recent works include *Le piano oriental* (Casterman, 2015) and *Prendre refuge* (with Mathias Énard, Casterman, 2021). She has also published books for children, including *Mouton* (Cambourakis, 2012) and *Le grand livre des petits bruits* (Casterman, 2020).

ABOUT THE TRANSLATOR

Award-winning translator Edward Gauvin specializes in contemporary comics and fantastical fiction. As an advocate for translators and translated literature, he has written widely and spoken at universities and festivals. The translator of more than 425 graphic novels, he is a contributing editor for comics at Words Without Borders. His collaborations with Lerner, ranging in setting from Lebanon to World War II France to modern-day Beijing, have been honored by the American Library Association and the Eisner Awards, and he is thrilled to be working with them again. Home is wherever his wife and daughter are.